SO-AKI-231

The Psychology
of
Today's Woman

The Psychology of Today's Woman

New Psychoanalytic Visions

Edited by

Toni Bernay

Dorothy W. Cantor

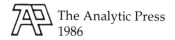 The Analytic Press
1986

The Analytic Press

Distributed solely by

Lawrence Erlbaum Associates, Inc., Publishers
365 Broadway
Hillsdale, New Jersey 07642

Library of Congress Cataloging in Publication Data
Main entry under title:

The Psychology of today's woman.

    Includes bibliographies and indexes.
    1. Women – Mental health.   2. Women – Psychology.
3. Psychoanalysis.   4. Psychotherapy.   I. Bernay, Toni.
II. Cantor, Dorothy W.   [DNLM: 1. Psychoanalytic
Interpretation.   2. Psychoanalytic Therapy.   3. Women –
psychology.   WM 460.5.W6 P974]
RC451.4.W6P77   155.6′33   85-22811
ISBN 0-88163-036-5

Printed in the United States of America
10 9 8 7 6 5 4 3 2

To
Mona, who began it all,
and
Gerry, with thanks and love

Contents

NEW VISIONS OF FEMININITY

TODAY'S WOMAN

ISSUES IN THE THERAPEUTIC RELATIONSHIP

Acknowledgments

As the months have gone by in the preparation of this book, we have come to appreciate how many people in our lives have contributed to its creation. We must express our gratitude to them as the book nears completion....

To Larry Erlbaum, who took a chance on an unknown quantity and gave us the privilege of being a part of his new baby; to friends and colleagues in the Women and Psychoanalysis Section of the American Psychological Association's Division of Psychoanalysis who helped provide us with an enlivening and congenial forum for much thinking and research.

Toni's special thanks to Joe Natterson, who encouraged and supported me through my transformations of understanding and definition; to Joan Willens and Harriet Wrye for their friendship, critical readings and helpful comments; to my secretary, Hannah Rosen, for her many hours of typing, retyping and mothering; and to my patients, who have shared their lives, selves and psyches with me. My gratitude to my son, Mitchell, who continues lovingly to help me to learn about motherhood and nurturance, and to my husband, Saar, who first, last and always stands by and encourages me in my creative work.

Dorothy's special thanks to the family of Rutgers Psy. D.'s, who are always supportive of my new ventures; to the many wonderful women who are friends, colleagues and patients, who have inspired my thinking about women's lives; and to my own family, Gerry, Laura, Josh and Karen, who have been willing, over the years, to modify their demands to make room for me to grow.

Lastly, we want to thank each other. As friends and co-editors we always found joy, giggles, and the strength to continue in the most frustrating of moments.

Toni Bernay, Ph.D.
Dorothy W. Cantor, Psy.D.

Contributors

Adrienne P. Applegarth, M.D.–San Francisco Psychoanalytic Institute, Department of Psychiatry, University of California School of Medicine, San Francisco.

Toni Bernay, Ph.D.–Private practice, Beverly Hills, California; Assistant Clinical Professor of Psychiatry (Psychology), Neuropsychiatric Institute, University of California, Los Angeles.

Dorothy W. Cantor, Psy.D.–Private practice, Westfield, NJ; Director of Continuing Education, Graduate School of Applied and Professional Psychology, Rutgers University.

Ruth-Jean Eisenbud, Ph.D.–Professor and Supervisor, New York University Postdoctoral Program in Psychotherapy and Psychoanalysis and Adelphi University Institute of Advanced Psychological Studies; faculty member, Long Island Institute of Psychoanalysis.

Eleanor Galenson, M.D.–Clinical Professor of Psychiatry, Mt. Sinai School of Medicine; member New York Psychoanalytic Institute.

Judith Lewis Herman, M.D.–Assistant Clinical Professor of Psychiatry, Harvard Medical School; founding member Women's Mental Health Collective, Somerville, MA.

Judith V. Jordan, Ph.D.–Associate Psychologist, McClean Hospital, Belmont, MA, Instructor, Department of Psychiatry, Harvard University Medical School.

Helen Block Lewis, Ph.D.–Professor Emerita (Adjunct) of Psychology, Yale University; President, Division of Psychoanalysis (Division 39), American Psychological Association; Editor, *Psychoanalytic Psychology*.

Stanley Moldawsky, Ph.D.–Private practice, Chatham, NJ; Visiting Professor, Graduate School of Applied and Professional Psychology, Rutgers University; training analyst, National Psychological Association for Psychoanalysis.

Joseph M. Natterson, M.D.–Training analyst, Southern California Analytic Institute; Clinical Professor, University of California, Los Angeles School of Medicine, Department of Psychiatry; Senior Attending Psychiatrist, Cedars Sinai Medical Center, Los Angeles.

Ethel Spector Person, M.D.–Director, and Training and Supervising Analyst, Columbia University Center for Psychoanalytic Training; Research Clinical Professor of Psychiatry, Columbia University.

Ellen Bassin Ruderman, Ph.D.–Clinical Social Worker and Psychoanalytic Psychotherapist, Encino, CA; Clinical staff member, Thalians Community Mental Health Center, Cedars Sinai Medical Center, Los Angeles.

Vicki Granet Semel, Psy.D.–Private practice, South Orange, NJ; faculty member, Psychoanalytic Center of Northern New Jersey, Morristown, NJ.

Natalie Shainess, M.D.–Faculty member, William Alanson White Psychoanalytic Institute; Training and Supervising Analyst, Long Island Institute of Psychoanaysis; Fellow and former Trustee, American Academy of Psychoanalysis.

Janet L. Surrey, Ph.D.–Assistant Psychologist, McClean Hospital, Belmost, MA; Instructor, Department of Psychiatry, Harvard University Medical School.

Margot Tallmer, Ph.D.–Professor Hunter College, Brookdale Center on Aging; faculty member, and Supervising Analyst, National Psychological Association for Psychoanalysis.

Susan L. Williams, Ph.D.–Private practice, Beverly Hills, CA.

Phyllis Ziman-Tobin, Ph.D.–Clinical Associate, Doctoral program in Clinical Psychology, City University of New York; Clinical Coordinator and Interviewer, The Video Archives for Holocaust Testimonies, Yale University; Psychoanalyst, New York City.

Foreword

Many years ago, while living through the transition from a life of the traditional woman to one of widening horizons, I had three dreams. In the first I stood looking into a full-length mirror. There was no reflection. Someone came to stand beside me, and I saw the two of us in the glass. The scene shifted and I was watching a slide show. With each click of the projector, a new picture was thrown on the screen. Each was a photograph of me – all at different times and places over the span of my life. With each click and each new scene I said the words, "I am." The scene shifted once again. I was standing on a mountain top high above the other mountains. There was a stillness that was almost like music, and the sunlight bounced off the snow, redoubling its own brilliance. Although I was totally alone I was happy and unafraid.

Only if we are able to move from a definition of self that is derived from role or defined solely by our relationship to another, to a new consolidation of the identity first built up out of our earliest experiences of self will we be able to flourish in the shifting social structure of our time. And – unless there is at one's core such chaos and despair that it must be sealed off in the interest of sanity – the loving self that first came into being within the interpersonal matrix of parental care will feel abandoned if we do not find new vehicles for its activation and its outward expression – whether in a lover, in creative work, or in motherhood.

From the start of life there is a bipolarity of experience that when integrated allows for a full breadth of human expression. The infant alternately focuses its attention inward and outward—either absorbed by experiences within the boundaries of its body, or intrigued with the face of the caretaking other. In healthy development, this bipolarity evolves into a secure identity, or sense of self, on the one hand, and the capacity for intimacy and caring on the other. This bipolarity and its particular significance for the little girl and the woman she will become is explored and elaborated in the following pages by Bernay, who writes of the importance of reconciling nurturance and aggression, and by Shainess, who calls for a vision of maturity that includes commitment both to oneself and to another. The two strands of development are intertwined from the start, with the structure of both self and object emerging from the primordial symbiotic oneness of the early months of life, a oneness made possible by the good-enough mother's sensitive and caring responses to her infant.

But in ways explored in this book, loving and being—intimacy and identity—come into conflct, and a variety of defenses may be called into play. Relating through roles is one of them. I am concerned that women may believe that a change of roles will change their lives in some profound manner. This is indeed a situation in which "the more things change, the more they stay the same." I like Lewis's recommendation that we "posit motherhood as a relationship rather than a profession." The authenticity we bring to our lives, an authenticity that allows for a full integration and owning of all we are, will provide a secure center of identity that both welcomes intimacy and enables autonomy, without fear. This integration includes our aggression, our sexuality, and that within us which may not be "nice." More than once I've heard female patients describe how they compete in the world by trying to "out-nice" the other, unaware of the hostility and competitiveness in that stance. The masochist is one who must preserve the sense of self as good at all costs, fearful of the rage that lies on the other side of the split. Owning the inevitable identifications with both parents, disentangled from their conflicting elements, may be the most difficult aspect of the integrative process.

Personhood, wholeness, structural integrity, authenticity—there are many ways to describe the sine qua non for being—and for loving as well, for love that comes from any other place will be compromised, as is the self. Our horizons open wide, offering opportunity and choice as to how to live our one and only life when these two threads of our humanity can be woven together in harmony. Today's woman lives in an era of unique potential and challenge. For the first time in all of history, if we can free ourselves from archaic constraints, despite the remaining obstacles, the world is indeed our oyster.

Althea J. Horner, Ph.D.

Introduction

To not be aware of or to be unable or unwilling to accommodate to a social reality that has been so profoundly transformed within our own generation is to unnecessarily and perhaps irreparably burden the delicate balance of transferences and countertransferences on which the progressive resolutions of our therapeutic analytic tasks depend. If the analyst and analysand have profoundly different visions of this reality — of the "proper" or normal role of women in society — an analytic impasse may readily ensue in which, the structure of the relationship being "tilted" (Greenacre) the way it is, the patient is the more usually bent into pseudo compliances with analytic interpretive pressures, though it can oppositely take the course of active withdrawals by the patient of major segments of psychic functioning from the analytic arena.
— Wallerstein 1973, p. 29

As women who have experienced both sides of the therapeutic dyad, we have been concerned with the applicability of analytic theory to the changing realities of today's woman and to our work with women patients. According to traditional psychoanalytic theory, women are seen as deviants from male norms with weak and compromised superegos; poor moral judgment; needy, dependent, and self-destructive personalities; and aggressive and competitive masculine strivings. These assumptions lead to the interpretation of women's customary passive resolutions, as well as their more contemporary assertive and achieving resolutions, as perversions. Such either-or, good-or-bad partisan thinking makes it difficult to differentiate between healthy resolutions and cultural mores or subjective personal values; between pathology and nonconformity; and between harmful choices arising out of psychic conflict and deviance from stereotype. In addition, such categorical definitions of what is "proper" and what is "deviant" derive from male developmental experience and notions partial to the objectivity and separateness of work rather than from the interdependence of nurturance and caring associated with feminine experience, development, and identity (Gilligan, 1982). Conceptualizing behavior as "sick" and "well" reifies and idealizes male characteristics and devalues rather than encompasses the female experience. In addition, simplistic classifications are no longer enough to capture the intricacies of intimacy and the human condition. We are not sure they ever were.

Living in an increasingly complex society and in a world of interdependent interests, today's woman presents us with problems that require us to encounter the gray and ambiguous zones of our value systems and our sense of morality. Among the problems are conflicts between self and other, compassion and autonomy, virtue and power. Can a woman successfully combine marriage, motherhood, and career without harm to her husband or mate, her child, her work, or herself? Can a woman put herself out into competitive arenas and reconcile a desire to care about and empathize with others with a need for success, achievement, personal integrity, and self-nurturance? Can a woman meet the demands of the biological clock and the aging process and still maintain a vital and creative life style?

There are no simple responses to such questions. We can no longer invoke the images of "a good man who's the sole provider for the family and a good woman who's home tending the children and fires" (M. Horner, quoted in Manuel, 1984). New and more complex images are needed to deal with women who can identify with a female Supreme Court Justice, a female astronaut, and a female vice-presidential candidate; women who have a very different experience of their femininity than did any previous generation; and women whose ego ideal has changed from passivity, dependence, and submission to assertiveness, independence, and achievement.

Freud (1933) acknowledged at age 75 that his understanding of femininity was "incomplete and fragmentary," and he invited those wanting to know more about the subject to "inquire of your own experience of life, or turn to the poets, or wait until science can give you deeper and more coherent information" (p. 135). Early psychoanalytic thinkers, beginning with Horney (1926) and Jones (1927), took up Freud's challenge, criticizing his theories, which echoed the envy and hostility of women recounted in ancient mythology and codified in Genesis. They turned the tables on Freud's ideas, positing men's envy of the breast, the womb, and women's nurturing and procreative capacities. Others (Thompson, 1942) attempted to support or rebut Freud's concepts, based on the effects of women's oppression within a patriarchal society. Still others (Zilboorg, 1944; Sherfey, 1966), attempted to disprove Freud's theories by pointing out his use of outmoded fin de siècle biological notions as the framework for his psychological equations causing him to construct fallacious analogies and reach fallacious conclusions.

Contemporary theorists and clinicians have again challenged their predecessors and the deficiency model of psychoanalytic feminine identity. They have responded to the current realities of today's woman with a reexamination and a reframing of conventional conceptions. They offer newly conceived constructs of feminine identity and psychology both based on elucidating women's lifelong experience of affiliation arising from the bond between mother and infant daughter. They have noted the fluid boundaries, sense of female continuity, and sexual as well as social identifications between mother and child, yielding women's special propensity for nurturance, caretaking, and interdependence. These new theorists have also attended to the differing needs presented by the cultural shifts, developmental opportunities, and psychological conflicts that women face at various stages in their adult lives.

We have developed this book with these ideas in mind, organizing the readings into four sections. The first, the reassessment of traditional visions of feminine psychology and the second, new visions of femininity address the need for a new understanding and transformation of the old into the new. The readings in these sections offer a view of women's development that integrates their unique developmental experience and life processes. The third section explores critical situations that contemporary women find themselves facing over their life span. The fourth section focuses on various facets of the clinical treatment of women, emphasizing the therapeutic relationship. As we worked on this book, we were flooded with ideas for additional chapters. If we didn't think of them, our colleagues suggested them! Thus, we offer *The Psychology of Today's Woman* as a beginning of an expanded perspective for understanding women.

TONI BERNAY, PH.D
DOROTHY W. CANTOR, PSY. D.

New York
October, 1984

REFERENCES

Freud, S. (1931), Femininity. In: New introductory lectures in psychoanalysis. *Standard Edition*, 22:112–135. London: Hogarth Press, 1961.

Gilligan, C. (1982), *In a Different Voice*. Cambridge, MA: Harvard University Press.

Horney, K. (1926), The flight from womanhood: The masculinity complex in woman as viewed by men and women. In: *Feminine Psychology*, ed. H. Kelman. New York: Norton, 1967. pp. 54–70.

Jones, E. (1927), The early development of female sexuality. *Internat. J. Psycho-Anal.*, 8: 459–472.

Manuel, D. (1984), New goal is to help students grow. *Los Angeles Times*, April 12.

Sherfey, M. J. (1966), The evolution and nature of female sexuality in relation to psychoanalytic theory. *J. Amer. Psychoanal. Assn.*, 14(1) : 28–128.

Thompson, C. (1942), The role of women in this culture. *Psychiat.*, 4 : 1–8.

Wallerstein, R. S. (1973), Psychoanalytic perspectives on the problem of reality. *J. Amer. Psychoanal. Assn.*, 21(1): 8–33.

Zillboorg, G. (1944), Masculine and feminine: Some biological and cultural aspects. *Psychiat.*, 7: 257–296.

TRADITIONAL VISIONS OF FEMININITY REASSESSED

1

Is Freud an Enemy of Women's Liberation? Some Historical Considerations

Helen Block Lewis, Ph.D.

Freud's discoveries were made in an intellectual tradition stemming from the Enlightenment— and indeed from classical antiquity (for example, the epic by Lucretius, *De Rerum Natura*)—which detailed the baleful effects of human civilization on human beings. One thread of that tradition holds that civilization itself is inimical to humanity. Rousseau, for example, described how civilized human beings had lost their compassion (*pitié*). Another variant of the tradition denies any intrinsic opposition between society and the individual, but rather sees an exploitative society as destructive of human nature. Thus, Marx emphasized the alienation of spirit that capitalism breeds; and, more recently, the Marxist Freudians—notably Wilhelm Reich and

Erich Fromm— have traced in detail how an exploitative society deforms human relatedness. Feminist social criticism is still another legacy of the Enlightenment. Although feminist thinkers are divided about the noxious role of the profit system, they are united in directing their criticism against the personal deformations that result from the widespread social inferiority of women.

Freud's critique of civilization posited an inherent conflict between the individual and a social order built on the painful repression of sexuality. Implicit in Freud's work is thus a critique of the morality on which the social order is based. Once the morality of the social order is brought into question, social inequality (in particular the subjugation of women) cannot be comfortably accepted; it must be "rationalized"— something Freud was skilled at doing himself as well as at describing it in others.

Freud's lasting contribution to women's (and men's) liberation derives from his opening of morality to scientific scrutiny. Freud's (1913) description of the origins of guilt within the emotional dynamics of the family system, however flawed by his attempt to conform his description to Darwinian instincts, has been a powerful stimulus to research on the hypothesis that sex differences in early experience with caretakers are critical in development. This research has led, in turn to such modern reformist concepts as "parenting" (Baumrind, 1980; Dinnerstein, 1976). Freud's description of the cognitive distortions, such as rationalization and projection, that can arise under the press of the moral emotions of shame and guilt have made the concept of emotional defenses a part of folk wisdom. In particular, we now understand how much gender identity is a "primary-process" resultant, involving symbolic transformations of many emotional experiences and defenses during development. We can now speak of sexism as a by-product of our passionately formed gender identity, and we can identify Freud's sexism, a (Freudian) concept that applies to many of Freud's writings about women.

Before coming to what has been most useful and lasting in Freud's contribution to women's liberation, it is necessary to understand the prevailing androcentrism in biology, which Freud accepted. It is also necessary to look at Freud's sexism as well as his misogyny. Let us look first at Freud's androcentric heritage.

ANDROCENTRISM IN BIOLOGY: FREUD'S HERITAGE

Evolutionary theory as Freud knew it emphasized male aggression that is, skill and cunning in fighting—as the primary factor for selection in human adaptation. Freud was also working in an atmosphere that took for granted that women, although childbearers, were the "second sex." One consequence is that Freudian instinct theory ignored the basic, long-lasting affectional ties that make human beings cultural animals, when Freud was actually describing the powerful emotional forces, including sexual feelings, that govern human attachment behavior in the nuclear family.

The prevailing androcentrism in biology is well illustrated by the history of ethology, one of the recently developed methodologies that has significantly altered the climate of thinking in the behavioral sciences. Relying on the "de novo" observations that were the hallmark of the nineteenth centruy naturalists, in which the behavior observed was altered as little as possible by the observation itself, ethologists have called attention to the *social* conditions governing even the narrowest neurophysiological responses (Chance, 1980). Chance points out, for example, that Pavlov did not inquire into the extent to which his experimental dogs were social creatures. Recognizing the social character of the animals, however, makes an enormous difference to even so narrow a function as conditioning the salivary reflex. Denton (cited in Chance, 1980), for example, showed that although sheep ordinarily salivate constantly, the rate of salivation can be augmented naturally, not at the sight of food, but at the sight of another sheep feeding. When food is brought to a solitary sheep in the laboratory, therefore, the salivary reflex is absent, and no conditioning by the experimenter is possible. But if another sheep is brought in and fed in the laboratory, conditioning of the first sheep becomes possible.

Another consequence of the neglect of the social interactions governing behavior has been the failure to recognize that the adult animal's social relationships "assume equal if not greater importance than his direct relationship to the physical environment" (Chance, 1980, p. 87). Two distinct patterns of social attention have been discerned in nonhuman primates. These are the *agonic* and *hedonic* modes of social cohesion. In the agonic mode, which is originally based on responses to the threat of danger, the threat has been encapsulated within the group by the existence of a dominant male who serves as a focus of social attention, but is also a "negative social referent." In the hedonic mode, which is also a mode of social attention fostering group cohesion, other animals are "positive social referents," in the context of which eating, resting, sleeping, and grooming take place.

Chance (1980) points out that the existence of a separate hedonic mode of social interaction has been the "single most important discovery" resulting from ethologists' focus on patterns of social attention in primate groups:

> The integrity of the . . . hedonic system has been hidden as its components – involving body contact (as in grooming, sitting or sleeping next to), relaxation and exploration . . . appear at different times . . . Only when the elimination of danger occurs, as within the core of a territory, or when the young are in the presence of the mother and in contact with her, has the hedonic system been seen as a single piece [p. 89].

Chance suggests that the reason for the relatively late discovery of a hedonic mode was that ethology developed initially from the study of birds and fishes whose social relations are phasic and constructed on agonic forms. Another reason, which seems equally plausible, is the prevailing androcentrism in science, which regarded affectional bonds as secondary derivatives of individualistic instinct or drives. The mother-infant interaction was neglected both as a factor in the evolution of species (see Morgan, 1972) and as a central "biological" source of humanity's long-lasting affectional and moral bonds. Freud was also a captive of such androcentric attitudes.

Another illuminating example of androcentrism in Freud's time comes from the history of embryology. In Freud's time (before the discovery of the chromosomal basis of sex) it was known that the reproductive system is undifferentiated in the very early fetal stages. The genital tubercle that forms in both sexes later becomes the clitoris in the female and the penis in the male. Freud shared the generally accepted doctrine interpreting these facts as meaning that the clitoris is a vestigal or abbreviated penis. On this basis, Freud developed the speculation that by adulthood women should have outgrown the need for this vestigal organ. In Freud's view, however, this speculation some-how gained the status of a phylogenetic fact.

Since the discovery of the chromosomal basis of sex and the hor-mones that chromosomes release, embryologists have discovered that without the operation of the Y chromosome, the embryo remains fe-male. This requires a concept of a model or template that is basically fe-male. Sherfey (1972) tells how hard it was for embryologists in the 1940's (mostly men) to grasp this concept. She says that it was not until she read the statement that "the neuter sex is female" that she herself grasped that some primary-process thinking was in evidence. Scientists were having a hard time announcing to the world that Adam's rib be-longed to Eve.

Freud was aware of the extent of his own ignorance about women. He lamented it frequently (Fliegel, 1973). At the same time (in a famil-iar Freudian mechanism called projection), he often cast the blame for his ignorance on the women themselves. So, he writes that the erotic life of women "partly owing to the stunting effect of civilized conditions and partly owing to their conventional secretiveness and insincerity — is still veiled in obscurity" (Freud, 1905, p. 151). Another example of Freud's prejudice against women is in his treatment of their sociability or moral development. Freud (1905) observed that the "development of the inhibitions against sexuality (shame, disgust, pity, etc.) takes place in girls earlier and in the face of less resistance than in boys" (p. 219). But this does not mean to him (as it might have, in terms of his own system) that the moral development of girls is faster and less diffi-cult than that of boys. Rather, in the same sentence just quoted, he suggests that the "tendency to sexual repression seems in general to be greater; and where the component instincts of sexuality appear, they prefer the passive form in girls" (p. 219). One does not need to be a very accomplished Freudian to recognize that the earlier and easier devel-opment of socialization in girls is being interpreted to their disadvan-tage as a function of their having a less active sexual instinct. There is now strong experimental evidence that girls are more sociable than boys (Maccoby & Jacklin, 1974) and that girls' aggressions are more "prosocial"—that is, more "moral"—than those of boys' (Sears, Rau, & Alpert, 1965)—a confirmation, as usual, of Freud's observations rather than of his theory.

Freud's androcentrism is particulary visible in the open contradic-tions within his own model of psychosexual development for the two sexes. In one model in *Three Essays on Sexuality*, Freud (1905) assumes that women's development is homologous to men's, an attitude that considers women to be the "other sex" but otherwise implies the equality of the sexes. The oedipal triangle is homologous for the two sexes, based on a component of heterosexual attraction that is the same for both. The sexual fantasies of the two sexes are equally incestuous and "differentiated owing to the attraction of the opposite sex – the son being drawn toward his mother and the daughter toward her father" (p. 227).

Freud, however, was actually contradicting his "homologue" version of the model of psychosexual development when he wrote, also in *Three Essays on Sexuality*, that "libido is invariably and necessarily of a masculine nature, whether it occurs in men or in women, and irrespectively of whether its object is a man or a woman" (1905, p. 218). Because libido is masculine, the model of psychosexual development is male for both sexes; women's task in development is to repudiate their masculinity. This is, of course, the model that brought much criticism within the psychoanalytic movement, as we shall see when we examine the history of Horney's controversy with Freud. But it is the model to which Freud clung; he repeated it in his final publication on the subject of women: "We are now obliged to recognize that the little girl is a little man" (1933, p. 118).

Freud's model was thus one of equality when he was thinking about "the object-relations" of the two sexes. It was when he was thinking of their genital zones that women could not be allowed to enjoy the clitoris. Freud apparently could not believe that the clitoris (even though it was a homologue of the penis) could be, or should be, a source of orgasm for the adult woman. The following quotation of a famous passage in his writings in which he was thinking about women's sexuality from the man's point of view, makes clear the operation of Freud's androcentric bias.

> If we are to understand how a little girl turns into a woman, we must follow the further vicissitudes of [this] excitability of the clitoris. Puberty, which brings about so great an accession of libido in boys, is marked in girls by a fresh wave of *repression*, in which it is precisely clitoridal sexuality that is affected. What is thus overtaken by repression is a piece of masculine sexuality. *The intensification of the brake upon sexuality brought about by pubertal repression in women serves as a stimulus to the libido of men*

and causes an increase of its activity. Along with this heightening of libido there is also an increase of sexual overvaluation which only emerges in full force in relation to a woman who holds herself back and who denies her sexuality [italics added]. When at last the sexual act is permitted and the clitoris itself becomes excited, it still retains a function: the task, namely, of transmitting the excitation to the adjacent female sexual parts, just as – to use a simile – pine shavings can be kindled in order to set a log of harder wood on fire. . . . When erotogenic susceptibility to stimulation has been successfully transferred by a woman from the clitoris to the vaginal orifice, it implies that she has adopted a new leading zone for the purpose of her later sexual activity. A man, on the other hand, retains his leading zones unchanged from childhood. The fact that women change their leading erotogenic zones in this way, together with the wave of repression at puberty, which as it were, puts aside their childish masculinity, are the chief determinants of the greater proneness of women to neurosis and especially to hysteria. These determinants, therefore are intimately related to the essence of femininity [1905, pp. 220–221].

It is amply clear from this passage that "femininity" is tailored to fit men's needs.

As Freud saw it, moreover, the assumption of their adult role was a harder task for women than for men. If one follows this line of reasoning, women should be more prone than men to disturbances of gender identity. We now know, in fact, that the opposite holds true. Men are more prone than women to severe mental illness in general, and are more prone not only to disorders of gender identity and sexual functioning, but also to obsessional neurosis and paranoia (Lewis, 1976).

Freud's androcentrism, which he shared with the rest of contemporary scientific thinking, thus led him astray about the psychology of women. Freud often lamented his own inability to understand women's psychology. So, for example, in a later postscript to *Three Essays on Sexuality*, Freud (1923) explicitly tells us that he can describe the infantile genital organization of the libido "only as it affects the male child; the corresponding processes in little girls are not known to us" (p. 142).

FREUD'S SEXISM

Something beyond the prevailing androcentrism was also operating in Freud's thinking, however – something more like sexism. This interpretation is based on the fact that misogynist statements in Freud's writings are not hard to find. As one example, in *Three Essays on Sexuality*, Freud (1905) likened the polymorphous perversity of children to the sexual behavior of women. As another, even more damaging example, in his paper "On Narcissism," Freud (1914) wrote that "complete object-love of the attachment type . . . is characteristic of the male. Women are by nature more subject to an intensification of their original narcissism. Strictly speaking, it is only themselves that women love" (p. 89). According to Freud, this narcissism is what gives women (as well as children and criminals) their special charm!

Freud's sexism, as well as his misogyny, is also apparent in his paper on "The Taboo of Virginity" (1918). Freud recognizes that the high value placed by civilized men on virginity is something needing explanation, instead of being taken for granted. His own explanation, however, goes no further than taking for granted the existence of (male-dominated) monogamy as a reflection of the development of civilization. A high value on virginity, he says, is the "logical continuation of the right to exclusive possession of a woman which forms the essence of monogamy" (p. 193).

How is it, then, that primitive peoples do not have the same regard for virginity as we do? Freud's interpretation is that the taboo of virginity is an instance of the generalized dread of women. "Perhaps this dread," Freud (1918) writes:

> is based on the fact that woman is different from man, forever incomprehensible and mysterious, strange and therefore apparently hostile. The man is afraid of being weakened by the woman, infected with her femininity, and of then showing himself incapable. The effect which coitus has of discharging tension and causing flaccidity may be the prototype of what the man fears; and the realization of the influence which the woman gains over him through sexual intercourse, the consideration she thereby forces from him, may justify the extension of this fear. In all this there is nothing obsolete, nothing which is still not alive among ourselves (pp. 198-199).

At this point, Freud is being very Freudian—that is, interpreting primary-process ideation in which women might be experienced as irrationally frightening. But in the next moment, he is arguing that "danger *really exists* [italics added], so that with the taboo of virginity a primitive man is defending himself against a correctly sensed, although psychical danger" (p. 201). The danger is that the woman's hostility will be evoked by her defloration "and the prospective husband is just the person who would have every reason to avoid such enmity" (p. 202). The woman's hostility, moreover, is evoked not by the pain of her defloration (and the invasion of her body) but by her penis envy! "Behind this envy for the penis, there comes to light the woman's hostile bitterness against the man, which never completely disappears in the relations between the sexes, and is clearly indicated in the strivings and in the literary productions of 'emancipated' women" (p. 205). Summing up, Freud writes: "A woman's *immature sexuality* is discharged onto the man who first makes her acquainted with the sexual act. This being so, the taboo of virginity is reasonable enough and we can understand the rule which decrees that precisely the man who is to enter upon a life shared with this woman shall avoid these dangers" (p. 206). Freud cites as evidence for the survival of this wisdom a popular comedy of the day entitled *Virgin's Venom*, which reminds him of the "habit of snake-charmers, who make poisonous snakes first bite a piece of cloth in order to handle them afterwards without danger" (p. 206). In this particular instance, the imagery he uses suggests more than a touch of misogyny.

FREUD'S SEXISM: THE HORNEY STORY

Perhaps the most significant evidence of Freud's sexism comes from the fact that even at the time Freud was working, androcentrism did not go unchallenged in all quarters. John Stuart Mill and Friedrich Engels are only two of the influential, eloquent voices calling attention to the subjugation of women. Not only did Freud ignore these challenges to androcentrism, but, as will be seen, he dealt harshly with critics within the psychoanalytic movement who questioned his view on the constitutional inferiority of women. In any case, even though Freud welcomed many women as his students, the combination of the prevailing androcentrism and Freud's sexism have made many of his clinical pronouncements on the sexuality of women demonstrably wrong, an unusual fate for Freud's clinical observations. For example, his dictum that it is necessary for women to overcome their liking for clitoral orgasm has been overturned by subsequent evidence (Masters & Johnson, 1970), but not without considerable harm to many women patients in the interim.

The history of the controversy between Freud and Karen Horney – a controversy that led ultimately to her defection from the Freudian movement and the development of her own school of psychoanalysis – has been carefully researched by Fliegel (1973). The story illuminates the issues with which Freud was dealing in an androcentric world. It also illustrates the fact that Freud did not use his own method of primary-process interpretation of the emotions engendered by the issues. If he had done so, the sexism inherent in his own views might have been more clearly apparent to him, as it was to Horney.

By the time Horney (1922) came to write her paper "On the Genesis of the Castration Complex in Women," Adler had already been read out of the Freudian movement for suggesting that "feelings of inferiority" in a competitive world were a source of emotional conflict and neurosis. Adler had also suggested that women are prone to inferiority feelings in response to their actual subordination in society. Horney's paper was written within the Freudian psychoanalytic movement; it was read at the Seventh International Congress of Psychoanalysis in Berlin. Horney took issue with the assumption of Abraham and Freud "as an axiomatic fact that females feel at a disadvantage because of their genital organs without this being regarded as constituting a problem in itself – possibly because to masculine narcissism this has seemed too self-evident to need explanation" (Horney, 1922, p. 38). Horney goes on to say that "an assertion that one half of the human race is discontented with the sex assigned to it and can overcome this discontent only in favorable circumstances – is decidedly unsatisfying, not only to feminine narcissism but also to biological science" (p. 38).

It is clear that Horney's suggestions in this paper rely heavily on the Freudian assumption that our ideas about the role of men and women are primary-process transformations representing conflicted feelings. As Fliegel says, one can hardly escape the judgment that Horney was more Freudian than Freud in grasping the importance of infantile sexual *fantasies* about the two anatomies, rather than clinging to a notion that the absence of a penis actually makes women constitutionally inferior.

Horney makes three specific suggestions about why little girls respond enviously to the realization that boys have a penis. Each of

Horney's suggestions is a very Freudian interpretation based on clinical material from her own cases. This evidence links penis envy to "urethral erotism," "scopophilia," and "masturbation wishes." In explaining urethral erotism, Horney suggests that children "narcissistically overvalue" all their excretory functions. Fantasies of omnipotence are more easily associated with the "jet of urine" passed by the male. Horney cites a common game played by two little boys in which they urinate to make a cross that will kill the person they are thinking of at the moment. As for scopophilia, little girls cannot see their genitals. "Women can arrive at no clear knowledge about her person and therefore finds it harder to free herself from herself" (Horney, 1922, p. 41). As for masturbatory wishes, girls have a harder time overcoming these, because they sense that boys do gratify themselves every time they hold their penis to urinate. It is apparent that each of these interpretations of early penis envy is made within the spirit and the letter of Freudian thinking.

Horney's (1922) major point of disagreement with Freud is voiced along with a grateful acknowledgement of how much Freud's paper on homosexuality in women helped her to understand the castration complex in women (p. 49). The point of disagreement is that women's neurotic attitudes toward the penis are not based on their early or primary penis-envy but on later disappointments and experiences of humiliation in their oedipal attachment to their fathers. Horney's view of the decisive importance of the later disappointments of women is based on her own clinical observations. She writes:

> The numerous unmistakable observations . . . show us how important it is to realize that . . . as an ontogenetic repetition of a phylogenetic experience the child constructs, on the basis of a (hostile or loving) identification with its mother, a fantasy that it has suffered full sexual appropriation by the father; and further, that in fantasy this experience presents itself as having actually taken place—as much a fact as it must have been at that distant time when all women were primarily the property of the father [p. 44].

Horney thus attributed the castration complex in neurotic women to the reactivation of their early penis envy as a consequence of disturbed object relations. Evidence from her own cases had persuaded her that women's castration complex was a defense against guilty fantasies of rape and castration at the hands of their fathers. She suggested, moreover, that healthy women get over their early penis envy by a positive identification with their mother, including a wish to be like her in having a child by a man. So far, in reading the text of her 1922 paper, there seems little to evoke controversy within the psychoanalytic movement. On the contrary, one might have thought that Horney's clinical observations would be welcomed as useful additional information about the development of women, especially since Freud had so often acknowledged his own ignorance of the psychology of women.

Horney's paper met a very different fate. Freud overtly ignored it, except for a passing reference to it in his famous paper on the anatomical distinction between the sexes (1925). In that paper he behaved as if there were no differences between her views and his own. In his 1925 paper, however, Freud for the first time laid down an authoritative description of girls' psychosexual development and from then on never revised it. As Fliegel (1973) observes, reading Freud's paper after reading Horney's suggests that Freud's "formulations constitute a direct reversal" (p. 389) of Horney's thesis. In Freud's formulation, a girl's oedipal wishes develop only out of frustrated phallic jealousy and only out of forced resignation to her actually castrated condition.

Fliegel's hypothesis to account for Freud's sudden adoption of an authoritative position on the subject of women was that he had developed cancer in the interval between Horney's 1922 paper and his 1925 publication. Freud's introduction to his 1925 paper is indeed explicit in his reference to a shortened life span. He also clearly suggests that he is publishing without waiting for confirmation of his views, a practice that he reminds his readers is not his custom ("Why do I not postpone publication . . . until further experience has given me proof?" [Freud, 1925, p. 248]). Freud calls on his collaborators who now exist in greater numbers than before to undertake the task of gathering evidence.

As Fliegel points out, this invitation was answered by his women students, Deutsch and Lampl-de Groot, who published clinical material supporting Freud's position, whereas Jones and Fenichel, two men students, could not support Freud. Fliegel notes further that all traces of the Horney controversy within the orthodox Freudian movement vanished from establishment psychoanalytic publications. Jones's disagreement with Freud was never recanted but Freud simply dismissed the controversy in subsequent publications. Jones's biography of

Freud contains only cryptic and bland references to the controversy. Fliegel contrasts this with Jones's detailed treatment of other controversies—for example, over how to proofread the *International Journal of Psycho-Analysis*! Jones is also quite bland about the subsequent career of Horney, noting simply that in 1932 Horney was on her way to New York and ignoring the fact that she was also on her way out of the Freudian school.

For her part, Horney, whose rich clinical observations had been given such short shrift by Freud, was much more polemical in her next publication on the subject, her famous paper on "The Flight from Womanhood" (1926). In this paper she clearly formulates the concept of womb envy on the part of boys, a concept that has led to considerable work on the part of anthropologists, beginning with Mead (1949). Horney also now personalizes the controversy. She pays tribute to Freud's genius but does not find it surprising that as a man he has difficulty understanding women. This paper contains a table in which boys' fantasies about girls are compared with psychoanalysts' ("our views") about women. The resulting similarity is compelling evidence for the sexism that Horney was trying to describe in Freud's thinking.

I have become very fond of Theodora Wells's (personal communication) satirical reversal of Freud's ideas about anatomy and destiny, because her script illustrates the irony that Freud's mistakes can best be illuminated by Freud's own methods of interpreting mistakes as primary-process thinking—in this instance accomplishing the aggrandizement of males. The script is Wells' account of how psychoanalysis might sound if women were in positions of power. It is designed as an introduction to therapy sessions for distressed, inferior males. Here is how it goes:

> Feel into the fact that women are the leaders, the power centers, the prime movers. Man, whose natural role is husband and father, fulfills himself through nurturing children and making the home a refuge for the woman. This is only natural to balance the biological role of woman who devotes her whole body to the race during pregnancy: the most revered power known to Woman (and to men, of course). Then feel further into the obvious biological explanation for woman as the ideal: her genital construction. By design, female genitals are compact and internal, protected by her body. Male genitals are exposed so that he must be protected from outside attack to assure the perpetuation of the race. His vulnerability obviously requires sheltering. Thus, by nature, males are

more passive than females and have a desire in sexual relations to be symbolically engulfed by the protective body of women. Males psychologically yearn for this protection, fully realizing their masculinity at this time and feeling exposed and vulnerable at other times. A man experiences himself as a "whole man" when thus engulfed. If the male denies these feelings, he is unconsciously rejecting his masculinity. Therapy is thus indicated to help him adjust to his own nature. Of course, therapy is administered by a woman, who has the education and wisdom to facilitate openness leading to the male's growth and self-actualization. To help him feel into the defensive emotionality he is invited to get in touch with the child in him. He remembers his sisters' jeering at his primitive genitals that "flap around foolishly." She can run, climb and ride horseback unencumbered. Obviously, since she is free to move, she is encouraged to develop her body and mind in preparation for her active responsibilities of adult womanhood. The male vulnerability needs female protection so he is taught the less active, but caring virtues of homemaking. Because of his vagina-envy he learns to bind up his genitals and learns to feel ashamed because of his nocturnal emissions. Instead, he is encouraged to dream of getting married, waiting for the time of his fulfillment – when "his woman" gives him a girl-child to care for. He knows that if it is a boy-child he has failed somehow – but they can try again. In getting to the child in him these early experiences are reawakened. He is, of course, led by a woman and in a circle of nineteen men and four women he begins to work through some of his deep feelings [of inferiority].

My point is that this script could not have been written without Freud's methods of interpreting as "primary process" what seems to be straightforward cognitive content.

FREUDIAN INTERPRETATIONS: INSIGHTS INTO GENDER IDENTITY

Freud's most enduring contribution to our understanding of sex differences comes from his insight into the extent to which primary-process transformations of conflicted feelings govern human attitudes about sex and sex differences. With this powerful instrument for unraveling conflicted feelings, psychoanalysis can predict with some success certain universals of experience for the two sexes. As Jahoda puts it (1977) "every child has to discover anew the existence and meaning of morphological sex differences" (p. 88) within the context of passionate attachments to his or her nuclear family. It may be useful to outline some of the ways in which attitudes of men and women are determined by their gender identity.

The linguistic and social connotations of the term *gender identity* suggest that sexual identity is a primary-process transformation of affects and self-images formed by each of us in interaction with our earliest caretakers. Gender, as distinct from sex, also suggests that identification of oneself as male or female is itself a complicated part of the socialization process, not an automatic consequence of chromosomal endowment. This supposition in turn suggests that adult heterosexual gender preference (like homosexuality) is the outcome of a long developmental process in which primary-process transformations—for instance, anaclitic and defensive identifications—play a decisive part.

Although all these concepts are implicit and explicit in Freud's writings on sex differences, Freud never actually used the term "gender identity." The term was first used by Stoller (1968) in his book about people with chromosomal sex abnormalities. Psychoanalysts and psychologists both have welcomed the term, however, because it helps to keep some of the manifold meanings of sex role disentangled.

In the sense that growing up in sexually different bodies inevitably produces psychological differences in the acculturation process, anatomy is one determinant of destiny. Although the term "acculturation process" has a modern ring, and although Freud actually talked more about unreconstructed instincts being constantly opposed by culture, Freud's basic assumption was that sex differences produced differences in the acculturation process. In Freud's system, primary-process transformations were bound to be different for the selves of the two sexes because of intrinsic differences in the parent-child relationship. The many experimental studies now demonstrating a sex difference in the mother-infant interaction are clearly a confirmation of this basic Freudian assumption. Sex differences in the mother-infant interaction must influence the courses of subsequent acculturation for each sex in some universal ways.

One of these predictable universals comes from the fact that women have a same-sex first caretaker, whereas men have an opposite-sex first caretaker as the first "object" of passionate attachment. Mead (1949) picked up the implications of this universal, suggesting that the boy's "earliest experience of self is one in which he is forced, in the relationship to his mother, to realize himself as different, as a creature unlike his mother . . . ." (p. 167). Lynn (1961) develops this point in a behavioral mode, suggesting that girls have only to learn a "lesson" in mother-person emulation, whereas boys have to learn to differentiate the gender of the self from that of the first caretaker and then to "solve the problem" of father-person identification. Lynn syggests that the actual consequences for developmental events differ from Freud's predicted consequences. For girls, the substructure of identity comes from assimilating "same sexedness" in imitation of a personal relationship; for boys, identity involves a more complicated cognitive process: abstracting a principle of identification from his being unlike his first caretaker and like his usually more distant father.

Still another universal of experience that influences acculturation for each sex stems from the fact that the first caretaker is of the opposite sex for boys and of the same sex for girls. Boys' very early frustrations at the hands of their (opposite sex) mothers form a substratum of experience when the time comes in adulthood for them to find a person of the opposite sex. Horney (1932) suggests that the little boy judges his genitals to be too small for his mother's vagina: "His original dread of women is not castration anxiety at all, but . . . the menace to his self-respect" (p. 142). Horney is careful to make the point that dread is not an inevitable characteristic of a man's relationship to the opposite sex, only a frequent stress point, on which later noxious events can build. In contrast, little girls' interest in their fathers usually occurs at a time when they are much older; their relationship to their fathers usually does not bear the imprint of earliest nurturance. On the contrary, experiences with father occur when the girl's self is quite well-formed. Disappointments with father can be better borne by a self that is already well developed; similarly, later disappointments in heterosexual relationships carry fewer scars of very ancient battles with mother fought mindless and alone.

Taken together with the more recent evidence of profound sex differences in the earliest mother-infant interaction, with boys being more difficult to pacify (Moss, 1974), the universal circumstance of same-sex nurturant figures for girls and cross-sex figures for boys suggests that boys should have greater difficulty assuming masculine gender identity than girls do assuming feminine gender identity. As noted earlier, findings from our own culture support this prediction (Lewis, 1976).

One of the most significant and puzzling findings of experimental studies of the mother-infant interaction that have developed from the questions raised about anatomy and destiny is the sex difference in primates' vulnerability to maternal deprivation, not only in adult sexual capacity but also in a variety of other social behaviors. Although the evidence from our own acculturated species is less unequivocal than that from nonhuman primates, there is more than a suggestion that human male infants are more subject to "inconsolable states" (Moss, 1974), and that maternal deprivation has a more clearly harmful effect on men than on women (Bayley & Schaefer, 1964). These experimental findings speak to the possibility of some intrinsic, genetic-hormonal differences between the sexes that may render females more resistant to the psychological stress of maternal deprivation. Another way of phrasing this difference is to say that women are more sociable than men.

Another line of investigation into the mother-infant interaction suggests that nonhuman mammal mothers not only can differentiate the sex of their pups but treat their male pups more "harshly". On the human level, there are studies suggesting that mothers have a harder time establishing a smooth interaction with their boy infants (Moss, 1974). This finding may itself be based, of course, on differences in mothers' attitudes toward the two genders, especially in a social system in which women are devalued. Differences in the symbolic meaning of boy and girl neonates to their parents have been demonstrated experimentally (for example, Rubin, Provenzano, & Luria, 1974). Girl and boy infants are differently perceived in the eyes of their beholders (girls being perceived as "softer"). This does not preclude the possibility that girl infants actually do bring something genetically different into the infant-caretaker interaction. Their smoother interaction with their same-sex caretakers may make a closer bond between the infant's self and mother. In turn, this closer bond may interact with women's social inferiority to foster women's proneness to states of shame (Lewis, 1976).

Another predictable universal of gender differences in sexual attitudes is the greater difficulty intrinsic for men in adult heterosexual intercourse. Wide-ranging explanations, using primary-process transformations of the emotional conflicts evoked by this circumstance, have included differences in men's and women's anxieties during intercourse (Horney, 1932) and characterological sex differences based on these differing anxieties (Fromm, 1943). Differential modes of experiencing the world, such as Erikson's (1964) "inner" and "outer" space, have also been suggested.

The fact that intercourse is intrinsically more difficult for men than for women is illuminated by the contrast between ourselves and nonhuman primates, for whom the estrus cycle still controls both male as well as female sexual arousal. The loss of estrus in the human species has brought intercourse under social much more than hormonal control. It has also resulted in the loss of a fail-safe stimulus. Yet, intercourse for men is still the same three-step process that can be seen among mammals: arousal-erection, intromission, and ejaculation-orgasm (Beach, 1965). A man's failure to have an erection or to maintain it prevents intercourse; no such burden of responsibility for intercourse is carried by women. A woman has only to be present and willing to permit penetration. A man must be aroused, a state not necessarily under his conscious control. The act of intercourse is thus more difficult for men and easier for women. A woman's orgasm, moreover, plays no role in her fertilization, while a man's ejaculation-orgasm is necessary for fertilization. As Horney (1932) put it:

> The man is actually obliged to go on proving his manhood to the woman. There is no analogous necessity for her. Even if she is frigid she can engage in sexual intercourse and conceive and bear a child. She performs her part merely by *being*, without any *doing*—a fact that has always filled men with admiration and resentment. The man, on the other hand, has to *do* something in order to fulfill himself. The ideal of "efficiency" is a typical masculine ideal [p. 145].

The gestalt of feelings and attitudes governing experience in sexual intercourse is thus "phallocentric" for men. The fear of his failure to have and maintain an erection is an intruder in a man's sexual experience. Fromm (1943) describes how the fear of impotence in a male increases his need for "mastery," an attitude that when coupled with resentment against women can readily turn into domination and rape. In contrast, women's attitudes toward sex are more embedded in the framework of possible maternity. Women's sexual experience has a frequent intruder in the image of herself as mother, with both the pleasurable and the fearful consequences of pregnancy.

Cross-cultural evidence suggests the accuracy of some of these interpretations of universal experience. Ford and Beach (1951) show that "love charms are much more often employed by men than by women" (pp. 108–109). Their survey of sexual behavior also shows that the majority of cultures studied believe that men should take the initiative in intercourse. This belief must in part reflect the acknowledgement of necessity. Mead (1949) makes the point that "the male who has learned various mechanical ways to stimulate his sexual specificity in order to copulate with a women he does not at the moment desire is doing far more violence to his nature than a female who needs only receive a male" (p. 210).

Horney's distinction between "being" and "doing" has stimulated a great deal of anthropological research on the development of sex roles (see, for example, Chodorow, 1971). The distinction between being and doing has an analog with the fact that women's gender identity is at lesser risk of malformation than men's, and it may be one component of the sex difference in proneness to depression and paranoia.

Another important primary-process resultant of the caretaker's gender is the way in which men's aggressions against women are fostered and rationalized by their relationship to their mothers. Dinnerstein (1976) has shown that the subordinate position of women is fostered by a family structure in which both boys and girls are predominantly reared by their mother. Boys' aggressions are especially exaggerated by the circumstance of earliest rearing by an opposite-sex caretaker. Baumrind (1980), summarizing new directions in socialization research, emphasizes the importance and usefulness of studies of one-sided rearing versus "parenting." Chodorow (1978) has also made use of Freudian concepts in her cross-cultural studies of the *reproduction* of mothering.

Erikson (1964) raised the question of human survival in his paper on womanhood and inner space. Erikson begins this essay by pointing with alarm to the fact that men have brought the species to the brink of destruction, and suggests that women may have to save it. "Maybe if women could gain the determination to represent publicly what they have always stood for privately in evolution and history (realism of upbringing, resourcefulness in peace-keeping and devotion to healing), they might well add an ethically restraining, because truly supranational, power to politics in the widest sense" (p. 604).

Finally, the recent work on psychological androgyny may reasonably be regarded as an outgrowth of Freudian interpretations. Freud carefully distinguished (as nearly always, with clinical accuracy) between masculine and feminine personality and the gender of a person's sexual object choice. Men homosexuals, he observed, are by no means always feminine in personality, nor are women homosexuals always masculine. Present-day work on psychological androgyny (for example, Bem, 1976), correcting earlier unipolar concepts of masculinity-femininity, represents an extension of Freud's view that masculinity and femininity are complicated resultants of emotional interactions with significant adults and significant cultural values.

The growing literature on psychological androgyny now questions whether masculinity and femininity are two poles of a single personality dimension. It suggests, rather, that masculinity and femininity may be independent personality dimensions or else orthogonally related. Even more important, androgynous sex-role identity is now considered to be more adaptive than conventional sex-role typing, since it allows greater flexibility of behavior. Thus, for example, androgynous women were found to be more nonconforming than feminine women; correspondingly, androgynous men were found to be more nurturant than masculine men (Bem, 1975; Bem, Martyna & Watson, 1976). Another study showed that in an experimental situation designed to elicit expressive behavior, androgynous men gazed at the person to whom they were speaking and smiled more often (when not speaking) than did masculine-typed men (LaFrance & Carmen, 1980). Thus, androgynous people are adding to their repertoire of useful behaviors rather than showing inconsistent and perhaps pathological "cross-sex" behavior.

FREUDIAN INSIGHTS AND COGNITIVE STYLE

My own interest in the psychology of women goes back to an unexpected finding during research in collaboration with H. A. Witkin and others some 40 years ago (Witkin, Lewis, Hertzman, Machover, Meissner, and Wapner, 1954). Women are slightly but significantly more field dependent perceivers than men. Field dependence is itself a significant reminder of the personal and emotional factors that Freud understood as underlying people's perception of the world. Beginning with middle adolescence and into adulthood, a sex difference in field dependence is found worldwide, except among the Eskimo, where cultural attitudes treat the two sexes as equal in the division of labor. (It is interesting to note also in passing that, according to evidence developed by Coates (1974), 5-year-old little girls in our own society are, if anything, more field independent than boys.) Field-dependent adults do well at tasks involving social skills—for example, they facilitate conflict resolution in group discussions better than field-independent performers; they are also more accurate at assessing other people's affective states. Field-independent people are better at tasks involving spatial visualization. Field-dependence is clearly a perceptual orientation appropriate for dealing with people, whereas field independence is more appropriate for dealing with things.

Most important for the development of my thinking was a study (Witkin, Lewis and Weil, 1968) in which we predicted and confirmed that field-dependent patients would be more prone to shame than guilt in their early psychotherapy sessions, whereas field-independent patients would be more prone to guilt than shame. (For this study we used Gottschalk and Gleser's, 1969 well-established method of scoring verbal content, clause by clause, for implied affective state.) In this study we also predicted and confirmed that field-dependent patients would be more likely to direct their hostility against themselves, whereas field-independent patients were likely to direct it both at themselves and outward. Moreover, there was a strong tendency for self-directed hostility and shame to occur together, whereas guilt involved hostility directed both ways. There is now considerable evidence for an association between field dependence and depression and hysteria (both phobias and psychosomatic illnesses) and, as one would predict, between field independence and obsessional neurosis and paranoia (Lewis, 1976). As is also well known, women are more prone than men (by a ratio of three to one) to depression and hysteria. In contrast, men are more prone than women to obsessional neurosis and paranoia—in the latter instance especially between the ages of 15 and 35.

This package of evidence involving field dependence led me to the hypothesis that women are more prone to shame than men and the converse proposition that men are more prone to guilt than women.

This formulation is close to the one Freud struggled with in his famous remark that women's superego is "never so impersonal" as men's. It came together with observations I had been making slowly over the years of practice as a psychoanalyst: namely, that the affective states of shame and guilt—the affective states that represent the forbidding internalized agency—have been much neglected in psychoanalytic work. I set out to do a phenomenological study of these states, (Lewis, 1971) and came to realize that shame and guilt are differing modes of maintaining the basic affectional ties by means of which human beings become acculturated and stay so. At this point let me digress for a moment to remind us that Freud did not have available to him the evidence from modern anthropology that acculturation is our species' unique adaptation for survival and that human beings are therefore uniquely moral creatures. Freud glimpsed this fact, but could not really integrate it into his theoretical system, because he had postulated that shame and guilt are narcissistic drive regulators or modifiers—even while he described clinically how these affective states serve to maintain affectional bonds, even at the expense of the self.

One striking observation that emerged from my phenomenological study was that shame, whether it occurs over a moral transgression or a failure to achieve, is an affective state in which the *self* is in the center of operations or, more accurately, the self-in-the-eyes-of-the-hostile-other. This aspect of the phenomenology of the self, I believe, has led to a confounding of shame and the so-called narcissistic personality. It was this error that led Freud to believe that women are more narcissistic than men. Guilt, in contrast, is about things or events in the world for which the self feels responsible. But the self is not the phenomenal center of the system at such moments; rather the center becomes the thing-in-the-world, the deed done or undone, and what one must do to remedy the wrong. There is a strong phenomenological affinity between shame and depression, which is an affective state about the worthless self. There is also a strong affinity between guilt and obsessive, paranoid ideation about the things one must do to make things right. Since guilt is more ideational than shame, which catches the self more "at the quick," shame is often quickly absorbed by guilty ideation. Guilt thus serves as a defense against the more painful, acute state of shame. In guilt the self is intact and busy, whereas in shame the self is divided and, for the moment, crushed.

My questions now became, how does it come about that women are more prone to shame? How do men become more prone to guilt? To answer these questions, I looked, as any psychoanalyst would, into the question of sex differences in the mother-infant interaction as well as into the ways in which an exploitative, warring society such as our own socializes men and women differently. As already indicated, there is evidence that little girls' socialization proceeds from a smoother and easier mother-infant interaction, whether this results from some genetic difference between the sexes or from the fact that little girls' first caretaker is same-sex as herself, or from some combinatin of these factors. No wonder women's gender identity is less subject to distortion than men's. But if women have some edge in sociability, they are also at greater risk of the other-connected "superego" experience, shame.

When I look at the impact of our exploitative society I am impressed by the way it injures the superego of the two sexes differently. Briefly, it suppresses the affectionate, social nature of our species in both sexes, but does so differently for men and women. Little girls, who may already have an edge in sociability over boys, are trained and encouraged into affectionate, nurturant roles. But by the time they are 2 years old, when their gender identity is well established, they discover that affectionateness is not really a useful commodity in an exploitative world; it is, in fact, a handicap that brings women into dependent relationships to others, relationships in which the other, not the self, is the center of the world. As a result, women have a terrible sense of loss and helplessness when the others around whom they have built their lives no longer need to be nurtured – and such feelings are intensified by the fact that women often have no other occupation. It is small wonder then, that women are prone to the shame of loss of love and to the shame of second-class rights in the world of power. It seems to me quite in keeping with the fact that women do not give up their affectionateness, however, only devalue it, that the clinical picture in depression and hysteria involves no bizarre distortions of gender identity. On the contrary, the symptoms of depression and hysteria are as familiar to all of us as mundane as depressed mood, anxiety, and bodily aches and pains.

For little boys, the internalized conflict between their affectionate natures and the exploitative demands of our social order assumes a different pattern. Little boys are not encouraged to develop their sociability; on the contrary, by the time their gender identity is well established at age 2, they are aware that they are expected to become aggressive and tougher than girls. Their gender identity involves extracting from their experiences with their first, opposite-sex caretaker that they are different from her and more like their distant fathers. Before they are 6 years old they are expected to "renounce" their affection for their mothers and become like their not only distant but also more aggressive fathers. They are required by our exploitative society to function in the world as if aggression and not affectionateness were the stuff of which they are made.

At the same time, the culture puts limits on just how aggressive— that is, just how guilty—men may be. No wonder they are more often obsessional than women. And no wonder that Schreber's personal mythology (Freud, 1911), by means of which he functioned for a few years at least, was that he had a special mission on earth to teach human beings that God's will is the cultivation of feminine voluptuousness. No wonder distorted gender identity is so often a hallmark of men's more frequent illness, paranoia.

PSYCHOANALYSIS AND FEMINISM: A RAPPROCHEMENT

As has been apparent throughout this essay, feminist themes have always been intrinsic in Freud's work, although clouded by his androcentrism and misogyny. A critique of the existing patterns of marriage was explicit in Freud's first descriptions of the suffering of hysterical women. For example, Freud (1908) gave the following sympathetic clinical description of women's plight:

> Let us, for instance, consider the very common case of a woman who does not love her husband because, owing to the conditions under which she entered marriage, she has no reason to love him, but who wants very much to love him, because that alone corresponds to the ideal of marriage to which she has been brought up. She will in that case suppress every impulse which would express the truth and contradict her endeavors to fulfill her ideal, and she will make special efforts to play the part of a loving, affectionate and attentive wife. The outcome of this self-suppression will be a neurotic illness; and this neurosis will in a

short time have taken revenge on the unloved husband and have caused him as much lack of satisfaction and worry as would have resulted from an acknowledgement of the true state of affairs. This example is completely typical of what a neurosis achieves [p. 203].

Feminist issues in Freud's work were entangled not only with his androcentrism, but also with the deeper question of the relationship between society and the individual. Having first observed the noxious effects of sexual repression, Freud then justified repression by considering it the necessary basis for the existence of civilization. The principal psychoanalytic revisionists – Adler, Horney, Fromm, and Reich – used socialist principles as a basis of their critique of civilization. They explicitly disagreed with Freud that all societies are based on the suppression of sexuality, distinguishing between the effects of more or less benign social orders. These theorists understood the interaction between sex roles and family dynamics as occurring within the framework of an exploitative and competitive society. They saw the actual difference in power between men and women as an important factor underlying primary-process fantasies about the "natural" sex roles of men and women.

Both Fromm and Reich, for example, characterized the patriarchal family as a reflection in miniature of the exploitative power relations in the societal background, and they suggested that, in this sense, the family serves as a transmission belt for attitudes that derogate women. Reich was most explicit in restricting Freud's critique of civilization to civilization's present forms. He followed Engels in assuming that the oppression of women makes its appearance in society at the same time as the establishment of an oppressing class.

Most important, however, both Fromm and Reich shared the conviction, which Freud did not have, that the abolition of exploitation would free human beings from the character deformations they now suffer as its consequence. Fromm (1955) for example, envisages the "sane society" as one in which the central value is human growth, not the use of human beings as commodities. In such a society, individuals would develop so that conflicts between the self and others are minimal. The implication of this view is that human beings of both sexes have a natural tendency toward peaceable relationships with each other. This is in effect a theory that postulates the social nature of human beings, with attachment emotions basic to their existence.

Psychoanalytically sophisticated political criticism of the social order has found recent expression in important works by feminists on rape (Brownmiller, 1975) and incest (Herman, 1981). Brownmiller's study makes clear that rape has been an instrument by which warring societies reward their soldiers and at the same time perpetuate the oppression of women. Herman points out that father-daughter incest is a frequent form of sexual exploitation. She interprets this fact as both a reflection of patriarchal power and a means of maintaining it. Both these studies make use of Freudian interpretation while explicitly disavowing the content of Freud's views on women.

Several recent attempts have been made to effect an explicit rapproachment between psychoanalysis and feminism. My own attempt (Lewis, 1976) was made from the psychoanalyst's side, and it built on the revisions suggested by the Freudian "left." Mitchell (1974), speaking from the political-feminist side, has made generous use of a more recent Freudian revisionist, Lacan (1975). Mitchell draws on Lacan's criticisms of Freudian metapsychology to help bring feminism and psychoanalysis together.

Lacan is particularly critical of Freud's metapsychology for its nonaffective formulations. In Lacan's system, the data of psychoanalysis derive from the dialogue between two selves (thus reflecting, in my view, the state of their emotional relatedness). Psychoanalysis is therefore a "science of mirages," which has developed a special language for these emotional transactions. This is a felicitous phrasing of Freud's concept of primary-process transformations of emotional conflict. Lacan (1975) brings his concept of the dialogue into line with more recent linguistic theories of universal grammar, criticizing Freud's concept of the unconscious as "inchoate," when it could better be understood as "structured like a language." From this Lacanian version of the Freudian unconscious Mitchell (1974) suggests that the psychoanalytic concept of the unconscious is the concept of mankind's transmission and inheritance of his social (cultural) laws. In each man's unconscious lies all mankind's "ideas" of history. Thus, understanding the laws of the unconscious amounts to a start in understanding how ideology functions. Of particular significance, of course, is the ideology of women's inferiority.

Although Mitchell effected this bridge between feminisim and psychoanalysis by a considerable looseness in her handling of Freud's writings (Fliegel, 1982), her effort to reinterpret Freud has met with some acceptance among feminist psychologists and psychoanalysts. Most important, the weakness in Freud's work is once again pinpointed by her work (as well as Lacan's): a thoroughgoing revision of Freud's meta-psychology is needed, to be replaced with a theory based on human social and emotional relatedness.

It is sometimes a source of ironic (and probably sexist) gratification to me that Freud's major discoveries were made as he analyzed the sufferings of hysterical women. They also were dissatisfied with their sex *roles* although their gender identity stayed clear. Psychoanalysis has since helped to open up protest against women's powerlessness and its symbolic forms.

I evaluate the changing sex roles that characterize our own times according to whether and how they foster our uniquely human affectionateness and morality. For example, the movement toward parenting by both sexes should, as its advocates suggest, increase the dimension of tenderness in men and so oppose the stereotypical linkage between manhood and war. In a time when we are all suffering the risk of mass extinction in nuclear war, this may offer us some small hope.

REFERENCES

Baumrind, D. (1980), New directions in socialization research. *American Psychologist,* 35: 639–652.

Bayley, N., & Schaefer, E. (1964), Correlates of maternal and child behaviors with development of mental abilities. *Monographs of the Society for Research in Child Development,* 29 (97).

Beach, F. (Ed.) (1965), *Sex and behavior.* New York: Wiley.

Bem, S. (1975), Sex-role adaptability: One consequence of psychological androgyny. *J. Personal. Soc. Psychol.,* 31: 634–643.

——— (1976), Probing the promise of androgyny. In: *Beyond Sex-Role Stereotypes,* ed. A. Kaplan & J. Bean. Boston: Little, Brown.

——— Martyna, W., & Watson, C. (1976), Sex typing and androgyny: Further exploration of the expresive domain. *J. Personal. Soc. Psychol.,* 34: 1016–1023.

Brownmiller, S. (1975), *Against Our Will: Men, Women and Rape.* New York: Simon & Schuster.

Chance, M. (1980), An ethological assessment of emotion. In: *Emotions: Theory, Research and Experience,* ed. R. Plutchik & H. Kellerman. New York: Academic Press.

Chodorow, N. (1971), Being and doing: A cross-cultural examination of the socialization of males and females. In: *Women in Sexist Society,* ed. V. Gornick & B. Moran. New York: New American Library.

_____ (1978), *The Reproduction of Mothering: Psychoanalysis and the Sociology of Gender*. Berkeley: University of California Press.

Coates, S., (1974), Sex differences in field dependence among preschool children. In: *Sex Differences in Behavior*, ed. R. Friedman, R. Richard, & R. Van de Wiele. New York: Wiley.

Dinnerstein, D. (1976), *The Mermaid and the Minotaur: Sexual Arrangements and Human Malaise*. New York: Harper & Row.

Erikson, E. (1964), Inner and outer space: Reflections on womanhood. *Daedalus*, 93: 582–606.

Fliegel, Z. (1973), Feminine psychosocial development in Freudian theory: A historical reconstruction. *Psychoanal. Quart.*, 42: 385–408.

_____ (1982), Half a century later: Current status of Freud's controversial views on women. *Psychoanal. Rev.*, 69: 7–28.

Ford, C., & Beach, F. (1951), *Patterns of Social Behavior*. New York: Harper & Row.

Freud, S. (1905), Three essays on the theory of sexuality. *Standard Edition*, 7: 125–143. London: Hogarth Press, 1953.

_____ (1908), "Civilized" sexual morality and modern nervous illness. *Standard Edition*, 9: 177–204. London: Hogarth Press, 1959.

_____ (1911), Psycho-Analytic notes on an autobiographical case of paranoia (*dementia paranoides*). *Standard Edition*, 12. London: Hogarth Press.

_____ (1913), Totem and taboo. *Standard Edition*, 13: 1–61. London: Hogarth Press, 1953.

_____ (1914), On narcissism: An introduction. *Standard Edition*, 14: 73–102. London: Hogarth Press, 1957.

_____ (1918), The taboo of virginity. *Standard Edition*, 11: 191–208. London: Hogarth Press, 1957.

_____ (1923), The infantile genital organization: An interpolation into the theory of sexuality. *Standard Edition*, 19: 139–145. London: Hogarth Press, 1961.

_____ (1925), Some psychical consequences of the anatomical distinction between the sexes. *Standard Edition*, 19: 241–258. London, Hogarth Press, 1961.

_____ (1933), New introductory lectures on psycho-Analysis. *Standard Edition*, 20: 5–182. London: Hogarth Press, 1964.

Fromm, E. (1943), Sex and character. *Psychiat.*, 6: 21–31.

_____ (1955), *The Sane Society*. New York: Holt, Rinehart.

Gottschalk, L., & Gleser, G. (1969), *The Measurement of Psychological States Through the Content Analysis of Verbal Behavior*. Berkeley: University of California Press. *Psychology*, ed. H. Kelman. New York: Norton, 1967.

_____ (1926), The flight from womanhood: The masculinity complex as viewed by men and women. In: *Feminine Psychology*.ed. H. Kelman. New York: Norton, 1967.

_____ (1932), The dread of women. In *Feminine Psychology*, ed. H. Kelman. New York: Norton, 1967.

Jahoda, M. (1977), *Freud and the Dilemas of Psychology*. New York: Basic Books.

Lacan, J. (1975), *The Language of the Self*. New York: Delta Books.

LaFrance, M., & Carmen, B. (1908), The non-verbal display of psychological androgyny. *J. Personal. Soc. Psychol.*, 38: 36–49.

Lewis, H. (1971), *Shame and Guilt in Neurosis.* New York: International Universities Press.

_____ (1976), *Psychic War in Men and Women.* New York: New York University Press.

Lynn, D. (1961), Sex role and parental identification. *Child Devel., 33:* 555–564.

Maccoby, E., & Jacklin, C. (1974), *The Psychology of Sex Differences.* Stanford: Stanford University Press.

Masters, W., & Johnson, V. (1970), *Human Sexual Inadequacy.* Boston: Little, Brown.

Mead, M. (1949), *Male and Female.* New York: Morrow.

Mitchell, J. (1974), *Psychoanalysis and Feminism.* New York: Random House.

Morgan, E. (1972), *The Descent of Woman.* New York: Bantam Books.

Moss, H. (1974), Early sex differences and the mother-infant interaction. In: *Sex Differences in Behavior,* ed. R. Friedman, R. Reichert, & R. Van de Wiele. New York: Wiley.

Rubin, J., Provenzano, F., & Luria, Z. (1974), The eye of the beholder: Parents' views on sex of newborns. *Amer. J. Orthopsychiat.,* 44: 512–519.

Sackett, G. (1974), Sex differences in rhesus monkeys following varied rearing experiences. In: *Sex Differences in Behavior,* ed. R. Friedman, R. Reichert, & R. Van de Wiele. New York: Wiley.

Sears, R., Rau, L., & Alpert, R. (1965), *Identification and Child-Rearing* Stanford: Stanford University Press.

Sherfey, M. (1972), *The Nature and Evolution of Female Sexuality.* New York: Random House.

Stoller, R. (1968), *Sex and Gender.* New York: Jason Aronson.

Witkin, H., Lewis, H., & Weil, E. (1968), Affective reactions and patient-therapist interactions in more and less differentiated patients in early psychotherapy sessions. *J. Nerv. Ment. Disease,* 146: 193–208.

_____ _____ Hertzman, M., Machoover, K., Meissner, P., & Wapner, S. (1954), *Personality Through Perception.* New York: Harper.

2

Early Pathways to Female Sexuality in Advantaged and Disadvantaged Girls

Eleanor Galenson, M.D.

The second year of life is, of course, a crucial time in the sexual development of young girls. Previous research carried out over a period of 12 years (Roiphe & Galenson, 1981) revealed much about the patterns of development of gender identity in a group of largely middle-class young children. These data have served in further research (Galenson, 1984) as the basis for comparison regarding gender identity formation in young children suffering from certain psychopathological conditions. In this article, the normal patterns of gender identity formation in the middle-class population studied previously will be summarized, and these findings will be contrasted with distortions in development found among a group of disadvantaged girls from a lower-class socio-economic background.

DEVELOPMENT IN MIDDLE-CLASS GIRLS

The original research was undertaken to investigate two hypotheses. The first was that all children regularly pass through a period of early genital discovery – an early genital phase – sometime between their sixteenth and twenty-fourth month. We also proposed that infants who experienced during their first year either some insult to the sense of bodily integrity – such as severe injury, operation, or illness – or a disturbed maternal relationship, would develop reactions to the discovery of the genital difference (Roiphe, 1968). These preoedipal castration reactions, it was postulated, would vary in the degree of their severity, depending on the extent of traumatization during the first year or so of life (Roiphe, 1968; Roiphe & Galenson, 1972, 1981; Galenson & Roiphe, 1971, 1976; Galenson, 1974).

The research, which extended over a period of 12 years, consisted of naturalistic observations of 70 infants (35 boys and 35 girls) and their middle-class parents during the infants' second year of life. All were white, and all families remained intact during the year of the study. The infants attended our nursery with their mothers four mornings a week, beginning when the infants were about 10 or 11 months old, and remained with us for the subsequent 11 months. Two of the 10 children selected each year were specifically chosen because of first-year experiences that would predispose them, according to our hypothesis, to the development of the preoedipal castration reactions when they reached the early genital phase.

This study enabled us to delineate the emergence of early gender identity in both sexes. From information supplied by the parents we learned that the boys usually discovered their penis during bathing or diapering sometime between 6 and 8 months of age, some two or three months prior to the girls' discovery of their genitals. This initial genital discovery was followed in both sexes by casual touching and intermittent handling of the genitals during the next few months. Boys and girls showed a difference in the quality of their genital play, however, girls' play being less persistent, less focused, and less frequent than that of the boys, probably because of the more direct mechanical stimulation of diapers and cleansing on the boys' more exposed genitals as well as differences in parental handling.

Toward the end of the first year, just when intentionality and upright locomotion began to emerge, intentional reaching for the genitals in both sexes was noted for the first time. This is probably an aspect of bodily discovery, but there is evidence of some pleasurable accompanying affect as well.

Our research data revealed much behavior indicating urinary awareness, a particularly rewarding finding in view of the paucity of such material in the infant observational literature. Awareness of the urinary-zone emerged in both sexes sometime between the twelfth and fourteenth month in most instances—usually, although not always, after anal awareness was already present and independent of attempts at toilet training. Urinary-derivative behavior followed soon afterward; both boys and girls now liked to play in the puddles of urine they produced, and they became curious about the urinary function in adults, peers, and animals. Their play now consisted of many sequences involving pouring and squirting liquids with faucets, hoses, watering cans, the mouth, and the like.

Most of the infants succeeded in being admitted to observe their parents' toilet functions during this period of their development, in spite of parental modesty in several families. Both boys and girls tried to grasp and sometimes mouth the father's urinary stream; as far as we could determine, this behavior was not connected with undue parental exposure, but was an expression of the intense curiosity and interest evoked by a newly discovered phenomenon connected with a newly emerging erogenous zone.

The girls consistently clamored to be in the bathroom with the mother to watch her urination, whereas many of the boys, after their initial exposure to the mother's urination, seemed to avoid it. We believe the boy's emerging awareness at this time of the genital difference promotes a defensive denial in relation to the mother's perineum that does not occur in the girl. (This denial may come to play an important role in the subsequent intellectual development of some boys.)

Parental reactions to the infants' urinary curiosity and exploration were intense; the infants' efforts to explore the male urinary stream by both oral and tactile means arouse considerable uneasiness, even in the most psychologically sophisticated fathers. Some fathers continued to allow occasional touching, whereas others rapidly banished their daughters from the bathroom during the father's urination, although the girls were permitted to enter during his bathing, showering, and shaving. The boys were not excluded in this way. Signs of reactivation of the parents' own infantile sexuality were evident at this point, and this led many of the parents to deny the presence of their infants' primitive curiosity. Within a week or two, many parents had forgotten about the information they themselves had given us; this was particularly true of fathers who had discussed daughters.

In the midst of the anal-urinary elaboration, genital self-stimulation of a qualitatively different variety emerged for the first time in all the infants. Sometime between their fifteenth and nineteenth month, a heightened genital sensitivity began to appear, which now served as a source of focused pleasure. At first, both boys and girls carried out repetitive, intense genital self-stimulation, either manually or by such indirect means as straddling objects, rocking, and thigh pressure, and both boys and girls attempted visual and tactile exploration of their genitals. This was accompanied by evidence of erotic arousal, including facial expressions of excitement and pleasure, flushing, rapid respiration, and perspiration. The infants also frequently made affectionate gestures and touched the mother's body during or following the genital self-stimulation, in a clear display of object-directed affect.

Masturbation was most common during bathing or diapering, when the infants had free access to their genitals. In the girls, the new quality of genital self-stimulation consisted of manual, repetitive rubbing, squeezing, and pinching of the labia at the area of the mons and clitoris. Several of the mothers reported that the little girl's finger had actually been introduced into the opening of the vagina itself, although this was not the main site of stimulation.

In both sexes, affectionate behavior toward the mother during masturbation began to disappear after the first few weeks as a result of subtle but defininte signals from the mother. It was replaced by an inward gaze and self-absorbed look, probably indicating that a fantasy feeling-state had become a regular concomitant of the genital self-stimulation. Various other behaviors now began to accompany the genital activity; many of the girls as well as the boys used their nursing bottles and objects such as blankets, stuffed animals and dolls to which the infants had become intensely attached (transitional objects) for direct masturbatory contact. The use of these objects would indicate the presence of early fantasy formation, probably based on memories of maternal contact during diapering and bathing.

The emergence of this true masturbation seemed to influence almost every sector of the infants' functioning. In the girls, doll play increased remarkably, and the quality of play changed in that dolls were continually undressed and the crotch area examined, phallic-shaped objects were placed at the dolls' pubis, and the dolls themselves were often used for masturbation or were positioned beneath the infants' genital area at bedtime. Many girls then went on to adopt one of the dolls as an obligatory companion, required during both waking and sleeping hours.

Curiosity about the sexual difference soon emerged in both boys and girls, leading to visual comparisons of the genitals as well as other parts of the body. Boys and girls tried to see and touch their mother's breasts and looked beneath the skirts of women and dolls quite persistently. Not too long after the emergence of curiosity about the sexual difference, the sexual development of the boys and girls began to diverge. During an initial period lasting several weeks, both boys and girls appeared to have shocklike reactions which consisted of a rather ubiquitous denial of the genital difference and displacement of interest to the mother's breast, umbilicus, and buttocks. Virtually all the girls went on to develop preoedipal castration reactions consisting of recrudescence of their recently allayed fears of object loss and self-disintegration as well as a variety of other regressive symptoms, depending on the severity of the reaction. There were also developmental advances in most of the girls, however, which took the form of a spurt of fantasy play and early attempts at graphic representation. Although this may have represented in part denial through fantasy, we believe the new developments also reflect early defensive efforts to cope with the anxiety provoked by the recognition of the genital difference.

In regard to object relations, the recognition of the genital difference led, in all but a few of the girls, to a heightening of ambivalence towards the mother and the emergence of a new erotic and flirtatious interest in the father. We regard this erotic turn to the father as an important preparation for the positive oedipal attachment, constituting an important step in the establishment of the girl's sense of female gender identity.

The eight girls in the sample who developed *severe* preoedipal castration reactions had all experienced an important threat to either the developing body image or their maternal relationship during their first year, as had been predicted by Roiphe (1968). However, since *all* the girls developed some degree of castration reaction, the data indicate that girls are overtly more vulnerable than boys to the effects of observing the anatomical difference. The girls' reactions affected almost every area of functioning. At the genital zone itself, manual masturbation was frequently replaced by indirect stimulation, and some girls abandoned masturbation entirely; several continued to masturbate, but without pleasure. In many girls distinct signs of shame and embarrassment were first observed during their fifteenth to eighteenth months, particularly in connection with loss of urinary control. This was not observed in the boys.

In regard to ego development, girls who had previously verbally differentiated boys from girls frequently confused the two labels, and their use of the word "boy" often ceased altogether. Also, the girls showed a greater tendency to regress temporarily to oral and anal self-comforting measures such as mouthing and sucking, anal masturbation, and anal and urinary retention, and displacement of masturbation to other body parts was common. Overall, the primitive anxieties of object and anal loss were now intensified and were reflected in renewed fears concerning separation. The castration anxiety itself was evident in the girls' new concerns over small bodily imperfections, such as minor bruises and scratches, and their avoidance of broken toys and foods.

The changes in the form of masturbation and its total inhibition in some girls appear to be related to the girl's effort to deny the sexual difference by temporarily avoiding the genital area. This avoidance soon disintegrated in most girls as sexual pressure rose and their reality testing supervened.

These castration responses influenced the sexual development of the girls from this time onward, both enhancing and inhibiting it. Thus, although both boys and girls had developed a special relationship with the father by the end of the first year, it was in the midst of their castration reactions that most of the girls approached the father in a new erotic manner. In contrast, the boys sought out the mother only at times of distress. The girls who now approached the father had all experienced a relatively successful first year. The reaction was different, however, among girls whose earlier relationship with the mother had been of poor quality or who had suffered important bodily traumata during the first year or had experienced the birth of a sibling during the second part of the second year. For these girls, hostile dependence on the mother became enormously aggravated, and the turn to the father did not ensue. Thus, these early psychosexual developments appear to decisively influence the girl's libidinal attachment to the father, determining whether a definitive erotic shift occurs toward the end of the second year or whether the tie to the mother becomes intensified and even more ambivalent. The milder castration reaction appears to facilitate the girl's turn to the father as her new love object, with a continuing albeit less intense attachment to the mother, whereas the more profound castration reaction appears to lead to a predominantly negative oedipal constellation, with the choice of the mother as the primary but ambivalently loved object.

In regard to affect, we noted that mood changes occurred in many girls concurrently with the preoedipal castration reactions. Mahler, Pine, and Bergman (1975) described the sadness and the loss of zest and enthusiasm in many little girls during the same chronological period. They attributed this change in mood to the rapprochement crisis, which seems to be of greater severity in girls than in boys. We believe that these mood changes, which may range from very mild reactions to the establishment of a basic depressive mood, can best be accounted for as reflecting developments in the psychosexual as well as the object-relations spheres.

As to ego functions, in addition to the advances (and the temporary regression) in the symbolic capacity already mentioned, many girls develop a type of attachment to dolls or other inanimate objects that is different from the earlier doll play in that the dolls and other inanimate objects are clung to tenaciously. We believe they serve as "infantile fetishes," representing the *father's* penis and body rather than the fantasied maternal phallus. Those girls who suffered the most intense castration reactions showed considerable constriction in their imaginative play along with a restriction in their general intellectual curiosity as their exploration of the world about them became definitely narrower in scope.

We originally postulated that all infants would show evidence of passage through an early genital phase sometime between 18 and 24 months of age. This condition was satisfied in all 70 subjects, except that the time of onset was several months earlier than anticipated. We also postulated that circumstances interfering with the developing sense of body intactness or with the mother-child relationship during the first year would lead to overt disturbances following the discovery of the genital difference that would constitute preoedipal castration reactions. This condition was satisfied in *all* the predisposed girls but in only *some* of the predisposed boys, suggesting that boys tend to utilize denial and motor discharge to deal with their anxiety at this time to a much greater degree than do girls.

Freud's (1905) original position that the organization of sexual drives exerts a special and exemplary role in development remains a valid one. With ongoing separation and individuation, the genital zone emerges as a distinct and differentiated source of endogenous pleasure sometime between 15 and 19 months of age, exerting a new and crucial influence on the sense of sexual identity, object relations, basic mood, and other aspects of ego functioning. We believe this era constitutes an early genital phase, preceding the oedipal period, which will inevitably be shaped by the preoedipal developments described.

The subtle, and perhaps not so subtle, differences in parental handling of the infant during the first year or so and communication of the parental attitude probably contribute to an incipient sense of gender identity in the child. But it is the emergence of genital awareness—an endogenous precipitate of anal and urinary awareness—that leads to the striking differences between boys and girls. The infant's reaction to the awareness of the genital difference seems to mark the divergent paths in sexual development that each sex follows thenceforth, a finding that suggests that the second half of the second year of life is a critical period for the development of the sense of gender identity.

We believe that Freud's (1931) original position regarding women was correct in that penis envy and the feminine castration complex exert crucial influences on feminine development. However, these occur earlier than Freud had anticipated, and they are closely intertwined with fears of object and anal loss.

DEVELOPMENT IN LOW SOCIOECONOMIC GIRLS

In contrasting normal preoedipal female sexuality with the preoedipal sexual development in girls from disrupted families, it should be stated at the outset that the data base for the disadvantaged group is as yet inadequate. Our own cases are few, and there is only an occasional case report in the literature. Thus far, we have treated eight infant girls from seriously disrupted families who have shown a variety of syndromes: child abuse, attachment disorders (including failure to thrive), and developmental lags of various types. Unlike the infants in our first study, these girls are black or Hispanic, and are from single-parent families; often the mothers are only in late adolescence. Economic and social deprivation are universal in this group.

Certain features in the quality and nature of the developing gender identity of the lower-class girls, as compared with that of the middle-class group, suggest basic differences between these two groups in regard to their early sexual development. These differences appear to parallel certain features in the sexuality of their mothers. The girls in the lower socioeconomic group seem to identify quite early with their mothers in their outward behavior, imitating their mannerisms and their nurturing activities with dolls and live babies, when these are available. However, their ambivalence toward the mother during the second year, despite the imitation and identification in their superficial behavior, is far more heavily weighted with aggression than is the behavior of the infants from intact families. The mother-daughter relationship begins to assume a sadomasochistic quality even as early as the end of the first year of life. Although these little girls take care of their doll babies, as their semisymbolic play develops, they are more often the strict and chastising mother than a tender and affectionate one.

Furthermore, this sadomasochistic tie to the mother is rarely attentuated by a reliable attachment to any male figure, although genital awareness and awareness of the genital anatomical difference emerge in the disadvantaged group toward the end of the second year, just as in the middle-class group. The little girls in these disrupted families are teasingly flirtatious, often actually provoking sexual advances by boys and adult men. However, these "sexual" encounters, even when they involve peers, tend to include aggressive and affectionate impulses in equal measure, and it is often difficult to distinguish their fighting from their loving behavior.

The eight female infants from disrupted homes seemed to wish to be both seduced and aggressively attacked, a type of female sexuality that differs profoundly from the admiration and responsiveness of a loving father with which the middle-class little girls were ushered into their preoedipal sexuality. This is all the more striking in view of the fact that the mothers from the lower socioeconomic group exhibit the same sadomasochistic quality in their relationships with the fathers of their children. Furthermore, these female children retain the preoedipal, highly ambivalent tie of infant to mother, rather than shifting to a male figure.

To the adolescent mothers from the same disrupted family backgrounds, their babies appear to represent the doll of their early childhood, and the babies are abandoned when the infantile period comes to an end, often as early as 12 months of age. The adolescent mother's abandonment of her baby seems to represent a repetition of her early relationship with her own mother and her dolls. Her relationship to her infant is sadomasochistic and therefore unstable in nature. It is complicated by the absence of a stable male figure to validate the small girl's sense of femininity and to offer the possibility of a true oedipal attachment. The following clinical vignette will illustrate the type of psychopathology and the treatment outcome of this low income group.

Fourteen-month-old Elaine stands in the middle of the room, fixed to one spot, legs spread widely, staring at her mother, a 26-year-old, 300 pound woman morosely spread out in a chair several yards away. The mother curses her child for being "crazy and stupid," and makes no move to rescue Elaine from the island of terror on which the child has become marooned. When Elaine is lifted to her mother's lap by a staff member, she is promptly turned upside-down, head squeezed between the mother's massive knees, her diaper inspected, and she is then plunked down hard in her stroller.

Elaine was hospitalized for the first time at 3 months of age because of an acute gastroenteritis. Her lethargy and poor physical development led to the suspicion of child abuse, particularly because of the mother's extreme verbal abuse of both the child and the staff, and Elaine was found to have suffered a subdural hematoma. Elaine was admitted to the hospital 12 times thereafter for various somatic complaints. The mother had an extremely poor relationship with the hospital staff, because of the mother's continued provocation and abuse with the exception of one social worker who befriended the mother by her reluctance to officially report the case as child abuse. The worker referred her to our therapeutic nursery instead.

The mother was one of 13 children of psychotic and alcoholic parents. She and one sister were the only children who were physically abused. At 15 years of age she was placed in the first of a series of foster homes, from each of which she eventually ran away. She returned to live with her mother several years later, and shortly thereafter became pregnant with Elaine. Four other children, ranging in age from 5 to 10 years, lived with Elaine and her mother, the mother acting as their foster parent.

With both mother and child in individual and group treatment, Elaine's development began to advance. She was no longer bound to her mother in terror, could ask other adults in the nursery for help, cried when her mother left the nursery, and initiated peek-a-boo games by age 16 months. Serious developmental delays were evident, however; she sucked her pacifier constantly or her bottle if it were available, chewed food minimally and without pleasure, had no awareness of bowel functioning, and her physical growth and fine motor coordination were delayed by several months. Furthermore, basic organization of patterns of sleeping and waking, eating, and distress and quieting had not yet been achieved. There was little or no joyfulness in this child, an absence of play and of affective reciprocity in the mother-child couple, and a definite mutually provocative quality in their interchange. Genital awareness and curiosity were just beginning to emerge.

We are most cautious about the outcome of treatment of infants like Elaine, even with continued intervention. Their unstable biological and early psychological organization appears to render them extremely vulnerable to the impact of even normal developmental stress. Most problematic, however, is the dilemma faced by children of such one-parent families regarding their early gender identity and the fusion and confusion of sexuality and aggression. The father's absence and the early sadomasochistic relationship with the mother places them in serious jeopardy with regard to heterosexual object choice later on.

CONCLUSION

In a small group of girls from disadvantaged families, the early tie to the mother assumes a definitely sadomasochistic quality very early in life, often by the middle of the second year. In contrast with the normal ambivalence of the little girl towards her mother observed in the middle-class group, the hostile aggression is far more intense in the disadvantaged girls and they remain bound in this type of maternal relationship, instead of turning towards a male at this time. Most of these children do not have access to a reliable male in their family constellation, so that the usual erotic turn to the father does not help them to disengage themselves from the overtly hostile ambivalent maternal attachment. This early distortion in the maternal attachment of the infants appears to replicate the experience of their mothers, and to lead eventually to the type of adult sadomasochistic sexuality characteristic of the mothers of these infant girls.

REFERENCES

Freud, S. (1905), Three essays on the theory of sexuality. *Standard Edition*, 7: 135–243. London: Hogarth Press, 1953.

_____ (1931), Female sexuality. *Standard Edition*, 21: 223–243. London: Hogarth Press, 1961.

Galenson, E. (1974), Emergence of genital awareness during the second year of life. In: *Sex Differences in Behavior*, ed. R. C. Friedman, R. M. Richart, & R. L. Vande Wiele. New York: Wiley.

_____ (1984), Psychotic disturbances in very young children: A clinical report. *Hillside J. Clin. Psychiat.*, 6(2).

_____ & Roiphe, H. (1971), Impact of early sexual discovery on mood, defensive organization and symbolization. *The Psychoanalytic Study of the Child*, 26: 195–216. New York/Chicago: Quadrangle Books.

_____ (1976), Some suggested revisions concerning early female development. In: *Female Psychology*, ed. H. Blum. New York: International Universities Press, 1977.

Mahler, M. S., Pine, F., & Bergman, A. (1975), *The Psychological Birth of the Human Infant: Symbiosis and Individuation*. New York: Basic Books.

Roiphe, H. (1968), On an early genital phase, with an addendum on genesis. *The Psychoanalytic Study of the Child*, 23: 348–365. New York: International Universities Press.

_____ & Galenson, E. (1972), Early genital activity and the castration complex. *Psychoanal. Quart.*, 41: 344–357.

_____ (1981), *Infantile Origins of Sexual Identity*. New York: International Universities Press.

NEW VISIONS OF FEMININITY

3

Reconciling Nurturance and Aggression: A New Feminine Identity

Toni Bernay, Ph.D.

Feminist ideologies and the sexual revolution have created new visions of femininity and new feminine ego ideals. Women have moved from a model of femininity that emphasizes passivity, dependence and submission to one that embraces aggression, assertiveness, and independence. Women have now grasped the freedom to dream of success and achievement and the courage to fulfill their dreams. In doing so, they have exchanged new demands for old—to become "superwoman" instead of "Stepford Wife"—and have incorporated these new norms into their definition of the competent woman.

An earlier version of this paper was presented at the annual meeting of the American Psychological Association, Toronto, Ontario, Canada, August 1984.

Moreover, this new emphasis creates new problems as generations of traditional parents continue to set the cultural pace for women's developmental journey. Parents still perpetuate dominant patriarchal notions based on the traditions of man as warrior and hunter and woman as childbearer, nurturer, and caretaker. Parents teach and demonstrate to their daughters that the feminine woman must be passive, dependent, loving, and conciliatory. She must relegate autonomy, aggression, competition, and control to the corners of her mind where conflicts are hidden and stored. For example, research on women's development supports the notion that women raised in this milieu have high affiliative needs that often motivate them to avoid success in the fear that deviation from the feminine stereotype will bring both social rejection and its accompanying guilt, anxiety, and depression (M. Horner & Walsh, 1974).

Clinicians' efforts to aid their women patients as they struggle to integrate the complexities of self and other and to explore and transform the old into the new have been complicated by female psychology's male-centered theoretical underpinnings. Such assumptions lead to the interpretation of both women's old passive and new assertive resolutons as deviant from male norms. These assumptions also lead to the interpretation of women's sense of ethics and morality as weak and corruptible—qualities arising from a flawed superego and eventuating in a lesser sense of justice and an inability to submit to the exigencies of life. In this view, women's judgment is marred by the vicissitudes of relational life and emotion (Freud, 1925). This deficiency view of woman's morality is perpetuated by Kohlberg (1981) in constructing his scale of moral development. Here, most women's sense of nonviolence and fairness to others fix them at the stage of pleasing others, so that they never reach the logical abstractions associated with a sense of universal justice.

Current thinking and empirically derived ideas (Mahler, Pine, & Bergman, 1975; Galenson & Roiphe, 1976; Chodorow, 1978; Galenson, 1982) are now giving greater credence to women's experience of attachment and connection. This work points toward developmental lines that include a relational self (Surrey, 1982; Jordan & Surrey, this volume) and a sense of morality arising from nurturance and responsible care (Gilligan, 1982). These female-oriented lines of development provide a new perspective on the psychological consequences of women's experience. From this point of view, attachment and nurturance can be seen as trends facilitating identity, maturity, and integrity, rather than as impediments to individuation or deviations from phallocentric norms.

In addition to addressing the reclamation and relegitimization of women's nurturant selves, which were disavowed during the 1960s and 1970s (see, for example, Friedan, 1963; Millet, 1969; Greer, 1970), theoreticians and clinicians are also addressing the importance of women's continuing to incorporate newly formed ego ideals. These include derivative strivings of autonomy, achievement, and assertiveness associated with male developmental notions of detachment and objectivity. To ignore either nurturant or aggressive components within the self is to ignore the human capacity for variability, alternative selves, and complex social roles, which contributes to an identity that can maintain sameness and continuity in the face of fluidity and change (Greenacre, 1958). To resolve ambivalence and bisexuality in favor of one side or the other would seem to forever fragment the images of the early omnipotent mother. Such a resolution alienates women from the generosity, creativity, secrets, power, abundance, and completeness of the good mother and estranges them from nondestructive expressions of primitive, aggressive feelings, which include desire and constructive action in the service of the "life force of growth" (Chasseguet-Smirgel, 1970; Greenacre, 1958; Parens, 1979).

It is the aim of this essay to describe and discuss the constructs of feminine identity and competence as they are evolving in the psychology of today's woman. Such a description of femininity in the 1980s circumscribes a reconciliation of nurturant and aggressive psychic trends. Illustrative clinical material will be used to discuss the effects of the clinical use of female-centered theories on women's efforts to creatively transform their experience of interconnection into a newly reordered sense of identity (Jordan & Surrey, this volume), including the moral domain of responsibility and care in relationships (Gilligan, 1982). Case material will also illustrate the importance of helping women to retain newly acquired assertive and competitive selves (Miller, 1976) as they attempt to recapture more traditional feminine and maternal identifications.

TRADITIONAL DEFINITIONS OF FEMININITY

In the words of de Beauvoir (1949): "Femininity is a fiction created by men, assented to by women untrained in the rigors of logical thought

or conscious of the advantages to be gained by compliance with masculine fantasies. Their assent traps them in the prison of repetition and
immanence which limits women's possibilities." Psychoanalysis has
made many contributions to the traditional definitions of femininity
women have, until recently, assented to.

Freud, by whose definitions women have so long lived their lives,
published his work on "Female Sexuality" (1931) at the age of 75. This
belated publication embodies his puzzlement, his ambivalence, his rev-
erence, his contempt, his passions, and his fears of the mysteries of the
"dark continent" of woman. A man of his time, Freud portrayed the
second sex as second class, vaporous, defective, and chattel. His work
became at once the entrée into the scientific study of the psychology of
women and a rallying point of feminists then and now. In
acknowledging the limitations of his understanding of women and in-
viting others to continue where he left off, Freud paved the way for the
serious, concerned inquiry into feminine psychology in which we are
now engaged.

Using the boy as the prototype and cornerstone for his developmental notions about women, Frued posited equal and parallel development for boys and girls (with the exception of object choice) during
the first three years of life. He felt that divergence of developmental experience occurred with the recognition of anatomical differences. At
this point, at the height of a time of "look at me" exhibitionistic pride,
the little girl is old enough and cognizant enough to compare her body
to others and realizes that she is missing a penis. Her primal fantasy of
the maternal phallus possessed by all, protecting and maintaining her
sense of inner wholeness, which until now has been unspoiled by perception, is ruptured. She tumbles from paradise and becomes aware
that mommy is also missing the vital organ. She blames mommy for
her own shameful, defective state. Feeling envious of the boy's penis,
deeming her clitoris analogous but inferior, she temporarily denounces
and renounces her sexuality. Envious of, angry at, and disappointed in
and by mommy, the little girl continues her struggle to leave the sensual, comforting emotional cocoon provided by mommy and her
body. She devalues mommy and turns toward daddy, substituting the
wish for a baby for the previously longed-for penis. Concomitantly,
she gives up the active stimulation she has enjoyed through clitoral
masturbation, and passivity gains the upper hand.

Meanwhile, the little boy, complete unto himself in organ, body,
and object choice, retains intact his love for mommy and comes to

know daddy as a dangerous, castrating rival. Undaunted by his fears and in control of his aggression, he identifies with and becomes pals with his dad, secure in the knowledge that he possesses a superior superego and a state of moral integrity unavailable to girls.

In formulating this conceptualization of the little girl's early attempts to find and define herself amidst sexual and generational differences, Freud posited that little girls were not aware of their vaginas or inner genital organs. He therefore did not consider the option that they could maintain a sense of internal wholeness by bringing imagined representations of their inner body with them as they separated from mommy to woo daddy, ultimately integrating these representations into their body image (Freud, 1925). Axiomatically, Freud thought, little girls did not have the capacity to use these mental images of the vagina and reproductive organs for reparation of self-esteem and body image and as part of developing active and positive selves.

Freud (1919) posited two stages of female development, indicating preoedipal and oedipal phases as the first significant developmental difference between boys and girls. Other theorists (Abrahm, 1920; Horney, 1926; Lampl-de Groot, 1933; M. Klein, 1975) elaborated on this notion, noting the importance of the girl's attachment to the mother in the first year of life. They reported that it is the characteristics and the fabric of this first relationship that the girl brings to the relationship with daddy and to all intimate relationships thereafter. Thus, the girl toddler brings the intense and ambivalent feelings experienced toward mommy—love, hate, envy, affection, frustration, longing, and rage—to her relationship with daddy, in hopes of repairing her damaged sense of self and self-esteem and avoiding further disappointments and disillusionments. The greater the girl's frustration with mommy, the greater are her longings toward daddy and the greater is her narcissistic vulnerability to futher wounds and disappointments in the new relationship with daddy and others to follow. For Freud, such disappointments represented a normal and important step in the girl's recognition and acceptance of herself as a castrated boy on the path toward the consolidation of femininity, renouncing masculinity and the clitoris on the way.

Investigators after Freud (Kestenberg, 1956) studied the girl's awareness of both early vaginal sensations and the capacities of the uterus as a container for a baby to see whether femininity does indeed develop at an early preoedipal point. Although the investigators arrived at no consensus, they did see the awareness of the capacity to have children and the awareness of the presence of a vagina and vaginal sensations as crucial to the development of feminine identity.

Other early psychoanalytic thinkers sought further understanding of femininity through the study of women's biology and drive organization. Benedek (1952) posited women's receptive tendencies and biological need for motherhood as the psychic and emotional correlates of the vicissitudes of the menstrual cycle. She saw motherhood not as a compensation for the missing penis, but as the manifestation of a survival instinct in the child and the primary organizer of her sexual drive and personality.

Freud (1931) characterized femininity as having "passive aims" and relegated women's aggression and active participation—other than that required for maternal behavior—to the realm of masochism. Masochism, Freud (1933) said, arises from the "suppression of women's aggressiveness which is prescribed for them constitutionally and imposed on them socially" (p. 90). Building on Freud's ideas on the fate of women's aggression, Deutsch (1930) defined femininity as the triad of passivity, masochism, and narcissism. Deutsch decided that masochism was "truly feminine" and considered feminine masochism analogous to "activity directed inward."

Horney (1926) and Thompson (1943) took a more psychosocial view, positing that penis envy and masochism were functions of the subordination of women in a patriarchal society, lack of acceptable outlets for female aggression, and unacceptable envy of men's social privilege. Horney (1931, 1932) further asserted that religious symbols and rituals, such as the Virgin Mary and taboos of sexual abstinence, are the result of men's narcissistic defenses against fears of the sexually active woman, envy of her breasts and procreative capacities, and rage at their limited access to the breast during the nursing period. These theorists suggested that women responded to social dictates by suppressing and binding erotically destructive tendencies, reluctantly turning them inward in a masochistic resolution of the problem of their aggression.

Abraham (1920) implied an alternative explanation, offering that penis envy is the beginning of love for an enviable object, alluding to a transformation of envy from a shameful to a laudatory feeling state. Freud, (1933) in contrast, stated definitively that "the effect of penis envy has a share in the physical vanity of women since they are bound to value their charms more highly as a late compensation for their original sexual inferiority" (p. 132). He also stated that women's greater degree of narcissism serves their greater need to be loved than to love. Freud characterized feminine love as passive in nature; that is, the woman lets herself be loved.

Throughout Freud's theory of female sexuality, statements such as these alluded to women's deficient and compromised superego and sense of morality, fairness, and justice. Freud thought that women's more personal, affiliative, emotionally responsive style demonstrated weakness and led to poor moral judgment. Mistaking rigidity for strength, he postulated that men have a greater capacity to be impersonal, objective, and detached—qualities necessary for separating sound judgment from the distracting influence of its emotional origin.

AGGRESSION IN FEMININE PSYCHOLOGY

Freud (1915) viewed aggression as a destructive force. He saw it as a component of the death instinct placed in the service of the sexual function, part of it directed outward as sadism and the remainder directed inward in erotogenic masochism. Freud struggled with derivative notions of aggression such as activity and its corollary, passivity; the former he associated with masculinity and the latter with femininity. He acknowledged, however, that maternal behavior is at once receptive and active and that some male behaviors, such as those involved in friendship, include the need for passivity.

Other theorists emphasize the nondestructive aspects of aggression. Some describe it in instinctual terms as an expression of the "life force of growth" (Greenacre, 1957; Parens, 1979). Others view it noninstinctually as springing from the tendency to grow and master life, so that anger, rage, and hate appear as response to obstructive forces (Rochlin, 1973; Miller, Nadelson, Notman, & Zilbach, 1981). Still others (Kohut, 1971) see aggression only as defensive, believing that when narcissism is threatened, humiliation, injured self-esteem, and aggression appear.

Winnicott (1950) stresses that aggression cannot be explained solely on the basis of anger and the death instinct. He draws together instinctual, innate, reactive, constructive, and destructive trends. Winnicott points out that the potential for aggression exists before ego integration occurs, making anger at instinctual frustration possible. The presence of aggressive potential makes the "erotic experience an experience." This then moves the infant to explore the environment, to develop a primary identity in a sense of simply *being*—to discover the "not-me" and to establish a sense of "me-ness." Without a fusion of aggressive and erotic components leading to an establishment of the "me," the infant lives separately from her[1] erotic life. She develops a false self, which never feels real and lacks impulsiveness, passion, and spontaneity. She lives "a purely aggressive, reactive life, dependent on the experience of opposition." For there to be movement rather than stillness, Winnicott says, "to get to something in terms of aggression corresponding to the erotic potential . . . we need a term such as life force" (p. 216).

In understanding the prerequisities of aggression, Winnicott emphasizes the crucial role played by the environmental mother in satisfying the infant's dependent needs. In fulfilling this role, the mother joins her infant in the maintenance of illusion and gently participates in the process of disillusionment. Through the mother's presence and availability, the infant can sustain her illusion of symbiotic oneness, feeling delight at commanding satisfaction at will, not yet recognizing that her gratification is dependent on the love of a willing maternal slave.

Winnicott (1971) requires acceptance of the paradox that the infant tends to create need-satisfying objects, but only if they already exist. This is played out in the infant-mother dyad as the infant-subject says to the mother-object: "I destroyed you. I love you. You have value for me because of your survival of my destructiveness of you. While I am loving you I am all the time destroying you in (unconscious) fantasy" (p. 90). In destroying the early maternal object, the infant relinquishes and transforms this simple mother into a more useful and complex maternal object. Through the use of fantasy informed by her developing capacities, the infant mobilizes her curiosity, spontaneity, experimentation, and activity in the service of interconnection, new affective identifications, and maternal transformations. In turn, the empathic environmental mother delights in and consistently validates her infant's efforts, enabling the child to begin to believe in her effectiveness and in the world around her. Initially, the infant's experience with the early mother is one of *communion*, not *communication* (McDougall,

---

[1]Because of the nature of the subject matter of this article, the feminine form is used for all generic personal pronouns.

1979), fusion rather than relatedness. As she feels more confident and more able to give up the illusion of omnipotence, the infant destroys her experience of communion and her sense of the early mother associated with it. By doing so, she creates a maternal object who is able to receive her communication.

Destruction of the object contributes to the beginnings of fantasy, aiding mourning and providing comfort, rapture, and gratification. The child's use of fantasy to continue to destroy or relinquish maternal objects who are no longer commensurate with her growing maturity, creating novel maternal objects along the way, carries with it the delight and playfulness of relatedness, discovery, and mastery. She learns that the object is beyond her omnipotent control and she learns the limits of herself, thus endowing both herself and mommy with autonomy, life, and externality.

This loving use of the object helps the infant to come to know and trust her aggression and her use of it and to feel trust and confidence in her effect upon the other. It brings her to the point of feeling safe enough to experience relatedness in which she experiences certain alterations in the self. By relinquishing omnipotent illusory control over her kingdom, she can allow and welcome others to become meaningful to her. Beyond this achievement, the assurance the infant gains through the process of destruction and repair facilitates her ability to "use" others, to destroy them as she destroys mommy – repeatedly, finding joy and love in mommy's survival – thereby strengthening affect and contributing to object constancy.

Despite the natural development of aggression described by Winnicott, and despite the emergence of superwoman and the feminist teachings of the last two decades, most women still feel that their own experienced, self-interested, directly expressed aggression is intolerable to them. It is felt as "evil" or "wrong" (Miller et al., 1981). This reaction is supported by centuries' old mythology, recounting with dread and horror the tales of how woman's anger and aggression destroyed the earth's live-giving and life-sustaining forces. In ancient literature, Medusa's rage turned men into stone. Scylla and Charubdis lured sailors onto the rocks of destruction. Demeter, the goddess of life, enraged by Hades' rape and abduction of her daughter, Persephone, railed: "If that be the natural fate of daughters, let all mankind perish. Let there be no crops, no grain, no corn, if this maiden is not returned to me" (Cavendish, 1983).

For most women, the unconscious ego ideal carries this legacy of aggression as wrong, evil, and unfeminine. Transmitted by a traditional mother (Chodorow, 1978) to her daughter, the unconscious feminine ideal still remains almost entirely associated with the care and nurturance of others and nearly devoid of aggression. In trying to meet the contrasting demands of the socially conscious, culturally touted assertive ego ideal, today's woman is confronted with the acknowledgement of her own aggression in the service of vital life activity. Recognition of aggression is often followed by guilt, anxiety, and depression.

Kaplan (1976) has reported evidence that gives credence to the idea that aggression in girls is often subverted or modified in a depressive direction. She offers that early inhibition of aggression in girls prevents sufficient sublimations, and restricts the development of healthy avenues for aggressive discharge. Kaplan observes the difficulties faced by delinquent girls in residential settings. When enraged, these girls often cry and/or respond to their anger in passive, inhibited, or self-effacing ways. When they become involved in fights, they are less apt to fight back than boys. When they do, they strike out, without regard to objective danger from their stronger attackers, in an unorganized, fiercely primitive and impulsive fashion. In contrast, boys usually size up their opponents before beginning to fight.

In pondering these observations, Zilbach, Notman, Nadelson, and Miller (1979) pose the question, given the unorganized quality of aggression, can aggression aimed at action and assertion be separated from aggression aimed at resisting, destroying or harming others? As one answer to their question, Zilbach et al. point out that for women, aggression is often experienced as if it were aimed only at destruction. Consequently, women often find the experience of aggression, regardless of its aim, disorganizing and overwhelming to the personality as a whole, adding to their tendency to fear aggression and to condemn themselves for having such feelings.

Following this, aggression engenders conflicts between the two ego ideals, with the traditionally oriented maternal imago stirring feelings of failure, inadequacy, shame, guilt, and depression. Self-esteem and the sense of competence plummets as the woman struggles to reconcile internalized, traditional ideals, desires for mastery and achievement, current female sex-role ideals, and the need to reconcile the demands of motherhood, marriage, and career.

Miller et al. (1981) contend that because aggression in the service of activity is *supposed* to be absent in girls, except to serve others, girls get much less opportunity to use, channel, practice, and refine their aggression than boys do. They continually repress and suppress their aggression, and it remains less organized, less modified, and less well tested than that of boys. The shaping of aggression that Miller and her coworkers describe is necessary for its organization and effective use. It is analogous to Winnicott's earlier description of the infant's use of the environmental mother, playfully destroying her and delighting in her survival, as one route to the confident use of aggression in the service of relatedness, competence, and joyfulness.

EFFECTS OF INHIBITED EARLY AGGRESSION: THE CASE OF CAROL

A case example will illustrate the disorganizing effects on women's personality of inhibited early aggression. Carol is a 35-year-old, recently divorced woman who has newly reentered the work force as an aerospace executive. She grew up in a chaotic, multigenerational family setting. Her mother was severely depressed, and her father was erratic and sometimes abusive. When Carol was 9 years old, her parents divorced and fought each other for custody of the children. Carol and her younger sister ultimately went to live with their mother but visited their father regularly. These visits were fraught with fear of his sadistic assaults. In early adolescence, Carol refused to visit him any longer.

There was little room for Carol to express her aggression within the family structure. The only outlets were running errands for her family and taking care of several elderly and frail grandparents, her younger sister, and her mother. Carol's grandmother opposed any conflict or expressiveness by engendering guilt and encouraging suppression: "How can you say that to your mother? She doesn't feel well" or "Don't make so much noise, it isn't nice."

When it came time to marry, Carol searched out a well-to-do, rigid, and orderly man with loving parents and siblings – the family Carol had always wanted. Marital life turned out to be more sterile than calm, and home was a "quiet museum." Carol became increasingly depressed. When she first entered therapy, she would come to sessions feeling terribly anxious because she had just left an angry husband at home to switch on the coffee pot and serve himself or because she had left only blueberries for breakfast instead of blueberries, strawberries, and peaches from which to choose. The idea of objecting to this tyranny never occurred to Carol.

When Carol divorced and started working, she found herself confused by the melee of the office world. She often felt attacked and hurt by her co-workers' competitive and self-interested responses to her nurturing and cooperative gestures. For instance, when her office moved, Carol offered to pack and move boxes while her officemate left for awhile. Later, Carol found out that her co-worker had used the time to write reports, stating that *her* reports were not going to be late. Carol felt helpless, resentful, and taken advantage of. At such times she would slip into explanations of mixed loyalties: "I had to help with the moving. It's just what you do — you pitch in and help, no questions asked!" She thought her boss would understand if her reports were a bit late. When that did not prove to be true, Carol became frightened and felt lost as she tried to reconcile her needs with those of others. These feelings were similar to ones she had had when she could not make peace between her parents.

Carol could not understand why some people were so "ill-mannered" and why she was so affected by "small altercations." Her quiet, polite descriptions of office politics were juxtaposed with panic and nausea and a desire to stop therapy and "run away" from the "pressure" of the job and life. As we explored her feelings, Carol realized that she was afraid to bring these events into therapy for discussion. At first she "forgot" to talk about them. They were unimportant, just part of her routine. Then she became aware that talking about intense feelings with me made her feel anxious and humiliated. "After all, you don't have such problems," she said. Subsequently, Carol became conscious that her aggression and ambition — her angry, competitive, and jealous feelings toward her co-workers and her vying for the boss's approval — felt so reprehensible and destructive to her that it was difficult and frightening to discuss them. She was also frightened at experiencing such feelings toward me. "All this ambition might hurt others — it feels like it comes from some poisonous place inside of me. If I feel competitive with you and tell you about it, it will weaken you, you'll get tired, drained, and disgusted with me. It will be the end of us and therapy".

In retracing the roots of her panicky feelings and need to run away, we would frequently return to a precipitant episode which would involve her mother. For example, her mother would call, whispering on the telephone that she wanted to speak to Carol but couldn't, because Uncle Joe, the family patriarch who was angry with Carol, was visiting. Carol would get furious and hurt and then swallow her anger. Following these calls, she would sometimes be horrified and terrified to find herself throwing a dish into the sink. However, she always made sure it landed where it wouldn't hurt anyone and that it already had a crack in it and was ready to be discarded. Anxiety attacks and desires to "run" would follow, nevertheless. She would often feel nauseated the next morning and find it difficult to go to work.

These incidents stirred feelings of deprivation, longing and rage and memories of Carol's mother sleeping or playing the piano for hours, preoccupied with herself, while Carol gave up school or peer activities to "stand on a stepstool so I could reach the stove and make dinner for my sister." She also remembered times when she wanted to participate in sports or school activities. Her grandmother would insist that she rest, because too much running around wasn't good for her: "It isn't healthy and it isn't ladylike." This reinforced Carol's diverting of aggression in the direction of depression and left her convinced that she was too frail and weak to ever maintain a strenuous work schedule.

The idea of being openly angry with her mother for her frightened, whispered phone calls and for not being able to have a separate and effective relationship with Carol because of the mother's fear of family disapproval felt evil and murderous to Carol. Expressing intensely felt feelings toward me felt equally destructive to her. Carol was also aghast at the idea that she envied senior executives and that she *wanted* to compete for promotions and make money. She was hurt and angry that her co-workers did not stop competing when she started nurturing. Recognizing her aggressive and ambitious desires came hard for Carol. Once she faced these aspects of herself, the work toward detoxifying and transforming her aggressive feelings into an effective internal resource began.

As Carol's example shows, a reassessment of feminine aggression, endorsing it as a source of life and growth, is needed to enable current and subsequent generations of women to validate their own aggressive strivings and to help their daughters (and sons) achieve greater comfort and confidence with their aggression from infancy on. The destructive effects of early inhibition of aggression, such as inhibition of anger and activity, can then be modified. The outcome can be a sense of adequate aggressiveness (Horney, 1935) which encompasses the "capacities for work, taking initiative, making plans, carrying through to completion, attaining success, insisting upon one's rights, defending oneself when attacked, forming and expressing autonomous views, recognizing one's goals, and being able to plan one's life according to them" (p. 228). Here again, Horney's concept of aggressiveness suggests Winnicott's notion of the use of aggression in the service of fulfilling the infant's erotic potential, as she actively experiences and explores her world and establishes her sense of self and me-ness.

FEMININITY AND NURTURANCE:
PAST, PRESENT, AND FUTURE VISIONS

There was a young man loved a maid.
Who taunted him "Are you afraid,"
She asked, "to bring me today
Your mother's head on a tray?"

He went and slew his mother dead,
Tore from her breast her heart so red,
Then towards his lady love he raced,
But tripped and fell in all his haste.

As the heart rolled on the ground
It gave forth a plaintif sound.
And it spoke in accents mild
"Did you hurt yourself my child?"
— J. Echergray,
"Severed Heart," Quoted in Bernard, 1974

Cultural stereotypes and traditional psychoanalytic thinking assume that "it is a woman's biological destiny to bear, to deliver, to nurse and to rear children" (Jacobson, 1950, p. 139). Following this thesis, caring and nurturance have been typically associated with femininity, motherhood, and suffering. Freud's biological emphasis on the pain of women's reproductive life, as well as on the forebearance and personal sacrifice necessary to rear children over extended periods of time, serves as the theoretical underpinnings for the psychoanalytic understanding of women's nurturing capacities.

Freud's women were steeped in the authoritarian and patriarchal values of their time. In the *Mill on the Floss,* Eliot (1860) characterized them as filling "their long empty days with memories and fears, while men characterized by purpose, lose the sense of dread and even of wounds in the ardour of action." Women's roles as wife, cook, nurse, and mother were timeless and predictable destinies rather than responsible choices. Mothers transmitted to their daughters attitudes of selfless love, blind devotion to husband and family, and deference to the options of others, continuing the chain of traditional maternal identifications.

Freud and his followers elaborated on his biologically determined notions of the links between femininity, suffering, and nurturance in their discussions of "women's deeply rooted passivity" (Benedek, 1952), "preference for passive aims" (Freud, 1931) and "truly feminine" (Deutsch, 1930) masochistic tendencies arising from and shaped by the suppression of women's aggressiveness. A more contemporary theorist, Blum (1976) states that "masochism is a residue of unresolved infantile conflict and is neither essentially feminine nor a valuable component of maternal female function and character. Though the female might be more predisposed to masochism, there is no evidence of particular female pleasure in pain" (p. 188).

In understanding masochism it is important to differentiate between the moral masochist, suffering for suffering's sake, and one who is suffering in the service of an enviable goal or larger ideal such as athletic prowess or childbearing. Shaness (this volume) refers to this positive concept of masochism as "audacity with caring" as opposed to "foolish masochism." Her example is Antigone's daring and life-threatening defiance of Creon by her insistence on burying her brother Polynices as a hero rather than leaving him, as ordered, to rot on the battlefield as a traitor.[2]

Others (Jacobson, 1964; Winnicott, 1950, 1960, 1963, 1971; G. Klein, 1976) have refocused the study of nurturance, emphasizing the wellspring of mutuality and mother-infant interconnectedness rather than biological perversions. Winnicott (1960) states that "there is no such thing as an infant, meaning of course that whenever one finds an infant one finds maternal care and without maternal care there would be no infant" (p. 39). Mutual adaptation, appreciation, communica-

---

[2]For a further discussion of women's morality, using Antigone instead of Electra as a model of female maturity, see Shaness, this volume.

tion, sharing, and a sense of being for the other pulsate between mother and child. A sense of relatedness and *we* identities become part of the infant's self.

Within this loving and playful milieu, the infant's capacity for nurturance and concern develops. Winnicott (1963) defines concern as "the fact that the individual cares, or minds, and both feels and accepts responsibility" (p. 73). He considers concern "the basis for the family where both parties in intercourse—beyond their pleasure—take responsibility for the result" (p. 73). In the larger sense, Winnicott considers a capacity for concern "at the back of all constructive play and work" (p. 73). This developmental milestone is an intrapsychic and intersubjective achievement. It presupposes health, a capacity for ambivalence, a complicated ego organization, and a reach for mastery.

To facilitate this developmental step, the "good-enough" mother becomes a reliable presence and a partner with her child in a benign cycle of object destruction and repair, demonstrating her survivability and her joy in the process over and over again. The infant's guilt over destructiveness recedes to an unfelt potential, appearing only when the opportunity for reparation fails to be present. The child becomes able to be concerned and to take responsibility for her instinctual impulses and the functions that belong to them. The opportunity for the infant to contribute to her world enables her to grasp the sense of concern.

Interconnections between mother and infant daughter go beyond the erotic intensity of bisexual sensuous unity to feminine sexual and social identifications. Jordan and Surrey (this volume) state:

> Through the identification with her mother as the 'mothering one' and through the mother's interest in being understood and cared for, the daughter as well as the mother becomes mobilized to care for, respond to, and attend to the well-being and development of the other. . . . . Through this mutual sensitivity and mutual caring, mothers are already teaching mothering, caring, relational practices to their female children [p. 90–91].

The moral issues inherent in women's subordination of self to the caretaking needs and desires of others are examined by Gilligan (1982) in her landmark work, *In a Different Voice.* Gilligan's perspective on the subject emanates from her studies of women's moral decision making, which challenges the findings of her mentor (Kohlberg, 1981) that in most women, morality is arrested at the point of needing to please and be approved of by others. Using a decision-making paradigm focused on conflicts about abortion and hypothetical moral dilemmas, Gilligan observed that women's sense of morality is mediated through the nonviolent "wish not to hurt others and the hope that in morality lies a way of solving conflicts so that no one will get hurt. The moral person is the one who helps others, if possible, without sacrificing oneself" (p. 165).

In contrast to women's moral ethic of nurturance and caring for others, men see morality as a matter of rules, rights, and the responsibility to carry out impartial justice, regardless of sacrifice. The effects of men's warrior ethic of dominance and submission are reflected in our millenium of world conflict. In today's world, where each person's interests are entwined with those of all others and nuclear holocaust is a daily threat, use of a moral ethic of concern and interdependent interests in conflict resolution would provide a temporizing note to the relentless furthering of destructive action.

Gilligan (1982) adds that the central moral problems for women are the conflicts between self and other, compassion and autonomy, virtue and power – dilemmas that demand as their solution recognizing and understanding the relativity of the multiple truths implicit in the reconciliation of femininity and adulthood. For women, the absolutes of caring and not hurting others become complicated by the need for personal integrity and self-nurturance to achieve an equality of self and other. For men, the absolutes of truth and fairness are challenged by the need for mutual equality and reciprocity. When equality moves toward equity, it gives rise to an ethic of generosity and care. Without such a balance, simplistic reductionism and categorization prevail. The "good woman" evades her true self and serves others to mask assertiveness, and the "bad woman" renounces the commitments that bind her to self-betrayal.

Such definitions of the "good" and "bad" woman derive from male developmental notions "partial to the separateness of the individual and the autonomy of work rather than the interdependence of nurturance, love and caring" (Gilligan, 1982, p. 160). The latter set of characteristics are viewed, even by contemporary theorists (Mahler, Pine, & Bergman, 1975), in regressive terms suggesting merger, symbiosis, and undifferentiation. In counterpoint, qualities that mark men's ethical conceptions, such as indepedence, objectivity, firmness, clarity, and logic, are considered signposts of maturity.

Women's more relational and nurturant style of judgment begins with a mother's experience of her daughter as continuous with herself, fusing the experience of attachment with the process of identity. Conversely, mothers experience sons as opposites who must differentiate themselves from her, tying the achievement of masculine gender identity to separation from mother (Chodorow, 1978), pp. 100, 166–167. From their more sexually diffuse beginnings, women develop perceptions of self and identity that are embedded in relationships and a sense of moral judgment that is insistently contextual. This relational bias in women's thinking is seen as a deficiency, just as the "bad" woman who departs from traditional roles and attitudes is viewed as deficient. Conceptually, this has left women as terminal children, forever locked in deviance.

Today's woman is both an expression and a disavowal of this feminine core identity of empathy and caretaking. The sexual revolution saw women burn bras and spurn their customary lives and roles as childbearers, homemakers, helpmates, and mothers. They discarded the soiled stereotypic feminine characteristics of nurturance, caretaking, and vulnerability and rallied to the call to arms of such militants as Betty Friedan, Kate Millet, and Germaine Greer. These radical feminists mobilized an army of women, urging them to vacate the tender traps of kitchen and nursery, conjugal bed and dinner table, suburbia and car pool, in favor of the waiting arms of the workplace, the dress-for-success suit, and the new college curricula aimed at the reentry woman.

Along the way, women have won the freedom to choose and build careers. They have emphasized the assertive and aggressive aspects of their personality, afraid that any need to be cared for, any desire to be taken care of, is treachery leading to a disastrous move backward to the prisons of tradition; afraid that any feelings of tenderness or yearnings for comfort provided by others are emotional and psychic betrayal, portending a loss of self-definition and a slide into passive oblivion. Having once struggled with and achieved some discernible differences between their mothers and themselves, having left passivity, conformity, and conventionality behind, many women are loathe to relinquish or modify newly constructed aggressive and competitive identifications.

Galenson (1982) suggests that the little girl's preoedipal, intense, and erotized tie to her mother compounds this dilemma. Strivings toward

separation are experienced as threats to the maternal bond and gener-
ate a sense of guilt, anxiety, depression, and shame about feelings of vitality, sexuality, and aggression. For the child this augurs loss of love
and love object, and loss of gratification of dependency needs. The
adult woman often experiences such feelings of vitality, sexuality, and
aggression paradoxically as inhibition, a sense of competence-loss,
helplessness and hopelessness, and loss of self-esteem (Bernay, 1982).

In her discussion of "The Refusal to Identify," A. Horner (1984)
notes that women often unconsciously experience their departures
from disparaged traditional identifications as a betrayal of the mother,
necessitating the suppression and denial of their own and the mother's
nurturing strengths. This leaves many women feeling "phony" or estranged from their own sense of accomplishments. Fearful of the destructive aspects of their own aggression, women cannot then claim
the effective and positive feelings associated with their achievements.
They cannot nurture themselves with caring validation because they
have been "bad" and feel the act of straying from stereotype as harmful
and as abandoning and abandonment of the maternal object. This discomfort with aggression and spontaneity often reflects a compliance
with false self-demands to identify with the empathic insufficiency of
the early mother, isolating the creativity of the true self from experience, affect, and expression.

These oft rigid resolutions in favor of achievement that are reached
by this transitional generation of women as they try to reconcile the
demands of marriage, motherhood, and career are now being questioned. Is superwoman a true self or yet another false self defending
against experience? Does she deprive women of the wholeness, full-
ness, and caring of the good mother? As Friedan (1981) states in her recent book, *The Second Stage*, "To deny the part of one's being that has,
through the ages, been expressed in motherhood—nurturing, loving
softness and tiger strength—is to deny part of one's personhood as a
woman."

New resolutions and reparations may be found in women's reclamation of previously disavowed aspects of themselves that are associated
with traditional, maternal and feminine identifications. Recast and informed by current thinking, such as that offered by Gilligan and by
Jordan and Surrey, and integrated with each woman's unique and essential self, these identifications can be transformed into more effective
selves and roles that transcend conventional conceptions. In this way,

feminine competence would include a sense of completeness and the tender and vital strength of maternal interconnectedness and nurturance as well as the empowering excitement of success, ambition, and achievement.

RECONCILING NURTURANCE AND AGGRESSION: THE CASE OF JOAN

Joan is a 32-year-old, never married executive, employed by a family-owned department store chain. She is personable, articulate, professionally assertive, and aggressive. An expert at closing deals, she has risen rapidly in the executive ranks. She entered therapy complaining of the need to break off her lengthy relationship with Ken, a married colleague and the boss's son, who had only recently separated from his wife. Joan was ambivalent about Ken, whose lack of integrity and manipulative and exploitive personality stood in sharp contrast to her own sense of integrity, idealism, and altruism and rigid moral code of right and wrong.

Joan came to realize that her "half a loaf" relationship with Ken represented both her internalization of her mother's disparaging and devaluing opinion of her father and her own guilt for being daddy's "favorite of all the girls in the family." By holding on to a relationship with a man of whom she felt fond but did not respect, whose scruples she constantly felt ashamed of, and who had been unavailable for marriage for so long, Joan felt she was paying penance.

Joan sometimes imagined Ken was her father during sex and became frightened by the fantasy. These experiences also helped her to realize that her incomplete relationship with Ken was a way of both having and not having her father alive inside her. It was also her way of not having any fulfilling love relationship of her own. Ken's lies and unscrupulousness were a corollary to Joan's isolation of childhood feelings of guilt: "I always felt like I lived a lie. I loved my father more than my mother. It felt wrong and unnatural. But he wasn't afraid of feelings. He was spontaneous, open, and excitable. I envied his life style. My mother's life was dull. Babies, housekeeping, talking on the phone—the existence of an unpaid maid. She was unenthusiastic and didn't seem to feel anything. I certainly didn't want to be like her."

In addition to breaking off with Ken, Joan felt the need to find herself separately from her mother and to stop feeling like "a puppet without a life of my own." She felt that her bubbly, spunky, intense self and feelings had been verbally "beaten" out of her by "shoulds" so that her mother would not have to feel frightened and inadequate in dealing with Joan and her feelings. Joan complained, "Since I've been a kid, I've lived my life as a series of reactions to my mother's picking criticisms. I get enraged and hurt, stifle my feelings, get an anxiety attack, and always end up feeling like the stupid kid. I'm tired of it." She would always have anxiety attacks during confrontations with maternal authority figures in her work and social world. Joan felt that she could never touch her mother or feel touched by her. "Mom was damaged goods, cold inside, not resilient. She was afraid of anything strong – a voice, a powerful feeling. I could never let loose with my feelings with her." Joan also felt that until she could touch her mother, she could never truly reclaim her own warmth and vitality or the capacities to comfort and soothe herself and to use her nurturing capabilities in a relationship as a wife and mother.

Although Joan's "stupid kid" reputation in the family was of long standing, she was the intellectually achieving child. Her sister Eva, five years Joan's senior, did poorly in school and was overweight and rebellious, but was considered the child with "good common sense." Eva became the mother's confidante. In contrast, Joan's curiosity, inquisitiveness and spontaneity were described contemptuously by her mother as "What's on the tongue is out. That child can never think before she speaks. She says such ridiculous and embarrassing things in front of the world."

Joan identified with her gregarious, generous, successful, and well-liked father, an attorney turned proprietor of the supermarket owned by Joan's family. Her mother spoke of father as a "decent, but silly and loud man." Joan also identified with her paternal grandmother, a successful businesswoman who Joan's mother thought was a crude peasant. Joan adored her grandmother and saw her as a "sharp-minded, sharp-tongued, straight-talking, warm Russian lady." Joan was secretly delighted at her mother's angry resentment about the close relationship Joan had with her grandmother. In retrospect, Joan also recognized her mother's envy of her father's and grandmother's competence.

When Joan was 14, her father died suddenly of a heart attack. Joan requested that her mother not cry publicly because it frightened Joan to see her "falling apart," so her mother grieved quietly in private. Joan said, "I was afraid she would cry herself to death – a frail, weak flower that would dry up and die." Joan's mother devoted herself to being a widow and to raising Joan. Joan threw a tantrum at her mother's one attempt at dating and asked her mother never to date again. Her mother complied.

Joan's transference to me centered around my having the right answers and knowing the right things to do and say and her having to guess what those right answers were. Any confusion or not knowing on her part felt like either a crime or a lie; any business trips she took felt like a shirking of her therapeutic responsibility. The expected punishment for these trespasses was to be labeled irresponsible and dismissed from therapy. When I did not react as expected, Joan felt that I was ridiculously reasonable and wondered whether anybody that reasonable could care about her. Caring meant telling her what to do and the right way to do it. Being reasonable, validating, and accepting or challenging, interested, and concerned was cold and irresponsible. Didn't I realize that she was a stupid kid and didn't know what to do? she would ask. "Besides", she said,

> your reasonableness feels like a lie sometimes – like my mom's coldness or even more, her platitudes. "Always tell the truth" really meant "Don't express your feelings." It's poor taste and it always ends up as a humiliating and hurtful experience. "Be whatever you want to be" really meant "Go and play around for awhile, but be sure you marry and to the right kind of man so that you're not ashamed of him like I am of your father." What if you're lying to me, too? If you tell me what to do, I don't have to worry about what you really think, I don't have to get anxious that you really can't handle my feelings, and I don't have to go out in the world and put myself on the line. I just have to follow orders.

Joan experienced all separations as final. For example, if I was a few minutes late for our session, she thought I had been killed or hurt in an auto accident, never to return again. When I left on vacation she had similar but more intense thoughts and feelings. After some time, Joan began to feel angry at my leaving. She remembered how angry she had been at being left at home when her parents went on vacation:

> My mother would get paranoid, cold. She was convinced my father would die of a heart attack when they were away. He anticipated and

planned for trips with excitement. She panicked and froze. It was like she left before she went away. Her feelings were always more important than mine. She was always so scared that I never felt that I could say that I was scared or lonely. For a long time in therapy, I needed to take a reading on your resiliency. I needed to find out over and over again that you can survive my loving, my anger, and my needing you.

Joan came to call her mother's empathic insufficiency "irresponsible," the same label she applied to Ken's behavior and to my "reasonableness." She fantasized that my trips out of town were always business and working trips. I would not go somewhere and lie on a beach and be "irresponsible." She also could not imagine me caring for a husband and family. That image conflicted with her idea of me as a responsible professional woman working hard on her career and, she added after awhile, "with me." When Joan got anxious about separations, she often had a comforting fantasy of a cloth doll attached to her with velcro. The doll was holding on to her as a baby might. She would never have to give up or lose the doll. This image was Joan's idea of her relationship to her mother, to myself, to all others close to her, and to her own, needy, frightened self. With closeness came crushing, dangerous, and suffocating fusion and the risk of loss and separation that felt ripping, tearing, deadly, and final.

I suggested that her wanting to feel close to me made it feel more painful to feel separated and separate from me – either ripped open and wounded, envious and left out, or terribly, finally alone. She responded:

> Yes, it hurts, and I envy you and others in your life, but it's important to me to know that feeling close to you and envious of you is survivable for me and for you. This gives me a clue that closeness was comfortable once and can be comforting again, that the ripping and tearing of separation is just disappointment and sadness and that anticipation and excitement and new beginnings are just on the other side of the hill.

After two and a half years of therapy, Joan's mother died following a complicated series of illnesses. By that time, Joan was feeling considerably better about her relationship with her mother. It had become more open, accepting, and expressive on both sides. As they had negotiated their relationship, Joan's anxiety attacks receded. About a year later, Joan separated from Ken and began to date other men. She also left her job and started her own consulting firm. Around that time, she had the following dream:

> I looked down at my breast. There was a milky white liquid pouring out of it in a thin stream. My breast opened up like the astrodome or like a flower with petals opening up. Inside was a good surprise: a ring of green. It looked like wasabi mustard – green, sensual, hot mustard that makes even the blandest sushi taste good.

At first Joan was horrified and sickened to think of her body opening up and draining out. The, she began to view her horror as representing her obsolete anxieties about wanting and needing – wanting to be a complete woman, wanting to be a nurturing woman, wanting to get from me what she felt she had been unable to get from her mother. I talked about the dream as representing her increasingly opening up and welcoming me in. It was also Joan welcoming herself in as a giving and generous woman, as well as an aggressive, hot, and sensual woman. She laughed at this and, referring to the thin stream of milk, said:

> It's about time I gave up the thinness of the stupid kid hiding behind "Miss Goody Two Shoes," always worried about and accommodating others so they won't get angry or disappear – a scared flower like my mother. It's time I gave myself a gift and enjoyed my warmer, fuller, bouncier personality – take a few chances and put myself out there – it won't kill me. The green mustard could also mean envy. That's okay. A ring, a bond of envy with you. I envied my father – his sense of excitement, his sparkle, his life style. And I envy you in the same way. I want more in every way – a marriage, a family, a career and fun. And I know I can have it all.

Joan has decided that her feelings, whatever they might be, are not evil, amoral, or frightening to me or to others, and that if conflict results, it can be transcended, even enjoyed. She has come to accept me as both a real and symbolic figure and role model who is interested and available, albeit in different ways than her mother. She has decided that caring and concern can be expressed in various ways, and each one can be the truth. She has a burgeoning interest in a relationship and marriage. For a long time, Joan felt that a relationship was so intense and complicated that she didn't know if she was capable of having one. "A career, that's easy. You get involved and excited. You set goals and you do it. But a relationship—it's so intimate, and it might lead to being a wife and a mother. You have to give up so much and be so responsible. Until now, it felt like I would lose too much of myself in the bargain. I now know that's not true."

Joan has begun to reclaim the enthusiastic and more vigorous aspects of herself from the jaws of guilt. She has become increasingly more comfortable and comforted by her warmer and more nurturing self, relinquishing compliant and isolating defenses in the process. She has also become more embracing of her own exploitive, envious, manipulative, irresponsible, and selfish desires. She is far more confident that her desire to be a complete woman—her tender yearnings to be continuous with her mother, myself, and all women—will result in a fuller sense of vitality and creativity, rather than a fatal fading of self-definition.

SUMMARY AND DISCUSSION

The current feminine ego ideal espouses aggression, assertiveness, and achievement rather than dependence, passivity, and submission. Having exchanged new selves and psyches for old, women are now questioning their bargain. Have they simply exchanged one oppressive destiny, one isolating and defensive experience for another? Is it time to reclaim the maternal strength and power disowned during the sexual revolution? And what of the assertive and achieving selves of recent construction?

This discussion has examined some aspects of the changing feminine identity of today's woman. It has also explored some newly emerging theories based on women's early experiences of maternal interconnectedness that are useful in helping women patients deal with the complexities of modern life and integrate the demands of traditional and contemporary ego ideals. The reconstruction of femininity I have offered here encompasses both aggressive and nurturant psychic and emotional trends as legitimate and valued dimensions of feminine identity. The various concepts of feminine competence discussed are all feminine, all human, including the strength of tenderness and caring; the enabling excitement of success, ambition, and achievement; and the creativity and vitality of relatedness, joy, and pride.

A review of the concepts of feminine aggression, including anger, assertiveness, and action, highlights the disorganizing effects of the early sensual inhibition of aggression that is common in female development. Following prior investigators who suggested that the roots of such problems lay in early maternal insufficiency and women's experience of their aggression as a destructive and evil force, I have explored a reevaluation of women's aggression as a source of life, desire, and growth. This includes women's perception of their departure from disparaged maternal identifications as autonomous, aggressive, and traitorous acts accompanied by anxiety, guilt, depression, and estrangement from their own self-validation, caring, and sense of accomplishment.

A corollary review and reassessment of women's nurturant tendencies reveals the possibility that women's early experiences of attachment are the genesis of mutual empathy and relatedness rather than the infantile oppression of masochism and passivity. In addition, contemporary thinking shows women's contextual moral judgment style as spawning a mature sense of morality based on interdependence, nurturance, and responsible care in contrast to the traditional notions of women's morality as deficient and subject to the corruptions of emotional distractions.

Winnicott's conception of the infant's use of the environmental mother in a loving and benign cycle of destruction and repair is reviewed. This represents a way of understanding how the infant comes to know and build trust and confidence in her aggression, develops the capacity for concern, creates and cultivates the spontaneity of the true self within the empathic milieu of mother-infant interconnectedness.

Winnicott's theories are juxtaposed with Gilligan's concepts of a moral ethic of responsible caring and concern and with Jordan and Surrey's ideas of maternal identifications as a pathway to feminine relational self and a sense of attentiveness and emotional responsivity. These concepts serve as organizing constructs for understanding women's early developmental experiences and as the theoretical basis for clinical interventions that are especially helpful to women patients.

REFERENCES

Abraham, K. (1920), Manifestations of the female castration complex. In: *Women and Analysis*, ed. J. Strouse. New York: Grossman, 1974.

Beauvoir, S. de (1949), *The Second Sex*. New York: Knopf, 1971.

Benedek, T. (1952), *Psychosexual Functions in Women*. New York: Ronald.

Bernard, J. (1974), *The Future of Motherhood*. New York: Dial.

Bernay, T. (1982), Separation and the sense of competence-loss in women. *Amer. J. Psychoanal.*, 42: 293–305.

Blum, H. (1976), Female psychology, masochism and the ego ideal. *J. Amer. Psychoanal. Assn.*, 24: 305–351.

Chasseguet-Smirgel, J. (1970), Feminine guilt and the Oedipus complex. In: *Female Sexuality*, ed. J. Chasseguet-Smirgel. Ann Arbor: University of Michigan Press, pp. 94–134.

Chodorow, N. (1978), *The Reproduction of Mothering*. Berkeley: University of California Press.

Cavendish, R. (Ed.) (1983), *Man, Myth, and Magic: The Illustrated Encyclopedia of Mythology, Religion and the Unknown* (s.v. Demeter, Rape of Persephone). New York: Marshall Cavendish.

Deutsch, H. (1930), The significance of masochism in the mental life of women. *Internat. J. Psycho-Anal.*, 11: 48–60.

Eliot, G. (1860), *The Mill on the Floss*. New York: New American Library, 1965.

Friedan, B. (1963), *The Feminine Mystique*. New York: Norton.

_____ (1981), *The Second Stage*. New York: Summit.

Freud, S. (1915), Instincts and their vicissitudes. *Standard Edition*, 14: 117–140. London: Hogarth Press, 1957.

_____ (1919), A child is being beaten. *Standard Edition*, 27: 179–204. London: Hogarth Press, 1961.

_____ (1925), Some psychical consequences of the anatomical distinction between the sexes. *Standard Edition*, 19: 248–258. London: Hogarth Press, 1961.

_____ (1931), Female sexuality. *Standard Edition*, 21: 223–243. London: Hogarth Press, 1961.

_____ (1933), New introductory lectures in psychoanalysis. *Standard Edition*, 20: 5–182. London: Hogarth Press, 1964.

Galenson, E. (1982), Preoedipal factors in the transference with special reference to women. Paper presented at the Scientific Meeting of the Southern California Psychoanalytic Society, Los Angeles, March 8.

_____ & Roiphe, H. (1976), Some suggested revisions concerning early female development. In: *Female Psychology*, ed. H. Blum. New York: International Universities Press, 1977.

Gilligan, C. (1982), *In a Different Voice*. Cambridge, MA: Harvard University Press.

Greenacre, P. (1957), The childhood of the artist. *The Psychoanalytic Study of the Child*, 12: 47–72. New York: International Universities Press.

_____ (1958), Early physical determinants in the development of the sense of identity. In: *Emotional Growth*, Vol. 1. New York: International Universities Press, pp. 113–127.

Greer, G. (1970), *The Female Eunuch*. New York: Bantam Books.

Horner, A. (1984), The refusal to identify: Developmental impasse. In: *Object Relations and the Developing Ego in Therapy*. New York: Aronson, pp. 345–369.

Horner, M. S., & Walsh, M. R. (1974), Psychological barriers to success in women. In: *Women and Success*, ed. R. B. Kundsin. New York: Morrow, pp. 138–144.

Horney, K. (1926), The flight from womanhood: The masculinity complex in women as viewed by men and women. In: Feminine Psychology, ed. H. Kelman. New York: Norton, 1967, pp. 54–70.

_____ (1931), The distrust between the sexes. In: Feminine Psychology, ed. H. Kelman. New York: Norton, 1967, pp. 107–118.

_____ (1932), The dread of women. In: Feminine Psychology, ed. H. Kelman. New York: Norton, 1967, pp. 133–146.   ᵥ

_____ (1935), The problem of feminine masochism. In: Feminine Psychology, ed. H. Kelman. New York: Norton, 1967, pp. 214–233.

Jacobson, E. (1950), Development of the wish for a child in boys. Psychoanal. Quart., 37: 523–538.

_____ (1964), The Self and the Object World. New York: International Universities Press.

Kaplan, E. (1976), Manifestations of aggression in latency and preadolescent girls. The Psychoanalytic Study of the Child, 31: 63–78.

Kestenberg, J. (1956), Vicissitudes of female sexuality. J. Amer. Psychoanal. Assn., 4: 453–475.

Klein, G. (1976), Psychoanalytic Theory: An Explanation of Essentials. New York: International Universities Press.

Klein, M. (1975), The effects of early anxiety situations on the early development of the girl. In: The Psychoanalysis of Children. New York: Delacorte Press, pp. 194–239.

Kohlberg, L. (1981), The Philosophy of Moral Development. New York: Harper & Row.

Kohut, H. (1971), The Analysis of the Self. New York: International Universities Press.

Lampl-de Groot, L. (1933), Problems of femininity. Psychoanal. Quart., 2: 489–518.

Mahler, M. S., Pine, F., & Bergman, A. (1975), The Psychological Birth of the Human Infant: Symbiosis and Individuation. New York: Basic Books.

McDougall, J. (1979), Primitive communication and the use of countertransference. In: Countertransference, ed. L. Epstein & A. Feiner. New York: Aronson, pp. 267–303.

Miller, J. B. (1976), Toward a New Psychology of Women. Boston: Beacon Press.

_____ Nadelson, C. C., Notman, M. T., & Zilbach, J. (1981), Aggression in women: A reexamination. In: Changing Concepts in Psychoanalysis, ed. S. Klebanow. New York: Gardner, pp. 157–167.

Millet, K. (1969), Sexual Politics. New York: Ballantine.

Parens, H. (1979), The Development of Aggression in Early Childhood. New York: Aronson.

Rochlin, G. (1973), Man's Aggression: The Defense of the Self. Boston: Gambit.

Surrey, J. (1982), The relational self in women: Clinical implications. In: Work in Progress. Wellesley, MA: Stone Center for Developmental Services and Studies.

Thompson, C. (1943), Cultural pressures in the psychology of women. Psychiat., 5: 331–339.

Winnicott, D. W. (1950), Aggression in relation to emotional development. Through Pediatrics to Psychoanalysis. New York: Basic Books, 1975, pp. 205–218.

_____ (1960), Ego distortion in terms of true and false self. The Maturational Processes and the Facilitating Environment. New York: International Universities Press, 1965, pp. 140–152.

_____ (1963), The development of the capacity for concern. *The Maturational Processes and the Facilitating Environment.* New York: International Universities Press, 1965, pp. 73–82.

_____ (1971), Use of an object and relating through identifications. *Playing and Reality.* London: Tavistock, pp. 86–94.

Zilbach, J., Notman, M. T., Nadelson, C. C., & Miller J. B. (1982), Aggression in women: Conceptual Issues and Clinical Implications. In: *The Woman Patient,* Vol. 3, ed. M. T. Notman & C. C. Nadelson. New York: Plenum Press, pp. 17–27.

4

The Self-in-Relation: Empathy and the Mother-Daughter Relationship

Judith V. Jordan, Ph.D.
Janet L. Surrey, Ph.D.

Freud recognized the importance of the early mother-daughter relationship as a major determinant in woman's psychological development, but he was unable to establish its exact significance within his
theoretical formulations. He did speculate that the necessity for a gender shift in sexual object choice for girls left females vulnerable to
bisexuality and to the failure to fully negotiate the oedipal crisis, which
he saw as the foundation of healthy development. This postulation is
an important example of the problems of "phallocentric" theory, in
which woman's development is viewed as the mirror image of male development and important sex differences may be overlooked.

    In this essay we introduce a reinterpretation of current psychoana-
lytic and developmental theory, which describes woman's develop-

ment from her own unique experience and perspective. Such reinterpretation often involves rethinking the "deficiency" model of female development, in which women are seen as lacking something important or as deficient in their development, resulting in psychological traits such as narcissism, passivity, dependence, and masochism.

This discussion reflects a beginning attempt to recast and reformulate notions of woman's development, focusing on aspects that may reflect hidden or neglected areas of human development — specifically, human relationships and the development of the capacity for relatedness. We postulate this capacity as fundamental to understanding woman's psychological development, her sense of identity and self-esteem. The self as an organizing psychological structure is seen as developing within the context of early mother-child interaction. Sex differences in the nature and development of this critical relationship over time form important differences in self-images, self-representations, identity, and ego ideals. The model of "self-in-relation" will be shown to be valuable to the therapist in understanding and validating women's unique experiences and conflicts, especially in a cultural milieu that often invalidates or challenges this mode of being in the world. We will also begin to reexamine current object relations theory as it relates to the development of the self-in-relation as established in the early mother-daughter relationship. Finally, we will illustrate the usefulness of this new model, offering clinical material and suggesting new clinical interpretations and interventions.

OVERVIEW OF EXISTING THEORY

Developmental and clinical theory has generally emphasized the growth of the autonomous, individuated self in such a way that early developmental milestones are typically characterized by greater separation from mother and an increasing sense of boundedness, self-control, the self as origin of action and intention, and use of logical, abstract thought. This particular bias, if we may call it that, probably derives from several influences: (1) the modeling of psychology as a science on Newtonian physics, which emphasized notions of discrete entities acting on each other in measurable ways; (2) the emphasis in Western, democratic countries on the sanctity and freedom of the individual; (3) a culture that perceives its task of child rearing as weaning the helpless, dependent infant toward greater self-sufficiency and independence; and (4) a study of the psyche that grew from an understanding of pathology in which the ego was seen as needing to protect itself from assaults both by internal impulses and external demands. Freud commented that "protection against stimuli is an almost more important function for the living organism than reception of stimuli" (Freud, 1920, p. 27). In traditional psychoanalytic theory the individual is seen as growing from an undifferentiated and later embedded and symbiotic phase into an individuated, separate state.

Freud's theory, which draws heavily on nineteenth century understanding of biology and physiology, is basically, as Horney (1926) stated, a "masculine psychology" (p. 54). Central to Freud's developmental model is the Oedipus complex, an important turning point. For boys, castration anxiety leads to identification with the feared parent — the father — and superego formation occurs. Bonding, identification, and the curtailment of self-interest are seen as derivative of the sexual and aggressive instincts; the little boy gives up his possessive, sexual interest in the mother out of fear of aggressive retaliation from the father. The resolution of the Oedipus complex is seen as crucial to the continued healthy development of the individual, both in terms of the capacity to function productively in society and the ability to engage in mature love relationships.

Although we might question the premises and development of this theory as it relates to males, such an exploration is beyond the scope of this paper. But the failure to account for female development, particularly in regard to the Oedipus complex, has been a major problem of Freudian theory. As Schafer (1974) points out, "Freud still puts the phallus, oedipal fantasies, castration anxiety and procreation in the center of his developmental theory" (p. 473). Freud's approach to female development was typically to conceptualize the female as deviating in some way from the male or "lacking" by comparison. The patriarchal and biological bias, as well as the materialistic determinism of the nineteenth and early twentieth centuries, is clear in this thinking.

Horney (1926) and Thompson (1942), among others, objected to Freud's understanding of women, particularly his emphasis on biological explanations. Sullivan (1940), turning from the focus on instinct theory, elaborated on the centrality of interpersonal relations. Erikson

(1963) emphasized environmental contributions to development in his psychosocial theory of development. He also noted the importance of adult stages of development.

Moving further away from Freud's drive theory and biological determinism, the school of object relations, led by Fairbairn (1954) and Winnicott (1971) suggested the importance of the earliest mother-infant relationship in the formation of the ego. The individual's relationships with his or her surrounding environment, particularly human contacts, are seen as more central to growth than the "taming" of the instincts. Moreover, object relations theorists began to address the mutuality of the exchange. For instance, Guntrip notes: "Personal object relations are essentially two sided, mutual by reason of being personal, and not a matter of mutual adaptation merely, but of mutual appreciation, communication, sharing and of each being for the other" (p. 111). The delineation of the separation-individuation phase of development (Mahler, Pine, & Bergman, 1975) emphasizes the importance of the interplay of the mother and the child before the oedipal stage. But the end point of the milestones in mother-child development suggested by Mahler is the establishment of a separated and autonomous self. Thus, although Mahler traces the path of early development quite differently from Freud, the movement is still toward establishment of the separate self.

More recently, Kohut's (1971) theory of self psychology has emphasized in the self/self-object unit the importance of the interrelation of self and other. As Ornstein (1982) notes: "The self cannot be conceptualized without the self-object environment nor can the function of the self objects be assessed without taking the state of this self into consideration" (p. 12).

George Klein (1976) made an important contribution to analytic theory in pointing to the imbalance in existing theories about the self. He posited two major lines of development of the self: "One is an autonomous unit, distinct from others as a locus of action and decision. The second aspect is one's self construed as a necessary part of a unit transcending one's autonomous actions. 'We' identities are also part of the self." "Like any biological 'organ' or 'part' the organism is . . . and must feel itself to be . . . both separate and a part of an entity beyond itself" (p. 178). Systems theorists have recently applied to development the idea of "a set of interacting units with relationships among them"

(Miller, 1978, p. 16). Stern (1980) has referred to the "self with the other"; Stechler and Kaplan (1980) have written about the coexistence of affiliative and autonomous tendencies; Kohut (1971) drew attention to the ongoing need for the self object; and Gilligan (1982), Miller (1976), and Surrey (1983) have all posited the special importance of what might be called a "relational self" in women.

Concomitantly, Newtonian physics has given way to the "new physics" and quantum theory, which emphasizes flow, waves, and interconnections. Instead of emphasis on static structure and discrete, bounded objects existing separately in space, then, we are seeing a growing appreciation of process, relationship, and interaction. In developmental and clinical theory, this is mirrored in growing attention to the line of development of interpersonal connection and relationship rather than to the view of the self as developing away from, or independent of, relationship. Too often, however, relational issues have been phrased in regressive terms, such as "merger," "symbiotic," or "undifferentiated," suggesting that intense interpersonal connection involves a movement into more primitive functioning. If the development of more complex, differentiated patterns of connection and intimacy is not appreciated, then the relational aspect of self-definition will continue to be inadequately understood and devalued.

Empathy is central to an understanding of the aspect of the self that involves "we-ness" — transcendence of the separate, disconnected self. It is the process through which one's experienced sense of basic connection and similarity to other humans is established. Kohut (1973) has described empathy as "a fundamental mode of human relatedness" (p. 704), "the recognition of the self in the other" (p. 705), and "the accepting, confirming and understanding human echo" (p. 713). Without empathy, there is no intimacy, no real attainment of an appreciation of the paradox of separateness within connection. Although empathy has often been construed as a mysterious and regressive process, the paradox of empathy is that in the joining process, one develops a more articulated and differentiated image of the other and hence responds in a more accurate way — quite the opposite of what regressive merging would lead to.

Given the importance of empathy to human relationships, it has been underestimated, even by those who have specialized in interpersonal theory. Thus, Sullivan (1940) p. 17 notes:

Empathy is the term that we use to refer to the peculiar emotional link-age that subtends the relationship of the infant with other significant people. Long before there are signs of any understanding of emotional expression there is evidence of this emotional contagion or commun-ion. We do not know much about the fate of empathy in the develop-mental history of people in general. There are indications that it en-dures throughout life, at least in some people. There are a few unstable instances of its function in most of us in our later years. I find it conven-ient to assume that the time of its great importance is later infancy and early childhood, perhaps age 6 to 27 months. So much for empathy (p. 17).

Although many theorists have studied or alluded to the importance of empathy in the early mother-infant relationship, there has been lit-tle comprehensive study of the development of empathy over the life span. How do women develop empathic mothering skills? Why is vicarious affective arousal, an important part of empathy, not shown as much by men? Perhaps the question is best posed: What facilitates empathic growth in females and what impedes it in males?

Without an appreciation of the elaboration and refinement of empa-thy as the individual grows, there is a tendency to resort to a regressive, oversimplified view of the empathic process, as illustrated by the quote from Sullivan. Empathy develops in the context of: an interest in inter-personal relatedness; well-developed perceptual discriminations vis à vis others; openness to the increasingly differentiated and articulated affects in oneself and others; increasing capacity to cognitively struc-ture these complex affective changes; ability to tolerate the tension of affective experiences generated by another's affect, over which one usually has no control; and a refinement of the capacity to "de-center" (cognitively and affectively to put oneself in the other's place). One cannot be so caught up with one's own self-interest or self-defense that one has neither the motivation nor the capacity to fully attend to the other.

The theory of the self-in-relation describes self-development within relationship, in which the goal of mutual empathy becomes the motivating force in the growth of the self. The early structure of the mother-daughter relationship and the elaboration of this relationship throughout the life cycle will be presented as a model for understand-ing the development of the self-in-relation.

EARLY DEVELOPMENT

There is evidence that relational capacities are present in some organized fashion very early in life. Simner (1971) and Sagi and Hoffman (1976) have demonstrated that one- to two-day old infants cry in response to the distress cry of another infant, a possible precursor to empathy. Sander (1980) and Stern (1980) have studied complex patterns of mutual regulation between mother and infant from an early age. This research challenges the old unidirectional model of development, in which the mother shapes and influences the infinitely malleable and unformed infant.

Reciprocity may be an especially important factor in the mother-daughter relationship. Chodorow (1978), drawing on object relations theory, proposes that the nature of the early identification differs for males and females. She suggests the period of "primary identification" continues longer for females than males and that the female child is more likely to be treated as an extension of the mother, whereas the male child is more apt to be treated as an object. Specifically, Chodorow notes the boy will be treated as a "sexual other" (p. 110) by the mother, who pushes the boy to differentiate from her. The preoedipal girl, on the contrary, is seen as an "extension or double of the mother herself" (p. 109), which leads to "boundary confusion and a lack of a sense of separateness in the world" (p. 110). Thus, Chodorow's analysis remains firmly entrenched in a Freudian theory that posits the importance of instinctual impulses as the basis of object relatedness. The theory also points to the pathological consequences of the early empathic bond between mother and daughter.

Although Chodorow seems to be making important observations regarding early mother-daughter relationships, she does not adequately explore the possibility that this early flexibility of boundaries and relational sensitivity is a positive developmental pathway. It is likely that maternal empathy differs with the sex of the child. Based partly on the sameness of their bodies and gender identification, the mother develops a rich set of assumptions about the girl, characterized by overlapping images of self and other. Thus, the mother draws on her own memories of herself in understanding her child. With a daughter, then, she may be less influenced by the obvious differences between herself and the child to form clearly separate images and expectations of self and other. Furthermore, the mother may feel more comfortable about encouraging a daughter to feel connected with her at an affective level. The process of understanding sons may be more "intellectual" and less based on identification and affective cues. Society also exerts influences on the mother to not view sons as being like her. Sons are to be raised to be like their fathers, like men. Since being a man is not something with which the mother has had immediate experience, she must act as she has seen others act with males or must imagine what should be done. All this leads to a less affectively tinged identification. As the boy begins to recognize his maleness, he too frequently distances himself from the mother and ultimately comes to devalue her differentness.

With mothers and daughters there is likely to be more frequent mirroring, mutual identification, and accurate empathy. This leads to the daughter's development of a sense of self that is anchored in relationship and connection. Some have referred to this ongoing investment in relationship between mother and daughter as "semisymbiotic" (Signe Hammer, quoted in Chodorow, 1978, p. 109). It may make more sense, given this new model, to look at it as an ongoing elaboration of a mutually empathic relationship. The exchange of affect, the attention to the relationship on both sides, is really quite dissimilar to the early mother-infant interaction. Rather than providing useful description, terms such as "semisymbiotic" merely reflect the paucity of our language and theory in describing relational development.

THE SELF-IN-RELATION: A DEVELOPMENTAL MODEL

The model of self-in-relation involves an assumption of a developmental pathway. The mother-daughter relationship can be seen as the earliest form of relationship, the foundation of the core structure of self that is necessary for empathic development. Articulating the structure of the formative mother-daughter relationship is fundamental to understanding women's unique development. The model presented here is a general model of relationship and is not totally specific to the nuclear mother-daughter relationship of early childhood. This relationship simply represents the beginning of a structure and process that will be developed through important relationships with other signifi-

cant people in childhood and throughout life. Such relational development will depend on the availability of early relationships and of relational networks which can foster and facilitate it. In fact, particular
crises and obstacles to the ongoing development of mutual empathy in
the mother-daughter relationship may become the spur to further relational development and growth within this relationship or others.

   This essay will focus on three structural aspects of the mother-
daughter relationship that have a crucial impact on the girl's developing sense of self. The first is the girl's ongoing interest in and emotional attentiveness to the mother. All children have a deep
fascination with early adult figures in their lives. This interest in people
as a primary part of the construction of reality and the exploration of
the feeling states of the parent, especially the mother, is probably reinforced much more in girls than in boys. For example, a patient described her 3-year-old daugher's frequent question, "What are you feeling, Mommy?" The mother would respond carefully and thoughtfully,
but would wonder why the daughter was asking. She was puzzled that
she recalled hardly any such interaction with her 5-year-old son.

   This early attentiveness to feeling states on the part of the daughter,
and the mother's corresponding ease with and interest in emotional
sharing, may be the origin of learning to "listen" to feelings, to orient
and attune to the other person — in other words, the origin of the capacity for empathy and the process of relational development. The
contrast with the development of this capacity in boys is shown by a
male patient's description of his childhood experience as "learning not
to listen," learning "to shut out my mother's voice, so that I would not
be distracted from pursuing my own interests." Following from this
early developmental difference, in adult life women experience "being
with" psychologically as self-enhancing, whereas men may experience
it as invasive, engulfing, or threatening. "Being with" here means both
"being seen" and "seeing the other," which is the experience of mutual
empathy. This early open connection is allowed to develop more naturally between mothers and daughters and probably forms the basis for
the girl's early maternal identification. This may be the origin of "seeing through the eyes of the other," as a natural intuitive process. A failure to differentiate or develop in this process might leave the girl feeling unclear about "whose feelings belong to whom," with a tendency to
experience the feelings of the other as her own, especially if she does
not have adequate opportunities for exploration and clarification. It is

through this normal process of describing and exploring feelings that one begins to know the other and the self-in-relation to the other.

This, then, is the second key aspect of the mother-daughter relationship: the experience of mutual empathy, developed in a matrix of emotional connectedness. The interest, ability, and involvement of the mother in listening and responding, empathizing and mirroring the child has been well described by Winnicott (1971), Kohut (1971), and others, who see this as the beginning of the development of experiences of the self. This experience of empathy also includes the girl's empathic connection to the mother through mutual identification, in a relationship that is open on both sides. The mother's easier emotional openness with the daughter and her sense of identification probably leave the girl feeling more emotionally connected, understood, and recognized than would a boy. The importance of this sense of mutual identification in forming the relational bond can, of course, lead to projection and overidentification. In healthy development, however, this sense of connection appears to form the framework for the process of differentiation and clarification. Thus, the mutual identification process fosters a sense of mutual understanding, connection, and finally differentiation. For boys, the importance of an early emotional separation and the formation of an identity through the assertion of difference fosters a basic relational stance of disconnection and lack of identification. Girls, then, develop the expectation that they can facilitate and enhance their sense of self through psychological connection and grow to expect that the mutual sharing of experience leads to mutual empathy. Reciprocally, mothers are likely to appreciate the enhancement of their own self-awareness through this process of mutual empathy because it compliments their own relational stance. Indeed, mothers often report a real deepening of self-awareness in their ongoing experience of relating to a growing child. Many mothers are finally able to come to therapy for themselves after their daughters have begun therapy.

These effects of the mother-daughter interaction demonstrate the last key formative factor of this early relationship: mutual empowerment. The emotional and cognitive connections based on shared feeling states and identification develop over time into a mutual, reciprocal process, in which both mother and daughter become highly responsive to the feeling states of the other over the life cycle. Through the girl's identification with her mother as "the mothering one" and through the mother's interest in being understood and cared for, the daughter as well as the mother becomes mobilized to care for, respond to, or attend to the well-being and development of the other. This is the motivational dynamic of mutual empowerment, the energizing force inherent in growth-enhancing relationships. Through this mutual sensitivity and mutual caring, mothers are already teaching mothering, caring, relational practices to their female children. By mothering, of course, we do not mean the traditional one-dimensional view of it, but rather attentiveness and emotional responsivity to the other as an intrinsic, ongoing aspect of one's own experience. Within the early mother-daughter relationship, and as it develops over the life cycle, we can begin to see the precursors of women's interest, comfort, and sense of purpose and empowerment in relatedness.

Another aspect of this reciprocity is the mutual self-esteem involved in the relationship. A "good relationship" is highly valued by both mother and daughter and becomes a fundamental component of women's self-worth throughout the life cycle. Self-esteem becomes related to the degree of mutual empathy in the relationship and to the shared sense of understanding and regard. Such a relationship is very difficult to maintain, especially in a culture that stresses separation as an ideal, and the validation of the need for relationship may become distorted and hidden. For women, guilt and shame may become tied to experiences of failure in mutual empathy. In growth-promoting situations, however, these failures can become challenges to relational growth. For example, as women reexamine their relationships with their mothers in therapy and develop a more empathic understanding, this understanding can be brought into the actual relationship to facilitate mutual empathy. A sense of self-worth becomes intricately involved in "good-enough" understanding and caring for the other and in a sense of mutual concern for the well-being of each other.

It is important to note that the development of accurate empathy involves a complex process that encompasses interactive validation of the differences between self and other and the recognition of the other as a growing individual with changing needs and newly developing competencies. Within the early mother-daughter relationship, the daughter is thus encouraged to learn to take the role of the mother (the provider, the listener, or the "surround") as well as of the daughter, (the receiver, the speaker, or the "figure"), depending on the needs of the situation or the individual at any given time. Clearly, in problematic situations both the mother and daughter can become overinvolved in feeling responsible and protective towards the other. But this model suggests that a healthy degree of reciprocity and role flexibility are essential for women's growth. The dynamics of such reciprocity establish in women the capacity to move from one perspective to another as the needs of a relational situation arise. This capacity we have termed the "oscillating self-structure."

There are a myriad of memory experiences that provide us with a sense of organization, coherence, and meaning—in other words, a sense of self. Conceptualizations of the self in the past have erred in regarding these as static, permanent structures. There is typically a fluid quality to these representations, however, that resembles Piaget's (1952) model for formation of schema. In the development of schema, the assimilation of new data to fit existing schema and the accommodation of the schema to the incoming material are ongoing processes that never reach a final, static equilibrium. Rather, there is a shifting balance in which first assimilation predominates, then accommodation becomes pronounced. Representations of self and other probably maintain a similarly shifting balance; the representations first overlap and then differentiate. There is room in such a model for what Klein (1976) called a sense of "we-ness"—affective joining with the other, as well as more autonomous self-definition. The process of empathy may be thought of as this oscillation of images of self and other—affective and cognitive overlap and distinctness. This notion challenges the old model in which self is seen as *either* distinct and autonomous *or* merged and embedded. One can feel connected and affectively joined and at the same time appreciate one's separateness. The emergent self, throughout the life span, needs to be seen as a structure (or a set of structures) providing a sense of coherent separateness and meaningful connection. Thus, the theory of the self-in-relation begins to develop a new model of growth through relationships.

Much attention has been given recently to the notion that there are important sex differences in the experience and construction of the self. A central theme of *Toward a New Psychology of Women* (Miller, 1976) is that "women's sense of self becomes very much organized around being able to make and maintain affiliation in relationships" (p. 13). Miller describes the necessity of developing new language and new concepts to describe women's unique experiences and to point out the problems that develop when principles of male development are cast as universal principles of human development. Gilligan (1982) further stresses the importance of women finding their own unique voice in describing "ourselves to ourselves." She shows that women's experiences of connectedness lead to differing conceptions of self, morality, and visions of relationship. It is essential to point out again that the inquiry into the nature of women's development is a step in the evolution of understanding human development. Women in Western society have been "carriers" of certain aspects of the human experience, and a full understanding of human development can only be derived from a thorough elucidation of both male and female experience.

The concept of the self-in-relation entails the recognition that, for women, the primary experience of self is relational; that is, the self is organized and developed in the context of important relationships. To understand this basic assumption, it is useful to use as a contrast some current assumptions about male (often generalized to human) development. Current developmental theory stresses the importance of separation from the mother at early stages of childhood development (Mahler, Pine, & Bergman, 1975), from the family at adolescence (Erikson, 1963), and from teachers and mentors in adulthood (in Levinson's [1978] phrase, "becoming one's own man"), in order to form a distinct separate identity. High value is placed on autonomy, self-reliance, independence, self-actualization, and following one's own unique dream, destiny, and fulfillment. Intimacy and generativity in adulthood (in Erikson's terms) are seen as possible only after the "closure" of identity. Relational "trust" is laid down in early childhood and does not reemerge as central until the end of adolescence. These values of individuation have permeated our cultural ideals as well as our clinical theories and practice. The notion of the self-in-relation emphasizes an important shift in emphasis from separation to relationship as the basis for the experience and development of self. For women, this relational pathway is primary and continuous although its centrality may be hidden and unacknowledged.

We have already described the early mother-daughter relationship as a model for relational development, using the concept of mutual empathy as the fundamental developmental process. The hyphenated expression, self-in-relation, implies an evolutionary process of growth and development through relationship. Such language is used to differentiate this from a static "self-construct" and to describe an experiential process of openness, flexibility, and change. On a practical level, listening to women in therapy describe themselves, we hear as a continuous theme that women's sense of self lies in establishing and maintaining emotional connection and identification with significant others, and that women's sense of personal worth, power, pleasure, growth, and well-being are experienced in the context of relationships and not in "splendid isolation." This is not to diminish the significance of other lines of self-development (such as agency, initiative, or creativity), but these other capacities are developed for women in the context of important relationships and need to be redefined in a relational framework. The idea of the self-in-relation is not in any way an attempt to idealize women's altruism or relational capacities. Rather, it is an attempt to develop a model that better fits women's unique experience, to develop more relevant and realistic self-images. By thus focusing and building on women's specific strengths, we can be more constructive in developing clinical, educational, and social strategies for fostering women's development.

A MODEL OF RELATIONSHIP: MUTUALITY AND INTERSUBJECTIVITY

We have thus postulated a theory of the development of the self through a particular mode of "being in relationship." This mode can be described as emotional and cognitive intersubjectivity – the ongoing, intrinsic inner awareness of and responsiveness to the continuous existence of others and the expectation of mutuality in this regard. We might term this "subject relations" theory to distinguish it from object relations theory, in which the object, based on the construction of the separate self, may not be fully experienced as a subject with a comprehensive personal construction of continuous reality. Our definition of relationship is not equivalent to the concept of attachment, extension of ego boundaries, or mutuality, defined as separate but equal coexistence, in which the needs and satisfactions of the other are as important as one's own. Our definition implies a sense of mutual interaction and continuity of dialogue. It connotes a way of being in the world as part of a unit larger than the individual, in which the whole is experienced as greater than the sum of the parts. The relationship or the new relational unit (for example, the couple, family, or group) comes to have a unique existence beyond the individuals, to be regarded, attended to, and cared about (somewhat akin to Klein's [1976] "we-ness"). In this model, relationship fosters and highlights self-experience, and the self is enhanced, not reduced or threatened, by connections. This form of relationship implies a two-way process of mutual empathy. Growth and communication in this model become processes of interaction and dialogue.

The ongoing process of intersubjective relationship obviously does not involve continuous physical connection. Rather, it involves a continuous psychological connection, in which the presence of the other forms a basic component of one's own experiences of self. The process and dialogue of relationship—the interaction, interconnection, and readiness to respond—is maintained on a psychological level. Such continuity is a basic aspect of the mother-child relationship, and mothers often report this as a major difference between themselves and their husbands in child care. Although a man may be highly committed to caring for the child, it is the woman who experiences the unceasing continuity of awareness. This experience of continuity is the "holding" of the other as part of the self and is a component of all growth-enhancing relationships.

The ability to be in mutually empathic or authentic relationships appears to rest on the development of the capacity for empathy. The experience of such a relationship involves the capacity for empathy in all persons involved. Kohut (1971) has emphasized the importance of experiencing parental empathy and mirroring in the child's early self-development, but almost no attention has been devoted to the problem of teaching and learning empathy. Rather, empathy has been construed as a highly subjective, intuitive, perhaps innate phenomenon. However, the "good-enough" mother, capable of providing a "holding" and facilitating environment for the growing child, does not suddenly appear with the birth of the infant. Much unrecognized learning must have taken place to allow the complex capacity for mothering to flower in response to the changes of the growing child. The development of the capacity for empathy needs to be carefully studied and elaborated.

Jordan (1983) has reexamined the concept of empathy in this light. She has shown that the ability to experience, comprehend, and respond to the inner state of another person is a highly complex process relying on a high level of psychological development and learning. Accurate empathy involves a simultaneous balancing of affective arousal and cognitive structuring as well as the ability to build on the subjective experience of identification with the other person. This process enables the individual to cognitively assimilate the experience as a basis for response. Such a definition of empathy implies highly developed emotional and cognitive operations requiring practice, modeling, and feedback in relationships.

The concept of the relational self relies heavily on this new definition of empathy and stresses the growth of such capacity as primary in women's development. The self-in-relation theory begins to sketch a developmental model to account for the development of empathic competencies in women, starting with the early mother-daughter relationship. This model assumes that the self is organized and developed through practice in relationships with the goal of increasing the capacity for reciprocal and mutually empathic relationships.

PATHWAYS OF DEVELOPMENT

It is difficult to find words to describe the process of relational development. We use the concept of "relationship-differentiation" as a contrast to the idea of separation-individuation. Differentiation here does not suggest as a developmental goal the assertion of difference or separateness. Rather, it is a process more like embryological development. By differentiation we mean a dynamic process that encompasses increasing levels of complexity, structure, choice, fluidity, and articulation within the context of human bonds and attachments. Such a process must be traced from its origins in early childhood relationships through its extensions to later growth and development. This new model emphasizes that the direction of growth is *not* toward greater degrees of autonomy or individuation or the breaking of early emotional ties. Rather, development is a dynamic process of growth within the relationship, in which all people involved are challenged to maintain connection and to foster, allow, or adapt to the growth of the other. This is the basic model inherent in parenting, but we are broadening this to include a more generalized dynamic of mutual, interactional growth within the relationship. It is not through separation, but through more highly articulated and expanded relational experience that individual development takes place. For example, the adolescent wants not necessarily to "separate" from her parents, but to change the form, distance, and content of the relationship in a way that affirms her own developmental changes and allows new relationships to develop and take priority. The ability to move and change in the relationship clearly depends on the capacities and willingness of all people involved to change and grow. The interconnection of generations over the life cycle, rather than the complete separation of the young from the parents, may distinguish the human species from other animals. As we have shown, the mother-daughter relationship represents this cyclic involvement of each generation in caring for the other. Clearly, continuity of relationship necessitates mutual growth, commitment, and responsiveness to the changing and evolving needs of all persons involved.

The other concept we have proposed is "relationship authenticity." This describes the ongoing effort to feel emotionally "real," connected, vital, clear, and purposeful in the relationship. It necessitates risk, conflict, and the willingness to challenge old images and patterns of relationship. Thus, the mutually empathic relationship that provides the energy for growth entails both the need to be seen and recognized for who one is and the need to see and understand the other with ongoing authenticity. This often creates problems for women in the attempt to differentiate from the early forms of the mother-daughter relationship.

The basic elements of the relational self in women, then, can be summarized as follows: (1) a basic emotional connection and ability to identify with the other; (2) the expectation of mutuality and the sharing of experience leading to a heightened experience of self-awareness, purpose, and motivation; (3) the expectation of relationship as a process of mutual sensitivity and responsibility and as an ongoing, intrinsic aspect of one's own growth and motivational framework; and (4) mutual empowerment developing in the context of relationships. Again, we are broadening Kohut's emphasis on empathy as a one-directional, parent-to-child phenomenon into a two-way, interactional model, in which it is as important to understand as to be understood, to empower as to be empowered. All people probably have a need to feel understood or "recognized" by others. It is equally paramount, but not yet emphasized, for women throughout their lives to "understand" the other. Indeed, women desire this as an essential part of their own growth and development. We will next discuss some problems in development that can arise based on such a model—at least in our own cultural context.

The pathways of development of the self-in-relation are only beginning to be charted. The nature of the development of empathy must be further elaborated, and the relational opportunities for such development must be more fully established. The actual application to other lines of self-development are only beginning to be understood. It is clear, however, that women's basic sense of self-worth and self-esteem are closely linked to the establishment of mutually empathic and reciprocally empowering relationships.

TODAY'S WOMAN

The special dilemma for women today lies in the fact that their "core relational self" exists in the milieu of Western industrial society, which is predicated on disconnection, autonomy, and individual achievement. The psychology that has arisen in this "culture of narcissism" has encouraged the notion that the self is a contained, separate unit. Miller (1976) has suggested that women typically become the carriers for the less valued human qualities. Thus, in a culture that devalues connection, women are the repositories of caretaking, relationship maintenance, and nurturance. Not only does the society tend to view the relational mode as less valuable, but it fails to validate women's experience of self. Psychoanalytic theory and developmental theory have contributed to this invalidation by supporting a point of view essentially aimed at explaining male development. Female psychology has then been seen as a deviation from the norm, or women's experience has been forced to fit men's experience.

As women have entered traditionally male arenas in our society, enormous stresses have been involved. These systems are not attuned to relational issues but are concerned mainly with production and mastery and view the individual as directed primarily toward protection and enhancement of the separate self. Naturally, they create conflicts in women whose very identity is bound up in relationship.

Clearly, what is needed is an integration of relationship, caring, and autonomous functioning. Women have been called on to do both: to act, think, and feel "like a man" when out "in the world" and to maintain traditional female norms "in the home." This assumes, again, a compartmentalization of functioning that is more characteristic of male psychology than of female psychology. It is a perpetuation of the tendency to make the female conform to the male model. Thus, women have to bear the burden of adding the role of the one out in the world to their traditional role of nurturer and caregiver. But if, on top of the drain on emotional energy involved in trying to fill two demanding roles, the woman feels unable to make the transition back and forth between the two modes, she is left feeling inadequate in each. Again, the models do not take into account the special psychology of women. For a real integration to occur, both males and females must be given the opportunity to fully acknowledge, express, and value the relational mode.

In clinical practice we see many adult women who experience difficulty in delineating, articulating, and acting directly on their own needs and perceptions. We see women who are unable to experience the sense of self necessary for self-determined motivation outside the context of a primary dyadic relationship and who become anxious and severely depressed at the real or perceived loss of an important relationship. Finally, we see many women who experience anxiety, confusion, guilt, and deep value conflicts when they attempt to meet the challenges of new opportunities with new self-definitions (such as the new "assertive" or " managerial" woman). It is extremely important to explore how these new models of female identity may be incongruent or directly in conflict with the powerful aspects of the early self-definition described in this model within the mother-daughter relationship. Women need to explore new relational patterns and constructs to support their growth in new arenas and new directions, or psychological problems may result. Many of these clinical observations can be reconstructed in the light of this new model. These reconstructions suggest new therapeutic interpretations, new forms of clinical intervention, and broader, more far-ranging mental health policies, specifically designed for women.

IMPLICATIONS FOR THERAPY

Therapists who appreciate the special developmental issues for women can play an important role in validating women's experience. Instead of viewing the importance of relationship to women as a sign of weakness, poorly developed ego, or pathological dependence, for instance, the therapist can validate the woman's sense of fragmentation and disorganization of self when there is a loss or dislocation of relationship. Although a part of the therapeutic task with such a loss is to help the person bear the pain of the aloneness and fragmentation, the therapist need not give the message that this is something the woman should be able to handle on her own, or that this is an indication of an overdependent attitude. Acknowledging the basic relatedness of the woman is also acknowledging her basic vulnerability to loss.

As Gilligan (1983) discovered in her research, women's basic orientation is toward caretaking. One of the typical areas of imbalance, however, is that women have trouble bringing caretaking to bear on themselves. Another important aspect of therapy may be encouraging the development of self-empathy. Although this is initially difficult to conceptualize, it is a process that bears some thought. Schafer (1964) referred to "intrapsychic empathy" (p. 294), Kohut (1959) wrote about the "ability of empathizing with ourselves, i.e. with our own past mental organizations," (p. 467) and Blanck and Blanck (1974) spoke of "retrospective self empathy" (1974, p. 251). Developing this capacity is a process by which the observing, often judging self can make empathic contact with some aspect of the self as object. This could occur in the form of a memory of oneself in an inner state that has not been fully integrated because it was not acceptable. To be able to now observe and tolerate the affect of that state in a context of understanding becomes a kind of intrapsychic empathy that can actually lead to lasting structural change in self-representations. The motivational and attitudinal states of nonjudgment, openness, taking an experience seriously, readiness to experience affect, and cognitive understanding may contribute to important shifts in self-images.

For example, one woman, who was quite identified with her critical, punitive father and spoke of herself in very derogatory terms, gave an extremely unfavorable description of herself going off for her first day of school. Every comment seemed to come from the rejecting paternal introject: "I was such an obnoxious kid. I wanted everyone to pay attention. No wonder my father got so mad." A therapeutic intervention was made indicating that of course she wanted to feel special as she went out into this new and perhaps scary part of the world, but at first it seemed to have no impact. The self-condemnations rolled forth like armored tanks. Looking at this same incident later in treatment, however, the woman burst into tears and said: "Suddenly I saw myself as the little girl, so scared and uncertain. My heart just went out to her. I could see myself, that little girl and really see what was happening inside. I feel it now for her – the pain. I feel it now for me. I couldn't feel it then. But I understand why I was acting that way." It was not simply that she became more accepting and less punitive of certain self-representations, although that was important for her. But she also connected with the affect that had been split off in the memory. Both the self as object and the experiencing self were modified by this exchange, and her identification with the critical father was altered so that she became less punitive and harsh in her self-judgments.

Another way of viewing the development of self-empathy can be described as developing the inner relational voice—or "becoming one's own mother." This involves helping the female patient to learn to "listen" and respond to herself and to mobilize around her own needs, interests, and perceptions. It means using new relationships to develop and articulate a new awareness of self. For instance, a woman in therapy felt that her mother had been unable to respond effectively to her anxiety as a child about her abusive and violent father. This patient has had great difficulty in her adult life in caring for herself in the face of anxiety. She has recently begun to meditate and had the experience of hearing a little girl's voice crying deep within her. She now listens to the little girl, who has begun to speak instead of just crying. The little girl asks the patient to allow her to "not know how to do something." She says "I can't do it and I can't learn unless it's okay not to know how." This patient, who works with emotionally disturbed children, has begun to be able to listen and be "with" the little girl and to accept that she will know how to help her. In essence, she has been going through a process of remothering herself, modeled on the therapy. She is also beginning to feel interested in having a child for the first time in her married life, as she begins to feel effective in taking care of herself. The focus in therapy has been on learning to *care* for herself, rather than on learning to *fight* for her rights and needs.

Another example of working based on the self-in-relation model involves helping the female patient to accept new self-images derived from new relationships—including, but not exclusively, the relationship with the therapist. This involves letting go of the early self-images developed in the mother-daughter relationship of childhood. Changing these early self-images can be extremely frightening if the woman has lacked the opportunity for practice in developing within this relationship or in other significant relationships. As discussed earlier, for today's woman, self-images idealized later in adolescence and adulthood can be quite incongruent with those elaborated in the early preoedipal relationship. The therapist needs to help the patient to develop the relational framework for growth to occur.

An example of this process took place with a 35-year-old, extremely attractive, vital and spirited single woman. She originally sought help because she was unable to develop a "good" relation with a man, which she thought she desperately wanted. Although she had a wide circle of close female and male friends, played the flute professionally, taught music to young children, and was quite creative and assertive in her life, she felt extremely depressed and guilty over both her "selfishness" (defined as "liking things my way") and her "sexuality" (she was quite interested and enthusiastic about sex). She shared letters from her southern Presbyterian mother, who emphasized the need for her to be less selfish, independent, and emotionally intense so that a man would want to marry her. In a deep sense the patient felt her mother was right, although she also felt quite angry and rebellious. A great deal of time in the therapy was spent allowing the patient to be able to admit that she enjoyed her life, although she missed having a steady, ongoing relationship with a man. To admit to feeling good about herself and accept her life meant that she would forever lose the chance to get married. Following a session in which she expressed a positive feeling about herself, this patient had a massive anxiety attack. Part of the therapy involved an active effort on the part of the patient to develop relationships with women who were also trying to establish new life styles. The therapist encouraged the patient to seek out older women with whom she could identify, including some of her musician friends.

In this case, the patient's mother was unable to accommodate to the daughter's changing self-image. The patient expressed her anger at her mother in the therapy, however, as well as her need to empathize with her mother's past history and the mother's definition and experience of her own role and obligations as a mother to a daughter. As this woman grew in her understanding, she was able to enlist her father and brother in helping her mother understand and accept her, but she was never totally successful. She has experienced much anxiety, sadness and grief over this loss. Yet she has also worked on finding new areas for sharing her life with the matter. When this woman was finally able to state that she enjoyed her life and accepted the possibility of a single life style, she soon developed an intense relationship with a man with whom she is currently involved. Now a new stage of relational development has begun, as she begins to test out and express her new self-images in a close relationship with a man.

SUMMARY

This paper has attempted to demonstrate the need for new models of the development and maintenance of self-images, sense of identity, motivation, and structures of the self in women. It has further posited the centrality to women's psychological growth of relationships based on mutual empathy. What we have called the self-in-relation suggests that women organize their sense of identity, find existential meaning, achieve a sense of coherence and continuity, and are motivated in the context of relationship. This need not be an actual, current relationship but can be an internalized relationship. The early mother-daughter relationship, in which mutual empathy plays an important part, is clearly a central and formative prototype. Mutual empathy, however, is elaborated and developed in complex ways, both within the mother-daughter dyad and in other relationships and communities over the life span. A woman's sense of self is ultimately connected to her ability to be in relationship, and her self-esteem suffers when she feels cut off. This model diverges from theories that emphasize the attainment of autonomy and separation as hallmarks of psychological maturity. It is important that therapists treating women begin to appreciate the special qualities of the female self-in-relation so that the understanding of women's conflicts is not distorted by application of principles of self-development that are essentially based on a male model. Such distortions seriously jeopardize the therapeutic enterprise.

REFERENCES

Blanck, G., & Blanck, R. (1979), Ego Psychology II: Psychoanalytic Developmental Psychology. New York: Columbia University Press.
Chodorow, N. (1978), The Reproduction of Mothering: Psychoanalysis and the Sociology of Gender. Berkeley: University of California Press.
Erikson, E. (1963), Childhood and Society (2nd ed.). New York: Norton.
Fairbairn, W. R. D. (1954), An Object Relations Theory of the Personality. New York: Basic Books.

Freud, S. (1920), Beyond the pleasure principle. *Standard Edition*, 18. London: Hogarth Press, 1955, pp. 3–64.

Gilligan, C. (1982), *In a Different Voice*. Cambridge MA: Harvard University Press.

Guntrip, H. (1973), *Psychoanalytic Theory, Therapy and the Self*. New York: Basic Books.

Horney, K. (1926), The flight from womanhood. In: *Feminine Psychology*, ed. H. Kelman, New York: Norton, 1967, pp. 54–70.

Jordan, J. (1983), *Empathy and the Mother-Daughter Relationship*. Wellesley, MA: Stone Center for Developmental Services and Studies.

Klein, G. (1976), *Psychoanalytic Theory: An Explanation of Essentials*. New York: International Universities Press.

Kohut, H. (1959), Introspection, empathy and psychoanalysis. *J. Amer. Psychoanal. Assn.*, 7: 459–483.

———— (1971), *The Analysis of the Self*. New York: International Universities Press.

———— (1973), The psychoanalyst in the community of scholars. In: *The Search for the Self: Selected Writings of Heinz Kohut*, Vol. 2, ed. P. Ornstein, New York: International Universities Press, 1978, pp. 685–724.

Levinson, D. (1978), *The Season of a Man's Life*. New York: Knopf.

Mahler, M. S., Pine, F., & Bergman, A. (1975), *The Psychological Birth of the Human Infant: Symbiosis and Individuation*. New York: Basic Books.

Miller, J. B. (1976), *Toward a New Psychology of Women*. Boston: Beacon Press.

Ornstein, A. (1982, December), Parental empathy and the troubled child. In: *Proceedings of the Silver Jubilee Professional Symposium*. Boston: Family Counseling and Guidance Centers, pp. 2–25.

Piaget, J. (1952), *The Origins of Intelligence in Children*. New York: Norton.

Sagi, A., & Hoffman, M. S. (1976), Empathic distress in newborns. *Develop. Psychol.*, 12: 175–176.

Sander, L. (1980), Investigation of the infant and its caretaking environment as a biological system. In: *The Course of Life*, Vol. 2, ed. S. Greenspan & G. Pollock, Adelphi, MD: National Institute of Mental Health, pp. 177–201.

Schafer, R. (1964), The clinical analysis of affects. *J. Amer. Psychoanal. Assn.*, 12: 275–299.

———— (1974), Problems in Freud's psychology of women. *J. Amer. Psychoanal. Assn.*, 22: 459–485.

Simner, M. D. (1971), Newborn's response to the cry of another infant. *Develop. Psychol.*, 5: 136–150.

Stechler, G., & Kaplan, S. (1980), The development of the self: A psychoanalytic perspective. *The Psychoanalytic Study of the Child*, 35: 85–106. New Haven: Yale University Press.

Stern, D. (1980, October), Early differentiation of self and other. Paper presented at the Psychology of Self Conference, Boston.

Sullivan, H. S. (1940), *Conceptions of Modern Psychiatry*. New York: Norton.

Surrey, J. (1983), *The Relational Self in Women*. Wellesley, MA: Stone Center for Developmental Services and Studies.

Thompson, C. (1942), Cultural processes in the psychology of women. *Psychiat.*, 4: 331–339.

Winnicott, D. W. (1971), *Playing and Reality*. New York: Basic Books.

5

Antigone: Symbol of Autonomy and Women's Moral Dilemmas

Natalie Shainess, M.D.

TRADITIONAL NOTIONS OF AUTONOMY

Freud's deficit model of feminine sexual and gender identity includes the notion that women have weaker superegos than men and a corrupt sense of social justice as a result of the "predominance of envy in their mental life" (Freud, 1933). Freud added that women were also

> weaker in their social interests, . . . having less capacities for sublimating their instincts than men, . . . [this deficiency] derived from the social qualities which unquestionably characterize all sexual relations. Lovers find sufficiency in each other and families too resist inclusion in more comprehensive associations. The aptitude for sublimation is subject to the greatest individual variation. (p. 134).

Implicit in Freud's ideas about sublimation and social interests is the notion that women are less capable then men of autonomous thought and action, which require variable interests and activities inside and outside of love relations and family life.

Feminist psychologists have attempted to debunk and replace Freud's concept of feminine metapsychology. Psychoanalytic thinkers, including this author, view Freud's notions of female psychology as essentially wrong when posited as *universal* descriptions. They are gender stereotypes, which reflect neurotic personality or character distortions formed because of the societal cocoon in which women were confined. They reflect the differences between men and women that result because men grew up as part of the patriarchal power structure and women grew up with the idea that achieving submission, passivity, masochism, and dependence typified the feminine ego ideal of the "good girl"—an ideal antithetical to the establishment of autonomy.

Psychoanalysts such as Horney (1926) and Thompson (1943) began to recognize and emphasize some of these cultural forces. Freud, however, became increasingly interested in theory and devoted to the ideas of instinct and instinctual unfolding in accord with the general scientific beliefs of his time. Today's concepts, stemming from ego psychology and from the imprinting work of Lorenz (1965), Hess (1949), and other ethologists and comparative animal psychologists, stress psychosocial influences and early learned behavior. Notions of instinct were simpler, though, and helped Freud fit things neatly, although not always appropriately, into the Procrustean bed of his theory. Continuing his biological emphasis, he abandoned his earlier consideration of culture, which was especially notable in his earlier work on humor (Freud, 1938).

In conceiving of psychological correlates for biological structures, Freud reached erroneous conclusions about the psychology of women. He noted women's tendency toward passivity, rather than recognizing their receptivity. If one follows biological determinism, as did Freud, then receptivity and not passivity would be considered the psychic equivalent of the taking in of the penis in sexual intercourse, of the sperm by the egg in fertilization, of the fertilized egg by the uterus in which it is implanted—and finally after birth, the infant by the nurturant care of the mother (Shainess, 1972). As receptivity and nurturance may be considered feminine psychic derivatives of biology, the psychic quality of being penetrating, strong and firm may be considered the male counterpart; one which strengthens the notion of the rigid, autonomous male self.

In choosing models to support his views of universal development, Freud understandably chose *prevalent* types, the most noticeable within the borders of his society. His assumption of the inevitability of instinctual forces led him to ignore the difference between *prevalence* and *universality*. This is comparable to assuming that an epidemic is normal. Had Freud pondered the difference between the prevalent and the universal, he would have had to confront the interpersonal and the societal as bases for sexual difference. Holt (1980) has reported that in his later years, Freud felt that "any theory was a kind of mythology which as such was ambivalent in that it disguised the truth while at the same time revealing it." This may be true, yet perhaps Freud was also reflecting his own oedipal blindness. As Miller (1976) has pointed out, the dominant group never studies itself, but turns outward to the supposedly inferior group in making its critical appraisal. So it appears that Freud was bound by his position in society and its temporal conditions in attempting to explain sexual differences solely in instinctual terms. Even Jones (1955), his disciple, acknowledged that Freud had an unduly "phallocentric" view (p. 421).

CONTEMPORARY DEVELOPMENTAL DATA

Contemporary theorists such as Lester (1976) have observed that the early sense of sexual identity is established through social, interpersonal, and intrapsychic channels long before the child is even aware of genitals. It is the result of gender assignment by the parents – a finding that gives little foundation to Freud's belief in instinctual drives as the basis for sexual development. Children's sense of gender identity develops from identification and affective ties with *both* parents and depends on the nature of the child's simultaneous and varied experience with each of them.

Baruch and Barnett (1975) have found that many early differences between boys and girls reflect the treatment of the infant or small child as girl or boy. They show that girls are influenced away from autonomy and success. Girls also identify with mother, who is perceived by both boys and girls as being generally weaker than the father.

Similarly, in a study of cognitive differences between the sexes, Block (cited in "Study Probes Differences in Sexes," 1980) found many variables relevant to the attainment of autonomy. She suggests that "boys have more opportunity in their social milieu to discover, invent and understand the world in which they live." Her study indicates that "where faced with conflicting information, girls get more reinforcement to assimilate discrepancies into their existing beliefs, rather than learn new accommodative strategies." Males are more "active-curious, exploratory, adventurous." The nature of the socialization process suggests that "boys more than girls are aided in constructing a premise system that presumes or anticipates the individual's mastery and instrumental competence," making the visions, dreams, and passions that inform life's autonomous thoughts and acts more accessible to boys and less so to girls.

Block's work also supports existing doubts about Freud's concepts of personality differences between men and women. Thus, if one ignores Freud's metapsychology of women, one may see the traits he described as a failure in the ability to be autonomous. This, then, is the basic problem of women as witnessed in its many forms, but it is undeniably a distortion resulting from the restriction of a complex nature. I suggest not that the traits Freud thought were inherent in women should be ignored, but rather that they are indications of low self-esteem, of ego deficit. They are important considerations for treatment, which will be considered later.

ELECTRA, OEDIPUS, AND ANTIGONE: CONTRASTING SYMBOLS OF AUTONOMY

In considering Freud's use of Oedipus as an example of adolescent maturational problems, I began to wonder why he did not look further for an illustration of the development of girls. The model presented by Antigone, the daughter of Oedipus, for instance, is an example not of difficulty, but of liberation from difficulty – an example of autonomy in a woman and something more: courage and potency – strong, healthy superego and ego. Instead, although Freud did not actually say so, he chose Electra, daughter of Agamemnon, in Aeschylus' *Oresteia*, as an appropriate model of his concept of feminine development.

A brief review of Freud's (1913) interpretation of Sophocles' tragedy will serve as background to consideration of Antigone as a female model. In choosing Oedipus as the model for his view of the specific problems of adolescence, Freud interpreted this phase as a time when the boy wants to kill his father and marry his mother, who is simply a passive prize. This interpretation distorts Sophocles' presentation of Oediups at Colonna, however. In fact, Oedipus was an abandoned child who did not know his father. Encountering an old man, who *happened* to be King Laius, his father, he slew him in anger because the old man would not let him pass down the road (symbolically, the road of life) – a clash of power, according to the interpretations of Fromm (1941), Mullahy (1948), and Schwartz (1978). Ultimately claiming the throne of Thebes, Oedipus "inherited" the queen who went with the throne, and who happened to be Jocasta, his mother. Thus, Freud's interpretation was both skewed and superficial. In fact, the Athenians believe that Oedipus was guiltless in the trilogy, because of his lack of *intent* to kill his father.

I would insist that Oedipus was guilty, however, not of intentionally killing his father, but of killing an old man – who happened to be his father. He was guilty of murderous rage, of the *unrestrained*, impulsive rage of youth. He could have picked up the old man and put him aside so that he might pass down the road. His rage may have been related to some deeply buried awareness of his abandonment as an infant, in addition to his annoyance at the current impediment. This would not justify his act, however, and the crucial question remains: Why could he not be gentle and yet succeed in passing? Oedipus' lack of a balanced ethical sense may be noted in Orestes as well, because the killing of his mother, Clytemnestra, was motivated by rage and vengeance. Of course, Orestes, too, was abandoned in childhood, and one is led to wonder whether abandonment of infants was common in classical Greek times, since both Aeschylus and Sophocles used this theme.

The rage found in these characters evokes the notions, suggested by many, that the male principle is one of clash, violence, power and rivalry. Fromm (1941) has interpreted the oedipal myth in terms of such a power struggle. Others, such as Bacon (1966), concluded that the Oedipus plays were *not* primarily concerned with a struggle for power but rather with the problem of *reconciling male and female principles*.

To find a nurturant female principle as corollary to the male principles of dominance and war represented by the murderous rage of Oedipus, let us return to Antigone, Oedipus' daughter (Shainess, 1982a). Antigone represents an active source of sustenance to the spirit, rather than just the passive nurturance of the womb. Her commitment to burying her brother's body embodies the qualities of independent ethics, caretaking, and autonomy.

In *Antigone* the sons of Oedipus, Eteocles and Polyneices, clash with each other for power, and kill each other in battle. Their uncle, Creon, who has taken over, decrees that Polyneices, having fought against his own city, must be left to rot on the battlefield. He is denied burial. His sister Antigone observes: "He must be left unwept, unsepulchered – a vulture's prize." She is ethically concerned with the indignity, the insult to his memory, and the threat to his afterlife. She notes: "And anyone who disobeys will pay no trifling penalty, but die by stoning in the city walls." Her decision to bury him, her defiance, is not impulsive – it is carefully considered. She is aware that she risks dreadful consequences in defying Creon's order.

Antigone's sister Ismene, to whom she appeals for help, refuses. Ismene is Freud's woman. She resorts to the dodge that women have used through the centuries: "[We must] remind ourselves that we are women, and as such are not made to fight with men. For might is right, and makes us bow to things like this, and worse. . . . I bend before authority. It does not do to meddle." Antigone does not press her, but replies, "I go to bury him. How sweet to die in such pursuit! To rest loved by him whom I have loved. . . . I shall not abandon him." She considers him, not herself; she is not narcissistic. She calls herself "sinner of a holy sin." Antigone is defiant, but her defiance is an idealistic precursor to ethical commitment, not self-centered rage. It is an act of love.

Here is also an act of independence, of autonomy. Creon fears this. His leader says, "Submission is a thing she never learned." Creon responds "No woman, while I live, shall govern men." Perhaps this is a special fear in men – that they may repeat their dependence on the mother and feel defenseless in adult life. Creon's edict and insistence on death for Antigone's defiance of it, follow his seizure of power in Thebes, and are part of an effort to maintain power by strict enforcement of discipline and quick dispatch of any threat. His punishment of the dead Polyneices and living Antigone stems from the danger of allowing the questionable circumstances surrounding his assumption of leadership to linger on and threaten his stability. The fact that Antigone is his son Haemon's betrothed cannot be permitted to sway him.

Antigone is not the average woman. But she is what the average woman might become – a person of autonomy and high principle; not narcissistically self-involved and not defensively suffering – that is, masochistic – but willing to take risks to live authentically. These are the qualities that made Haemon love and respect her. Under more fortunate circumstances, she might have used these qualities to live, rather than to die. And this, of course, applies to women's lives and to the possibilities available to them.

Developmental perspectives offer further contrast between Oedipus and Antigone. Bacon (1966) has suggested that Oedipus does not become "Knowing Foot" until he has progressed through much of his life. Through blinding himself—a symbolic self-castration to atone for his youthful "blind rage" and murder—he destroys his outer vision and is able to see more truly within. He can lead into groves where darkness makes outer vision unnecessary. But it is a belated transformation, a change in one to whom power and the structure of interrelated life can no longer matter.

Antigone, on the other hand, makes a loving choice, takes a life-affirming action that may lead to her death. Her choice, made in youth, does not call for self-mutilation. She is not blinded by rage; she can *see* in her youth. She symbolizes a mature, if not full-grown, person in her youth, someone further down the road to self-definition. This vision of maturity includes commitment both to herself and to another.

In spelling out an "Electra complex"—involving a passive, father-worshipping woman—Freud again used a model of immaturity in adolescence as a symbol of adult femininity. In doing so, he froze the definition of womanhood in time, implying that every adult woman is a case of hopelessly arrested development. Electra and Ismene belong together. They are father-worshippers, women who do not think for themselves. Electra is fixated on her father, who is the be-all and end-all of her existence. The relationship inevitably has erotic elements. Thus, Electra exemplifies the unresolved "oedipal" relationship with the father that so many women carry throughout life. She epitomizes denied penis envy and obvious penis worship.

Electra is incapable of autonomy; she turns to others for direction at the funeral ceremony of her father, Agamemnon: "Bondswomen . . . give me your advice . . . What words contrive to please my father's ear? . . . . Shall I use the customary prayer . . . or pour [oil] in silence without ceremony? . . . I beg you to advise me. . . . Do not be afraid to unfold your thoughts to me." An allegedly loving daughter, Electra does not know what to say or how to worship at her father's grave; she cannot act without direction. Her life process of hero worship has left her empty and has not promoted the development of any substance within herself. She is passive; she is indecisive. What a contrast to Antigone, who needs no advice from others, who is a person in her own right and able to take direction from her love, who can see and act on her life's dilemmas!

Whatever the outcome of their lives, Oedipus is a model for youthful intemperance, Antigone for the balance of audacity with caring. Antigone can be likened to Shakespeare's Cordelia (Shainess, 1982), who in a quiet way also combines autonomy with loving in rejecting her father's sophistry and refusing his command to prove her love through words. Her father, King Lear, realizes much too late that he has cast out his pearl. This suggests that autonomy in women is a most intolerable quality to men. It is interesting that both Sophocles and Shakespeare gave these women men who truly loved and admired them and were their match in love and devotion.

Antigone's betrothed, Haemon, is in every way her counterpart, and is as much a contrast to the youthful Oedipus as Antigone is to Electra. Threatened by his father, Creon, Haemon does not become enraged. He simultaneously declares his love and confronts his father: "You know my father how I prize your happiness. For sons and fathers crown each other's glory with each other's fame. Then, don't entrench yourself in your opinions as if everyone else were wrong. The kind of man who always thinks that he is right, that his opinions, pronouncements, are the final word, when once exposed shows nothing there. But a wise man has much to learn without a loss of dignity." As Creon's threats become more heated, the dramatic confrontation between father and son is heightened by a dialogue of rapier-sharp responses, creating a remarkable intellectual duel. Through it all, Haemon retains his calm dignity, ultimately saying "I speak for you, for me and for the gods below." Creon's response is, "You shall not marry her alive." He is a man obsessed with outrage. His youthful son retains a more mature, calm vision. Again, the message of Antigone's committed stance, auguring and defining mature morality, is repeated through her male counterpart's voice.

ANTIGONE'S AUTONOMY: MASOCHISM OR AUDACITY?

It has been surprising to find how many colleagues view Antigone's behavior as masochistic because it brought her life to a close. But audacity such as Antigone's differs from masochism. Audacity is often an expression of courage combined with caring. It is rooted in love, rather than defiance or hate. Many adolescent expressions of protest contain both but do not embrace autonomy and maturity.

The difference, then, between masochism and autonomous audacious behavior that may result in harm to the person is in the *motivation* of the behavior, not the end result—and of course this includes unconscious motivation as well. Masochism (Shainess, 1984) is a group of defensive behaviors and expressions in which the individual *anticipates* hurt or harm and fears the power and authority of others—almost *all* others. The individual attempts to avoid this harm by "second-guessing" the other—that is, by attempting to anticipate what the action will be and to ward it off before it occurs. But this attempt is doomed to failure, because it is based largely and compulsively on the person's experience in infancy and childhood with one or two (usually one) significant adults—a very limited experience in relationships. The individual then assumes that all people will act like the hurtful adult of early life. The premise of masochism, that submissive behavior *avoids* trouble, is faulty.

Because masochism is primarily defensive, it is essentially an expression of self-concern and self-preoccupation. Love and concern for others do not really enter into consideraton. Contrast this with Antigone's reason for defying Creon: She is unwilling to let her dead brother be harmed spiritually or his remains lose dignity. A similar example is found in Gage's (1983) story of his courageous mother, Eleni, who accepted torture and death to send her children to freedom during the Greek civil war. Gage comments that "Like Antigone, my mother acted out of love, not hate." Both Antigone and her modern-day counterpart, Eleni, were courageous, idealistic women, making the only choice they could consider: to protect their loved ones. Hence, they were nurturant in their autonomy.

Still another instance of audacious autonomy is that of Joan of Arc, who risked her life to save her people and underwent the most horrible of deaths, being tortured psychologically and burned at the stake. Jung's (1964) interpretation of her actions is unsatisfying, since he sees them as the result of her masculine side, the animus. It appears that when women are courageous, they are seen as men or as expressing their so-called "masculine side." But in the play *St. Joan*, Shaw (1951) saw his heroine's courage as feminine and she pleaded for nurturance and acknowledgement of her audacious self and acts: "Oh God, who

made this beautiful earth—when will it be ready to receive its saints—
how long, Lord, how long?"

AUTONOMY AND DEVIANCE FROM STEREOTYPE

Over the centuries women have faced great difficulties when they
have deviated from stereotypic feminine behavior and turned to autonomous and assertive behavior. Illustrations of the implications of
deviance from stereotype have been beautifully portrayed in Holly-
wood films made following World War II, an era when sex roles in films
were clearly delineated along traditional lines.

In *Witness for the Prosecution*, the lawyer, played by Charles
Laughton, had all the famous traits of Winston Churchill. He resem-
bled him physically, was irascible, and insisted on his brandy and ci-
gars despite his doctor's cautions regarding his hypertension. His
talent for an apt and nasty word, unpleasantness to women, and brilliance made him an interesting, perversely delightful, and oddly
enough, acceptable and competent figure. Yet, one might ask, would a
woman lawyer who had acted as Charles Laughton did have been as
acceptable?

Indeed, Marlene Dietrich, who played the wife of the accused mur-
derer, was cast in a suspicious role because she was calm, taciturn, and
self-assured, and refused to accept the advice men offered. Obviously,
her femininity was suspect because she "acted like a man." Yet in no
sense could Dietrich's behavior have been called aggressive or penis
envying. I would consider her an Antigone, doing what *she* thought
best and taking the risks involved.

Dietrich's ego ideal was one of competence and autonomy—the ego
ideal of today's woman. However, contemporary social and psychological demands to achieve such an ideal often engender conflict and fear
of autonomy in women. One aspect of this has been described by
Bernay (1982) as competence-loss. The woman experiences a sense of
helplessness and hopelessness when threatened with fantasied or actual separation from a maternally cathected object; such maternal
abandonment is often stimulated by assertive or autonomous behavior such as Dietrich portrayed. In the wake of her assertiveness, as the
woman relives the early experience of abandonment, she feels herself
unworthy and incompetent, and fails on this basis. This competence-

loss experience seems in some ways equivalent to fears of success. Passivity and masochism are expressions of the capitulation part of the competence-loss process, while competence and autonomy are expressions of its triumphant aspects.

TRANSFORMING MASOCHISM INTO AUTONOMY: A CLINICAL EXAMPLE

Increasingly, in clinical practice I observe masochistic traits in women, both subtle and overt. The task with such women is to uncover the childhood identifications and experiences at the hands of significant adults that led them to fear the power of the other. These women must be helped to discover their own capacity for autonomy — to become less fear ridden and to integrate autonomy into their ego ideal. The therapist must recognize masochistic thought and behavior as anger turned back upon the self, resulting in self-mutilation and self-damage. Women's dreams are particularly revealing of these difficulties. In such dreams, women occasionally appear to engage in sadistic retaliation. This is in fact an eruption of rage when the abuse can no longer be contained.

Marital gender stereotypes have been particularly troublesome. They foster the concepts of the "good wife," who enters marriage with a heavy sense of obligation, while the husband enters with a sense of entitlement. In such a relationship, both partners lose their autonomy. This consolidates the wife's submissive dependence on the husband in all areas, including the sexual. The following example from practice illustrates some of the root causes and problems of masochism.

Selma was the oldest of two girls by two years. Her mother was strident, demanding, and constantly critical while her father was passive and submissive. Selma came into treatment at age 25, embattled on every front. Although she was gifted and capable in her work, her male boss seemed an unpleasent replica of her mother. Her boyfriend perpetually derided her, while her father constantly pleaded with her to "be more agreeable to your mother." She and her sister quarreled constantly. Selma was probably the provocateur, as evidenced by the fact that although she became quite obese at adolescence and her younger sister was slight, she constantly borrowed her sister's clothes, both with and without permission. Selma had to struggle to get into the garments, often playing havoc with them. It was as if she gained some sense of worth in her sister's "skin." At the start of therapy, Selma also suffered from severe migraine headaches, often precipitated by arguments with her boyfriend, and she was incapacitated much of the time. In sum, Selma seemed to continually recreate her assaultive and emotionally unavailable mother in contemporary peer and work relationships. Frightened of maternal abandonment, she buried her autonomy and sense of self in self-destructive strivings and behaviors, and in psychosomatic symptoms.

As we reviewed her early experience, and she began to develop a sense of self (admittedly rudimentary, initially), she resolved to change. Her first step was to end the relationship with her boyfriend. "I thought a boyfriend would make me feel like a woman," she said, "but he repeats my mother's attacks and makes me feel like nothing. I'm better off without him." This step in itself seemed to occasion considerable relief. To my surprise, within a few weeks Selma announced that she could no longer put up with her boss and was searching for a new job. She found a good one. It would be nice to be able to say that all was smooth sailing at that point, but, as might be expected, she soon had difficulties with the new boss.

Selma's mother was truly expert in continually inciting guilty feelings in her. Her statements ranged from the common variety, such as "You're killing me by doing such-and-such," or "It will be your fault if I drop dead," to somewhat more subtle examples. One of the latter occurred in relation to Selma's new and better job. As a fringe benefit, Selma was given a car by the company, and she was allowed to choose whatever type of car she wanted within a certain price range. Delighted, she chose a sporty, red two-seater, and drove to visit her mother, who lived in another state, to show it off. Her mother's comment was, "Don't you think it is selfish of you to buy a two-seater?" The car was irrelevant to the mother, as she lived far away; but this kind of comment had perpetually damaged Selma's sense of worth and her pride.

Progress was slow for Selma, but her determination that she *would* change was striking. Perhaps an indirect indication of this was the fact that she met another young man with whom she became involved in a reasonably respectful mutual relationship, and they eventually married.

Selma's problems came to a head when her boss was replaced with a new man whose snarling remarks left her constantly distraught. He would generalize any small oversight or omission on her part and imply that it was part of a major defect, he had anticipated it, he would have to do something drastic about it, and so forth. I wondered what I could do to help, as we had examined the sources of the problem almost endlessly. I told her the story of Antigone, suggesting that we must all take risks in order to live more fully. I added that with each success, things got a little easier, although one could never say there would be no setbacks.

Several weeks later Selma told me that this man started the day with a typical comment: "You women just can't be relied on." With much pride, she reported that "to her surprise," she found herself saying: "I'm tired of this. Why must you always accuse others? You better have real cause the next time, because I am not going to continue being blamed without reason. I try hard and I'm willing to discuss any mistakes and try to improve, but I don't want to live in a state of war!" She added, "I didn't even feel concerned! And he came back later and acknowledged he was feeling grouchy that morning."

Selma remained in treatment for some time, continually relinquishing her defensive and self-abusive maternal identifications for autonomous and risk-taking ones. She eventually went into business for herself, with great success. This transformation of her maternal representation to be more nurturing and caring was manifest in her changing feelings about becoming a mother. Selma spent an entire session talking about a friend's delightful daughter. She said that she was no longer afraid to be a mother and was looking forward to having children.

Within the transference, Selma relived her competitive dynamic, perceiving me as a berating, competitive mother and herself as the angry, berated and long-suffering daughter. Transference manifestations in this young woman were expressed indirectly, largely because she repressed and revealed no signs of anger, until in a few situations her angry feelings became overwhelming. The first blow-up came when Selma met the young man she eventually married. She began seeing him virtually every day. After about a month, she said that they had already been talking about marriage, and she intended to marry him soon. I asked what the haste was about and suggested that in view of her previous relationship with a man, it would be a good idea to take some time to examine the nature of their relationship before rushing into marriage. Selma stormed out of my office.

In the next session, she accused me of not wanting her to get married. After all, she had learned that I was divorced. I must not like men, and I must not want her to have any pleasure in life. This incident ushered in a stormy period. Some time back, Selma had given me a diary she had written in her adolescence, in which she had documented her mother's attempts to prevent her from maturing as a woman and her own angry and frequently defiant responses to her mother's thwarting efforts. In this diary, she had cited the fairy tale of Snow White, in which the stepmother asks the mirror on the wall who is the fairest of them all, as a way of illustrating the competitive and vengeful mother-daughter relationship. The tale and its meanings became a symbol and part of our private language in ultimately working out her "paranoid" belief that I wanted to take revenge and harm her, like her mother – a belief which left Selma unable to take in the help, caring and concern which would ultimately enable her to develop self-comforting and self-caretaking capabilities of her own.

Selma's anger surfaced on another occasion. Selma's new husband was unemployed and began to become psychologically disturbed. He indicated that since she worked, there was really no reason for him to find a job. He would be her poet and playmate. I suggested that he was having problems with low self-esteem, was trying to evade reality, and should see a therapist, and I gave Selma the name of a psychologist. Selma was enraged and believed that I was seeing her husband in a bad light. She felt that I really did not want their marriage to work out well. At the same time, it was hard for her to ignore the fact that I was trying to be helpful, and she ultimately gave her husband the name of the therapist. He consulted this man, began to feel better, and again sought work, with positive results.

Toward the end of therapy, we reviewed this process. We noted that it was in the area of Selma's life *as a woman* that she had felt threatened and that transferential behavior was most significantly elicited. She particularly observed that her conflicts seemed to center around her hopeless feelings of always expecting to be abused and to have her autonomy thwarted; feelings she associated with her relationship with her mother. We discussed the importance of her having resolved these conflicts in a way that allowed her to give up her self-effacing and constricted maternal identifications in favor of feelings of spontaneity, creativity and expansiveness, even though such feelings had for so long made Selma feel frightened, helpless and alone.

SUMMARY

In examining Freud's gender concepts in theory, it seemed surprising that he turned to the story of Oedipus as a universal problem of adolescent maturation, yet ignored Antigone, the daughter of Oedipus, as a model of feminine *maturation* – an example of an autonomous person with a high ethical sense, commitment, and courage. Although Freud did not directly formulate an "Electra complex," his view of femininity is more appropriate to Aeschylus' Electra, the helpless father-worshipping daughter of Agamemnon, or to Ismene, Antigone's sister.

Although in the Freudian metapsychology of femininity, women are seen as developing *weaker* superegos than men, this is at odds with women's role as caretakers and nurturers. Antigone is portrayed by Sophocles as actually having a stronger superego than Oedipus and her brothers, the sons of Oedipus. Her clash with Creon – a man ruthless in his pursuit of power – results from her insistence on honoring her brother's memory, an act expressing her sense of dedication, and her courageous assumptions of risk in this cause.

Clarification of these issues leads to a new perception of gender difference, as perceived in therapy or in society's expectations of women's behavior.

REFERENCES

Aeschylus (525–456 B.C.), *The Oresteia Trilogy*, ed. W. Corrigan (G. Thomson, trans.), New York: Dell, 1965.
Bacon, H. H. (1966), Woman's two faces: Sophocles' view of the tragedy of Oedipus and his family. In: *Science and Psychoanalysis*, Vol. 10, ed. J. Masserman. New York: Grune & Stratton.
Baruch, G. K., & Barnett, R. C. (1975), Implications and applications of recent research on feminine development. *Psychiat.*, 38: 318–327.
Bernay, T. (1982), Separation and competence-loss in women. *Amer. J. Psychoanal.*, 42 (4): 293–305.
Freud, S. (1900), The interpretation of dreams. *Standard Edition*, 4 & 5. London: Hogarth Press, 1953.

———— (1905), Three essays on the theory of sexuality. *Standard Edition*, 7: 135–243. London: Hogarth Press, 1953.

———— (1905), Jokes and their relation to the unconscious. *Standard Edition*, 8. London: Hogarth Press, 1960.

———— (1925), Some psychical consequences of the anatomical distinction between the sexes. *Standard Edition*, 19: 248–258. London: Hogarth Press, 1961.

———— (1931), Female sexuality. *Standard Edition*, 21: 225–243. London: Hogarth Press, 1961.

———— (1933), New introductory lectures on psycho-analysis. *Standard Edition*, 22: 5–182. London: Hogarth Press, 1964.

———— (1940), An outline of psycho-analysis. *Standard Edition*, 23: 144–207. London: Hogarth Press, 1964.

Fromm, E. (1941), *Escape from Freedom*. New York: Farrar & Rinehart.

Gage, N. (1983), *Eleni*. New York: Random House.

Hess, E. H. (1949), Imprinting. *Science*, 100: 133–141.

Holt, H. (1980), Some fundamental ideas in existential analysis. *Mod. Psychother.*, 3: 1–26.

Horney, K. (1926), The flight from womanhood: The masculinity complex in women as viewed by men and women. In: *Feminine Psychology*, ed. H. Kelman. New York: Norton, 1967.

Jones, E. (1955), *Life and Work of Sigmund Freud*, Vol. II. New York: Basic Books.

Jung, C. G. (1964), Approaching the unconscious. In: *Man and His Symbols*. New York: Doubleday.

Lester, E. (1976), On the psychological development of the female child. *J. Amer. Acad. Psychoanal.*, 4: 515–529.

Lorenz, K. (1965), *Evolution and Modification of Behavior*. Chicago: University of Chicago Press.

Miller, J. B. (1976), *Toward a New Psychology of Women*, Boston: Beacon Press.

Mullahy, P. (1948), *Oedipus: Myth and Complex*. New York: Grove Press.

Schwartz, E. K. (1978), Fathers and sons: Who will destroy whom? In: *Psychoanalytic Perspectives on Aggression*, ed. G. Goldman & D. Milman. Dubuque, IA: Kendall-Hunt.

Shainess, N. (1972), Toward a new feminine psychology, *Notre Dame J.*, 4: 293–300.

———— (1982), Antigone: The neglected daughter of Oedipus. *J. Amer. Acad. Psychoanal.*, 10 (3): 443–456.

———— (1982), Shakespearean women and women today. *Bull. N. Y. Acad. Med.*, 58 (7): 640–660.

———— (1984), *Sweet Suffering: Woman as Victim*, Indianapolis, IN: Bobbs-Merrill.

Shaw, G. B. (1951), *St. Joan*. In: *Seven Plays*, New York: Dodd, Mead.

Sophocles (495–406 B.C.), *Three Theban Plays*, New York: Oxford University Press, 1958.

Study Probes Cognitive Difference in Sexes (1980, January 4), *Psychiatric News*.

Thompson, C. (1943), Penis envy in women, *Psychiat.*, 6: 123–131.

6

Working Mothers:
Impact on the Self, the Couple,
and the Children

Ethel Spector Person, M.D.

The major unsolved problem for contemporary women is how to integrate work with family life. Most of the psychological reports on working women have focused on upwardly mobile professionals and have stressed the barriers to their success, either external or internal (psychological) ones.[1] When these women marry and have children, they become part of what has been designated as the "dual-career family."

---

[1]There are a few notable exceptions, including Nadelson and Notman (1981, 1982; Nadelson, 1981), who have written extensively and to the point about the problems in integrating work and family, and the effects on the self and the children.

An earlier version of this paper was presented at the New York University School of Social Work Symposium, "A New Look at Changing Sex Roles: Impact on Child Development and Family Life," New York, New York, April 22, 1983.

But the economic and social realities of our time are such that, unless we are so narrow as to restrict our interest to the upper-middle class, most women work of necessity, not out of any primary wish for self-fulfillment or self-actualization. Poor women have always worked, whereas whether middle-class women worked used to be primarily an elective decision. However, current economic conditions and the ongoing reorganization of society dictate that most women today must expect to work. (Kamerman, 1979; Mogul, 1979).

The number of women in the work force has increased dramatically, and there is an ongoing erosion of the number of families conforming to the traditional nuclear family composed of the working father, homemaker mother, and dependent children. Despite the continuing expectation that young people will fall in love, marry for life, and have children whom they jointly raise to adulthood, in actuality one sees more and more variations in family configurations. Along with such emerging patterns as serial (multiple) marriage, divorced parents, communal bonding, and single mothers, many more married mothers are entering the work force. A recent *New York Times* report on "The State of Families," estimates the proportion of traditional nuclear families at less than 10 percent (Collins, 1984b), and Notman and Nadelson (1981) have suggested it is only 6 percent.

Notman and Nadelson (1981), quoting from a variety of sources, also estimate that the number of women in the work force increased by 60 percent over the 1970s, and that 30 percent of children under 6 have working mothers. As Notman and Nadelson further point out, although most working mothers are married, live with their husbands, and have school-age children, over 15 million working women are single, separated, widowed, or divorced, and a large percentage of these also have young children. Lash, Sigal, and Dudzinski (1980), report that 40 percent of all New York City mothers participated in the labor force in 1976. Although this figure was only 31.4 percent for mothers with preschool children, this group experienced the greatest increase in labor-force participation, rising from 21.5 percent in 1971.

The exodus from the home to the workplace has created a "crossover generation," so named because this group of women has, of necessity, broken with the conventions of their mothers. Both because of the break in tradition and the realistic difficulties involved, this generation is confronted with special problems. In the current workplace, women suffer from conflicts in internal belief systems: They feel it is necessary to try to be a perfect wife, perfect mother, and a perfect career woman, all at the same time, and to reconcile their guilt over abandoning the ideals of their mothers. But the biggest problem facing most of these women, whether they are working to support their families or to fulfill their wishes for self-actualization, are the everyday problems of managing the dual responsibilities of job and family. This unsettling situation is often compounded by real concerns over who will look after the children. One of the most serious difficulties is the lack of adequate day care or home care facilities.

Some problems are common to all women who work, and others are specific to women in dual-career families. Frequent difficulties are the stress of managing two full-time obligations, worry about the effects of working on the marital relationship, and concerns about the effects of their absences on their children. The possible effects on children are passionately debated, often with preconceived opinions and without regard to the growing body of literature on the subject. Despite popular prejudices to the contrary, there is no evidence that children of working mothers suffer, or at least not school-age children (Rossi, 1964; Johnson and Johnson, 1977). Although many have grown accustomed to the idea of mothers of school-age children reentering the work force, the current controversies center on the needs of infants and preschoolers and the implications for them of having a working mother.

This essay will address the subjective problems of working mothers and will review some of the pertinent thinking on the effects of day care on young children. It will also focus on the curious paradox that although most women work out of necessity, the working mother's absence from the home is often blamed for increasing family stress and inadequate care of children. (For a review of the work-family dichotomy, see Kamerman, 1979). The working mother is, in fact, blamed for the very conditions that led her into the work force in the first place, particularly the destabilization of the nuclear family. But mental health professionals cannot allow themselves to be polarized between advocates for the working mother and those who stress the needs of the child. The needs of one cannot be understood to preclude those of the other. Most mothers do not rest easily if they believe the best interests of their children are threatened. Although this discussion focuses on the problems of working mothers, it should also be noted that some research has shown that benefits may accrue to the self, the couple, and the children when the woman works outside the home. (For a brief overview of some of this research, see Nadelson & Notman, 1981; see also Baruch, 1972; and Marantz & Mansfield, 1977).

CONFLICTING IDEOLOGIES OF MOTHERHOOD AND SELFHOOD

In addition to the inherent complications of integrating a work life with a personal life and the care of children, women's lives are further complicated by some dubious "shoulds"—ideologies of what constitutes ideal womanhood.

For many years, the ideology of dedicated motherhood dictated that a woman define herself primarily as wife and mother, and she was seen as being almost totally responsible for shaping the destiny of the child. This ideology, a relatively recent phenomenon, reflects the "professionalization of motherhood." Once a relationship, motherhood has become either a job, an identity, or both. In contrast, mothers in earlier generations performed economic tasks alongside their husbands, and care of children was shared among an extended family group. In more recent years, the ideology of dedicated motherhood has come under intense scrutiny, in part due to questions raised by the woman's movement.

As Rothman (1978) points out, the woman's movement was born in conservatism. Essentially a plea for civil liberties for women, the movement saw women as a minority group. In the 1960s, ". . . the organizers of NOW (The National Organization for Women) believed that ending sexual discrimination in the work force and establishing a national network of daycare centers would immediately accomplish the social and economic equality of American women" (p. 243). This did not occur. The failure led to a shift in the ideology informing the women's movement from an emphasis on civil liberties to women's liberation per se. In the beginning, NOW (and the women's movement in general) had perpetuated the already reigning ideology of educated motherhood and the ideal of the wife companion as its model for ideal womanhood; it was later replaced by the "woman as her own person." Even more dramatically, according to Rothman, "Just as the civil rights movement would move from brotherhood to black power, so the woman's movement too would shift from a partnership to a war between the sexes" (p. 236).

But the empahsis on the woman as a person and self-fulfillment outside the roles of wife and mother did not come about simply because of the philosophy of the women's movement or that of the so-called "me-generation." It was and is the natural outcome of economic conditions and the reality that so many married women must work to maintain the family's standard of living. Furthermore, the social realities suggest that even women who adhere to the values of dedicated motherhood and do not identify themselves as feminists may well have to support themselves and their children at some point during their lives, owing either to divorce or death. This knowledge, conscious or unconscious, subtly shapes women's plans, survival strategies, and values.

One more reality, the implications of which have not yet been fully confronted, is the effect on parents of the knowledge that old people are no longer cared for by their grown children. The expectation that one may end one's days in an old-age home or retirement community may erode the absolute commitment to provide for children no matter the degree of selflessness required. If, as Doctorow (1975) suggests in *Ragtime*, Houdini was the last of the great mother lovers, and passionate attachment to mothers has passed from fashion, such a shift in the cultural sensibility has consequences for mothers' love of children. As one woman patient in her fifties put it, hers was the last generation to be bound by duty to both parents and children, but with no expectation that such consideration would be paid to her in turn.

The current shift toward female employment, whatever its causes, has occasioned a radical shift in our perceptions of family obligations and mutual interests. As Rothman (1978) suggests, it is no longer assumed that what benefits a woman automatically benefits her husband and children. In fact, it is sometimes feared that what benefits husband and children depletes the woman. This leads to a novel social predicament. As Rothman puts it, "When one could no longer assume that a woman was primarily a mother, that her needs were identical with and indistinguishable from the child's, then child advocacy took on a novel meaning" (p. 248).

Even so, most mothers are still devoted to the best interests of their children. They do not abandon a commitment to mothering but face the problems inherent in simultaneously mothering and working, a prime example of "role proliferation." As Johnson and Johnson (1976) point out, "Such proliferation . . . requires deep commitment to both role expectations which constantly pose competitive concerns and demands" (p. 15).

Obviously, the simultaneous commitment to motherhood and work can conflict. Much of the argument over the potential conflict of interest between mother and child centers on fears like those suggested by Fraiberg's (1977) book, *Every Child's Birthright: In Defense of Mothering*. Although Fraiberg is disapproving, she never explicitly says that mothers should not work. Instead, she focuses on the hazards to the child's mental health if the child is turned over to a succession of caretakers. Actually, as the fragmentary research (which will be assessed later) suggests, the negative effects of alternative forms of child care are nowhere as clear as Fraiberg would have it. However, the crucial point is that her message has no relevance to the majority of working mothers who have no choice about whether or not to work—other than to increase their worries about their children.

PROBLEMS OF WORKING MOTHERS

As already noted, many women are caught in the crosscurrents of change. Despite the dramatic shift in cultural values, both old and new values coexist. In the absence of absolutes, women are subjected to enormous conflicts of values, which often result in role conflicts. Furthermore, social support systems have not evolved to keep pace with the increasing demands made on women in their disparate roles. No new form of organization has replaced the extended family. The real difficulties of combining marriage, motherhood, and full-time commitment to work cannot be overestimated. To cite just one major example, the decade from 25 to 35 years of age is critical both for childrearing and establishing successful professional strategies. Working mothers express guilt over neglect of their maternal duties and anger at children for taking them away from their professional commitments. Many women have written about the stress of trying to be "superwoman"—doing it all, working a full day, and putting dinner on the table.

Many attributes necessary to a woman's autonomous self-fulfillment are fundamentally at odds with the personality characteristics associated with the traditional role of nurturer and mate. The individual woman is often literally caught between two worlds, without the guarantees and protection of the traditional marriage and the extended family or the role-models and psychological skills necessary for achievement at work.

Although success in a job or career reinforces a male's gender identity, the same success threatens the current definition of the female role. Although this definition of femininity is not logical and lags behind current economic and social realities, women nonetheless sometimes perceive themselves as deviant, unfeminine, and unattractive to men to the extent that they define themselves by working (Person, 1982). Such feelings are not eased by the realization that some men do in fact consider competent and self-reliant women threatening and unattractive.

Women who defy traditional definitions of feminine behavior often jeopardize marital relationships or fear that they do so. In our society the man is far freer to remarry or enter into a series of relationships with women if he loses a mate. Both sexes subconsciously know this, and so a working woman who is married, or who hopes to be, becomes the keeper of the marriage. With individual exceptions on both sides, a woman who challenges definitions of her femininity and risks male disapproval reduces the possibility of future relationships. Insofar as this is the case, it adds to the stress working women feel and tends to lower their work ambitions and their performance on the job. But it is not the marital relationship or the job that suffers most—it is the women, as the result of the subjective strain they experience in fulfilling disparate and contradictory roles.

Essentially, insofar as we consider the integration of working and mothering, working mothers suffer from two major ailments: guilt and, most important, "role strain," as it is euphemistically called.

Guilt

Nearly all working women feel guilty. Obviously, whether a mother is forced or chooses to work may lead to different problems. Women who work out of necessity, when there is no alternative, may have somewhat less guilt than those who work in order to pursue their own careers and self-development. The former view their work as providing for their children, but they have more difficulty in supplying good substitute care. If they live in extended families, they may, however, be supplying the best possible substitute care. It is interesting to note that women who most often have the least guilt about leaving their children are not working woman at all, but upper-class women who have themselves been raised by nannies, governesses, and housekeepers and who automatically turn over the care of their children. It is much more common among both the lower and upper classes than among middle-class women to leave children in the care of other people for extended periods of time without suffering undue guilt. Poorer women are fulfilling the ideology of motherhood to the best of their abilities, and the more affluent are generally following the customs of their class.

It is among women who voluntarily choose to work that guilt is paramount. And even for them, only part of the impetus to work comes from the desire for self-development. Many more families today require two incomes. In addition, a form of self-preservation comes into play with the realization that the tendency toward closer spacing of children and reduction of family size will reduce mothering to a fraction of one's life (Hill & Rodgers, 1964; Rossi, 1964, 1972). Consequently, some women conclude that they will have to pursue not just jobs but careers in order to fill their lives. Some women work as an escape from the demands of small children. Women are sometimes subject to depression when "forced" to stay home. Working then can be a very wise decision, but one that usually provokes undue amounts of self-criticism and guilt.

There are typical ways in which almost all working mothers struggle to keep guilt within tolerable limits. By and large, they focus on the quality rather than the quantity of time spent with the children and try to compensate with special activities and material benefits.

Role Strain

As Johnson and Johnson (1976) suggest, role strain arises from the problems inherent in managing separate and sometimes conflicting roles. The phrase *role strain* does not adequately describe the level of stress working mothers experience. It in no way captures the chronic fatigue, the anxiety, the sense of always being behind, or the near panic that working mothers often feel. This remains true no matter how much a father participates in the actual tasks of running the house and the family. The reason seems to be that the woman, by and large, maintains her role as the "psychological" parent.

The psychological parent is the one who actually takes responsibility for remembering where the child is, and how the child must be transported, who covers for the child if the child care arrangement is inoperative, and so forth. Although the father may perform the work of taking care of the child, he is better able than the mother to put the child out of his mind, enabling him to concentrate on his other work. He is rarely "in two places at once," though it is precisely this feeling that causes the intense inner strife of many mothers. This is particularly true for the mother with younger children, who may be acutely concerned about the inadequacies of her substitute child care arrangement but may have no alternative. Concern for her children's emotional, social, and intellectual development as well as empathy for their needs for nurturance and dependence create intense anxiety and guilt in the mother. She may fear for the safety of the child and does not have the security of knowing that the child has enough command of the language to protect itself. Mothers of infants and young children have the additional problem of being awakened during the night, and they live in a state of sleep deprivation for several years.

Even those rare women who put together work and mothering with relative ease testify to the strain, whether it is periodic exhaustion; neglect of the self (exercise or appearance); or most commonly, the utter lack of private time, solitude, and the privilege of thinking one's own thoughts. Those with creative aspirations are hardest hit.

Johnson and Johnson (1977), reporting on the research on dual-career families, stress the difficulties for career women: "Although some present ideology has promulgated the importance of father's sharing in the vicissitudes of child rearing, motherhood, in most segments of society, remains a sacred task that demands high dedication and commitment and specifically involves the mother rather than the father" (p. 392). Thus, even in the two-career family, the mother's parenting role is disproportionately added to her working role. Johnson and Johnson add: "Despite the prevalence of supportive husbands, all wives reported major concerns over the conflict between their career and their children" (p 393). The wives' role strain was evident in fatigue, emotional depletion, and sometimes guilt. Their statements were in marked contrast to those of the husbands, who felt that they were occasionally overworked but that they were only going through a stage. The findings involving only those marriages regarded as "good" indicate that, given the high level of marital adjustment and support from the husbands, the source of role strain could conclusively be identified with child rearing rather than marriage.

Johnson and Johnson suggested that there were certain typical ways that role strain was kept within tolerable limits. In addition to the means by which the women sought to alleviate their guilt, they very often lowered their career ambitions. They also invoked patterns of child rearing geared to fostering self-reliance and independence in the children rather than focusing on behavior. Paradoxically, these mothers espoused the expectations of traditional dedicated mothering and they, like many women of the middle and upper classes, assumed responsibility for the child's success or failure. But while the husband concentrated on management problems, the wives worried about the emotional cost. Finally, these families socialized predominantly with other two-career families.

For almost all working mothers, the overwhelming problem, both objectively and subjectively, is that of providing good alternative care. Aside from the question (to be discussed later) of the possible effects on children of *any* kind of alternative care whatsoever, the immediate problem remains obtaining consistent and dependable care. One anxiety for a working mother is her nagging awareness that alternative care is never 100 percent available or reliable. The nanny may get sick or quit without notice, or the child may get sick and not be able to go to the day care center. The school child has holidays and vacations. There is almost no fail-safe system that affords the working mother the security that she will be able to go to work everyday. This uncertainty takes its toll both on the job and in the home but, most of all, in a kind of chronic unease lying just below the surface of emotional life.

Mothers at the professional end of the spectrum often hire full-time "help," yet still live in terror. Typically, however, it is a "pass-along" system, with the poor suffering most. Housekeepers and maids farm out their own children in order to take care of more affluent women's children. In some communities, very old women take in four or more children.

THE EFFECTS OF ALTERNATIVE CARE ARRANGEMENTS

As already made clear, working is a necessity for many women for both external and internal reasons. Many of the aspects of stress and role strain can be reduced, and many benefits — not just problems — can

accrue. A major boon to women and children alike would be the provision of quality-controlled, reliable, alternative care options along
with the reassurance that such alternative care was not damaging to
young children. As I have already suggested, many problems have diminished by the time children are enrolled in school programs, although working mothers are still subjected to inordinate demands.
The most pressing questions, however, involve the problems of working mothers with infants and preschool children.

There is a schism in contemporary life. On the one hand, women
work and, increasingly, those with very young children enter the work
force. On the other, growing attention is being paid in the literature to
the necessity for infant-maternal attachment and bonding and to the
negative effects of maternal deprivation, which is often attributed to
absences imposed by the mother's work life. Unfortunately, women's
rights and needs and children's rights and needs seem to collide in both
the real world and, almost invariably, in the scientific literature.

It has been suggested that the focus on the potential hazards of maternal separation may reflect a hidden agenda (see, for example,
Arney, 1980). As Arney notes:

> Much of the research on bonding is methodologically flawed, yet
> bonding theory has been widely accepted despite its demonstrable sci-
> entific problems. One must ask how flawed science can slip through the
> critical screens of the medical profession, which presents itself as scien-
> tific, at least in part. The answer is that scientific production of knowl-
> edge based on bonding theory is, in fact, pseudo-science used to rein-
> force and defend social institutions that are suffering attacks on their
> legitimacy [p. 547].

This is no longer an isolated charge in the feminist literature and may,
in fact, have merit. It is certainly true that people speak passionately on
both sides of the debate with somewhat incomplete knowledge and
considerable emotional bias.

Before turning to the evidence indicating that good alternative child
care is far from damaging, and in some instances is beneficial, it is important to reiterate the common beliefs that almost sanctify maternal
bonding. Kagan, Kearsley, and Zelazo (1978) have suggested that the
ideologic foundations of modern developmental psychology are related to three a priori suppositions. The first is that the experience of
the infant exerts an influence on its contemporaneous development—
that is, that its behavior during the observed time span reflects con-

temporaneous experience (day care for example). The second is that the experiences of the early years of life influence not only those early years themselves but also adolescence and adulthood. The third supposition—which is related to the ideology of dedicated mother-hood already discussed—suggests that the optimum environment for an infant is an emotionally close, nurturant relationship with a single caretaker, preferably the biological mother.

This last supposition provides the intellectual rationale for the ideology of dedicated motherhood. It is a position that has been most systematically espoused by Bowlby (1969) and, most recently, by Fraiberg (1977). However, this supposition has never been demonstrated. Maternal bonding or attachment theory postulates that a special relationship grows between the mother and the infant immediately after birth. Closely related to the idea of maternal bonding is the reverse concept of maternal deprivation. As Bowlby suggested in 1951, "Mother love in infancy and childhood is as important for mental health as are vitamins and proteins for physical health" (quoted in Rutter, 1981, p. 13). Bowlby went so far as to suggest that individuals with any psychiatric disorder invariably showed an impairment of the capacity for affectional bonding that was frequently related to a disturbance of bonding in childhood. Maternal deprivation too often has been cited as an explanation for a wide variety of conditions, including cognitive abnormalities, delinquency, depression, dwarfism, acute distress, and affectional psychopathology.

Although relying heavily on observations of institutionalized children made by Spitz (1965) and the observations of Bowlby (1969), the ideology of dedicated mothering draws on many other prominent voices who have declared maternal bonding to be absolutely central to infant development. Many feminists were extremely disappointed when Rossi (1977) raised doubts about the viability of any alternative to the biological mother for child care, dramatically revising her previous thinking (Rossi, 1964). Rossi, too, apparently now believes that the maternal-infant bond is the key developmental factor for the infant, that men probably cannot fill that role adequately, and that it is unlikely that any kind of alternative or institutionalized child care can provide an adequate substitute. Fraiberg (1977), as already mentioned, also subscribes to this position. She emphasizes the importance of the child's first attachment to the mother for both cognitive and emotional development. All this implies that a mother's employment puts the child at serious risk.

Yet very serious questions have been raised about the validity of these various assertions. Rossi (1972) had herself previously pointed out that homemakers spent less than two hours a day in direct interaction with their children; she believed that house care rather than child care kept women at home. Furthermore, there is no evidence that a working mother automatically endangers her child's attachment behavior.

The most systematic and compelling critique of any simple maternal bonding theory has come from Rutter (1981) in his review of the evidence on maternal deprivation. As he points out, Bowlby's exposure of the institutional care of children had profoundly positive effects by revealing the deplorable conditions that existed. In fact, Bowlby's work has been compared in importance to the exposure of abominable prison conditions in the nineteenth century. But, as Rutter notes, Bowlby's claims of the effects of maternal deprivation outside institutions have met with considerable criticism and theoretical dispute. For example, Bowlby's findings were not controlled for selection of children to institutions, hereditary conditions, biological damage from malnutrition, birth complications, and so forth.

Rutter's main contribution to the discourse on maternal bonding, however, is in pointing out that the general rubric of maternal deprivation refers, in fact, to many different experiences. Rutter raises several crucial distinctions. First, as he makes clear, separation need not involve destruction of the mother-child bond. Therefore, the fact that a mother or a child is hospitalized may have no deleterious effects; the emotional sequalae of such separations are related to many variables. Most important, Rutter disassociates himself from Bowlby's view that the child is innately monotropic and that the bond with the mother is different in kind from all other bonds. Rutter finds that, although the evidence is not yet complete, it appears that children develop bonds with several people and that the bonds do not differ in kind. The chief bond need not be with the biological parent, it need not be with the chief caretaker, and it need not be with a female. In fact, the relationship with the parent of the same sex seems to have a special role at certain times in development.

Rutter suggests that more important than disruption of bonds may be the qualities attendant on the distortion of relationships. Therefore, rather than decry separation per se, he focuses on the quality of the interaction. Rutter cites quality of mothering as the critical variable. Consequently, he focuses on the nature of the mother-infant bond rather than on its simple presence or absence. For example, the depressed mother who is home full time may have a negative impact on her children. Multiple caretakers were not found to be harmful if there was stability and predictability. Significant bonding between fathers and children often takes place.

Kagan, Kearsley, and Zelazo (1978) investigated the effects of group care outside the home on the young child's psychological development. They place their study in its broad context, pointing out with great cogency: "Of the millions of children who do not receive adequate amounts of early affection, only a small proportion develop pathology, and of the group with adult pathology, a large proportion may have been loved during early childhood" (p. 36). They base their conclusions on formal and informal assessments and observations of children over a period of 2 ½ years. Using a sample of children both in a day care center and at home, these authors found that a child's attendance at a day care center staffed by conscientious and nurturing adults "does not seem to produce a psychological profile very much different from the one created by rearing totally in the home" (p. 260).

Kagan, Kearsley, and Zelazo reported no dilution of the child's bond to the mother among the children in day care, even though the children had multiple contacts with other adults. They did not find that day care had hidden psychological dangers. Nonetheless, they wisely recommend that we continue to assess the data. Moreover, these authors found no evidence to suggest that good quality group care makes a positive difference. They suggest that the primary tie and the continuing priority of the experience in the home are related to the salience of the highly charged affective relationship between the parents and the children, not to the more dispassionate relationships at the day care center. In sum, they suggest that if the ratio of children to caretakers is not large, the staff is conscientious and well-supervised, and there is some professional monitoring of the child's development, group care does not seem to have an important effect on the infant's development.

The conceptual error in most of the literature on alternative child care arrangements is to compare bad institutional care with idealized home care. However, I by no means intend to minimize the difficulty of obtaining good care outside or inside the home.

EFFECTS OF THE IDEOLOGY OF DEDICATED MOTHERHOOD

One argument does not come up in discussions of children yet seems to be quite critical, particularly for the middle-class population that private practitioners see primarily. Most of these private patients do not suffer from a disruption of maternal bond. If anything, they seem to suffer more from a zealous invasiveness on the part of the mother. In this regard, the ideology of dedicated motherhood may be pernicious, not only for the burden of guilt it imposes on mothers who choose or are forced to work, but also for the overidealized expectations and hypertrophied hopes that it imposes on both mother and children. I would agree with Rossi's (1964) early assessment that both extremes of maternal rejection and maternal overinvolvement have a negative impact on child development.

Chodorow and Contratto (1982) suggest that the idealization of mothers creates the counterpart of the omnipotent child whose needs and demands for maternal care are taken as totally realistic. This is a shrewd appraisal and suggests that the child's willingness to blame the mother and the adult's willingness to blame her own childhood derives from the ideology of dedicated motherhood. This ideology fosters a lack of internalization of responsibility and consequences. It also fosters the grievous notion that everyone is an underachiever and that were it not for some impairment in the parent-child relationship, life would also go smoothly and all ambitions be fulfilled. Our fear of maternal deprivation sometimes tempts us into suffocating overcare and the resultant stifling of autonomy.

CONCLUSION: TOWARD A RESOLUTION

I am certainly not suggesting that mothers give up mothering; nor am I suggesting that all young children should be reared in day care centers or by nannies. I am suggesting that the way we look at the subject is imbued by distortion and myth centering on the mystification of the mother-child bond. I am suggesting that many of the beliefs we have cherished must be reexamined, particularly in the light of current social realities. It is probably better, for instance, to posit motherhood as a relationship rather than as a profession.

It is untenable to cling to positions that are irrelevant to the vast majority of women and might not be desirable even if plausible. Sheila Kamerman, professor of social policy and planning at Columbia University, has aptly stated: "You can't debate whether children should be in some form of daycare or other—that's nonsense. It's a fait accompli for women in every sector of society, and the question is not whether, but how to do it in as enhancing and supporting a way as possible" (quoted in Collins, 1984b, p. 311). Yet no effective social policy has been implemented to provide the best child care facilities for infants and preschool children of working mothers. It is crucial for mental health professionals to address the issues involved in formulating pertinent social policy on the question of day care and its implementation. It would be a grave error to restrict our skills and expertise solely to ministering to the internal conflicts of individual women, when many problems shared by the majority of working mothers are normative and must be attributed to a situational conflict in which there are few viable alternatives. This is one more instance in which some problems experienced in terms of personal distress or shortcomings derive not from unconscious conflict or personal inadequacies but from pressing external circumstance. (But obviously they intensify preexisting conflicts.)

Establishing quality day care centers is one of the most critical issues facing our generation. In addition, there must be provisions for professional training programs and licensing in child care for qualified individuals to staff these centers and to provide for home care of children as well. Studies seem to indicate that few children are ever harmed by excellent alternative care but that damage can be done by inferior methods. A woman can work without sacrificing a child, but if inferior care is creating a generation of emotionally disabled children, it is in the interest of society to acknowledge it and legislate for improved child care immediately.

REFERENCES

Arney, W. R. (1980), Maternal-infant bonding: The politics of falling in love with your child. *Feminist Studies*, 6 (3): 547–570.

Baruch, G. K. (1972), Maternal influences upon college women's attitudes toward women and work. *Development. Psych.*, 6 (1): pp. 32–37.

Bowlby, J. (1969), *Attachment*. New York: Basic Books.

Chodorow, N., & Contratto, S. (1982), The fantasy of the perfect mother. In: *Rethinking the Family: Some Feminist Questions*, ed. B. Thorne & M. Yalom. New York: Longman.

Collins, G. (1984a), Experts debate impact of daycare on children and on society. *New York Times*, September 4, p. B11.

_____ (1984b), Study finds family bears brunt of social change. *New York Times*, October 6, p. B48.

Fraiberg, S. (1977), *Every Child's Birthright: In Defense of Mothering*. New York: Basic Books.

Doctorow, E. L. (1979), *Ragtime*. New York: Random House.

Hill, R. & Rodgers, K. (1964), The developmental approach. In: *Handbook of Marriage and the Family*, ed. H. Christensen. Chicago: Rand McNally, pp. 171–211.

Howell, M. C. (1973), Employed mothers and their families (I). *Pediatrics*, 52(2): 252–263.

Kagan, J., Kearsley, R. B., & Zelazo, P. R. (1978), *Infancy: Its Place in Human Development*. Cambridge, MA: Harvard University Press.

Kamerman, S. (1979), Work and family in industrialized societies. *Signs: J. Wom. Cult. Soc.*, 4 (4): 632–650.

Johnson, C. L., & Johnson, F. A. (1977), Attitudes toward parenting in dual-career families. *Amer. J. Psychiat.*, 134(4): 391–395.

Johnson, F. A., & Johnson, C. L. (1976), Role strain in high-commitment career women. *J. Amer. Acad. Psychoanal.*, 4(10): 13–36.

Lash, T., Sigal, H., & Dudzinski, D. (1980), *State of the Child: New York City II*. New York: Foundation for Child Development.

Marantz, S. A., & Mansfield, A-F. (1977), Maternal employment and the development of sex-role stereotyping in five-to-eleven-year-old girls. *Child Devel.* 48: 668–673.

Mogul, K. M. (1979), Women in mid-life: Decisions, rewards, and conflicts related to work and careers. *Amer. J. Psychiat.*, 136(9): 1139–1143.

Nadelson, C. (1981), Alternative life-styles in the mental health of children. In: *American Handbook of Psychiatry* (2nd ed.), Vol. 7, ed. S. Arieti & H. Brodie. New York: Basic Books, pp. 204–226.

_____ & Notman, M. (1981), Women, work and children: Child psychiatry perspectives. *J. Amer. Acad. Child Psychiat.*, 20: 863–875.

_____ _____ (1982), Maternal work and children. In: *The Woman Patient* (Vol. 2): *Concepts of Femininity in the Life Cycle*, ed. C. Nadelson & M. Notman. New York: Plenum Press, pp. 121–134.

Person, E. (1982), Women working: Fears of failure, deviance and success. *J. Amer. Acad. Psychoanal.*, 10(1): 67–84.

Rossi, A. (1964), Equality between the sexes: An immodest proposal. *Daedalus*, 93: 607–652.

_____ (1972), Family development in a changing world. *Amer. J. Psychiat.*, 128: 1057–1066.

_____ (1977), A biosocial perspective on parenting. *Daedalus*, 106: 1–31.

Rothman, S. (1978), *Woman's Proper Place: A History of Changing Ideals and Practices, 1870 to the Present*. New York: Basic Books.

Rutter, M. (1981), *Maternal Deprivation Reassessed*. Harmondsworth: Penguin. (First published 1972).

Spitz, R. (1965), *The First Year of Life*. New York: International Universities Press.

7
Anger in the Mother-Daughter Relationship

Judith Lewis Herman, M.D.
Helen Block Lewis, Ph.D.

In our exploitative, warring, male-dominated society, men are socialized to the expectation that they are entitled to power, not only over
their own destinies, but also over other people, especially women.
Women are socialized to the acceptance of men's power and of their
own inferior place. Women's power as mothers stands as the only exception to this order of things. The power of mothers can be transmitted only to daughters. It is a special kind of power, based not on the
ability to kill, but on the ability to create and foster life.

Anger in the mother-daughter relationship has a special configuration based on the contradiction between women's inferior status and
their special power as mothers. The social subordination of women inevitably creates a condition of chronic anger at the same time that it

renders dangerous any expession of this anger or even conscious identification of its true source. Moreover, this chronic anger conflicts with
the nurturant and loving feelings that have been the most consistent
basis of women's dignity and power. Anger between mothers and
daughters is therefore an especially painful state for both; first, because
it is often a displaced anger that cannot find its true source, and second, because it violates their shared role as affectionate nurturers.
Even in the midst of intense conflict, both may have the sense that anger does not properly *belong* in their relationship, and both may long
for reconciliation.

MOTHERS AND DAUGHTERS IN RECENT WOMEN'S LITERATURE

Women's literature of the past ten years is filled with the voices of
daughters seeking their mothers. The quest generally begins from a
point of estrangement, anger, and reproach and moves toward solidarity. One can detect the longing for closeness behind the anger in this
daughter's complaint:

> Women in modern Judeo-Christian societies are motherless children.
> Painting after painting, sculpture after sculpture in the Christian world
> portray Madonnas comforting and worshipping their infant sons. . . .
> The fierce bond of love, continuity, and pride between the pagan De-
> meter (the Earth Mother) and her daughter Persephone (the Kore-
> Maiden) does not exist between women in Catholic mythology or cul-
> ture. It cannot. Mothers have neither land nor money to cede to their
> daughters. Their legacy is one of capitulation [Chesler, 1972, pp.
> 17–18.]

Chesler's lament connects the alienation of mother and daughter with
their mutual subordination, and looks backward to a lost culture that
worshipped their fertility. Implicitly, in her version of a paradise lost,
she asserts the possibility of a society in which daughters might inherit
power. If mothers and daughters are not doomed to servitude and inferiority because of their sex, the alienation between them, based on
mutual inferiority, may be overcome.

Feminist historians and anthropologists, searching for evidence of
other social possibilities, have indeed established convincing evidence

that male domination is not a universal condition of human society and that the biological fact of motherhood does not inevitably relegate women to a position of inferiority. Sacks (1979), for example, relates the status of women in general, and of mothers in particular, to their ownership of the means of production. She cites as examples pre-colonial African societies in which women were "sisters," members of a kin corporation of owners in which they have the status of "an adult among adults, a decision maker." Sacks points out that the capitalist view of motherhood as a socially dependent state does not fit the facts:

> Women, and mainly mothers at that, have been significant producers of food, clothing and shelter almost universally. They have combined their work with child care as universally. . . . Moreover, mothers and female nonmothers have wielded power and authority over children, husbands, brothers, villagers and subjects. . . . In addition, many nonclass societies lack a first and second sex and lack the distinctions between gender-related and important and menial work [p. 93].

In a complex analysis of preliterate cultures, Sanday (1981), relates the power of women not only to their control of a significant and valued sphere of production, but to the culture's recent experiences of plenty or famine, permanence or migration, and to the religious framework within which its historical experience is understood. Male dominance appears to be most severe in cultures like our own, in which creation myths recognize the power of a male deity only, and in which the formative experiences of the group involve migration, hunting, and warfare. Cultures whose creation myths recognize an original mother or couple, and whose formative experiences are of reliable attachment to a particular part of the earth, tend to be far more egalitarian. Although women are everywhere the primary caretakers of children, nurturance of the young tends to be a segregated, inferior occupation particularly in exploitative, warring societies, which all societies are not. Our own culture represents an extreme along the continuum that Sanday describes, and much of the apparent universality of male dominance can be ascribed to the conquest of most of the world's cultures by our own.

Even within our own culture, the status of women and the material basis of the female inheritance has shown considerable variability. Alienation between mothers and daughters in its present extreme form is a rather recent historical development, related to the degradation of the mother's role within the family.

One hundred years ago, although mothers had "neither land nor money" to bequeath to their daughters, many mothers did possess a body of knowledge and skill that commanded the respect of an artisan's craft and that was regularly transmitted to their daughters on the model of apprenticeship. Production and preservation of food and clothing; nursing the young, old, and sick; and attendance at birth and death were the province of mothers and the birthright of daughters. These valued and necessary skills, handed down from mother to daughter, formed the material of a segregated, domestic society that Smith-Rosenberg (1975) has named "the female world of love and ritual." This is a version of what Sacks calls "sisterhood." The rearing of daughters took place within a complex and intricate social network formed by female kin – mother, sisters, grandmothers, aunts, cousins – and by the mother's girlhood friends and their daughters. Although men, then as now, controlled the women's fate, this highly segregated society of women seemed to provide some limited measure of dignity, protection, and solidarity. Within this female world, anger and hostility among women, as well as ambition and heterosexual curiosity, were vigorously suppressed, while lifelong loving and nurturant relationships between women were expected and promoted.

Expressions of unreserved affection and tenderness between mothers and daughters, which today strike us as quaint and artificial, were common in the documents of family life in the last century. Here, for example, is a letter from a mother, Sarah Alden Ripley, to her recently married daughter, Sophy Thayer. The year is 1861.

> You do not know how much I miss you, not only when I struggle in and out of my mortal envelope and pump my nightly potation and no longer pour into your sympathizing ear my senile gossip, but all the day I muse away, since the sound of your voice no longer rouses me to sympathy with your joys or sorrows. You can't know how much I miss your affectionate demonstrations [quoted in Smith-Rosenberg, 1975, p. 15].

Or consider the following document (quoted in Friday, 1977, pp. 51–52), which dates from the early part of our century. It is part of a farewell letter from a mother to her 14-year-old daughter, written when the mother, the strong-willed wife of a wealthy and powerful man, was about to run away from her husband, leaving three younger children in her daughter's care:

My darling Jane:

. . . To me, motherhood has been the most beautiful thing in my life. The wonder of it never ceases for me. . . .

All my life as a child I looked forward to the time when I would have children of my own. . . . And when I held you, Jane — my first baby — in my arms, I had the greatest thrill I have ever experienced. I felt almost saintly, as if I had really entered heaven. . . .

I am telling you this, Jane, just so you will understand my love and feeling for you. Always remember this as you grow older, think of me sometimes and try to understand what I am trying to convey to you. . . .

This is the hardest, bitterest moment of my life, leaving you, but I cannot do anything else. I cannot see through my tears. God bless you all,

Mama

Daughter Jane obeyed her mother's injunction against angry thoughts or feelings. In spite of her mother's desertion, she reportedly spoke of her mother in later years with an unmixed love bordering on adoration. Jane's daughter, Nancy, gained widespread public attention in our time with an immensely popular book about mother-daughter relationships. It is a book filled with disappointment, recriminations, and complaints. Its opening sentences read: "I have always lied to my mother. And she to me" (Friday, 1977, p. 19).

This progressive alienation between mothers and daughters over three generations parallels the destruction of the female apprenticeship system and the impoverishment of the home as a workplace. As more and more skilled tasks that were formerly the province of women working within the home were taken over by hierarchical corporate institutions controlled by men (the factory, the hospital, the school), mothers had less and less to hand down to their daughters. With the degredation of its material base in knowledge and skill, the female world of love and ritual lost its meaning and importance. All that currently remains of a once elaborate and rich social world are its restrictions, and even these are diminishing in force. Whatever survives of segregated female culture today is the object of ridicule; all-female society is generally scorned for its supposed narrowness, its (hetero)sexual repressiveness, its backwardness, its triviality. The masculine world is seen as the source not only of wealth and power, but even of knowledge, competence, imagination, and skill. The mother of 100 years ago

initiated her daughter into an artisanate; the mother of today socializes her daughter into a female proletariat.[1]

This is an inherently conflictual task. The mother, herself dependent and inferior, has the job of preparing her daughter for a life of dependence and inferiority. She must adapt her daughter to a world in
which women compete for the scarce favors and rewards that are
granted by men. She must teach her daughter to please men—that is,
to be "feminine"—and to serve them—that is, to do housework. She
must also protect her daughter from the worst excesses of male exploitation, teaching her to avoid molestation, rape, incest, prostitution,
and physical assault. Although men create these dangers, it is the lot of
women to explain them to their outraged and uncomprehending girl
children. To protect their daughters, mothers are often forced to be
their daughters' jailers. Given the conditions of this initiation into
servitude, hostility and conflict in the mother-daughter relationship is
indeed inevitable. But because it arises between members of the gender
whose special power is nurturance, hostility between mother and
daughter is especially difficult for both. For this reason, anger in the
mother-daughter relationship is simultaneously full of both scorn and
longing for rapprochement. Behind the agonizing ambivalence toward
each other is the mother and daughter's shared need to establish their
freedom from male domination. It is when this underlying theme is
most available to their consciousness that mothers and daughters can
find their way to reconciliation.

A CONTRAST: THE FATHER-SON RELATIONSHIP

A brief contrast with hostility in the father-son relationship will illu-
minate the special nature of anger between the inferiors who are also
the reproducers of the species. Fathers and sons are both striving for
something they value and that has a reality based in our world: power.
Since the exercise of aggression is essential to the maintenance of
power, aggression is a highly valued norm of men's behavior. This is
not to say that fathers are immune to the values of nurturance and to
feelings of affection for their children. But the confusion between

---

[1]The feminist revival of traditional women's skills such as needlecraft, herbal medicine, and midwifery can be understood as an attempt to reclaim the productive base of
"sisterhood."

power and masculinity that our society perpetuates also makes aggression between fathers and sons more acceptable and inevitable between them. The conflict between their affectionateness and their anger at each other exists between fathers and sons, but it does not contradict a gender role of nurturance. Fathers usually have little of this role in any case.

So, for example, Freud could easily write the script for the conflict between fathers and sons as a struggle for (sexual) power over the mother, in which the son renounces his love for her out of fear of the father's castrating power and in return for the promise of the father's patriarchal powers in the future. This is a family version of the "social contract" in a hostile world. Fathers' and sons' affection for each other plays a minor role in this drama (although Freud did not always ignore it). Rather, men's socialization is accomplished by a heavy reliance on "identification with the aggressor." In contrast, a woman's socialization into femininity involves her in an identification with an ideal of nurturance and affection.

Experimental observations of mother-infant interactions have developed a body of data that is generally consistent with earlier psychoanalytic formulations of sex differences in both nurturance and aggression. Evidence from studies of both non-human and human primates suggests that throughout the life-cycle, males are both more aggressive and less sociable than females. It should be emphasized that the possibility of some biological substrate underlying these differences in no way implies support for a doctrine of biological determinism.

Within many primate species, for example, mothers are more rejecting and punishing of their male infants than of their females. Mothers not only punish male infants more, but they hold them and carry them around less than females. There is speculation that the mothers' greater aggression is elicited by the greater aggression of the male infants (Jensen, Bobbitt, and Gordon, 1968; Mitchell and Brandt, 1970). Evidence from studies of maternal deprivation among primates shows, further, that female infants are injured much less by maternal deprivation than males (Sackett, 1974). Male infants raised in isolation are more damaged sexually, socially, and in exploratory behavior than female infants raised under comparable conditions. As Sackett puts it, females are the "buffered sex"; they are somehow less vulnerable to earliest social loss. This may be interpreted as meaning that females have something more of sociability to begin with.

Differences between the sexes in what may be regarded as the fore-
runners of later sociability can also be observed in human neonates.
Newborn girls suck, mouth, and smile more than newborn boys, who
startle more (Korner, 1969). Although the smile of a two-day old infant
is not a social smile, it is a possible forerunner. Newborn girls are more
sensitive than newborn boys to the sound of other newborns crying
(Simner, 1971).

The interaction between mothers and their new babies is also different in the two genders. On the whole, mothers have an easier time of it
with their girl infants than with their boys, who are not only irritable
and fussy to begin with, but are more subject to "inconsolable states"
(Moss, 1974). Among human beings as well as primates, moreover,
there is some evidence that boys are injured more than girls by maternal deprivation (Bayley & Schaefer, 1964), which suggests, once again,
that women's "sociability" is sturdier than men's.

However it comes about, the picture of aggressive men and less aggressive *and* more affectionate women has been overwhelmingly documented by psychological studies over the past 30 years (Lewis, 1976). A
bibliography (Oetzel, 1966) of the evidence on the question of which
sex is more aggressive turned up 49 separate studies by different investigators, all unanimous in finding men more aggressive. Maccoby and
Jacklin's (1974) review of this question left the answer unchanged.
Some of these studies reported observations of children's behavior;
others were self-report studies of adults; still others used projective
techniques. The people studied ranged in age from 3 years to adulthood. Whatever the mode of inquiry, the answer is uniform: men are
more aggressive than women. Three-year-old boys in nursery school
quarrel and fight more than 3-year-old girls. College men form more
"hostile sentences." In a structured interview, men describe more overt
aggressive behavior than women. Our society, which trains men to be
exploiters and warriors does a thorough job of inculcating the required
higher level of aggression.

The same bibliography of psychological studies (Oetzel, 1966) also
documents the overwhelming evidence that women's attitudes toward
other people are more positive than men's. These studies are important
because they make the point that women are both less aggresssive and
more positively oriented to other people (including men) than are
men. Forty-seven studies are listed under the headings of "interest in
and positive feelings for others," "nurturant behavior," and "need for

affiliation" (sociability, affectionateness, friendliness, and gregarious-ness), covering people ranging in age from 3 to adulthood, and with a wide variety of experimental techniques. A strong majority of these studies (42) showed women to be more "positive" in their attitudes to-ward others; the remaining 5 studies showed no difference.

Even in their dreams, men and women show differences both in ag-gression and in positive attitudes toward others. Brenneis (1968) for ex-ample, found a greater frequency and higher intensity of aggression in the manifest content of men's dreams. Hall and Van de Castle (1966) found that women's dreams more often contained a greater number of people, more familiar people, and a greater number of references to parents than men's dreams. Even in their symbolic conceptions of the Deity, men and women have different modes of responses. A Rorschach study (Larson & Knapp, 1968) showed that fear of God was more characteristic of men, whereas benevolent representations of the Deity were more characteristic of women.

Some of the experimentally observed differences between the sexes are particularly important because they reflect the combination of higher sociability and lesser aggression in women. When it comes to achievement motivation, for example, boys are more highly motivated when the circumstances are competitive; girls are more motivated when what they are striving to achieve is a "social goal," such as help-fulness. Women invest more heavily in affiliative relationships; men are more involved in status and power (Maccoby & Jacklin, 1974).

A man's level of aggression becomes characteristic of him in early childhood. By age 4, the "pattern of feminine-maternal qualities . . . has all but broken down [in boys] under the requirement that males model themselves after males. The anaclitic quality of the initial social-ization process is evident in girls but does not appear in boys" (Sears, Rau & Alpert, 1965, p. 262). Aggression remains characteristic of boys through childhood. Follow-up studies of the same person later in life (Kagan & Moss, 1962) show unequivocally that the more aggressive boys turn into the more aggressive men. And the more aggressive boys choose or prefer toys and activities that are assigned to masculine la-bels in our society. One investigator sums it up as follows: "Aggressive adolescent boys become aggressive, easily angered men. . . . Appropri-ately sex-typed, they become 'instrumental' i.e. self-sufficient, lacking in sociability and introspection" (Mussen, 1969, p. 712).

When they become fathers, men retain this combination of traits. A number of experimental studies ask the questions, Which sex is more punishing in the family, and to which sex child? The answer is that fathers are more punishing than mothers, but *only* to boys, not to girls (Lewis, 1976). When the corresponding question is asked—Are mothers more nurturant and affectionate within their own families than fathers?—the answer is an unequivocal yes. Mothers are more nurturant and affectionate than fathers to both boys and girls.

And so the scene perpetuates itself: Aggressive fathers make aggressive sons who turn into aggressive fathers. Nurturant mothers make affectionate daughters who turn into nurturant mothers. No wonder anger in the mother-daughter relationship is especially difficult for both parties to sustain! "Identification with the aggressor" is not women's style.

The framework for women thus involves functioning at a lower level of aggression and a higher level of affectionateness than men. This difference has traditionally been valued ambivalently in our culture. On the one hand, women's nurturance has been culturally fostered as a means of ensuring that women will function as a refuge or haven for men, a relief from their exploitative behavior. On the other hand, these same qualities are denigrated as inferior in a culture that valorizes aggression (Miller, 1976). Feminist thinkers, too, have often viewed women's nurturance with ambivalence, and for good reasons. First, there is always the danger that any observation of widespread sex differences can be cited in support of biological determinist theories which rationalize women's oppression as part of the natural order. Second, feminist thinkers cannot help but share in the attitudes of an extremely aggressive culture, in which female nurturance is alternately sentimentalized and despised (Chodorow, 1979). And finally, even if the nurturant qualities of women are positively and unambivalently valued, the danger that these very qualities sometimes render women more vulnerable to exploitation must be recognized. The attachments which are a great potential source of female strength can also be a potential trap.

These ambivalent attitudes are nowhere more apparent than in the mother-daughter relationship. It is in this arena that each developing girl must resolve for herself the contradictory feelings toward a mother who is at once nurturant and socially inferior, and face the danger that the bonds of affection can become the bonds of servitude.

EARLY CONFLICTS IN THE MOTHER-DAUGHTER
RELATIONSHIP

Psychoanalysis recognizes three important life stages in which daughters angrily reject their mothers: the oedipal, pubertal, and young adult periods of life. Each stage originates in a sudden period of growth, expanded curiosity and understanding, and interest in sex and the relation between the sexes. Each precedes entry into a wider social world. At each stage, the daughter comes to a fuller awareness of the relative place of males and females in society. At each stage, she reacts with shock, disappointment, and anger against her mother. Fueling this anger is a deeper, often unconscious, reaction to the injustice of women's second-class status, and an implicit demand that a truly nurturant mother should struggle against her own (and her daughter's) inferiority.

In Freud's formulation, the first and prototypic crisis occurs when the girl child discovers that both she and her mother are "castrated." In rage and disappointment, she blames her mother for having failed to provide her with a penis, and despises her for lacking one herself. Henceforth she withdraws love from her mother and transfers it to her father who, if he will not supply her with the desired penis, at least has the virtue of possessing one himself. Freud's main criticism of women was that they did not carry out this process as completely as he considered desirable and that they retained considerable attachment to their mothers.

Generations of feminists have thoroughly criticized Freud's formulation of the so-called castration complex in women. Horney (1926) aptly pointed out 40 years ago that castration is a male, not a female fantasy and that Freud's conception of the castration complex in girls corresponds exactly to fantasies ordinarily entertained by a 5-year-old boy. Her criticism still stands.

Nevertheless, psychoanalytic theory still challenges us to explain the hostility between mother and daughter, which does occur predictably at this crisis in the daughter's life. And Freud's formulation takes on new meaning if it is understood as a description of the way in which children experience the contradiction between the nurturant power of mothers and the dominant powers of fathers. Both sexes originally see the mother as all-powerful and learn only later that she is inferior in power to the father. The boy's repudiation of his mother involves him in a repudiation of his earliest attachment figure, at the same time that it rewards him with the uncertain hope of admission to a superior caste. The girl's repudiation of her mother also involves a denigration of her earliest attachment figure, but with no hope of the future reward of superior power. Her outrage at this double loss compounds her fury at her mother. It is only when both sexes disentangle gender from its confusion with aggressive power that both sexes can regain their original attachments.

It is indeed a shock when the little girl first recognizes what it means to be female in a world where power and privilege are the province of males. At the same time that she recognizes her own inferior status, she is forced to reevaluate her estimation of her mother. The woman who once appeared all-powerful to her is now revealed as subservient and weak. Outraged and disappointed, the daughter reproaches the mother for their common fate. It is as if she said to her mother: "How could you have allowed this to happen? Why didn't you fight harder, for yourself and for me?"

Chodorow (1978) emphasizes both the role of disappointed love and the role of male superiority in the young daughter's rejection of her mother. The daughter's pride is deeply wounded by the discovery that even her mother prefers males to females, placing her love for her husband (and often for her sons as well) above her love for her daughter. The mother's preference is experienced not only as a rejection but as a betrayal, as if by choosing a man as her primary love object the mother affirms the superiority of males and acquiesces in her own inferior status. At this age, the daughter may also become aware of her mother's deferential behavior toward her father or other significant men. Not only does her esteem for her mother suffer, but her own self-esteem is endangered by the thought that she might share in her mother's inferior status.

The daughter initially attempts to resolve her disappointment in her mother by turning to her father for rescue. Realizing that all the world, her mother included, sees the father as the source of freedom and power, she attempts to form a privileged relationship with her father that might exempt her from the onerous fate of an ordinary female. But this solution brings her into still greater conflict with her mother. And it increases the danger that the father will be tempted to transform this special relationship into a seductive or incestuous one.

Psychoanalysis emphasizes the competitive aspects of this conflict: Mother and daughter become rivals for the same love object. Certainly competition between mother and daughter is unavoidable, given that both are subservient to the father, and both depend on the favors that he alone has the power to confer or withhold. However, competition represents only one aspect of the conflict between mother and daughter that occurs at this time. Commonly overlooked is the fact that the mother is often required to interfere in the father-daughter relationship to protect her daughter. In a society in which roughly 5 percent of all girls are incestuously involved with their fathers or stepfathers, no mother can regard her daughter's emerging sexual interest without anxiety (Russell, 1983). The more conscientious the mother, the more she will seek to interpose herself between father and daughter, to prevent development of an exclusive and privileged relationship between them.

Girl children, furthermore, are exposed to a very real risk of sexual abuse, not only by their fathers, but also by other adult males with whom they come into contact. One girl out of three experiences at least one sexual encounter with an adult male before the age of 18 (Russell, 1983). In most instances, the offender is not a stranger, but a man known to the family who is able to gain the confidence of the child. Girls who are molested are usually warned and threatened not to tell anyone, especially their mothers; and most obey.

Mothers, therefore, cannot fail to be alarmed by their daughter's growing sexual awareness and curiosity. Although the statistics on child sexual abuse are only now reaching public consciousness, the fear of sexual abuse has *always* informed the consciousness of mothers. After all, many mothers have their own childhood experiences to draw upon. Mothers know the dangers that their daughters face, even if the rest of us choose not to know.

The most common result is an anxious concern for "modesty" that mothers attempt to instill in their daughters. Mothers restrict sexual curiosity and exhibitionism in their daughters and supervise their behavior more closely than that of their sons. This surveillance of the daughter's sexual activity often extends to a general interference with autonomy, adventurousness, and initiative. The mother teaches her daughter that there are severe limits to society's toleration of these qualities in little girls, and the hazards of exceeding these limits are very real. In families where mothers are unable to fulfill this protective

function, however, daughters are particularly vulnerable to victimiza-
tion and abuse of all sorts (Finkelhor, 1979). Daughters in these families feel far more deeply betrayed than those who merely complain of
their mothers' restrictiveness. They feel that they have been offered as
a sacrifice in order to propitiate a powerful male, and they bitterly de-
spise their mothers for their utter helplessness (Herman, 1981).

Because daughters are generally unaware of the dangers of preda-
tory male sexuality, and because mothers rarely explain these dangers
clearly, appropriate maternal protectiveness is generally experienced
as "overprotectiveness"—restrictive, prudish behavior. In the daughter's perception, it is her mother who inhibits her expression of pride,
autonomy, and sexuality; mother who fearfully clings to her and will
not let her go; mother who jealously stands in the way of her freedom;
mother who constantly interferes in the special relationship she would
like to have, first with her father, and later with other men.

The daughter's common grievances find mythical expression in
three popular folk tales. The conflict over housework (that is, female
servitude) is central to the story of Cinderella, in which a wicked stepmother confines one daughter to kitchen slavery, while her lazy step-
sisters go free. In reality, of course, it is fathers and brothers, not
mothers and sisters, who are exempted from household drudgery and
who impose it on women and girls. The conflict over sexuality appears
symbolically in the story of Sleeping Beauty, in which a witch's curse
puts Beauty into a deathlike sleep at the moment of puberty. The image of the mother as rival finds its clearest representation in the story of
Snow White, where an innocent heroine is persecuted by a jealous
queen who will not tolerate the existence of a younger female more
beautiful than herself. In each legend, the young girl's enemy is an
older female; in each, her rescuer is a male.

The resolution of the fairy tales, in which the daughter-heroine is
lifted onto the prince's horse, represents not merely sexual fulfillment,
but escape from the degraded female condition. Each girl is encouraged in the fantasy that an exception will be made for her; that, as a
princess, she will be chosen by a man to be elevated above the common
drudgery of feminine existence, the drudgery to which she sees her
mother consigned.

The enduring popularity of these three tales, each in recent times en-
shrined in American mass culture through the cartoon art of Walt
Disney, attests to the importance of daughters' fury with their mothers
and their attempt to rely on powerful men for their salvation.

The oppressed condition of women is thus the ultimate, usually hidden, source of the daughter's disappointment in her mother, and it fuels the daughter's desire to separate and be different from her mother. The failure to discern the larger context in which the daughter's contempt arises can make it appear as if the mother-daughter conflict is inherernt in their gender and thus almost impossible to resolve. This is the mistake Freud made. It is also one that is currently being repeated in some present-day feminist-psychoanalytic writings.

MOTHERS' AND FATHERS' ROLES IN EARLY DEVELOPMENT

A theme in recent psychoanalytically oriented feminist literature is that because mothers are devalued people, it is harder for them to provide adequate mothering for their daughters than for their sons. Thus, for example, Flax (1978), following Mahler's (Mahler, Pine, & Bergman, 1975) description of the phases of "symbiosis," "differentiation," and "rapprochement" in the process of separation and individuation, suggests that little girls naturally fare worse with their mothers in all of these important phases of development.

Le us look more closely at each phase of early development. Flax contends that during the symbiotic period, mothers are not available to their daughters in a consistent way because the mothers identify "more strongly" with their daughters than with their sons. This identification evokes more conflicted feeling and more infantile wishes in the mother. Flax rests this belief about the symbiotic period primarily on retrospective evidence from patients in therapy. But such evidence, although suggestive, is always subject to distortion, both in the patient's report and in the therapist's observation. As already indicated, the evidence from direct observation of sex differences in the mother-infant interaction (at least in white, middle-class families) is that mothers have an easier time forming a smooth relationship with their daughters than with their sons.

On the assumption that girls have already been more stressed than boys by their mothers in the symbiotic period, Flax suggests that girls receive less "emotional refueling" from their mothers when they attempt to develop their capacities in the next phase of growth, differentiation. There is no evidence whatsoever for that assertion, which is entirely speculative. In fact, a study of 1-year-old infants' reactions to a strange situation (Ainsworth, Blehar, Waters & Wall, 1978) suggests that mothers who are ambivalent do indeed have infants who are anxiously rather than securely "attached." But this finding held with equal frequency for boys and girls.

By the time of the so-called rapprochement period, when gender becomes explicit in its implications, Flax supposes that girls, who are already vulnerable because of presumed deficiencies in the first two stages, are subject to a gender-specific lessening of self-esteem. Boys enjoy their functioning in their widening world, while girls are more enmeshed in an ambivalent relationship with their mothers. Although Flax disagrees with Mahler's focus on the anatomical distinction between the sexes as the reason for girls' loss of self-esteem, she does use a concept of "symbolic" penis-envy to explain girls' relative lack of an autonomous ego. The girl cannot identify with her father because of the difference between her gender and his; nor can she repress the female part of her self. She is thus in the painful bind of having a strong, unfulfilled need for fusion that interferes with her need to be autonomous. "Her experience has shown her that her mother does not wish her to individuate, so perhaps she can please her mother by remaining in a more infantile state. In either case she must choose between what feels like nurturance—the love of her mother, no matter how ambivalently expressed—and autonomy" (Flax, 1978, p. 178).

Once again, however, direct studies of early childhood appear to contradict this gloomy picture. On the specific question of the effects of recognizing anatomical differences between the sexes, Galenson and Roiphe (1980) offer some new findings from their psychoanalytic studies. When boys in the second year of life perceive the genital difference between the sexes, they deny the difference. Moreover, this need to deny apparently has an effect on their symbolic capacities. They are less likely to use fantasy as a symbolic elaboration, and their image of their own body is also affected. Boys' play is repetitive. Boys remain distant from their mothers, presumably because their mothers remind them of castration. (Galenson and Roiphe report that some words could not be learned by boys from their mothers but could be learned from their fathers.) Girls, in contrast, do not deny the genital difference; their symbolic activities also flourish. They are extremely flexible in their play and are interested in trying new things. This is a picture in considerable contrast with Flax's portrait of the clinging little girl with low self-esteem.

Early wounds in the formation of female self-esteem do occur in many, perhaps in most, families. But the origin of this injury may frequently be traced not only to a primary failure in the mother-daughter relationship but also to the influence of the father. Although the role of the father in early development is generally ignored in psychological theory, we do know that infants of both sexes form early attachments to their fathers as well as to their mothers (Pederson, 1980; Lamb, 1981). But fathers, at least traditional fathers, do not reciprocate their daughters' attachment as wholeheartedly as they do that of their sons. To the extent that they are interested in children at all, most fathers prefer sons (Hoffman, 1977). The paternal desire for a son and heir often influences patterns of childbearing. It is still common in this country, as in many parts of the world, for mothers of girls to continue having children until a boy is born; then and only then is the family considered complete. The reverse pattern rarely occurs. Sex discrimination begins in infancy. Both fathers and mothers have sex-stereotyped perceptions of their newborns, describing boys as sturdy and girls of equal weight and size as delicate (Rubin, Provenzano & Luria, 1974). Fathers stimulate, talk to, and even look at their baby boys more than their baby girls and spend more time with infant sons than with infant daughters (Lewis & Weintraub, 1981).

From the second year of life on, fathers tend to have stricter notions of sex-stereotyped behavior and to insist on sex-role conformity more than mothers (Langlois & Downs, 1980; Biller, 1981). Although they may be more overtly punitive toward their sons, they are also more interested in them and more able to encourage their sons' intellectual and social development (Radin, 1981). Fathers' ambitions for their sons focus on achievement and dominance; their ambitions for their daughters focus on submissiveness and pleasing others. In one study of white, middle-class fathers, the wish most commonly expressed for their girls was that they might not become too "bossy" (Aberle & Naegele, 1952).

The effect of this neglect and devaluation of daughters by their fathers has never been incorporated into any developmental theory. When the influence of fathers has been studied at all, it has traditionally been the result of social concern about the effect of the absence of fathers on *boys*. (Boys do indeed demonstrate their vulnerability to paternal abandonment, often in antisocial ways.) It is our impression, based on clinical experience, that daughters often displace their anger at their critical, aloof, neglectful, or absent fathers onto their mothers. Fathers' lack of interest in their daughters is accepted as an inevitable, even natural state of affairs, while any slight on the part of the mothers is bitterly resented. Like everyone else, daughters expect more from mothers.

ESTRANGEMENT IN ADOLESCENCE AND YOUNG ADULTHOOD

Estrangement between mother and daughter reaches its peak during the daughter's adolescent and early adult struggles to develop a satis-factory identity and an intimate relationship. Young women express the greatest scorn for their mothers at this time, the greatest desire to be different from their mothers, and the greatest fear that nevertheless they will turn out to be just like their mothers. The mother's efforts to warn and protect her daughter result in the greatest conflict at this time, for the daughter is interested in exploring her sexuality and is most unwilling to hear her mother's warnings about what she can ex-pect from men. Here is the way two mothers described their ex-perience:

> I consider the adolescent period of my daughter's life difficult, and I have noticed that this is characteristic of a lot of mothers. I did not have this problem with my son. It was very heavy for me, that she had such contempt for me.

> When my daughter was about seventeen she was going out with this guy who was beating her up, and she accepted it; as much as I told her "How could you think of a thing like that? You were never raised that way, where a man could be violent and beat up a woman." She said that was because I was never with working class men and that's what they do. All that meant to me was that when they're that age they're so anxious to get a guy they'll do anything [Arcana, 1979, pp. 208–209].

The mother's response to her daughter's hostility and rejection varies with the extent to which she esteems herself as a woman. Mothers who value themselves highly will find themselves more able to tolerate their daughters' emancipatory struggle than mothers whose own self-esteem is badly injured. The mother's own repressed anger and discontent is unlocked by her daughter's anger, and she may respond with terrifying rage or with depression.

The oppressive conditions under which mothers are condemned to bear and rear their children engender feelings of resentment against both sons and daughters. But there is a particular kind of anger that mothers are apt to feel only in relation to their daughters, an anger that arises in identification. In each stage of her life, the daughter reawakens the mother's own childhood and adolescent struggles to come to terms with her identity as an inferior female, and reopens all the narcissistic wounds the mother suffered in growing up. The daughter challenges and disrupts whatever peace the mother has made with her place in the world. Through the daughter, the mother relives her own rebellion, her own discontent, her own shame at being a woman. In the words of de Beauvoir (1949): "In her daughter the mother does not hail a member of the superior caste; in her she seeks a double. She projects upon her daughter all the ambiguity of her relation with herself" (p. 488).

A mother who has herself been abused, victimized, and neglected may come to see her daughter as a despised and disavowed part of herself, sometimes even as the embodiment of her angry self. For example, a 25-year-old divorced woman who was raising her three children alone described her 7-year-old daughter in the following words: "She was a rotten cranky baby. She's fresh but she gets her way. She's spoiled rotten. She's defiant; she needs discipline. She answers back, she's sassy. She keeps her distance." This mother, herself severely abused in childhood, felt that the best time of her life had been in early adolescence, before she got pregnant, when she felt grown-up and independent enough to defy her mother. Even earlier, she had been a rebellious, tough little girl: "I was a rotten kid. A flip little bitch. I had tantrums. I hit and kicked at bedtime. I told my foster mother it had to be her fault; she spoiled me rotten. I wasn't scared of anybody." The words in which the mother described her scapegoat daughter and her childhood self are virtually the same. In her daughter, she saw the rejected and furious child she had once been. The feelings reawakened by this daughter were so unbearable that she sought to banish them by physically attacking the child, thus reenacting her own experience of abuse.

At the other extreme, mothers may project onto their daughters not the most despised, but the most idealized part of themselves. They may

wish and expect their daughters to be only nurturant, affectionate females, devoid of anger. To the extent that other relationships have
been disappointing, they wish for special closeness, unmarred by aggression and conflict, with a "sweet little girl." Like everyone else,
mothers are quite capable of sentimentalizing females and developing
unattainable expectations of loyalty and devotion from themselves
and their daughters. During their daughters' crises of emancipation,
such mothers experience the inevitable conflict as a cruel disappointment. At the same time, because they labor under an idealized expectation of selflessness and affection, they cannot respond to their
daughters' hostility in kind. Instead, such mothers resolutely try to understand and forgive their daughters. But their refusal to engage in
conflict only exacerbates their daughters' anger by adding an additional burden of guilt. The resulting impasse leaves mothers feeling rejected, covertly furious, and particularly susceptible to depression.

A third form of identification involves the mother's projection onto
the daughter of another kind of idealized self: the liberated woman she
would like to become. We presume that all mothers in this society perceive themselves to some extent as trapped, devalued, and oppressed.
Such feelings are usually only partly conscious; the mother's state of
disappointment is usually ascribed not to the general condition of
women, but rather to the particular choices and circumstances of her
life. Almost all mothers have some fantasies of what they might have
become if they had the possibility of other choices in work, marriage,
and childbearing. Because, in fact, the range of choice for girls and
young women remains a narrow one, mothers continue to experience
anxiety lest their daughters make what they perceive as the wrong
choices. The more dissatisfied a mother feels with her own life, the
greater will be her worry that her daughter might repeat her "mistakes," and the more difficulty she will have tolerating her daughter's
attempt to arrive at her own decisions.

RAPPROCHEMENT BETWEEN MOTHER AND
DAUGHTER

Rapprochement between mothers and daughters generally begins at
the point when the daughter herself becomes a mother—either literally
in giving birth to children, or in committing herself to a prolonged task

of creating and care. During this maturational crisis, the daughter simultaneously assumes a new position of power with respect to her infant and reexperiences in memory her mother's care. As she forms an affectionate attachment to her own child, her own positive experiences of maternal nurturance are reawakened. In the words of Rich (1976):

> Mothers and daughters have always exchanged with each other—beyond the verbally transmitted lore of female survival—a knowledge that is subliminal, subversive, preverbal; the knowledge flowing between two alike bodies, one of which has spent nine months inside the other. The experience of giving birth stirs deep reverberations of her mother in a daughter; women often dream of their mothers during pregnancy and labor [pp. 221–222].

In experiencing the demands and frustrations of motherhood, the daughter may also become more tolerant of her mother's shortcomings.

The birth of a grandchild likewise represents a maturational crisis for the grandmother. This milestone, like menopause or the departure of her children from home, brings her into confrontation with the passage of time and her own aging. In addition, the birth of the grandchild begins a recapitulation of her own experience of mothering. But this time, the social and psychological circumstances of the relationship are profoundly changed. She is no longer primarily responsible for the child's upbringing. She is free, not only from the routine, exhausting duties of child care, but also from the onerous duty to bend her grandchild to the oppressive reality of a violent, male-dominated society. She is no longer the instrument by which her little girls are socialized to acceptance of inferior status.

Moreover, the grandmother herself may be relatively freer from male dominance than she was at an earlier stage of her life. She is no longer required to be "feminine" and sexually pleasing. A certain degree of assertive behavior, forbidden to younger women, is permitted to her. The possibility and risk of pregnancy are over. She is not bound by the duties of child care. She is no longer subservient to her own father. Her husband's power declines relative to hers as his physical strength and economic power diminish. The longer she lives, the more likely it is that she will be a widow. The world of older women is a female world; the endurance of women, and of women's relationships, eclipses the power and importance of men.

As the daughter enters into the childbearing years and the mother leaves them behind, their interlocking maturation creates the possibility of resolving earlier conflicts. The reconciliation between mothers and daughters in later life is not simply a sentimental fantasy, but apparently a common experience. Like other women's relationships, especially those that are relatively harmonious, it has also been almost universally ignored in psychological literature.

One recent exception is a study by Bromberg (1983), who interviewed 75 Jewish mother-daughter pairs. The mothers, ranging in age from 65 to 84, were all living independently (within an hour's travel) of their daughters. The study's primary finding was that

> despite all of the stories about pathological relationships involving terrible hostility between mothers and daughters [there was a] positive connection, interdependence and mutual exchange of a range of affective and instrumental tasks. Even where there were fluctuations in their past or present quality of affective relationship each did what needed to be done for the other. That interaction remained unaffected by the number of external demands made on the daughter through her employment, marital status, or by conjugal family. While generalizability may be limited by the ethnicity of the sample, it must be noted that other researchers working with multi-cultural, ethnic and class groups are reporting similar findings.

As Bromberg aptly remarks, the lack of previously normative studies of aging mothers and their daughters "can be traced to cultural forces which provided only one legitimate content for women: their lives with men." Bromberg also suggests that it is not realistic to view the relationships of later life as merely a reenactment of earlier interaction. "Filial maturity" is a concept that clearly describes the relationship between these adult daughters and their aging mothers.

The reconciliation between mother and daughter and the establishment of a sense of continuity from one generation to the next proceed best when both mother and daughter are able to affirm the value of their common womanhood. Even under the most severe conditions of oppression, lacking land or money, craft or skill, mothers do have an inheritance to hand on to their daughters. The powers of creation, nurturance, affection, and peacefulness are real, even though they are denigrated and sentimentalized by dominant, warring men, and even though these very qualities often render women more vulnerable to exploitation. Women's capacity for attachment, care, and endurance is not evidence of inferiority but of courage and strength. In reclaiming this heritage, daughters overcome their anger and disappointment in their mothers and discover a sustaining source of pride. In the words of Walker (1983):

> I notice that it is only when my mother is working in her flowers that she is radiant, almost to the point of being invisible – except as Creator: hand and eye. She is involved in work her soul must have. Ordering the universe in the image of her personal conception of Beauty.
>
> Her face, as she prepares the Art that is her gift, is a legacy of respect she leaves to me, for all that illuminates and cherishes life. She has handed down respect for the possibilities – and the will to grasp them [pp. 241–242].

REFERENCES

Aberle, D. F., & Naegele, K. K. (1952), Middle class fathers' occupational role and attitudes towards children. *Amer. J. Orthopsychiat.*, 22: 336–378.

Ainsworth, M., Blehar, M., Waters, E., & Wall, S. (1978), *Patterns of Attachment.* Hillsdale, NJ: Lawrence Erlbaum Associates.

Arcana, J. (1979), *Our Mothers' Daughters.* Berkeley: Shameless Hussy Press.

Bayley, N., & Schaefer, E. (1964), Correlations of maternal and child behaviors with development of mental abilities. *Monographs of the Society for Research in Child Development*, 29 (97).

Beauvoir, S. de (1949), *The Second Sex.* New York: Bantam, 1961.

Biller, H. (1981), The father and sex role development. In *The Role of the Father in Child Development* (2nd ed.), ed. M. Lamb. New York: Wiley.

Brenneis, C. (1968), Differences in male and female styles in manifest content. *Dissertation Abstracts*, 28: 3056.

Bromberg, E. (1983), Mother-daughter relationships in later life. *J. Gerontologic. Soc. Work*, 6.

Chesler, P. (1972), *Women and Madness.* New York: Doubleday.

Chodorow, N. (1978), *The Reproduction of Mothering: Psychoanalysis and the Sociology of Gender.* Berkeley: University of California Press.

Chodorow, N. (1979), Feminism and difference: Gender, relation, and difference in psychoanalytic perspective. *Socialist Review*, 46: 51–69.

Finkelhor, D. (1979), *Sexually Victimized Children.* New York: Free Press.

Flax, J. (1978), The conflict between nurturance and autonomy in mother-daughter relationships and within feminism. *Feminist Studies*, 4: 171–189.

Friday, N. (1977), *My Mother/Myself*. New York: Dell.

Galenson, E., & Roiphe, H. (1980), The preoedipal development of the boy. Paper presented to a panel on Gender and Gender Role at the Annual Meeting of the American Psychological Association.

Hall, C., & Van de Castle, R. (1966), *The Content Analysis of Dreams*. New York: Appleton-Century-Croft.

Herman, J. (1981), *Father-Daughter Incest*. Cambridge, MA: Harvard University Press.

Hoffman, L. W. (1977), Changes in family roles, socialization, and sex differences. *Amer. Psychologist*, 32: 644–658.

Horney, K. (1926), The flight from womanhood: The masculinity complex in women as viewed by men and by women. In: *Feminine Psychology*, ed. H. Kelman. New York: Norton, 1967.

Jensen, G. D., Bobbitt, R. A., & Gordon, B. N. (1968), Sex differences in the development of independence in infant monkeys. *Behaviour*, 30: 1–14.

Kagan, J., & Moss, H. (1962), *Birth to Maturity: A Study in Psychological Development*. New York: Wiley.

Korner, A. (1969), Neonatal startles, smiles, erections and reflex sucks as related to age, state and individuality. *Child Devel.*, 40: 1039–1053.

Lamb, M. (Ed.) (1981), *The Role of the Father in Child Development* (2nd ed.). New York: Wiley & Sons.

Langlois, J. H., & Downs, A. C. (1980), Mothers, fathers, and peers as socialization agents of sex-typed play behaviors in young children. *Child Devel.* 51: 1217–1247.

Larson, L., & Knapp, R. (1968), Sex differences in symbolic conceptions of the Deity. *Journal of Projective Techniques and Personality Assessment*, 28: 303–306.

Lewis, H. (1976), *Psychic War in Men and Women*. New York: New York University Press.

Lewis, M., & Weintraub, M. (1981), The role of the father in cognitive, academic, and intellectual development. In: *The Role of the Father in Child Development* (2nd ed.), ed. M. Lamb. New York: Wiley.

Maccoby, E., & Jacklin, C. (1974), *The Psychology of Sex Differences*. Stanford: Stanford University Press.

Mahler, M. S., Pine, F., & Bergman, A. (1975), *The Psychological Birth of the Human Infant: Symbiosis and Individuation*. New York: Basic Books.

Miller, J. B. (1976), *Toward a New Psychology of Women*. Boston: Beacon Press.

Mitchell, G., & Brandt, E. M. (1970), Behavioral differences related to experience of mother and sex of infant in rhesus monkeys. *Develop. Psychol.*, 3: 149.

Moss, H. (1974), Early sex differences in mother-infant interaction. In: *Sex, Differences in Behavior*, ed. K. Friedman, R. Reichert, & R. Vandeweile. New York: Wiley.

Mussen, P. (1969), Early sex-role development. In: *Handbook of Socialization Research*, ed. D. Godin. Chicago: Rand McNally.

Oetzel, R. (1966), Annotated bibliography and classified summary of research in sex differences. In: *The Development of Sex Differences*, ed. E. Maccoby. Stanford: Stanford University Press, pp. 223–321, 323–351.

Pederson, F. (Ed.) (1980), *The Father-Infant Relationship: Observational Studies in a Family Setting*. New York: Praeger.

Radin, N. (1981), The role of the father in cognitive, academic, and intellectual development. In: *The Role of the Father in Child Development* (2nd ed.), ed. M. Lamb. New York: Wiley.

Rich, A. (1976), *Of Woman Born: Motherhood as Experience and Institution*. New York: Bantam.

Rubin, J., Provenzano, F., & Luria, Z. (1974), The eye of the beholder: Parents' views on sex of newborns. *Amer. J. Orthopsychiat.*, 44: 512–519.

Russell, D. (1983), Incidence and prevalence of intrafamilial and extrafamilial sexual abuse of children. *Child Abuse Negl.*, 7: 133–146.

Sackett, G. (1974), Sex differences in rhesus monkeys following varied rearing experiences. In: *Sex Differences in Behavior*, ed. R. Friedman, R. Reichert & R. Vandeweile. New York: Wiley.

Sacks, K. (1979), *Sisters and Wives*. Westport, CT: Greenwood Press.

Sanday, P. (1981), *Female Power and Male Dominance: On the Origins of Social Inequality*. Cambridge, Eng.: Cambridge University Press.

Sears, R., Rau, L., & Alpert, R. (1965), *Identification and Child-Rearing*. Stanford: Stanford University Press.

Simner, M. (1971), Newborn response to the cry of another infant. *Development. Psychol.*, 5: 136–150.

Smith-Rosenberg, C. (1975), The female world of love and ritual: Relations between women in nineteenth century America. *Signs: J. Wom. Cult. Soc.*, 1: 1–29.

Walker, A. (1983), *In Search of our Mothers' Gardens*. New York: Harcourt Brace Jovanovich.

TODAY'S WOMAN

8
Reproductive Motivations and Contemporary Feminine Development

Susan L. Williams, Ph.D.

An individual's choice to become a parent has been labeled the ". . . most fateful decision of your life," in that it is "unpredictable and irrevocable" (Whelan, 1975, p. 14). This essay attempts to elucidate how this decision is confounded and complicated for the woman in contemporary American society. It is a decision that many consider, wrongly and simplistically, to be "primarily emotional" (Whelan, 1975, p. 13). Rather, a woman's relationship to her reproductive capacities is fraught not only with the mysteries of her own unconscious and the conflicts of her own personal familial history, but also with a social, political, and economic history of patriarchy and oppression. It is dangerously reductionistic to consider a woman's choice of motherhood to be singularly personal, because direct economic, political and social constraints on the reproductive options available to different groups of women affect, and are affected by, a range of cultural and social conditions: women's own consciousness and perceptions of their medical and sexual needs, the kinds of sexual and family relations they have to rely on, and the strategies they adopt to negotiate sexual and familial conflicts about birth control and childbearing [Petchesky, 1981, p. 60].

In short, there is no single or simple route that a woman travels to come to her decision to have a child or remain child free.

This paper attempts to delineate some of the complex routes women travel toward their reproductive decisions. Several theses will be offered. First, reproduction of the species exists at the intersection of the personal, the biological, social, and political. A useful theory of reproductive motives must address not only all these arenas of human functioning, but must account for their interactions. Second, the recent development of contraceptive methodology has drastically changed the material conditions under which a woman matures and comes to her reproductive decisions. This external (social) change mandates a concomitant internal (psychological) change – the development of psychic structures that specifically regulate reproduction. These intrapsychic alterations are evidenced most particularly by female patients, and clinical illustrations will be offered. Finally, although old and new theories of reproductive motivation offer insights and elaborations on components of women's reproduction, they do not fully explicate a working paradigm of women's motivations to have children. This essay offers a beginning in revising, formulating, and reformulating how we have come to understand a woman's relationship to reproduction.

HISTORICAL AND SOCIAL PERSPECTIVES ON REPRODUCTION

... the long and violent campaign against voluntary motherhood ... [Rich, 1979, p. 263].

It is of profound significance that the female of the species reproduces. Although she does not do this alone, she accepts, through her biology and anatomy, an enormous responsibility for the perpetuation of the species. This responsibility not only includes conception, gestation, and birthing of offspring, but more often than not, involves caretaking of the young.

For the human being, it is of profound *psychological* significance that the choice for parenthood, and thus a woman's control over her reproduction, is a relatively new arena of biological control (Russo, 1976). Gordon (1976) presents a cogent analysis of the history of contraception, tracing its roots back to the folklore and folk culture of women. Magical rituals and symbols, such as incantations, potions that were believed to induce abortions, and prayer, appear to be women's first attempts at controlling conception (Gordon, 1976, pp. 30–31). In preindustrial societies, forms of the "rhythm" method have been documented, along with coitus interruptus, and abstinence. However, as Gordon states, these methods result "in hit-or-miss population limitation" (p. 32). Consequently, infanticide was often viewed as a viable means of population control. Whether infanticide was utilized for economic reasons or to increase mobility in nomadic tribes, in societies in which it was a legal practice, "men almost always governed its application" (p. 33). Gordon goes on to say that "Abortion is just a step away from infanticide," and that "Almost all preindustrial societies accepted abortion" (p. 35). Abortion and coitus interruptus appear to be two of the most common forms of birth control in history.

Contraceptive methods were "used for several thousand years before Christ" and "the fact that skills at preventing conception were so advanced so long ago tells us something about how much people wanted control over reproduction" (Gordon, 1976, p. 26). It is noteworthy, however, how recently contraception was addressed by the medical community. To say that contraception has been utilized for centuries is misleading, because more often than not, contraception was controlled by men or "practiced illegally; its technology passed on by an underground of midwives and wisewomen" (p. 26).

Margaret Sanger coined the term "birth control" in 1915; yet it was not until the 1920s that the medical community had correctly recorded ovulation (Gordon, 1976, p. 206), and it was not until the 1930s that most American physicians understood the ovulation/menstruation cycle (p. 101). Finally, the relatively recent development of the birth control pill in the 1960s by Carl Djerrassi ushered in for American women what has been labelled the "contraceptive revolution" (Whelan, 1975, p. 11).

Throughout history and in the present day, we see both women's wishes to exercise control over conception and the multiple forces that fight against that control. Patriarchy, religion, government, and education are all mobilized to keep contraception out of the hands of women. The present-day legal and social attacks on women's right to make their own reproductive decisions is but a continuation of this historical tradition.

This historical and political lack of control over one's own body creates an important psychological reality for all women. As Fenichel (1945) states, "The character of man is socially determined" (p. 464). His use of sexist language notwithstanding, Fenichel's point remains, as many others have concurred, that men *and women* exist only within the group, or social context. He goes on to say:

> . . . Insight into the formative power of social forces upon individual minds does not require any change in Freud's concepts of instincts. . . . Different "biological constitutions" contain manifold possibilities; yet they are not realities but potentialities. It is experience, that is, the cultural conditions, that transforms potentialities into realities, that shapes the real mental structure of man by forcing his instinctual demands into certain directions, by favoring some of them and blocking others, and even by turning parts of them against the rest [p. 588].

Thus, women's "biological constitutions" — that is, their reproductive capabilities — are not "realities," but "potentialities." A woman's capacity to procreate is but a potential in a society that offers means of controlling conception. When a society obstructs a woman's control over her own body, this potential becomes a forced reality. In such a social order, there is no such thing as voluntary motherhood, only a policy of pronatalism and what has been labeled "coercive motherhood" (Bernard, 1974).[1]

---

[1] In my experience, many clinicians have witnessed in the consulting room the effects of coercive motherhood: women who did not want to be mothers but who through ignorance, poverty, or the unavailability of contraception, were "saddled" with pregnancy after pregnancy; children and adults who were told they were "accidents" or unplanned pregnancies and are now riddled with a basic sense of not being wanted, desired, or valued. A colleague has related a case of a severely schizophrenic boy whose mother reported that she had attempted three self-abortions during her pregnancy. (This is not to say that all unwanted children are marred by their origins. Certainly, compensatory measures on the part of the parent play an important part in the upbringing of an originally unwanted child.)

Today's woman lives in a time that offers readily available means of birth control.[2] Most likely, the mother of today's woman was not brought up in such an atmosphere, and certainly her grandmother's options were even more limited. A woman growing up in the early 1900s most likely tried to prevent conception by means of coitus interruptus, abstinence, rhythm, or illegal or self-induced abortion. Unwanted pregnancy was to be feared, medically and economically. Women's sense of control over this ubiquitous threat was shaky; much was left to chance. The woman of the mid-twentieth century had considerably more control over reproduction. Armed with her diaphragm and spermicides, as well as the old methods, she was able to exercise more conscious intention over her reproduction than her counterpart of the 1920s. Yet, we know from clinical and anecdotal data that this woman did not do a great deal to educate her daughter about contraception. Although this lack of dialogue between the mother and daughter of the 1950s can be attributed to taboos against sex education, it was not until the "sexual revolution" of the 1960s that contraception came out of the closet. Still, we see clinically mothers of the 1980s who are struggling with sexual and contraceptive information. Do they make contraception available to their adolescent daughter? If so, at what age? If so, what method? Herein lies the intersection between women's sexuality and their reproductive capabilities. The mother becomes the conduit of information about sex and contraception for her maturing daughter. Silence on such subjects becomes a statement that leaves the daughter to fend for herself on a major developmental process: the regulation and understanding of her sexuality and her capacity for motherhood.[3]

---

[2] I agree with others who have stated that there exists an economics of contraception (Michaelson, 1981). Economic conditions create a social strata of white, middle- and upper-class women who have obtained biological control over their reproduction, while the working-class woman is still encumbered by de facto involuntary motherhood. However, the political economy of motherhood must be left for another analysis.

[3] Although patients are able to report voluminous examples of toilet training, dietary regulation, taboos against masturbatory or sexual activity, and general self-regulation, it continues to amaze me how many women (and men) cannot recall any contraceptive information conveyed by their parents. Such anecdotal material is exceedingly sparse and, in my experience more common to men—warnings from the father not to "knock up" some girl, for example. Fathers seem more willing to pass on the "right" to sexuality granted by the condom, than mothers are to acknowledge their daughters' sexuality and therefore their capacity to become pregnant. It is well documented that women's

For many women, this newly obtained control over reproduction brings a challenge, if not an outright crisis in their decision for or against motherhood. Contemporary women are still conflicted in their development of psychic structures to negotiate the control of their reproduction. The alteration in the material conditions of society by the introduction of available means of birth control introduces, through processes of internalization, a new arena of required self-regulatory mechanisms. For all human beings, self-regulation through zonal development – that is control over one's bodily functions – contributes to identity. Men and women alike must deal with conflicts involving evacuative functions, feeding, sexual orientation and expression, and body ego. Yet, because of the psychological and biological consequences of a potential pregnancy, a woman's relationship to reproduction is markedly different than that of a man:

> Roughly 400 times in her life a woman must make a sober choice. Either she will leave herself open to pregnancy, or she will deny her uterus its animating powers. For a woman there is no such thing as casual noncommitment. If she wants to wander free, it requires an act of negation every month. And a good deal of psychic energy is involved in that denial. She can never simply not think about it because that in itself is a way of tipping her destiny [Sheehy, 1976, pp. 238–239].

The development of effective contraception offers the contemporary woman many avenues to express her reproductive drive. A woman may postpone childbearing or eliminate it altogether; she may prevent conception with the magical omnipotence of the birth control pill or an intrauterine device (IUD); or she can decisively, in anticipation of intercourse, use a method of contraception that involves vaginal insertion, such as the diaphragm, spermicidal creams or jellies, the cervical cap, or the cervical sponge. Finally, she may elect to have her partner use contraception. Although these decisions are affected by cultural, social, political, economic, and religious conditions, each woman must decide for herself how she chooses to exercise control over her reproductive capacity.

---

sexuality is less sanctioned by society than men's. The irony is that although men might receive more warnings about the perils of impregnating a woman, contraceptive methodology is almost solely designed for women, the condom and the vasectomy being the two exceptions.

CLINICAL DATA

Extending the complexities of the historical, political, economic and social factors integral to reproductive decision-making to each woman's unique psychology, we find that

> it is true that individual psychology is concerned with the individual man and explores the paths by which he seeks to find satisfaction for his instinctual impulses; but only rarely and under certain exceptional conditions is individual psychology in a position to disregard the relations of this individual to others. In the individual's mental life someone else is invariably involved, as a model, as an object, as a helper, as an opponent; and so from the very first individual psychology, in this extended but entirely justifiable sense of the words, is at the same time social psychology as well [Freud, 1921, p. 69].

Female patients manifest and present their individual and social psychology relevant to the topic of reproduction and contraception in emblematic ways. For example, two adolescent patients, both 18 years old, reported that they used no contraception during intercourse because, in essence, no one had ever talked to them about it. Both young women were raised in an urban area, attended public schools, and began treatment in the early 1980s. Although they were both consciously aware of their capacity to become pregnant, their ideas about contraception were marked by defensive confusion, denial, and magical thinking. In essence, these two women understood the physiology of reproduction, yet neither one of them had any sense of control or self-regulation over this phenomenon.

Reproductive Conflicts and Contraceptive Methodology

Conflicts about reproduction often emerge in the choice of birth control methods. Adult women patients who use contraception and who have changed their method of birth control from the pill or IUD to cervical block devices, such as the diaphragm, report a growing awareness of both their bodies and the psychic concerns involved in their sexual activity. They frequently complain of diminished spontaneity in their sexual life because of the new method of contraception. Although representing a realistic concern, these complaints also seem in many cases to represent resentment and anger at bringing into consciousness a heretofore predominantly unconscious process—namely, the splitting off of their reproductive conflicts. Such dissociation is frequently enhanced by routinely taking a pill each morning or evening, disconnected from the actual sexual activity. Likewise, IUDs are inserted by a physician and are passively contained by the woman. In contrast, the conscious intention and action involved in manually inserting a contraceptive device prior to intercourse confronts the woman psychologically and phenomenologically with the dilemmas of reproduction.

Thus, in the routinized behavior of ingesting a pill, the meaning of the act of contraception can be lost. Similarly, women who "don't think" about their IUD incorporate it, literally and figuratively. These acts of dissociation raise issues involving internalization and decision making. Schafer (1968) states that internalization "refers to all those processes by which the subject transforms real or imagined regulatory interactions with his environment, and real or imagined characteristics of his environment, into inner regulations and characteristics" (p. 9). Internalization encompasses the processes of incorporation, introjection, and identification. Specifically, incorporation

> may be said to refer to ideas that one has taken a part or all of another person (or creature or thing) into one's self corporeally, and, further, that this taking in is the basis of certain novel, disturbing, and/or gratifying sensations, impulses, feelings, and actions of one's own and of correlated changes in one's experience of the environment. This set of ideas is usually unconscious . . . [Schafer, 1968, p. 20].

By definition, all contraceptive devices are introduced into the body. However, use of the birth control pill or the IUD seems to create in some women a stronger and more unconscious incorporation, because their utilization is constant, whether intercourse occurs or not. In using a cervical block method of contraception, the "self" acts on the body. The woman establishes a dichotomy between the self, who at each opportunity for conception elects to not conceive, and the body, which is able to conceive. This act of volition is presented with each sexual act—a challenge to choose, to think. In using a method like an IUD, in contrast, the "self" is not required to think and therefore decide. The differentiation between the self/body who can conceive and the self/body who uses contraception is blurred. Rather, the self/body is one that cannot conceive. The woman is unable to stop the mechanism of the IUD without outside medical assistance. Thus, she has incorporated a device through her vaginal orifice that alters her self-representation. Whereas the IUD is foreign to the self/body who can conceive, the device is syntonic with the self/body who is essentially infertile. In contrast, the self/body of a woman who uses a cervical block method of contraception consists of a self who can conceive and a body that is temporarily and volitionally rendered infertile. It is not surprising then that one patient reports, "Oh, I can't get pregnant, I *have* an IUD," in contrast to another woman patient who states, "I *use* a diaphragm."

There appears to be a psychologically differentiated meaning to actively creating a barrier between a woman's internal self/body and her sexual partner. The meaning of this act of barricading the cervix against both one's sexual partner and one's capacity to conceive is highly variable; however, certain themes emerge from patients' self-reports. These include concerns involving the exploration and awareness of one's own body, the concepts of "inner" and "outer," and purposefulness and responsibility in one's behavior. Finally, the use of vaginally inserted contraceptive devices offers the woman a means of acting out conflicts that use of the birth control pill and the IUD often preclude, such as forgetting and rationalizing.

Meanings of Contraceptive Failure

Although "contraceptive failure" is an appropriate medical term, it is psychologically inaccurate. The "failure" essentially refers to forgetting or rationalizing. In two such clinical cases, the women became pregnant after a marked loss. One woman "forgot" to use her diaphragm after the death of her mother. The second patient failed to remember to insert her diaphragm before sex after a divorce from her husband of seven years. Both women rationalized this "failure" to use their diaphragm by thinking that the body would magically cooperate with the thought—that they did not want to become pregnant.

Both these patients stated they had no conscious intention of becoming pregnant, and both elected to terminate these "unwanted" pregnancies. However, the decisions about their pregnancies were highly conflictual and ambivalent. They both wished to fill up the "hole" left by their object loss and feared being pregnant with a damaged, bad object. Psychologically speaking, the "failure" of contraception represented a defeat for only one part of the personality—the conscious wish to avoid pregnancy. A competing part of the personality, the unconscious wish, triumphed. The unconscious wish included the belief that the loss of the real objects could be denied by the pregnancy. Thus, the women were in a sense conceiving and incorporating a dead mother or a lost husband—which led to ambivalent fantasies of being pregnant with a dead or poisonous object as well as a longed for, beloved object. After their abortions, each woman mourned the aborted object, representing the idealized mother or lost husband. Clearly, neither woman became pregnant because she wanted a child; rather, she longed for what she had already lost. In essence, these women were unconsciously deluded into a belief in compensation and replacement.

When the Partner Uses the Contraception

Some women choose to have their partners use the contraception. In one such case, the patient's object relations, her experience of herself as a damaged, unimportant female in society, and her defensive structure were neatly captured in her relationship to sex and contraception.

The patient, Ms. A., had originally come into treatment because of problems that she viewed, quite concretely, as "stress-related headaches." She had originally sought biofeedback treatment for these headaches, and only after their slight and temporary amelioration was she open to a referral for verbal, face-to-face psychotherapy. She was remarkably unpsychological in her approach to herself and to her world. She lived in a world where things *were* what they appeared to be. She had almost no curiosity and certainly no delight in inquiry and exploration. Her relationship to her husband was markedly flat and unexciting; yet the patient did not complain of boredom. This existence was merely a matter of fact: "That's the way things are." The patient's work in computer science provided her with her only limited sense of gratification, which stemmed from her competence and the approval of peers and superiors.

Ms. A. was the only daughter of a socialite mother and a financially successful businessman father. Her upbringing was primarily handled by maids, who apparently approached their charge as a job. Ms. A. herself approached almost every endeavor in her life as a job requiring mastery, and this became a theme in the treatment. The patient perceived her father as extremely powerful, driven by greed and the need to dominate. He treated his wife and daughter as a business. Her perceptions of her mother mostly involved appearance – her mother's job in life was to put on a show, through entertaining, socializing and dress. Her father showed no respect for her mother's endeavors. He frequently ridiculed her for her frivolous and "feminine" pursuits.

During the course of her treatment, Ms. A. elaborated on the pleasure she obtained from knowing that "nothing would be dumped into her" because she insisted that her husband use a condom. She was relieved by the artificial boundary of the condom and could only experience orgasm when her partner used one. It seemed that this woman felt threatened by using cervical barrier methods of contraception because this put her in touch with an internal orifice and bodily contents. By association, it put her in touch with her internal life. Anxiety about her own bodily contents was prevalent, accompanied by many fantasies of something bad and rotting existing within her. Her insistence that her partner be the one to use the contraception provided this patient with an external boundary between herself and what was perceived as a threatening and poisonous penis. In short, the condom served as a means of transforming a dangerous part object into a safe one. This artificial membrane protected her bodily and psychic integrity. In this manner the patient was able to defend against her self-percepts as a contaminated and bad woman and to deny her rage at and fear of men. Thus, what appeared to be a sexually active and well-adjusted young woman gave way to a woman who was bitterly angry toward men and full of self-hate. It is noteworthy that when this patient became pregnant for the first time, she miscarried. Her second pregnancy was fraught with many physical difficulties, and she complained bitterly of severe morning sickness, self-loathing, and anger toward her sexual partner.

Thus, the patient, by means of very strong identifications with both her parents, came to live life by "going through the motions." Anything internal was feared, dirty, and dark. This was expressed concretely by her insistence on using sanitary napkins instead of tampons. Penile penetration was also feared – both because of the feared, dominating, ridiculing male object and the loathsome condition of her interior. It is no wonder that sex and motherhood were merely dutiful for this young woman – again, a matter of fact, something one simply does. Ms. A. found no real joy or excitement in any of these pursuits.

Conflicts Manifested in the Transference

In another case, a woman expressed many of her conflicts about her reproductive capabilities and her femininity through the transference. The patient, Ms. C., came into treatment at age 38 because of intermittent drug use, problems in her relationships with men and women, and disruptive experiences of derealization and depersonalization. The patient had been married three times, each time to verbally or physically abusive men, and each marriage ended in divorce. When Ms. C. entered into psychotherapy, coming four times a week, she was living with a man who was five years her junior, as well as with her 7 year-old son, the product of her previous marriage.

Ms. C. had been raised in an affluent community in northern California. She was the second among five siblings, with an older sister, a younger sister, and two younger brothers. She described her mother as extremely petite and feminine, a homemaker who never worked outside the home—in short, a devoted mother who spent all her time tending to her immaculate home and to her five children. Ms. C. described her father as an ambitious, successful corporate executive who had little involvement with his children and would come home after 12-hour days expecting his dinner ready and peace and quiet. Ms. C. saw her mother as extremely accommodating, putting up with her father's demands in quiet, martyred suffering.

Ms. C.'s eldest sibling had been diagnosed as schizophrenic during her adolescence and had spent much of her life in and out of psychiatric facilities. The younger siblings seemed to lead marginal existences and were unsuccessful in their work and relationships. All Ms. C's siblings manifested problems with impulse control, whether through alcoholism, drug addiction, or bulimia.

One of Ms. C.'s presenting problems involved her current love relationship. She described her lover as the first man she had been involved with who did not abuse her. He worked at a rather boring job and was moderately successful. He seemed commited to a relationship with the patient and had spoken of marriage and having children with Ms. C. Although Ms. C. reported feeling genuinely cared about for the first time in her life, she complained of being unexcited by this "nice guy."

Initially, Ms. C. was opposed to having any more children, but about seven months into treatment, she began fantasizing about having one more child with her lover. Her fantasized child was a beautiful, petite, feminine little girl. Although Ms. C. was considered quite beautiful, she was a large, statuesque woman. All her life she had received much attention as a result of her good looks, yet she never felt "feminine" or attractive. She was convinced that to be "pretty," a woman must be small. Ms. C. also regretted not pursuing a formal education and felt lacking in intelligence. Finally, she regretted that she had not pursued treatment earlier in life and felt that she had wasted much of her time and potential. Consequently, Ms. C., in her fantasy, believed that she would offer her daughter the best education and would raise her, with my help, in a "conscious" and "enlightened" manner. It seemed that for this patient, the fantasized daughter represented a union with a safe and "good" object – her lover – and, more important, an idealized and split off part of her own personality. This fantasy daughter was the embodiment of Ms. C.'s femininity, while Ms. C. consciously viewed herself to be large and masculine.

During this phase of treatment, the transference was overtly positive, marked by references of great hostility. Ms. C. would occasionally make references to my being "too small," plain, frail, sickly, and unstylish in appearance. She produced a fantasy in which I was unmarried, lived with a maiden aunt, read voraciously, and had no social life and certainly no sex life. Clearly, she saw nothing about me that was admirable or enviable. However, I made up for all that I lacked in appearance to Ms. C. by being a devoted, hard-working "lady doctor."

Fifteen months into treatment, Ms. C. was unexpectedly hospitalized, resulting in an emergency hysterectomy. She missed three weeks of consultations, and returned to treatment looking drawn, affectless, and depressed. She did not verbalize any depression or sense of loss, however. Instead, she spoke of the relief she experienced not only because she had received such swift and expert medical treatment, but because she would never have to worry about an unwanted pregnancy or bother with menstruation again. To hear this patient, one would think a hysterectomy was a serendipitous godsend, but to look at her, one would gather quite a different impression. Ms. C. spent little time addressing her hysterectomy and quickly moved on to other preoccupations, namely, her job, her son, and her relationship with her lover.

It was not until her third year of treatment with me that Ms. C. mourned the loss of her reproductive capacity. Her mourning was ushered in through the transference material. In analyzing the negative transference, a very different picture of me emerged. Ms. C. complained of feeling terribly envious of me and viewed me as all that she was not. I was felt to be pretty, feminine, and, most important, petite. Ms. C. frequently complimented me on my dress or appearance and wanted to steer her sessions in the direction of "girl talk," emphasizing clothes, makeup, and hair styles. To make matters worse, my Ph.D. was the hallmark of a formal education and my practice a sign of success. Ms. C. began to worry that I might become pregnant. This fantasy was unbearable for her. She imagined that I would come out to the waiting room one day in maternity clothes and that she would end treatment then and there. Of course, I would have a daughter who would be the ideal, feminine little girl of Ms. C.'s earlier fantasies.

Ms. C. believed that her hysterectomy had made more of a man out of her than she already was. She felt alternately empty and filled up with something that was decaying and rotting. For her, I was already pregnant: pregnant with reproductive organs, femininity, education, life, and hope. She was hopelessly empty. The fact that she had had a child was of little consolation. She felt that her son was damaged like her. She said that she did not know what she was doing when she had him and bitterly attacked herself as a mother.

In exploring this material with Ms. C., it became clear that Ms. C. had always believed she could never measure up to her petite and feminine mother. There was only room for one woman in Ms. C.'s family, and the patient and her mother seemed to agree that it was the mother. Moreover, there was only one definition of femininity: to be a petite mother. Although the patient had always felt masculine, she had at least been able to reproduce and by having a daughter perhaps create someone who was feminine. The loss of her reproductive capacities left Ms. C. with no hope for a creative outlet. Ms. C. was finally able to redefine her ideas about femininity, coming up with her own notions involving strength, softness, creativity, and the generation of life in all her activities.

THEORETICAL CONSIDERATIONS

Definitions of Motherhood: The False Dichotomy

Throughout history there have always been women who were mothers and women who were without children. With the increased options for expressing one's relationship to reproduction, however, the distinction between these two categories has become more marked. More and more women are electing to postpone childbearing until their thirties, creating a growing class of women in their twenties who are childless. Moreover, some women forego motherhood alto-gether. The psychological literature contains many investigations of these women (Popenoe, 1936; Garland & Poloma, 1971; House-knecht, 1977; Ory, 1978; Fabe & Wikler, 1979; Williams, 1980). The choice of parenthood – how one woman elects maternity while her co-hort opts for childlessness – presents an array of psychological and so-ciological questions revolving around a woman's relationship to her own sexuality, her parental identifications, her assessment of herself as creative and achieving, her sense of herself as mother or nonmother as well as her religiousness, socioeconomic status, and educational level.

On its face, the distinction between women as childed or not is natu-ral and makes sense. The states of motherhood and childlessness are contrasted ubiquitously in the psychological and sociological litera-ture, art, literature, poetry, and music. Historically, the joys and fulfill-ment of motherhood have been publicly endorsed to the extent of be-coming dogma, whereas the failure and shame of nonmotherhood or infertility are viewed as a personal and social tragedy. Although the so-cial zeitgeist seems to be changing to some extent, the polarization of mother and childless woman still prevails. This dichotomy serves only to describe an external condition, however, leaving much to be desired in describing a woman's internal, psychic condition. As Rich (1976) puts it:

> The "childless woman" and the "mother" are a false polarity . . . . There are no such simple categories.
>
> . . . Is a woman who bore a baby she could not keep a "childless" woman? Am I, whose children are grown-up, who come and go as I will, unchilded as compared to younger women still pushing prams, hur-rying home to feedings, waking at night to a child's cry? What makes us mothers? The care of small children? The physical changes of pregnancy and birth? The years of nurture? What of the woman who, never having been pregnant, begins lactating when she adopts an infant? What of the woman who stuffs her newborn into a bus-station locker and goes numbly back to her "child-free" life? What of the woman who, as the eldest girl in a large family, has practically raised her younger sisters and brothers, and then has entered a convent [pp. 254–255]?

Rich's questions speak to the problem of reductionism surrounding the topic of motherhood. We have come to define motherhood by means of biological determinism. The adoptive mother appears to be the one exception to this definition; we consider her to be a mother even though she has not biologically produced any offspring.

Wyatt (1976) points out that the motivations for reproduction are pluralistic, both collective and idiosyncratic, conscious and unconscious, and that they are fluid, in that they change over time. We can speculate that a woman's motivation for having a first child differs from her reasons for having a second or for adopting. These differences can and are influenced by social forces such as peer pressure—for example, attitudes toward small or large families. It is also common to hear that a couple wants a second child for reasons of the child's gender; they may have a boy and now want to "try for" a girl. A woman who was an only child may elect to have numerous pregnancies as a reaction against her own lack of siblings. A child of Holocaust survivors reports that she wants to have a lot of children as a means of replenishing her ethnic group. A female patient reports not wanting children because her own childhood was so traumatic that she is certain she would be a "bad" mother.

Although these are conscious, stated reasons for variation in family planning, we can glean from these rationales the multidetermination of choices regarding parenthood and the fluidity of these choices over time. *Reproduction is a developmental process.* Simple categorizations of women as mothers or nonmothers thus lose intrapsychic as well as social significance. Child-free women may have strong propensities to nurture, succor, and create and still express these qualities outside the role of mother. These "mothering" drives are often exhibited in friendships with other women. Or, the woman may channel mothering qualities into her work, whether in a creative endeavor or through achieving a particular goal. Veevers (1971) points out that dichotomizing women along the lines of motherhood and nonmotherhood was not even useful in his research on infertility. He found that whereas one infertile woman may pursue *every* avenue available to her so that she might conceive, another woman in the same position may quickly stop the search for medical intervention and accept her infertility, never seeking to alter it. How then would we categorize these two women? Clearly, both are "child free." Clearly, both have some chance, no matter how minimal, to seek out motherhood. Yet, one woman vigorously pursues her chance, while the other "resigns" herself. We must conclude that categorizing these women on the biological level of fertility is not elucidating. Rather the drive toward creating, whether by means of procreation or other avenues, exists along a continuum for all women. In this light, the reproductive drive is viewed generally as a creative drive, an expression of Eros.

To speak of reproduction as simply one expression of a greater libidinal aim, then, is to more clearly articulate a dialectical process. The expression of the life instinct, Eros, is not, as we are led to believe, simply reduced for women to the production of life. The drive toward life is expressed in creativity, curiosity, exploration, and expansion. We have psychologically endorsed this for men, for men are not subject to the dichotomy of father-nonfather. This same endorsement must apply to women. Any theoretically sound understanding of reproductive motivation for either sex must grapple with the multiple expressions of libidinal drives.

Existing Models of Reproductive Motivation

Psychoanalysis has struggled to create a paradigm to explain women's reproductive motives. In my opinion, a comprehensive theory is still forthcoming.

Freud (1925) put forth the original psychoanalytic hypothesis regarding women's unconscious motivation to bear children. At the center of his argument is the notion of the female's penis envy. The young female child notes a physical state of castration. She blames her mother for this state of affairs. In doing so, she turns away from her primary libidinal cathexis to the mother and embraces the father, the possessor of the penis. In her oedipal seduction of the father, Freud believed the little girl is attempting to reconcile herself to her castrated fate. As an adult, she seeks out as object choice a male who is able to impregnate her, and she is able to produce, through the mechanism of displacement, the fantasized phallus — a baby. If the infant is a male, the fantasy is concretized; the woman literally has produced a penis of her own.

At the crux of this thesis rests Freud's ideas about identification, that is, the distinction between "being" and "having" (Freud, 1921). The female behaves like the mother (being) which constitutes the feminine identification. But her object choice, the male, indicates what she chooses to have. For Freud, the woman's having the man as an object choice denotes having a child.

Freud's theories about women are admittedly incomplete. His understanding of the girl's feminine identifications with the mother indicates
that Freud believes that women want to *be* like the mother. However,
his explanation of what the woman obtains (has) from being like her
mother – the aim of the identification – is a point of great confusion in
his writing.

Discussion of problems with Freud's explanation for the wish for a
child are well represented in psychoanalytic and feminist literature
(see, for example, Strouse, 1974). A quid pro quo of sorts has been established by many theorists who indicate that not only is the female
envious of the male's genitalia, but the male is envious of the feminine
capacity to reproduce (Jaffe, 1977). Galenson and Roiphe (1976) as well
as Chodorow (1974, 1978) and others have cited ways in which
children come to differentiate between the sexes irrespective of differences in genitalia. But in Freud's theories the notion of the castration
complex is integral to the woman's wish for a baby. As Chodorow
(1978) states:

> Thus, Freud does not tell us only that a little girl *thinks* or *imagines* that
> she is castrated or mutilated or that she *thinks* she is inferior or an in-
> complete boy. Rather she is so [pp. 144–145].

Freud makes a leap from the internal fantasy life of the young girl to a
statement of fact. In doing so, he violates some of his basic tenets of the
workings of the unconscious. At the basis of displacement exists what
Lacan (cited in Lemaire, 1977) would say is the linguistic counterpart
of metonymy. In displacement, one thing is substituted for another; in
metonymy, "one word is put in the place of another word whose meaning is to be understood" (Lemaire, 1977, p. 193). While Chodorow cri-
tiques Freud for turning fantasy into fact, it is equally important to understand that envy of the penis on the girl's part represents a condensation – that is the phallus signifies more than one psychological meaning. Again turning to Lacan, we can then view penis envy, when
present, as metaphorical, and any displacement existing between
phallas and baby as metonymic. The little girl unconsciously envies
much more than the presence of a phallus; rather she envies what it
stands for. In displacement, the adult woman uses the baby as a
stand-in for all that the phallus might unconsciously represent. Thus,
an adult woman may in fact become pregnant as a means of making

herself feel important, potent, grand, special, valued, creative, achieving—in short, the manifold meanings that were archaically attributed to the possession of a penis.

Understanding the metaphoric and metonymic processes that elaborate the unconscious processes of condensation and displacement aids in our understanding of the multiple expressions of libidinal aims. Unconscious determinants of the expression of Eros result in a myriad of configurations. Hence, a woman may express her wish to create, to expand her life and her sense of self in many ways. Having a baby is but one expression for many women, but is certainly not the sole metaphor of creativity.

In viewing reproduction as an expression of a more superordinate libidinal drive, we do not, however, have to eliminate the notion of subordinate, reproductive drive. Benedek (1959) comes closer to outlining the developmental features of "a primary reproductive drive . . . expressed by the adult tendency to give, to nurse, to succor" (p. 383). Yet, as we can see by her definition, she confuses her exposition of a drive by describing features of that drive. We know from clinical data that many women who are compelled to reproduce seem to lack any of the features of giving, nursing, or succoring. Yet, Benedek (1960) views procreation as instinctual and states that women only give up the instinct associated with reproduction "under compelling conditions" (p. 411), without ever outlining these conditions. The problem with Benedek's thesis is that it is so biologically deterministic that she loses the flavor of psychoanalytic investigation, that is, the role of mental determinism in mediating biological constitutions. Benedek does not establish a theory of a continuum of reproductive motives, which I think more accurately describes the intrapsychic mechanisms involved in the choice of motherhood. Instead, we are to believe that there is a biological drive, developed through the female's experience with her parents, and then expressed by the implicitly healthy choice of motherhood or by the implicitly pathological turning away from motherhood. Kohut (1975), however, makes a distinction between a "healthy woman's wish for a child" (p. 786) and that of a woman who wants a child in an attempt to repair some internal sense of damage. Although not detailed, Kohut's discussion makes it clear that a woman's wish for a child is a form of self-expression.

The kind of thinking represented by Benedek omits that there are perhaps many ways in which a woman comes to a reproductive choice;

that there may exist some generic themes in that choice; that the decision is overdetermined, and that choices for as well as against motherhood can be healthy or pathological. A general theme emerges from female patients' reports of a wish to have a special, all-important relationship with another human being, a desire to be powerful and essential in relation to another. This need, in my view, reflects psychic overdetermination: a relationship to her parents in which the young girl did not feel important, influential, and powerful; and a position in a larger social order that is not valued, in which a woman's avenues to achieve a sense of potency and influence are severely constrained. This is not to say that a society that valued women and offered them equal opportunities for achievement would produce women who did not want to mother. Rather, I think such a social order would alter the external conditions that are then internalized by both men and women. Such external social conditions would, at least, set the stage for a healthier developmental process.

TOWARD A NEW PARADIGM OF REPRODUCTIVE MOTIVATION

If we are to treat reproductive choices, based on multiply determined motivations, as an expression of the self, then the course of female development and resultant identity formation is paramount to our analysis. It is of profound importance to reframe our understanding of a woman's relationship to her procreative abilities in this light. Instead of viewing women as compelled to reproduce because of some anatomical deficiency or lack in their personality organization or propelled by the rise and fall of hormonal levels, we can work toward a paradigm of reproductive drives that embraces woman's relationship to herself, to her own unconscious, to her culture, and to her object relationships.

Chodorow (1974, 1978) has attempted to describe how women mother and in turn reproduce mothers. Like Dinnerstein (1976), Chodorow stresses the psychological impact of asymmetrical parenting arrangements, which mean that for most people, male and female alike, the first object is a woman. Without citing the anthropological evidence for the extended caretaking relationship between women and children, it is sufficient to note that "women as mothers are pivotal actors in the sphere of social reproduction" (Chodorow, 1978, p. 11). Chodorow's major thesis is that "women's mothering . . . [is] fundamental to the social organization of gender" (p. 34) and that "the sexual division of labor both produces gender differences and is in turn reproduced by them" (p. 38).

Chodorow sees feminine development as markedly different from male development. Because the female child has a primary caretaker of the same sex, who is less likely to view her daughter as separate from herself, the female's preoedipal attachment is more intense, retentive, and long lasting. Whereas the mother can more easily differentiate herself from her son, such an important differentiation is not so easily achieved between daughters and mothers. This creates a protracted symbiosis and a relationship that is often highlighted by narcissistic features, in which the mother sees the daughter as an extension of herself.

Chodorow (1974) points out that the boy achieves his identification with the male parent by inference. Most likely the boy is involved on a daily basis with women: mother, caretakers, and teachers. He develops a secondary identification with his father based on what little time he spends with him and from viewing males on television, and in children's stories, and so forth. For the girl, primary and secondary identifications are achieved with an object that is concrete and ubiquitous and with whom she has daily contact. No inferences need to be made.

This difference results in a fundamentally different constellation of ego boundaries for the woman. Chodorow (1978) believes that the female remains more attached to the mother and more involved with preoedipal and oedipal issues than the male:

> From the retention of preoedipal attachments to their mother, growing girls come to define and experience themselves as continuous with others; their experience of self contains more flexible or permeable ego boundaries [p. 169].

This permeability serves women's procreation well. To become pregnant, the woman must tolerate intrusion, sometimes welcoming it, sometimes with ambivalence. She then must share her body for nine months with another human being. In this endeavor, the "good-enough" mother (Winnicott, 1956) must empathically identify with the fetus she gestates and ultimately cares for. She must suspend her own ego boundaries, decathect, to some extent, from the outside world, and cathect to the unit of self and infant. Still, this account does not directly address why one woman elects motherhood and another childlessness.

It would seem, based on Chodorow's view, that the nulliparous woman has achieved a markedly different identification with her mother than the woman who seeks maternity. Competing objects in the girl's development can account for this different identification. The mother-daughter symbiosis is clearly mediated by the girl's relationship to her father and her resulting identification with him. Thus, the nulliparous woman may be symbiotically merged with her mother; yet this lack of differentiation is broken, to some extent, by an overlay identification with father. In such cases – particularly illustrated by the high-achieving woman – an identification with a powerful paternal object covers a symbiotic tie with a maternal object who is actually or is imagined as less powerful. Although the early incorporative and identificatory relationships with the mother are at the base of personality structure for women, the additional information with the father, as well as the strength of this identification, clearly play an important role in the woman's relationship to reproduction.

The confluence of social and psychological influences is represented in the microstructure of the family – the first set and prototype of relationships for all people. As a result of this early experience, some women come to believe that "feminine success" (Bardwick, 1972, p. 12) is "largely defined by success in establishing and maintaining love relationships and by maternity" (p. 3). Others conclude that success involves achievements in those arenas dominated by men. The object relations school of thought, endorsed by Chodorow (1974, 1978) and others, addresses the psychology rather than the biology (Guntrip, 1973, p. 69) of early and resultant object relationships.

M. Klein (1932), who can be considered the "mother" of object relations theory, notes that a woman's relationship to both her mother and her father is fundamental in feminine development and the wish to procreate. She points to the forceful impact of greed and envy on the female's development. The young girl envies the mother, who has the father (his penis), the attributes and potency of adulthood, and the capacity to reproduce rival siblings. The envious attacks launched against the mother create a fearful dilemma for the girl. She is afraid that the mother will retaliate and rob her of her own contents and qualities. To ward off this anticipated attack from mother, the girl turns to the father in an attempt to enrich herself. The father may offer the girl a secure and nourishing relationship, or he may subtly or overtly reject her approaches.

If the girl's experience with the father is predominantly nourishing, she will view herself not as robbed, barren, or spoiled, but rather as worthy and filled with potential, creativity, and hope. If the father is rejecting, hostile, and devaluing, the girl's sadistic and destructive features are only intensified. On this line of experience also rest the young girl's developing attitudes about adulthood. She essentially envies her mother because she is the adult – all powerful, mobile, in possession of the riches of adult life. The mother is the source, whereas the father is a prized possession of the mother. The daughter thus turns to the father not only as a "cushion" between her and mother, but also to discover what she may grow to have as an adult woman. This triadic configuration is pivotal, then, for the girl's developing object relations and wish to have a baby.

Klein makes it clear that the wish to procreate stems from one's sense of object relations – that is, one's sense of self, others, and self in relation to others. This seems to agree with Kohut's (1975) formulations and is borne out by clinical examples. The girl who has a rejecting father and whose destructive features are thus intensified, may grow into adulthood and choose a husband whom she is bound to hate. Klein (1932) believes that "women who have a strong sadistic attitude to their husbands usually look upon their child as an enemy" (p. 230). In this circumstance, the woman imagines that the husband deposits hateful introjects into the woman and that she will give birth to a poisonous and feared object. When this dynamic is particularly intense, I believe, may women opt out of reproducing altogether.

Given the importance of the father's role in feminine development and the significance of the parental dyad in outlining gender arrangements for the developing girl, Klein, along with most psychoanalysts, ignores a most crucial factor: the father's attitude toward women. Women have been raised in a society in which sexism is a predominant and insidious social condition. Sexism, like racism, permeates every aspect of human relations. Any man maturing in such a society is bound to be influenced by its sexist ideas. Thus, a man's relationship to his daughter is likewise bound to be influenced by social, cultural, economic, and finally, personal sources of sexism and oppression. Fathers, like mothers, are agents of social as well as biological and psychological reproduction.

The impact of a sexist father on a woman's development cannot be underestimated. A father's sexism is not only expressed directly to his daughter, but is communicated, by inference and example, in his relationship to the daughter's mother. Hence, a mother who openly accepts a position of subservience to her husband teaches her daughter a tragic lesson. In short, many women have had fathers who are misogynistic, fearful of women's creativity and potency, and who actively attempt to socialize their daughters into a life of oppression. These women are then betrayed by their mothers who accept, rationalize, and condone such conditions.

It is no wonder, then, that female patients frequently describe themselves to be damaged. Freud would have us believe that this is a product of their anatomical castration. Instead, I believe this to be a result of a social (macrostructural) and familial (microstructural) mutilation of the feminine personality. Women cannot be raised by oppressed women and oppressive men and come to any other conclusion about themselves. Parental misogyny, the hatred of women by both parents, underscores any woman's development. A woman who experienced a father who devalued her because she was female and a mother who betrayed her because she did not defend her daughter against such assaults, internalizes a maternal object who is oppressed, enslaved, devalued, and powerless, and a paternal object who is oppressive, dominating, and hostile toward women. Such internalizations and the resultant identity configurations leave women with a highly conflicted relationship to their reproductive abilities and their creative capacities in general. As Bardwick (1972) concludes, "in our middle class culture the best that can be hoped for, in psychologically healthy girls, is an ambivalent attitude toward sex and reproduction" (p. 6).

SUMMARY

Although a choice to have a child is in itself a major decision in any woman's life, it extends beyond simple personal considerations. It is a decision that is influenced by and in turn influences social, political, and economic conditions. In American society, women's decisions about reproduction exist within a social and historical context that biases women toward having children. Women have had to struggle and continue to do so in order to have control over their own bodies.

The relatively recent development of effective means of contraception has brought into sharp focus the many conflicts involved in a woman's relationship to her reproductive capacities. These conflicts are often elucidated by women's choices for or against certain contraceptive methods; their "failures" to use contraception; their choices for or against motherhood; and their relationships with husbands, lovers, and other women. Clinical material has been offered here as a sampling of some of the conflicts that emerge for women when confronted with their capacity to reproduce.

Traditional theory came out of a social and historical context in which readily available means of contraception did not exist. In addition, traditional theory is marred by phallocentrism and is frequently overly biologistic. A new paradigm has been offered that seeks to delineate the multidetermination of reproduction, the influence of sexism on women's development, and the resulting conflicts that frequently emerge for women in coming to terms with their roles as reproducers and caretakers of the species. Instead of emphasizing biology and instinct, this new paradigm focuses on the internalization of certain object relations and the resulting identifications that then become the template through which women view themselves as reproducers. Because of ubiquitous social misogyny and sexism, women then internalize a conflicted picture of men and women and are consequently bound to be conflicted about continuing to reproduce the prevailing gender arrangements and social order. A comprehensive model that seeks to clarify our understanding of women's conscious and unconscious reproductive motivations must address the manifold determinants of biology, sociology, culture, economics, politics, and the family.

REFERENCES

Bardwick, J. (1972), Psychological conflict and the reproductive system. In: *Feminine Personality and Conflict*, ed. E. L. Walker. Belmont, CA: Brooks/Cole.

Benedek, T. (1959), Parenthood as a developmental phase. In: *Psychoanalytic Investigations: Selected Papers of Therese Benedek*. New York: Quadrangle, 1973, pp. 377–407.

———— (1960), On the organization of the reproductive drive. In: *Psychoanalytic Investigations: Selected Papers of Therese Benedek*. New York: Quadrangle, 1973, pp. 408–445.

Bernard, J. (1974), *The Future of Motherhood*. New York: Dial.

Chodorow, N. (1974), Family structure and feminine personality. In: *Women, Culture, and Society*, ed. M. Z. Rosaldo & L. Lamphere. Stanford, CA: Stanford University Press.

———— (1978), *The Reproduction of Mothering: Psychoanalysis and the Sociology of Gender*. Berkeley: University of California Press.

Dinnerstein, D. (1976), *The Mermaid and the Minotaur: Sexual Arrangements and Human Malaise*. New York: Harper & Row.

Fabe, M., & Wikler, N. (1979), *Up Against the Clock: Career Women Speak on the Choice to have Children*. New York: Random House.

Fenichel, O. (1945), *The Psychoanalytic Theory of Neurosis*. New York: Norton.

Freud, S. (1921), Group psychology and the analysis of the ego. *Standard Edition*, 18: 67–143. London: Hogarth Press.

———— (1925), Some psychical consequences of the anatomical distinction between the sexes. *Standard Edition*, 19: 241–258. London: Hogarth Press.

Galenson, E., & Roiphe, H. (1976), Some suggested revisions concerning early female development. In: *Female Psychology*, ed. H. Blum. New York: International Universities Press, 1977, pp. 29–57.

Garland, T. N., & Poloma, M. M. (1971), Cribs or Careers? Professionally employed married women's attitudes toward motherhood. Paper presented at the 66th Annual Meeting of the American Sociological Association, Denver, Co, August 30–September 2.

Gordon, L. (1976), *Woman's Body, Woman's Right: A Social History of Birth Control in America*. New York: Grossman.

Guntrip, H. (1973), *Psychoanalytic Theory, Therapy and the Self: A Basic Guide to the Human Personality in Freud, Erikson, Klein, Sullivan, Fairbairn, Hartmann, Jacobson, and Winnicott*. New York: Basic Books.

Houseknecht, S. K. (1977), Reference group support for voluntary childlessness: Evidence for conformity. *J. Marriage Fam.*, 39: 285–292.

Jaffe, D. (1977), The masculine envy of woman's procreative function. In: *Female Psychology*, ed. H. Blum. New York: International Universities Press, pp. 194–239.

Klein, M. (1932). The effects of early anxiety-situations on the sexual development of the girl. In: *The Psychoanalysis of Children*, trans. A. Strachey. New York: Delacorte, 1975.

Kohut, H. (1975), A note on female sexuality. In: *The Search for the Self: The Selected Writings of Heinz Kohut: 1950–1978*, Vol. 2, ed. P. Ornstein. New York: International Universities Press, 1978, pp. 783–792.

Lemaire, A. (1977), *Jacques Lacan*. London: Routledge and Kegan Paul.

Michaelson, K. (Ed.) (1981), *And the Poor Get Children: Radical Perspectives on Population Dynamics*. New York: Monthly Review Press.

Mitchell, J. (Ed.) (1983), *Feminine Sexuality: Jacques Lacan and the Ecole Freudienne*, trans. J. Rose. New York: Norton.

Ory, M. G. (1978), The decision to parent or not: Normative and structural components. *J. Marriage Fam.*, 40: 531–539.

Petchesky, R. P. (1981), "Reproductive choice" in the contemporary United States: A social analysis of female sterilization. In: *And the Poor Get Children: Radical Perspectives on Population Dynamics*, ed. K. Michaelson. New York: Monthly Review Press, pp. 50–88.

Popenoe, P. (1936), Motivation of childless marriages. In: *Pronatalism: The Myth of Mom and Apple Pie*, ed. E. Peck & J. Senderowitz. New York: Thomas Y. Crowell 1974, pp. 278–283.

Rich, A. (1976), *Of Woman Born: Motherhoood as Experience and Institution*. New York: Bantam.

_____ (1979), *On Lies, Secrets, and Silence: Selected Prose, 1966–1978*. New York: Norton.

Russo, N. F. (1976), The motherhood mandate. *J. Soc. Issues*, 32: 143–153.

Schafer, R. (1968), *Aspects of Internalization*. New York: International Universities Press.

Sheehy, G. (1976), *Passages: Predictable Crises of Adult Life*. New York: Dutton.

Strouse, J. (Ed.) (1974), *Women and Analysis*. New York: Grossman.

Veevers, J. E. (1971), Differential childlessness by color: A further examination. *Soc. Biol.* 18: 285–291.

Whelan, E. M. (1975), *A Baby? Maybe: A Guide to Making the Most Fateful Decision of Your Life*. New York: Bobbs-Merrill.

Williams, S. L. (1980), *Reproductive motivation and feminine identifications*. Unpublished doctoral dissertation, California School of Professional Psychology, Los Angeles.

Winnicott, D. W. (1956), Primary maternal preoccupation. In: *Through Peadiatrics to Psycho-Analysis*. New York: Basic Bookks, 1975, pp. 300–305.

Wyatt, F. (1967), Clinical notes on the motives of reproduction. *J. Soc. Issues*, 33; 29–56.

9

Marriage and Divorce: The Search for Adult Identity

Dorothy W. Cantor, Psy.D.

Despite the near universality of the experience of marriage and the increasing incidence of divorce, the psychoanalytic literature pays relatively little attention to either. Indeed, Kernberg (1980) observed recently that "psychoanalytic contributions have dealt more with the psychology and psychopathology of sexual life than with the psychology and psychopathology of love relations" (p. 281). Horney writing in 1927, was equally astounded that there had been no thorough analytic exposition of the problems of marriage. She hypothesized that

> the whole question touches us too closely to form an attractive object of scientific curiosity and ambition. But it is also possible that it is not the

Portions of this paper have appeared previously in "Divorce: Separation or separation-individuation?" *American Journal of Psychoanalysis*, 1982, 42, (4), pp. 307–313.

problems but the conflicts that touch us too closely, lie too near some of
the deepest roots of our most intimate personal experience. And then
there is another difficulty: Marriage is a social institution" [p. 84].

If marriage and divorce are perceived as sociocultural phenomena,
then perhaps they can be left to be explored by social psychologists and
family therapists who look at concepts such as group cohesiveness as
related to material, symbolic, and affectional rewards; the intergen-
erational transmission of marital instability; or the economic determinants of marital breakup. However, marriage and divorce also involve
developmental and transferential phenomena that psychoanalysts
cannot ignore, particularly when they are undergoing tremendous
change. The literature is sparse. Two essays by Horney, written in 1927
and 1932, address problems of marriage and the problems of the monogamous ideal. Kernberg (1980) and Benedek (1977) have made
passing reference to marriage, observing that the changes in women in
our society may threaten men, shift the balance between the sexes, and
increase the aggressive components of marriage. The Blancks (1968)
addressed the issues from the point of view of ego psychology, a major
step. The literature seems to have stopped there, and no analytical
work has specifically addressed the issues surrounding marriage and divorce as they specifically relate to women. The goal of this essay is to
provide a psychoanalytic perspective on marriage and divorce as factors in women's development in adult life. The focus will be on the
marital dyad and not on the role that children play in marriage.

MARRIAGE

Although we observe that times are changing and we see couples establishing alternatives to marriage, it is also true that women in the
1980's continue to choose to marry. Horney would not be surprised.
Writing in 1927, she observed, "We are likely to be extremely skeptical
when we hear it prophesied that the institution of marriage will soon
come to an end" (p. 85). Her skepticism came from her perception that
the drive toward marriage was based on the expectation that in it
would be found the fulfillment of oedipal desires. However, she added
that the same wishes would lead to inevitable disappointment and feel-

ings of guilt. Horney was thus quite dubious about the possibility of successful, rewarding marriages.

For today's woman, a successful, rewarding marriage depends on her having achieved her own sense of identity, along with the ability to give and receive love, and on finding a partner who is at an equivalent stage of development so that both can experience themselves as part of the couple and as individuals. They can "open up, merge and separate without fear of loss of self or loss of the other person" (Eichenbaum & Orbach, 1983). Willi (1982) defines a healthy relationship in terms of the inner and outer boundaries of the dyad. He sees normal functioning as an appropriate position on a continuum between total fusion and rigid separation of the partners.

Marriage is a developmental task that requires the establishment of new object relations, permits further separation from parents, and allows for expression of autonomy. To conceptualize it as a developmental task assumes that psychological development continues into adult life. According to Blanck and Blanck (1968), marriage provides an "average expectable environment in which a love relationship offers potential for continued growth of the partners" (p. 17).

Finding Identity Through the Husband

Historically, women have been expected to find their identities through their husbands, rather than achieving their own sense of self—a situation that precludes a healthy marriage. Woman's social role requires that she shape her life in accordance with a man's (Eichenbaum & Orbach, 1983). One of the most blatant cultural statements of this is the expectation that a woman will assume her husband's name. Many women today are maintaining their own names after marriage or are hyphenating their name with that of their husband. Up to now, it has been considered socially correct for women to be referred to as "Mrs. Husband's Name." And only in 1984 did the local newspaper in Westfield, New Jersey, begin to print a bride's first name under her wedding picture.

Erikson (1968) described girls as holding their identity in abeyance. Their task is to attract males whose status will define them. Intimacy goes along with identity. By contrast, Erikson sees males as developing their identity via learning and mastery. It is not surprising that generations of little girls have succumbed to the fairy tale dreams that have taught them their happiness as adults will be attained by marrying the prince!

On the other hand, a number of women today are choosing to delay marriage until they have established their own identities, through education and career development. These women focus their energies during their twenties on self-development analogous to that which Erikson described for boys. They avoid commitment to serious relationships with men that might distract them or seduce them into a false sense of identity through the partner. When they approach age 30, however, these women often become frantic as they recognize their state of aloneness and become fearful of its permanence. They want to marry in order to have the satisfaction of attachment and sharing, to have a stable sexual relationship, and to have children.

Even if they had apparently accomplished a healthy separation from mother, women have been expected to regress to an early state of merger and dependence when they married. Earlier psychoanalysts considered it normal for women to resolve their Oedipus complex only incompletely, partially separating from mothers by idealizing their fathers and remaining dependent on men. Lebe (1982), however, challenged the normalcy of the incomplete resolution, which prevented women from competing actively and fully with men. As recently as 1978, Meissner, in an otherwise modern discussion of marriage from a psychoanalytic perspective, wrote: ". . . The woman can become more secure and confident of her own capacities for meaningful endeavor and self-assertion in a variety of intellectual and work pursuits by *identification with her husband*" (p. 45; italics added). Implicit in such formulations is the notion that it is normal for women to develop their sense of initiative and assertiveness through their husbands. They are not expected to develop it, as men do, during the stage of "industry vs. inferiority" (Erikson, 1968).

Two cases of women in their sixties will serve to illustrate the degree of dependence on their husbands that women have experienced. One woman, Mrs. A., entered treatment at the age of 61, having been widowed nine years earlier. She was acutely depressed and had been taking Librium for most of the nine-year period. Her late husband's clothing still hung in the closet. She comforted herself in the evening by sitting in his bathrobe.

Her husband had been something of a tyrant, frequently "blowing his top." Mrs. A., however, was ever-smiling and "swell." Her husband had carried the angry feelings for her. The therapy centered on her being able to own her own anger, which she had repressed since childhood in order to be a good girl. As her own development proceeded, Mrs. A. discarded her husband's things, began dating, and eventually moved in with a man, all without discussion in treatment. Her new relationship did not compromise her newly found sense of self.

Mrs. B. was widowed at 68. She was a college graduate and very bright, but in her marriage she regressed to a helpless position in relation to her husband. She had never written a check, nor could she tune the television. She was in a state of panic when her husband died, but quickly learned that she had the capacity to do things for herself. She met a man who wanted to marry her, but she refused. "I did that once," she explained to her therapist. As she perceived it, she had abdicated her sense of self to her husband, and she did not trust herself to maintain it were she to remarry.

Had their husbands lived, neither of these women would have been likely to develop. Their sense of self was activated by the loss of the object. Not all women are able to mobilize and grow as these women did, as will be shown in discussing women whose husbands leave them.

Although the women's liberation movement has created a social milieu in which women are freer to develop and express themselves, a large number of women, both young and older, have not completed the process of separation from parents. For these women, marriage still serves as a means of avoiding the task of individuation while appearing to separate from the family. I am surprised at the number of women in their twenties who still see marriage as the only path to happiness and whose fantasies of marriage incorporate fantasies of merger with the other as well as unresolved oedipal longings.

One such young woman is Ms. C., a moderately depressed, 22-year-old college student who has been in treatment for several years. She describes her father as explosive, abusive, and unloving, but wishes she could be close to him. Her mother is an intrusive person who has directed every aspect of her daughter's life, including her social life and career choice. The patient believes that the only way in which she can be happy is to be married. In her fantasies of marriage, she clearly achieves the closeness with the oedipal father and the attachment to the preoedipal mother. As she begins to establish her own identity in the course of treatment, Ms. C. has changed career direction and made many new friends. Yet she clings to the marital fantasy and resists interpretations of its meaning to her.

Marriage and Attachment

I am indebted to Gilligan (1982) for pointing out a unique feature of women's development that has been previously ignored by psychoanalysts. In Gilligan's words: "The elusive mystery of women's development lies in its recognition of the continuing importance of attachment in the human life cycle. Woman's place in man's life cycle is to protect this recognition while the developmental litany intones the celebration of separation, autonomy, individuation and natural rights" (p. 23). To accept Gilligan's view is to recognize that the "concept of identity expands to include the experience of interconnection" (p. 173).

   Thus, it is possible to view marriage as a healthy developmental milestone for a mature woman. Otherwise, we would have to view all marriage as an indication of the immaturity of a nonindividuated person. From this perspective, marriage can be an opportunity to experience love, closeness and sexual gratification with one man, to provide an environment for raising children and experiencing motherhood, and to provide opportunities for satisfaction of appropriate needs to nurture and to maintain relationships.

DIVORCE

The divorce rate has just leveled off after climbing for the past 20 years. It reached a record high in 1981 of 53 per 1000 people and then declined for three years to 49 per 1000 in August, 1984, according to the National Center for Health Statistics. Part of the reality behind the figures is that the dependent women of earlier generations were unlikely to precipitate divorce because they felt unable to take care of themselves. The generation of women in transition from this dependent state created marital instability as they changed in midmarriage. We may hope that succeeding generations of women, who potentially will enter marriage at a healthier point in their development, will be able to sustain marriage more successfully.

Horney's Oedipal View of Divorce

In her paper, "Problems of Marriage," Horney (1932) considered the impact of the early oedipal love experiences on later relationships with the opposite sex. Horney observed such attitudes in the male as recoiling from the forbidding, intimidating female; the notion of the saintliness of women, which interferes with sexual desires for the wife; and the dread of being unable to satisfy the woman. "The less such attitudes have been overcome in the course of his development," she wrote, "the more uncomfortable the husband must feel in relation to his wife" (p. 127). Horney postulated that these unconscious feelings could lead to tensions and conflicts within the marriage. She suggested that the tension might be relieved in work or in the company of other men or other women. Today, we would expect divorce to be used as an alternative means of relieving the tension.

For many woman, according to Horney, frigidity is a problem brought to marriage from early development. However, she saw the total attitude toward the husband as more serious than the symptom. Frigidity represents a hostile, resentful attitude toward males, who are seen as always having the advantage. It also represents the anxiety associated with satisfaction of instinctual drives.

In summary, Horney stated: "As the spark goes out of a marriage, or a third person intrudes, the very things we usually hold responsible for the breaking down of a marriage, are already a consequence of certain development" (p. 131). To Horney, then, divorce would be seen as associated less with "the annoying qualities of the partner, and much more with the unresolved conflicts we bring into the marriage from our own development" (p. 131).

Divorce as Separation-Individuation

An alternative to the oedipal model of marital failure is the hypothesis that many divorces result from working through the task of separation-individuation at an adult level. Whereas the outcome of failure in the childhood separation-individuation process is serious psychopathology, the outcome of failure in the marital separation-individuation process is divorce.

The marital couple may be seen as analogous to the mother-child dyad. The psychodynamic process in all loving relationships follows that of the original mother-child dyad (Benedek, 1977). In a marriage, through the gratification of the sexual desires, each partner introjects the other as a gratifier of needs and becomes a part of the self-system of the other. The symbiotic merger is an idealized fantasy, extolled in love songs and novels that proclaim "we are one." For an individual who has an excessive fixation at the narcissistic level, the gratification in the symbiotic marital relationship is a satisfying experience. For example, Mr. D., a 38-year-old man who had been married for 15 years, described his relationship with his wife as follows: "I feel like a part of her and she of me—like metals fused into a solid block—a single unit. But there's a precarious quality. The separate parts don't exist. If the unit is pulled apart, it shatters into pieces."

As we better understand object relations theory, we find that an increasing number of the people seen in clinical practice exhibit narcissistic and borderline features. I suspect that these features were equally present in the neurotic patients of earlier times, but that they went unrecognized. What we see in practice is a crystalization of what exists in the nonpatient population. We can conclude, therefore, that many people experience their marital relationships to some degree like Mr. D. does.

Differentiation. The normal developmental thrust of a physically maturing infant is to begin to differentiate, or "hatch out," from the symbiosis with the mother (Mahler, 1972). A safe anchor in the symbiotic orbit enhances the differentiation process. In adults, the developmental thrust comes from a different source.

Historically, men differentiated as they developed increasing ego strength in their educational or employment spheres. Marriages dissolved because men "outgrew" their wives. In recent years, however, we are seeing a developmental thrust in women, who are becoming increasingly aware of their own capacities outside the marital dyad. Like the infant's first steps, their initial movements toward differentiation are tentative. They move out slowly, taking a course or working part time. The differentiation phase is overlapped by a practicing period, akin to the infant's practicing subphase, during which the infant delights in new-found skills but returns periodically to the mother, seeming to need her physical proximity from time to time.

An example of a woman in this differentiation phase was Mrs. E., the 43-year-old mother of four children, who had worked as a bank teller from the time her youngest child started school. Her marital relationship was similar to that described by Mr. D. She said that her husband "shadowed" her: "At home, I've got to be in his sight all the time. He constantly comes to look at what I'm doing." She recognized that she was too insecure to move away from his shadow. About a year before seeking treatment, Mrs. E. was promoted to a lower level managerial position at the bank. Although she had authority over her children, she had never exercised it independently without consulting with her husband. The authority she exercised in her new job served as the developmental thrust, and she found herself "rebelling" at home, wanting to go out shopping or to visit friends without her husband and even without reporting to him. However, she looked forward to spending her evenings and weekends at home and telling her husband about her experiences.

The differentiation of the child is experienced by the mother in varying ways. The borderline mother, who has experienced significant gratification during her child's symbiotic phase, is available when the child clings and behaves regressively, but withdraws as the child attempts to separate and grow (Masterson & Rinsley, 1980). The paradox for the child is that he or she needs the mother's supplies of nurturance in order to grow and has no other source; but if the child grows, the supplies are withdrawn. For the child, the result is the split object relations unit.

In the marital dyad, the nondifferentiating spouse assumes the role of the mother in the mother-child dyad. The response of the husband to the differentiating wife will have profound effect on the outcome for the marriage. For example, in the case of Mrs. E., the husband was furious at Mrs. E.'s differentiating behavior. Indeed, her reason for seeking treatment was to fortify herself against the pull back into the symbiotic orbit and to continue the separation-individuation process.

If the husband's symbiotic needs were previously being met in the relationship and his response to the wife's growth is withdrawal, the wife has the option of looking elsewhere for nurturant supplies rather than enduring the discomfort and frustration. The marriage, at this point, is in danger of dissolution.

The mother whose symbiotic needs were being met by her infant may recreate the symbiosis by having another child. The husband may achieve the same end by finding another symbiotic partner and giving up the marriage, which is no longer gratifying. Mr. D., whose symbiotic marriage has already been described, followed such a pattern. As the oldest of five children, Mr. D. felt that his own mother had replaced him and his younger siblings as they differentiated. Every two years, a new child was born. Mr. D. recalled his mother's affinity for babies and how much more attention she gave them than she gave to her growing children. His initial response to his wife's differentiation was a repetition of his mother's behavior. He sought another woman with whom he could fuse, so as not to have to experience the terror of being alone.

Some husbands, like some mothers, experience a sense of relief at the ending of the symbiotic union. These husbands are supportive of their differentiating wives, but may have diffuclty adjusting to the next phase of development.

Rapprochement. When the toddler becomes more aware of being physically separate from the mother, he or she loses some of the previous imperviousness to frustration and begins to actively seek the mother's presence. The child seems to have lost some of the grandiosity associated with the first steps into the world and to recognize him-/or herself as a relatively helpless, small, and separate individual. Thus, in the rapprochement phase, the child seeks the mother, and her continued emotional availability is essential if the child's autonomous ego is to attain optimal functional capacity (Mahler, 1972).

Similarly, the differentiating wife discovers that being entirely independent is lonely. It is comforting to be able to share problems, get emotional support, and be loved by the husband. The wife seeks the husband, and his emotional availability is essential for the continuation of the marriage.

The husband, like some mothers, may take pleasure in the new object relationship that is possible with the differentiating individual (Mahler, Pine & Bergman, 1970). If so, the marital relationship can be recreated on a new basis. If the husband has experienced relief at the loss of the symbiotic union, however, the rapprochement may be experienced as a new threat. The husband may either ignore the wife when she seeks attention or encourage her to take care of matters alone. A child, forced to adjust to such a mother, makes use of splitting and denial, and a borderline personality structure ensues. A wife who has sufficiently differentiated can break up the marriage and seek to fill the rapprochement needs with another partner or through other emotionally supportive adult relationships.

On the Way to Object Constancy. Mahler (1972) conservatively designated the fourth stage of the separation-individuation process as the "child on the way to object constancy." The important thing about this stage is its implicit developmental and ongoing character, which acknowledges that the child is still growing. For the marital dyad, if the marriage has survived the differentiation, practicing, and rapprochement subphases, the husband and wife can acknowledge themselves as separate individuals with firm boundaries who have in their sexuality "a capacity for empathy with – but not merger into – a primitive state of symbiotic fusion" (Kernberg, 1980, p. 293). Because the marital relationship exists between two separate individuals, it will continually change and develop as the individuals do. Therefore, survival of the marriage through the separation-individuation of one of the partners does not preclude other marital crises in the future.

Developmental Crisis: When a Husband Leaves

In discussing divorce as a possible outcome of a separation–individuation process, it was assumed that the woman would be the developing and changing partner. In many instances, however, the husband differentiates and leaves the wife. If the woman has a well-established sense of herself, she can mourn the loss appropriately and move on, either on her own or by establishing a new relationship. The less individuated woman will find herself in a developmental crisis, similar to that of the widows described earlier. Such women frequently seek treatment because of their depression, loneliness, and emptiness. Clinical intuition suggests that abandoned women who choose male therapists enter treatment resistant to change and looking for another man on whom to depend. Abandoned women who choose female therapists are looking for another kind of woman with whom to identify in the process of developing their own identity.

The less individuated women have rarely considered, prior to therapy, what they themselves wanted. Such a woman was Mrs. F., whose husband left her after 20 years of marriage. Although she had no previous history of mental illness, Mrs. F. became suicidal. She was hospitalized for a five-week period, after which she returned to school and began to talk about the future. It became clear in treatment, however, that she had little sense of self to sustain her. She believed that the only way for her to have a happy future would be to find another man. If she were to succeed this early in treatment in establishing such a relationship, she would no doubt leave therapy, feeling instantly "cured" by borrowing the new man's ego.

Mrs. F. spoke frequently of the women she met in the singles' world, women who were still miserable after years of divorce. Many of these are women who have not accepted the developmental opportunity provided by their being alone for the first time in their lives.

Other women grow when on their own. Lebe (1982) has suggested that the decade between ages 30 and 40 is an opportune time for women to develop because "there have been sufficient narcissistic achievements, . . . enough distance from the pre-Oedipal mother and an opportunity to observe that their own anal-sadistic impulses towards men have not castrated or destroyed them . . ." (p. 72).

Remarriage

It seems clear that remarriage has the same chance of being successful and rewarding as a first marriage. If a woman has individuated before, during, or subsequent to her first marriage, she can establish a mature relationship with a man that can meet her needs for attachment without being overly dependent. If she has not grown, the prognosis for her remarriage is no better than the first time around. Not surprisingly, the divorce rate for the second marriages is even higher than that for first marriages.

IMPLICATIONS FOR TREATMENT

We see many people who are undergoing marital stress and who consider divorce as a means of solving their problems. For some—and as yet there are no statistics to indicate how many—the marital stress is related to the separation-individuation of one spouse and its impact on the other. For others, the marital stress is a reflection of unresolved oedipal conflicts. As in working with any patient, regardless of the overt presenting problem, the first task of the therapist is to determine the developmental level at which the patient is functioning. That determination will help the therapist understand whether the marital stress is of a preoedipal or oedipal nature. The therapist's understanding of the developmental level of the conflict will color the evaluation of the decision to separate as being healthy or unhealthy.

In Mrs. G.'s case, for example, the wish to separate stemmed from unresolved oedipal wishes. Mrs. G. entered therapy at the time that she was considering her second divorce. She had had two abortions during her teens and had also given birth to a child whom she had given up for adoption. Her first marriage to an older professional man had been childless. The divorce, she reported, had been the result of his refusal to have children. Her second marriage was to a businessman who already had three children by a previous marriage. Mrs. G. was considering divorce from him, ostensibly because he was not sufficiently attentive to her. It seemed evident that she had never resolved the childhood wish to have a child by her father and that her marriages would be doomed to failure until the wish was resolved in therapy.

In contrast, the decision to separate was healthy and appropriate for Mrs. E., who was working through the separation-individuation process. Unable to convince her husband to change in any way, Mrs. E. made the difficult decision to leave him in order to maintain her individuated state. She leased an apartment and, despite her fear, moved into it.

About three weeks prior to her intended move, Mrs. E. opened her therapy session with a report of her husband's query, "Doesn't anyone try to keep marriages together?" However, therapy did not cause Mrs. E.'s decision to leave the marriage, as her husband implied. She had begun the separation-individuation process on her own, and therapy helped her to understand her needs, her inability to individuate earlier in life, her anger, and so forth. When a patient's goal in therapy is individuation and the development of a sense of self, however, it can be a contributing factor in divorce if, as in Mrs. E.'s case, the husband cannot tolerate the loss of the symbiotic union.

Mrs. E. had tried to convince her husband to seek treatment, but he refused to acknowledge his own need to change. He blamed his wife for the failure of the marriage. Had he sought treatment for himself, the outcome for the marriage might have been like that experienced by

Mr. D. and his wife. After almost two years of treatment, Mr. D. was still married. He had concluded, "It would be better to develop a sense of myself, to exist on my own, without this type of arrangement of having to merge into something. I want to be unafraid to venture out, to take that risk." Gradually, he has come to value his wife's separateness and is looking forward to his own.

Mr. D. was able to use therapy to help him cope with the symbiotic loss and to provide him with the developmental thrust for his own individuation. The developmental task is difficult for the partner who feels abandoned by the spouse's individuation because the impetus is external. However, therapy can help the "mother" spouse to achieve individuation. As therapists, we have a responsibility to encourage the spouses of differentiating partners to seek treatment for themselves.

Because the success of marriages like these depends on tremendous movement from borderline symbiotic state to a separated-individuated state, marriage counseling cannot be expected to save such marriages. Each partner needs to work separately in a psychoanalytic developmental approach to achieve his or her own sense of self, which can then be brought to a mature love relationship. The therapist who works with today's women, as Menaker (1983) has pointed out, must be particularly sensitive to the transitional phase of sociocultural evolution in which these women find themselves. Traditional views of marriage and divorce have changed, and women cannot look to the generations that preceded them for role models as wives.

REFERENCES

Benedek, T. (1977), Ambivalence, passion and love. *J. Amer. Psychoanal. Assn.*, 25: 53–80.
Blanck, R., & Blanck, G. (1968), *Marriage & Personal Development.* New York: Columbia University Press.
Eichenbaum L., & Orbach, S. (1983), *Understanding Women: A Feminist Psychoanalytic Approach.* New York: Basic Books.
Erikson, E. H. (1968), *Identity: Youth & Crisis.* New York: Norton.
Gilligan, C. (1982), *In a Different Voice.* Cambridge, MA: Harvard University Press.
Horney, K. (1927), The problem of the monogamous ideal. In: *Feminine Psychology*, ed. H. Kelman. New York: Norton, 1967, pp. 84–98.
_____ (1932), Problems of marriage. In: *Feminine Psychology*, ed. H. Kelman. New York: Norton, 1967, pp. 119–132.

Kernberg, O. (1980), *Internal World and External Reality.* New York: Jason Aronson.

Lebe, D. (1982), Individuation of women. *Psychoanal. Rev.,* 69 (1): 63–73.

Mahler, M. S. (1972), Rapprochement subphase of the separation-individuation process. *Psychoanal. Quart.,* 41: 487–506.

_____ Pine, F., & Bergman, A. (1970), The mother's reaction to her toddler's drive to individuation. In: *Parenthood: Its Psychology and Psychopathology,* ed. J. E. Anthony & T. Benedek. Boston: Little, Brown, pp. 257–274.

Masterson, J. M., & Rinsley, D. B. (1980), The borderline syndrome: The role of the mother in the genesis and psychic structure of the borderline personality. In: *Rapprochement,* ed. R. F. Lax, S. Bach, & J. A. Burland. New York: Jason Aronson, pp. 299–330.

Menaker, E. (1982), Female identity in psychosocial perspective. *Psychoanal. Rev.,* 69 (1): 75–83.

Meissner, W. W. (1978), The conceptualization of marriage & family dynamics from a psychoanalytic perspective. In: *Marriage and Marital Therapy,* ed. T. J. Paolino, Jr. & B. S. McCrady. New York: Brunner/Mazel, pp. 25–88.

Willi, J. (1982), *Couples in collusion.* New York: Jason Aronson.

10

Women and Work

Adrienne Applegarth, M.D.

Work has always been a conspicuous feature of the lives of human beings. From the beginning, psychoanalytic authors have taken an interest in the psychological basis of this function, elaborating the intricate interplay between instinctual and ego forces in its various forms, including inhibitions. Hendrick (1943), Menninger (1942), and Oberndorf (1951) have addressed problems of work in men, and Halpern (1964), Hellman (1954), and Mahler (1942) have described learning inhibitions in normal and gifted children. Work in the lives of women has been scarcely mentioned in the analytic literature, however, and the problem of work inhibitions in women has not in general been addressed, although there has been more recent interest (Applegarth, 1976).

This lack of attention is somewhat understandable in view of the smaller numbers of women who sought and carried out full-fledged careers from the turn of the century until World War II. Even though the numbers were relatively small, however, enough women undertook careers that one might have expected more specific attention to this problem. Undoubtedly, both social and analytic misconceptions have played a role in this neglect, especially the idea that it is less natural for women to seek careers, so that the seeking was more apt to receive analytic attention than was an inhibition in this function.

Until recent years, the shape of the psychoanalytic theory of female psychosexual development has supported the idea that women's strivings toward a career represent misdirection of normal drives and, in general, are the expression of masculine currents. Even in the early days of psychoanalysis, Horney and Jones raised objections to most or all the theories then being crystallized to account for female development. For various reasons, however, these voices were ignored and fell silent. The women's movement has not only had the effect of forcing open the doors for women to seek careers on broader fronts than before, but has also brought added energy to the attempts within psychoanalysis at reexamining our theories of female psychology. The increasing numbers of women seeking careers or now established in them has provided analysts with a considerable group in which to observe the adaptations, both successful and unsuccessful, of these women.

Two constellations emerge with striking clarity among those women who have experienced enough work-related difficulties to have consulted me over the past 15 years. The first of these consists of inhibitions of varying degrees of severity; the second consists of patterns of conflict over the attempt to reconcile the demands of work and motherhood.

THE NATURE OF WORK

The urge to work is itself a subject of considerable difference of opinion, the details of which cannot be reviewed here. Freud, in his famous dictum that normality represents the ability to love and to work obviously took work much more for granted than he did love. Naturally, the overwhelming preponderance of the world's population works because it must in order to live, but this apparent response to reality may hide many other important motivations and functions for work.

Psychoanalysts have considered that work represents a sublimation of the two great instinctual drives, and it would therefore express these drives in an altered and aim-inhibited way. In later years, however, the concept of sublimation has been seen to be far more complex and difficult to agree upon (Hartmann, 1955). Freud (1915) himself pointed out that certain great achievements seem to occur in connection with a particularly open expression of drive (p. 195), and others (Loomie et al., 1958) have noted the appearance of markedly instinctual material accompanying what would usually be regarded as sublimated activities. White (1963), on the other hand, considered the possibility that work and other ego functions may not be best explained as a vicissitude of instinctual drive, but may represent the expression of ego interest or drives, which he called *effectance*.

It seems to be a universal observation that children will tend to play when their basic life needs are met; and work, at its best, may be regarded as developmental stage of play. Work is intimately connected with important identifications and represents a large part of the sense of identity. Clearly, there can be great pleasure in this function, which we would regard as the expression of not only the instinctual drives but also as a gratification of narcissism. The frequency of depressions seen in men after retirement would attest to these factors. For both sexes, work clearly also satisfies important social needs as well as the working out of important object relationships.

In view of the importance of these forces, it would be no surprise that inhibitions of this function should occur on a variety of bases. Many of these both men and women would have in common. Organic brain disease and severe mental illness characteristically interfere drastically with the ego functions in general and so impair the ability to work, although it is sometimes remarkable how the work function can remain an island of almost normal activity in a sea of mental disturbance. Other mainly neurotic inhibitions of the work capacity are shared by men and women, but this essay will focus mainly on those aspects of the problem that affect women more strongly or, in a few cases, exclusively.

Work inhibition will be used here to refer to a relatively definite and localized disturbance of the work function. The observations I will describe have been made with patients in both psychotherapy and analysis over a period of about 15 years. I will not include data on patients whose work difficulty is only part of a larger and more serious ego disruption. Also, I will focus on patients who were seeking or already involved in a serious career that evolved out of their own interest and that they intended to pursue over the course of a lifetime. This exludes a fairly large group of women who work to help out the family finances or to put a spouse through school, but who do not have a career goal in mind for themselves. These patients' careers include medicine, law, psychology, social work, teaching, writing, business, and administration. Work inhibitions in these patients fall into some rough categories, which I will attempt to outline, but clearly there is a good deal of overlap in the dynamics among these categories.

NARCISSISTIC INHIBITIONS IN WORK

Various problems around narcissism underlie many disturbances in work among women. Most patients with this type of problem would not even be given a diagnosis of narcissistic character, although their narcissistic conflicts color their pathology to a considerable degree. The pattern shown seems to depend strongly upon the level of the narcissistic difficulty. A common problem is that such patients will energetically avoid the risk of failure, or even the risk of error, which to them amounts to the same thing. Naturally, a person who is devastated by mistakes will have great difficulty learning to do anything well. Many of them also quite evidently have the idea that those who can do things well are somehow born with their ability; they seem almost to lack the concept that one can progress from lack of skill to skill by practice.

Since these women can conceive of no way of progressing to the point achieved by the figures they admire at work, they can only helplessly envy those whose powers awe them. Typically, such patients are convinced that people who achieve have a magical edge or tool of some kind that allows them to attain their level of performance. Severely narcissistic patients feel that their envy is corrosive and destructive, and they fear producing such envy in others by any achievements of their own—a further root of inhibition of work.

Another important feature of such patients is their resentment at having to make an effort or having to put up with discomfort. Experiencing difficulty in an endeavor may therefore produce in them considerable rage. This rage is often unconscious at first, and their conscious experience is one of inexplicable loss of interest in a project they had been eagerly pursuing.

It is often difficult for patients with such narcissistic conflicts to find pleasure in the functions involved in their work. Typically, when their pathology is more severe, they select their field more for reasons of status or to copy an envied figure than for reasons of satisfaction. This is not surprising in view of the impediments to pleasure in their work, as already noted. Anything that is so dangerous to the self-esteem can hardly be enjoyed in a relaxed manner.

Extreme and opposite family backgrounds may sometimes be associated with these constellations. For example, one such patient grew up with a single parent, the mother, who continually told the child how perfect and how talented she was. For her own reasons, the mother needed to reassure herself about her child in this way and to be reassured in turn by her daughter's admiration. The daughter felt any criticism, even her own, to be an assault and an indication that she was attempting the wrong activity. She was therefore never able to carry through any activity beyond the point to which her native talents would carry her without practice and learning. By giving up what she attempted, she avoided what she felt to be a disastrous disillusionment. The patient naturally did not enjoy any sense of excellence, inasmuch as she never really achieved anything. As might be imagined, she was also unable to withstand the work of an analytic treatment.

A more likely family background for a woman with this type of inhibition is one in which little was expected of the child and her efforts were undermined by derision. It has frequently been observed that children who are raised by parents who view them in a negative light often assume this view of themselves in order to join forces with the parent in some way and so preserve some bond (Berger & Kennedy, 1975). Severe conflicts also arise around surpassing a parent with a strong feeling of defectiveness, and these conflicts add to the patient's need to preserve her own inadequacies.

Another interesting group of patients are those who have represented a narcissistic fulfillment for a parent. This situation seems to occur more with boys who fulfill many of the mother's renounced aspirations, but it is also seen in the case of precocious and gifted girls. It may lead to high achievement; at times, however, it produces a strong paralysis of performance if the motivation to thwart and disappoint the parent is present. The patient may feel this is necessary to establish separateness, or it may be the vehicle of aggression that cannot be expressed more openly.

Penis Envy and Work Disturbances

The phenomenon of penis envy occupies a special place among the narcissistic disturbances of women. From the time it was first described, controversy has swirled around the concept. The various opinions range from those who flatly deny its existence, through those who observe it as a phenomenon but offer differing explanations, to those who entirely support Freud's classical description of its central role in female sexual development (Freud, 1925, 1931).

Few analysts would take the first position; this point of view seems to be held mainly by those who do not have child or psychoanalytic observations available to them. Among analytic writers, the interpretations of the cause of penis envy have varied, and there is currently a good deal of scrutiny of the topic. Horney (1924, 1926, 1933) of course was the first analytic writer to take issue with Freud, followed shortly by Jones (1927, 1933, 1935). Essentially, Horney's position was that penis envy does not represent the irreducible bedrock which Freud assumed it did, but that it requires explanation. She felt that this was especially true in view of her impression that girls were not little boys preoedipally as Freud considered them to be, but showed every evidence of being unmistakably little girls. Horney suggested that a milder, primary penis envy develops normally, simply on the basis of the boy "having more" – something he is free to handle and with which he can do interesting things in urination. The later, stronger penis envy develops as a defensive response to the dangers of the feminine oedipal constellation. It also is strengthened by narcissistic considerations, namely, that the man or boy's position of value and power in the family and society is much greater. In addition, the freedom of the male is greater, as is his range of life choices. Thus, Horney's theories were organized more around fantasied dangers of genital mutilation arising from the Oedipus complex and realistic narcissistic insults, however amplified through fantasy.

A number of recent contributions call into doubt the centrality of penis envy as the organizer of female sexual development and also question whether it is in fact mainly a conflict of the genital level of development. There seems to be rather general agreement around the position taken by Stoller (1976), for example, who points out that gender identity and the sense of the self as feminine are established long before the phase when penis envy might play a role. Also, Grossman and

Stewart (1971) point out that penis envy in neurotic women may indeed represent mainly a genital level conflict, but in more disturbed women, e.g., borderline, it may act as a metaphor expressing their general, far more serious and pervasive sense of deficiency and worthlessness and envy in a way that is defensive and may act as a major resistance to the analysis of these aspects of their personality. Roiphe and Galenson (1981) confirmed, through their longitudinal observations of children from 12 months to 3 years of age, the impact on both sexes of the discovery of the anatomical difference. However, they were also able to differentiate children for whom this impact was more or less severe, depending on their current object relation, especially the relationship with the mother, and illnesses and injuries either at that time or previously.

Thus, the role of penis envy is coming to be understood within a wider context of personality development and structure than in Freud's day. The phenomenon remains observable, however, both in children and adults. No matter how one explains it, the consequences may be quite marked in development, especially in the work function. For example, women with this problem commonly complain of a pervasive feeling of doubt as to their abilities, although when pinned down about it, they find such doubt difficult to justify. Intense penis envy may also be present in women who do not suffer from work inhibitions, who, on the contrary, have developed a high level of attainment that one might expect to reassure them. It is startling, therefore, to find that they share a sense of doubt, of being fraudulent, of having fooled people or having their success by a fluke. Thus, a well-developed conflict around penis envy does not necessarily result in a work inhibition. It may, in fact, result in other adaptations as well, one of which may be a high level achievement on the basis of "I'll show them."

In any case, women suffering from penis envy feel that men have an extra "something" necessary for success that they lack. This "something" is typically located in the brain, based on a conviction that men have more confidence or more mechanical or mathematical aptitude. Some women may find it difficult to define the superiority that men possess. The vigor with which these women put forward this view is striking. They assume the existence of a superiority in men that they cannot demonstrate or defend, yet I rarely hear women consciously express envy of those areas in which men do, in fact, have a certain superiority, such as muscular strength. Nor do these women always consciously envy the penis, even though it represents a real difference between men and women. Perhaps it is easier to envy a difference that is not real than one that is.

These women often feel that they can only attain their ends through special manipulations using their sexual charms or capitalizing on their weakness. They experience a strong sense of deprivation or injury and insist on redress of their grievance. They admire men, even to the point of worship, and are generally contemptuous of women. However, their conscious attitude may for a long time be hostility or contempt toward men, as consciousness of the envy and worship produces real rage.

As noted, women of achievement may feel they have succeeded by fraud or stolen their success. This feeling seems to be related to the attribution by all these women of a masculine character to achievement, especially in fields such as science, medicine, mechanical facility, etc. As a result, these patients may resign themselves to being unable to achieve, or may react to difficulties in the course of learning as a disastrous confirmation of their defectiveness. As a result, they may abandon further attempts to achieve and withdraw into other adaptations. Their identification of certain careers as masculine arouses fears that they will frighten men off. An important component of this idea is the fantasy that the only way they can compete with men is to steal something from them or to gain revenge by humiliating them (Abraham, 1922). There is some degree of reality in this idea. Men do have a tendency to fear strong and aggressive women inasmuch as they too have fantasies of being envied for their superior penis, with its magic strengths. This convergence with reality makes the fantasies difficult to analyze as fantasies.

The normal channels of marriage and childbirth have provided one of the adaptations for such conflicts in women. It is possible for a woman to renounce the discouragement and humiliation of struggling with achievement in favor of vicarious satisfaction of these wishes through a man of high status. In fantasy, by some variety of fusion with a man, the woman may acquire the penis that she feels is the touchstone of success. A similar adaptation is to have a child who can be idealized in the same way. Of course, these solutions may put heavy pressure on the one selected to fulfill the renounced ambition. In addition, much disruption may be created in work or school situations by skirmishing among wives and mothers who are freer to support someone else's ambition with aggression.

Treatment Issues

The course of treatment of these narcissistic problems is not easy for either patient or analyst. Avoidances that have become characterological are particularly stubborn. In addition, these avoidances receive a good deal of societal support. Girls are so often told, for example, that they need not bother with achievement because they will marry instead.

Still, women seem to cling to the conviction of inferiority based on penis envy with particular strength, which reinforces the picture of the complex forces that act to maintain it. One would expect that a complex based on a narcissistic blow alone would yield with relief to the adult patient's scrutiny, once the ideas came into consciousness. In my experience, this does not happen as a rule; rather, patients attempt to reestablish and bolster their impression of inferiority, so that the other roots of penis envy need to be worked through with care.

Freud (1937) also observed this difficulty, but had no clear explanation for it. Today, we are aware that we need to explore for the presence of at least the following overdetermining factors that may be supporting the complex: (1) fear of the dangers of the positive Oedipus complex, including genital mutilation; (2) phallic wishes toward the mother; (3) pregenital conflicts and fantasies expressed through the metaphor of penis envy; (4) rationalization of feelings of deprivation and wishes for revenge at the oedipal level; (5) rationalization of the complex insistence on being taken care of; (6) family and societal influences; (7) injury to narcissism, as classically formulated; and (8) defense against aggression.

AGGRESSION IN WORK CONFLICTS

The handling of the aggressive drive seems to be somewhat different in women and men, but both show the effects of conflicts around this drive in their work performance. It is generally agreed that overt aggression is more commonly manifested in males than in females. This difference extends some distance down into the animal kingdom, although it is not universal. Marked exceptions to this are seen in the behavior of a mother with her young. Thus, there is some evidence that constitutional factors play a role in aggressive behavior, but in human beings, learning is far more important. There is no doubt about the common tendency of parents to inhibit aggressive behavior in girls, especially fighting or boisterous physical behavior, while more or less encouraging it in boys.

Nevertheless, as we know, both sexes have severe conflicts with aggression. Certainly, work inhibitions have been often described in men centering around fear of the dangerous aggression involved in the competition which is felt to be inherent in achievement, and which is exaggerated in fantasy. The oedipal fears of triumphing over the father show vividly in such patients. Women may experience much the same conflict with regard to achievement, but the triumph they fear may involve either parent. They may see the mother as weak and ineffectual—"only a woman"; and the wish or actual fulfillment of the wish to best the mother and to share work with the father is a thinly disguised oedipal gratification that may provoke much guilt and fear. The conflicts in the girl may be intensified greatly when the mother is in actuality jealous of the daughter's freedom to pursue ends that the mother chose or felt obligated to renounce.

Patients whose problems are centered more at the pregenital level have many difficulties around aggression in their work, because they feel an exaggerated, omnipotent sense of the power of their impulses. For example, one borderline patient, a physician, was heavily invested in such omnipotent ideas of her power. In certain ways it helped her in her profession, as she felt that she could always hold off disease and death. This conviction led her to extraordinary heroics in behalf of her patients, some of which were quite successful. At such times, however, she would feel herself expanding in size and power as she became elated, and she almost literally felt that she had then the power to squash and eclipse everyone around her. She would then experience panic, which disturbed both her personal and professional life.

A second example is presented by a somewhat less disturbed woman, who is extremely successful in her own business. She has found it almost impossible to act successfully as a boss, because she is so fearful about the aggression involved. She has to befriend her employees to an excessive degree, soliciting accounts of their home life and problems in which she is actually not the least interested. She finds herself enmeshed in these problems, helping take care of them and making allowance for employees' shortcomings at work, all of which she condemns. She really has a lively contempt for these employees, who are so much less competent than she is, but she is too afraid of hurting them and incurring their virulent wrath to be able to require them to do their jobs efficiently. Her adaptation at work has been to hire a manager to deal with the employees. At times, when she is setting up a new aspect of her business, she begins to feel elated and powerful as she sees that it will work. At the same time, she becomes irritable and fearful of any small difficulty, fearing that these difficulties are the signal that fate's retribution for her exercise of power is at hand. She then becomes depressed for a time and unable to accomplish her necessary work.

Both these examples represent not only various pregenitally based fears of aggression, but also important superego attitudes toward it. Men will more often complain that they lack competitiveness, while women complain that they are too aggressive and competitive. In the view of many female patients, competition is an entirely pejorative word. This ideal of passivity and nonaggression is, of course, fostered by society's standards for women, just as the aggressive ideal is fostered for men. Much has been written about the true natures of men and women in this respect, but most of it remains the personal predilection of the writer. As noted, it is possible that there are innate differences between the sexes in these qualities, but one hardly needs to invoke this explanation in view of the intense social pressure brought to bear on both men and women to conform to these ideals.

For this conformity, both sexes pay quite a price. In women, difficulties arise in work or school performance when serious conflicts exist around competition. Female patients frequently describe how they refrain from doing as well as they could in the classroom because they fear showing up their classmates and incurring their envy. Such concern for the feelings of the loser in the competition and consequent propitiating behavior and remarks are much more common among women than men.

A similar, quite striking response of women to aggression is their nearly universal concern about whether or not others will like them. Women are also concerned about their sexual attractiveness to men, of course, but the worry over being liked is separate and quite prominent.

Many women seem to consciously guide their behavior in terms of this worry, so that superficially, they seem to be guided more by the opinions of others than by their own standards. However, women's fantasies about whether others will like them seem to rest upon their own struggles with guilt about their impulses, especially aggression. Interpretations directed toward this guilt have been quite effective.

FEARS OF BEING ALONE

A whole constellation of difficulties arise for women around the problem of being alone, and some of these affect the work performance. Although men also worry about being alone, this concern seems to play a larger role in the life of women. Many women pass from home to college, perhaps to graduate school, and then to marriage, without ever having really lived on their own, although they may have had the illusion of doing so. Therefore, one of the major fears of women deciding on divorce, for example, is their conviction that they cannot make it on their own. Women may complain of feeling incomplete in a narcissistic sense without a man, as well as feeling that traditionally masculine tasks are beyond her. I have heard some astonishing fantasies about the dangers and impossibility of these activities.

These fears play a perhaps more subtle role throughout development. Girls are discouraged, often for good reason, from venturing into lonely places by themselves, and their families make an effort to impress on them some of the hazards the world offers females. This influence, coupled with the girl's own fantasies, help to establish fears about venturing forth alone. In addition, families do not usually make the same efforts with girls to instill courageous behavior that they do with boys. Moreover, unlike girls, boys are expected to be curious, to explore, and even to get into trouble.

Something of these attitudes seem to carry over into the academic and work spheres and may limit some women's ability to think independently or to range in new directions, particularly in creative pursuits. Both independent thought and conscience may be inhibited, leading to an emphasis on conforming behavior.

A gifted, creative writer showed this type of inhibition in marked form when her work was repeatedly rejected. She not only suffered the narcissistic blow of the rejection, with its negative connotation, but also felt it meant that she should not be indulging in writing as a process and questioned its content as well. She had the conscious conviction that if her work was right and good, people would like it and accept it, even though she also knew that many gifted, creative people suffer long periods of rejection. She maintained this split in her thinking in order to avoid confronting the way in which she condemned the pleasures of her creative work.

THE NEED TO BE TAKEN CARE OF

A fascinating pattern of work disturbance, which may utilize any or all of the dynamics already mentioned, lies in the frequent expression of a wish to be taken care of. At its most extreme, this wish represents an entire life plan for the solution of neurotic conflict. Naturally, this is not the normal wish to have a sexual partner with whom one shares life and perhaps children. This normal wish does not eclipse other aspects of life as does the need I referred to here.

Patients with this extreme "need" to be taken care of have as their sole objective the plan to find a man—usually handsome, tall, and wealthy with a prestigious job and high social status—who will fulfill their "need." Exploring the details of that "need," however, reveals the conflict that finding this ideal man is expected to resolve. It may represent the depressed patient's fantasy of being filled up by or uniting with the mother of the pregenital years, narcissistically and libidinally gratifying the patient to make up for early disturbances in the relationship and eliminating rage. Or, having such a man may be seen as sparing her the conflicts surrounding competition and performance, especially the narcissistic ones described earlier. Marriage to a sadistic man may offer some women the man's apparent strength, in particular to control what the woman feels to be her own highly dangerous, omnipotent, aggressive impulses. Other women may experience total self-sacrifice for even a normal man and children as a defensive solution to a struggle with both libidinal and aggressive drives. The peremptory need for a man illustrated in these few examples usually involves marriage, with all its connotations of possession. Although this plan may appear to resolve certain neurotic conflicts, it may also seriously interfere to one degree or another with the ability of an otherwise capable woman to carry out her work. A patient who has the plan of finding a man as her solution usually gives the impression of waiting or marking time. Her investment in whatever work she is in is somewhat absent minded; and she does not regard it as a serious objective in its own right or at least has inner reservations about her commitment to it. Naturally, her performance in her chosen field will be less than the best possible under the influence of such dynamics.

The analytic treatment of these patients presents many difficulties. It has often been observed that the entrance of any patient into analysis with a specific objective constitutes a formidable resistance; the patient usually finds it difficult to become interested in any subject that does not obviously involve the objective. The patient's objective serves as a limitation on free association and a rationalization of the patient's intention not to change internally—that is, not to face renunciation of some infantile objective. This type of difficulty may also be seen in patients with symptoms such as alcoholism, drug use, or certain phobias and is a common theme in many patients whose treatment has not progressed.

CREATIVITY

Another pattern of work inhibition may also have as its foundation different combinations of the dynamics already mentioned. In this case, patients, usually those with really outstanding or even extraordinary creative gifts, may become frightened about the strength of their creative capacity. In particular they are uneasy about their lack of control over their creativity. It seems to have a life of its own—they cannot rely on it to appear when they want it to, nor can they put aside its peremptory claim on their lives when it is in full bloom. These individuals feel themselves set apart from others, often quite accurately. They not only feel the loneliness of being different, but also are uneasy about why they have this gift and others do not. Some may feel it is stolen and may expect retribution at any time, producing some reluctance to use it.

Patients who are particularly uneasy over their inability to control their creativity also show the same concern over their more ordinary impulses. As they become more at ease with this aspect of themselves, they usually become more confident about the creative process.

WORK AND CHILDREN

I have referred in a number of connections to the defensive use of certain normal functions, such as marriage, for purposes of conflict resolution and the interference with work that results. There can be no question, however, that marriage and especially motherhood produce certain conflicts with the work function that are inherent in the activities themselves. One such conflict is between working and having children.

In the past few years, considerable numbers of married or unmarried women between the ages of about 31 to 37 appear to be experiencing an urgent wish to bear children. This wish seems far more intense for these women than it was earlier in their lives. This phenomenon seems to have arisen out of women's new freedom to follow careers and postpone motherhood. Whereas previously, the onset of childbearing occurred at a younger age and almost automatically, its postponement seems to have increased the force of the wish. It is true that the fact that these women are approaching the end of the time in which pregnancy is best undertaken lends urgency to the wish. Nevertheless, this is a cognitive recognition that does not seem to sufficiently account for the drive quality of the wish. These women come to feel that they are being seriously deprived by not having children and that they must then make some very difficult choices about how to manage work and children. Furthermore, these women also feel keenly the separation from their children in their younger years if they elect to return to work early. Of course, giving up or severely curtailing work at this time may or may not express a work inhibition. It may represent an essentially nonneurotic decision to give freer rein to an important life current.

It seems that analytic theory is somewhat inadequate when it approaches the phenomena of the wish to bear a child and the wish to raise one, which are two quite different issues. Freud's formulation of the matter was that the wish for a child arises out of penis envy as a partial restitution, as it were, with the oedipal interest in the father resting very much on his ability to give the girl a child. Much of the analytic literature stresses this formulation of the wish for a child as well as the burdens and sufferings of motherhood. This trend led to theories of motherhood as embodying masochistic trends. Horney (1926), again, dissented, being one of the few who emphasized that the joy of motherhood was being overlooked. Parens et al. (1976) have suggested that the wish for a child represents a maturational stage of the libidinal drive that cannot be shown to be inextricably connected to penis envy. They observed girls from birth to 3 years of age, studying the order in which evidence of penis envy, an evident wish for a child, and the onset of the libidinal wish for the father appeared. They reasoned that if Freud's formulation was correct, penis envy always had to precede the other two. In fact, they did not find this to be the case and concluded that penis envy was an inadequate primary cause for the wish for a child in girls. It would seem that the psychoanalytic theories of motherhood could stand some reworking the same way that the theories of sexual development have been reexamined.

The urges both to have a child and to carry on productive work make heavy demands on the mother. Although we have certain general ideas about what influences are important in the development of small children, we are not able to state precisely what balance between maternal care and substitute care is necessary or optimal. It obviously depends very much on the quality of each and on the nature of the child in question. Therefore, the door is open for the mother to have all sorts of fantasies about what is necessary for the child and, therefore, what she is obligated to provide.

One of the ways in which a woman can deal with this uncertainty is to try to become "supermom." She may feel reassured if she is able to provide for every conceivable need of her child, to say nothing of her husband. She can then submerge any guilty sense that she does not love her child enough, which might arise if she becomes angry at the child or bored or if she longs to return to work and a secondary process world. The "supermom's" ideal of motherhood may be one of total provision and self-sacrifice based on an identification with a mother who emphasized that as her role. Or she may be giving her mother lessons in adequate mothering if she felt that her own mother had serious shortcomings. In any case, her attempts at perfection assist her in the struggle against her own impulses, which she feels are selfish and destructive. In particular, if she feels that she is acting selfish and self-centered by being interested in her work, she may develop an inhibition in its performance. The sublimations involved in work may also be threatened when the balance between instinctual wishes and defense is altered, as it may be during pregnancy and childbearing. A woman's tendency to need to become "supermom" may also be stimulated by any feelings of omnipotence, so that she feels that she not only must be but can be equal to all challenges. Some of the forces that affect her work performance may also contribute to the woman's trouble in either disciplining or gratifying her children. For example, the same problems with aggression that may have hampered her work may also be expressed in an inability to say no to or curb her children, thus intensifying the conflict between work and home.

INTERNAL INFLUENCES ON THE FREEDOM TO WORK

In considering women and work, we might wonder what sorts of influences are responsible not only for inhibitions in work but also for especially good functioning. After all, many of the same conflicts and histories are to be found both in women who perform very well and those who have problems with achievement. One would find it difficult to predict which women would run into trouble in work arising out of these influences and which would not.

In comparing women in my practice who fall into either group, my rough impression is that the group who showed most interference had a close and sticky relationship with their mothers, based at least in part on the mother's excessive need to keep the child close. Although these relationships had a good deal of conflict, they seemed to have provided quite a good deal of reward for staying close. These mothers characteristically were not themselves achievers; indeed, some of them were quite disturbed, putting pressure on the child to help the mother by not being too competent and by not leaving her. Women who seem freer to achieve, in contrast, had more conflicted relationships with their mothers, who were themselves stronger figures. These mothers also tended to work at a career themselves, although this was not uniformly true. These initial impressions at least suggest that being "bound by the apron strings" may be bad for girls as well as boys.

In these remarks on work I have tried to outline some of the many internal obstacles to the progress of women in work. Naturally, I do not intend to imply that the many social obstacles to women's success in work are not exceedingly important; however, these external impediments have been considered elsewhere. As analysts, our role is to pay meticulous attention to the way in which these realistic obstacles can also be used as the focus of resistance, without at the same time denying their existence.

REFERENCES

Abraham, K. (1922), Manifestations of the female castration complex. *Internat. J. Psycho-anal.*, 3: 1–29.

Applegarth, A. (1976), Some observations on work inhibition in women. *J. Amer. Psychoanal. Assn.*, 24 (suppl.): 251–269.

Berger, M., & Kennedy, H. (1975), Pseudobackwardness in children: Maternal attitudes as an etiological factor. *The Psychoanalytic Study of the Child*, 30: 279–307. New Haven: Yale University Press.

Freud, S. (1915), The unconscious. *Standard Edition*, 14: 161–215. London: Hogarth Press, 1957.

_____ (1925), Some psychical consequences of the anatomical distinction between the sexes. *Standard Edition*, 19: 241–258, London: Hogarth Press, 1961.

_____ (1931), Female sexuality. *Standard Edition*, 21: 223–243, London: Hogarth Press, 1961.

_____ (1937), Analysis terminable and interminable. *Standard Edition*, 23: 209–255. London: Hogarth Press, 1964.

Grossman, W. I., & Stewart, W. A. (1976), Penis envy: From childhood wish to developmental metaphor. *J. Amer. Psychoanal. Assn.*, 24 (suppl.): 193–213.

Halpern, H. (1964), Psychodynamic and cultural determinants of work inhibition in children and adolescents. *Psychoanal. Rev.*, 51: 173–189.

Hartmann, H. (1955), Notes on the theory of sublimation. *The Psychoanalytic Study of the Child*, 10: 9–28. New York: International Universities Press.

Hellman, I. (1954), Some observations on mothers of children with intellectual inhibitions. *The Psychoanalytic Study of the Child*, 9: 259–274, New York: International Universities Press.

Hendrick, I. (1943), Work and the pleasure principle *Psychoanal. Quart.*, 12: 311–330.

Horney, K. (1924), On the genesis of the castration complex in women. *Internat. J. Psycho-anal.*, 5: 50–65.

_____ (1926), The flight from womanhood. *Internat. J. Psycho-anal.* 7: 324–339.

_____ (1933), The denial of the vagina. *Internat. J. Psycho-anal.*, 14: 57–70.

Jones, E. (1927), The early development of female sexuality. *Internat. J. Psycho-anal.*, 8: 459–472.

_____ (1933), The phallic phase. *Internat. J. Psycho-anal.*, 14: 1–33.

_____ (1935), Early female sexuality. *Internat. J. Psycho-anal.*, 16: 263–273.

Loomie, L. S., Rosen, V. H., & Stein, M. H. (1958), Ernst Kris and the gifted adolescent project. *The Psychoanalytic Study of the Child*, 13: 44–58. New York: International Universities Press.

Mahler, M. (1942), Pseudo-imbecility. *Psychoanal. Quart.*, 11:149–164.

Menninger, K. (1942), Work as a sublimation. *Bull. Menn. Clinic*, 6: 170–182.

Oberndorf, C. P. (1951), Psychopathology of work. *Bull. Menn. Clinic*, 15: 77–84.

Parens, H., Pollock, L., Stern, J., & Kramer, S. (1976), On the girl's entry into the Oedipus complex. *J. Amer. Psychoanal. Assn.*, 24 (suppl.): 79–109.

Roiphe, H., & Galenson, E. (1981), *Infantile origins of sexual identity*. New York: International Universities Press.

Stoller, R. J. (1976), Primary femininity. *J. Amer. Psychoanal. Assn.*, 24 (suppl.): 39–79.

White, R. W. (1963), Ego and reality in psychoanalytic theory. *Psychological Issues*, Monogr. 11. New York: International Universities Press.

11
Empty-Nest Syndrome: Possibility or Despair

Margot Tallmer, Ph.D.

The common expression, the "empty-nest" syndrome, reflects the current psychoanalytic emphasis on the association between aging and loss. Psychological changes in late adulthood are generally explained as reactions to loss and, ultimately, to the most basic fear of death. Two examples of this thinking will suffice. Sternschein (1973, p. 637) sees

> middle age as a time of maximal and autonomous engagement with objects and of definitive self-delineation and self-realization. . . . The idealization of this age period also has a definitive purpose aimed at coping with the, by now, critical issue of "growing to dying," . . . an unevenly unfolding process involving painful confrontations with the inevitability of death and the limitations of time.

Jaques (1981, p. 11) similarly asserts that "it is this fact of the entry upon the psychological scene of the reality and inevitability of one's own personal death that is the central and crucial feature of the midlife phase – the feature which precipitates the critical nature of the period."

In fact, however, loss is the dominant characteristic of the very end of life rather than of the aging process itself. Nevertheless, current thinking has designated loss as part of the "midlife crisis," a phenomenon that by now has assumed a certain cachet. Midlife crisis is considered to be a period of appraising one's life situation, assessing past losses, and regarding potential routes for dealing with the remainder of life – a remainder now briefer than the time already lived; that is, one's life is more than half over. Gould (1980) suggests, perhaps facetiously, that the pervasive popularization of this midlife crisis may actually reflect a need on the part of writers to explain their own age-related intrapsychic difficulties within the framework of an acceptable, nonthreatening label.

Two popularly designated specific losses for middle-aged women (approximately 45–60 years of age) are the cessation of the menses, a biological event, and the departure of the children from the home, a psychological phenomenon. Both these so-called losses, occurring at about the same time, are said to usher in the postulated midlife crisis for women and to mark the onset of aging. The empty-nest syndrome has been defined as a depressive reaction to the woman's loss of her children and her maternal functioning.

This phenomenon of the empty-nest syndrome must be viewed in terms of general adult development and the meaning of parenthood – motherhood in particular. The effects of other variables such as the role of the spouse and the family must also be considered.

THEORIES OF ADULT DEVELOPMENT

We have been obliged, belatedly, to extend our theoretical notions of personality development into adulthood, recognizing that adults, like children and adolescents, go through dynamic, ongoing developmental processes. Influenced by adult experiences as well as by factors from the past, primary themes of oedipal relationships, separation, and identity continue to press forward throughout life, demanding attention; physiological and neurological events also affect the organism throughout the lifetime (Rangell, 1953; Colarusso & Nemiroff, 1979). Adulthood is a time of personality integration and change – not as clearly limned as in childhood, but of equal power. Adulthood is not just a period of marking time until death.

Psychoanalysts are latecomers to adult psychology. Jung actually stressed midlife individuation, but his concepts relating to this period of life have only recently become popularized. Erikson (1959) and Levinson (1977) are two major contributors to stage theories that encompass the entire life cycle, using age as the key variable. Levinson's work, innovative and well researched, was unfortunately limited to the study of males. Erikson, actually the first psychoanalyst to take a broad view of development over the life span, was hampered by the lack of an adult psychology at the time of his writing. He did define the developmental tasks of the later years; however, his attention to adulthood was minimal in comparison to an extended focus on childhood and adolescence.

Erikson's ideas are appealing and thoughtful, often serving the function of interpreting empirical data. He moved beyond Freud into concerns with the impact of the society on the individual's perception of the world. Erikson envisioned progressive, unfolding psychological processes, or epigenetic stages, that lead a person to become a more complex, better integrated self as she or he ages. Each stage offers positive possibilities and challenges for growth and expansion. Middle adulthood, for example, is a time for confronting the particular developmental task of achieving generativity rather than stagnation.

At this time of life, the individual must experience a sense of having contributed to the future of society, with the belief that some of those contributions will continue after one's death. Because losing oneself in the physical and mental life of others leads to the expansion of ego interests, this is a period of enrichment. Inadequate original parenting may prevent the next generation from achieving the goal of generativity. Maturity is demonstrated by parental sacrifices and a lack of selfishness in relationship to children; in Erikson's view, giving up a career or other pleasures for offspring is a hallmark of adult personality.

Erikson's final stage of ego development is concerned with achieving integrity as opposed to despair – two abstract, rather global concepts. On the positive side, this includes acceptance of one's life for what it has been, relating to the past by embracing both successes and failures, concentrating on the large scope of humankind rather than on self-absorption, and accepting mortality without an unreasoning fear of death. In Erikson's words (1968, pp. 139–140):

> In the aging person who has taken care of things and people and has adapted himself to the triumphs and disappointments of being, by necessity, the originator of others and the generator of things and ideas — only in him the fruit of the seven stages gradually ripens. . . . [Ego integrity] is the ego's accrued assurance of its proclivity for order and meaning — an emotional integration faithful to the image-bearers of the past and ready to take, and eventually to renounce, leadership in the present. It is the acceptance of one's one and only life cycle and of the people who have become significant to it as something that had to be and that, by necessity, permitted of no substitutions. It thus means a new and different love of one's parents, free of the wish that they should have been different, and an acceptance of the fact that one's life is one's own responsibility. It is a sense of comradeship with men and women of distant times and of different pursuits who have created orders and objects and sayings conveying human dignity and love. . . . Despair expresses the feeling that time is short, too short for the attempt to start another life and to try out alternate roads to integrity.

How does Erikson deal with the psychological differences between men and women? (The use of masculine nouns and pronouns in the previous quotation gives us a ready clue.) He uses observations of play activities in prepubescent youngsters as empirical evidence that differences in modes of spatial organization are gender-likened. Girls' designs reflect their biology — their spaces are quiet and protective, mirroring the womb and the vagina. Males are interested in active, productive, thrusting spatial compositions obviously conforming to phallic configurations. For Erikson, the unique biological blueprints of the sexes determine personality. Women are endowed with psychological capacities to care for others.

Erikson's innovative ideas about the adolescent identity crisis have been well popularized. In his formulation, identity achieved in adolescence is a precursor to the subsequent stage of intimacy, wherein one's identity is fused with another, while one still maintains a sense of self bolstered by unselfish, mature love. Women, according to Erikson, achieve their identity through marriage, committing themselves firmly to caring for others, in line with their innate biological and psychological capacities. Issues of identity do not become critical for women until their child-rearing responsibilities diminish in their late thirties or early forties. For Erikson, then, only at this point, corresponding to the empty-nest syndrome, does the woman need to consider her identity as separate from her husband's and from those she cares for. Erikson did not account for women who do not choose motherhood, nor did he adequately consider sex-linked cultural conditioning. Moreover, women are most often responsible for aging parents, thus continuing in the caring role and, supposedly, further deferring the need for achieving an identification. Interestingly, men do not require women for the same task of identity formation.

Recently, Erikson has dealt more fully with this issue of the capacity for caring in the older person, designating caring as a fundamental task of adulthood. That is, the individual must learn how to spend his or her reservoir of caring resources. Conceding the reality of feminist criticism, Erikson admits to having slighted identity formation in women. Currently, Erikson has recanted to some degree and now wants women involved in formerly male-dominated institutions because of women's specific modes of experience, their altruism, and their value systems. He acknowledges that men are conflicted about the value of the penis, corresponding to the hypothesized notion of penis envy in women, and that males are jealous of the maternal capacities of females. Erikson (quoted in Evans, 1981) states that "Freud's general judgment of the identity of the female was probably the weakest part of his theory. Exactly what is to blame for that I don't know, except that he was a Victorian man, a patriarchical man" (p. 43).

Erikson has his own problems with female issues, however, because his observations, discussions, and examples are based largely on upper-middle-class men or professional persons. The male, once again, is the touchstone of personhood. It is true that the departure of children from the home may present the mothering person with many choices and decisions to be made about the next period of life. I do not agree, however, that this is now a matter of identity formation or necessarily a time of depression. (In all fairness to Erikson, he does not connect the stage with depressive affect as other writers have done.) Any shift in life offers the potential for both positive and negative outcomes. Freedom may bring its own difficulties. Reaching a plateau in development is a natural sequence in the life cycle, not an exclusive domain of the woman; nor is it marked by the pejorative connotation of an empty nest.

For Peck (1968), the stage of ego integrity or despair, covering as it does nearly the entire second half of life, must be further divided into smaller categories based on the developmental tasks to be accomplished. One such task is the reevaluation of wisdom as being of higher value than physical prowess. Physical strength inevitably declines with age, despite any accent on body maintenance and care. Greater prestige must therefore be accorded to those who achieve gains in problem solving, judgment, and other cognitive developments. Society and the individual must award plain, old-fashioned respect for the wisdom of the mature adult. Concomitantly, as the primacy of sexuality also decreases with age, people must be assessed in terms of more basic integrity, rather than measured as sex objects. Lest this seem too Pollyannish, Peck would have other attributes as the basis for human relationships to avoid sexualizing interpersonal exchanges. The relevance of Peck's thinking to the position of older women is self-evident. Given society's emphasis on retaining a youthful appearance, a totally impossible feat, women's alterations in physical appearance are treated far more harshly than men's. Mature women suffer the indignities of aging to a much greater degree.

Cathectic flexibility, the ability to withdraw emotionally from roles and people, and then to reinvest oneself in others or in different activities and interests is a positive attribute, particularly in adulthood. Such tasks are often mandated by the environment or by a reassessment that proves some activities to be now unworthy of further commitment. Mental flexibility is of equal importance, permitting the person to alloplasically alter the environment rather than adhering rigidly to former positions and attitudinal sets. In the period of old age, the work role has to lose some of its former importance, yielding to other means of ego differentiation. Similarly, the main stress on the body must be relinquished, while the emphasis on the major importance of human relationships is maintained. Finally, achieving ego transcendence rather than ego preoccupation permits the aging individual to accept personal death, knowing that he or she has contributed to future generations.

Other psychologists have been instrumental in developing an adult psychology, dealing in particular with role theory. Cumming and Henry (1961) developed a disengagement theory that purported to explain the patent withdrawal of the elderly from society. In the course of their work, they made the assumption that women's passage through the life cycle is smoother than the route traversed by men. Their explanation is that women's pivotal roles as homemakers and nurturers continue throughout their life, while their aging male counterparts are obliged to confront critical life alterations, such as retirement. They view work as central to the lives of men, occupying the most role space and offering the greatest social as well as monetary rewards.

Later research on life span psychology (Kutner, 1961; Heyman, 1970; Lopata, 1971; Kline, 1975) has suggested that, on the contrary, discontinuity is a major characteristic and a central adaptation of women's lives. Role shifts and vocational changes mandated by child bearing, child care, and a husband's job changes and consequent geographical moves all demand a great deal of flexibility – a resource helpful in aging and pertinent to the empty-nest syndrome. Moreover, the role of spouse disappears far more frequently among women than men – 70 percent of those widowed are women. Thus, women can adjust better to role change because they have been so frequently obliged to do so. A lifetime of differing roles and demands can be a positive experience.

In 1968, Neugarten presented rather startling empirical data on middle age that questioned much of the then current psychoanalytic thinking. Her research confirmed the theory that middle age is a time of self-scrutiny and self-appraisal. It did not confirm the notion of the depressed middle-aged women, however, but rather found that midlife women feel freer and more energetic, liberated, excited, and satisfied than when they were younger.

Additionally, research (Neugarten & Gutmann, 1968) has revealed personality changes in both sexes with age: Men and women were found to reverse their roles as authorities in the family, with women taking over the role as heads of the family in later life. Concomitantly, women become more accepting of their aggressive impulses, while men deal more easily with their nurturant and affiliative needs. Others have confirmed these findings (Kerckhoff, 1966; Thurnher, 1974). Kuhlen (1963) has further explicated how individuals satisfy or frustrate their needs at different times in the life cycle.

In summary, these researchers did not find depression to be present in middle-aged women – the leave-taking of the children caused women to assess occupational possibilities and plan for the next 30 years. Men, having explored their aggressive capabilities in the work area, become concerned with other areas of their lives – areas women formerly took care of for them. Men try to express the "caring" parts of their personalities. Both genders, but women in particular, are better able to monitor their bodies and to become alert to the effects of stress.

PARENTHOOD

A basic component of our psychological makeup is structured around becoming a parent. This event absorbs and organizes much of human energy from early adulthood well into middle age and, indeed, continues to absorb us in an attentuated form throughout life. Not many will quarrel with this assertion, but few have paid sufficient attention to parenthood. Psychoanalysis has stressed evidence of pathological parenting, based on patients' recall of their childhood experiences, rather than on reports of parents themselves. Indeed, Michels (1981) notes that Anna Freud et al.'s Outline for Metapsychological Assessment of the Adult Personality (1965) refers to parenthood in only one instance, and excludes it from a list of life episodes that should be specifically assessed. There is an extraordinary dearth of objective data, psychoanalytically based research, or theoretical speculation on the topic of parenthood. Benedek's (1960) contribution was a milestone in the literature; but was her frequently acknowledged contribution so noteworthy and innovative, or is its importance exaggerated because others have continued to slight the topic and must rely upon her speculations? Whatever the cause, social psychologists, sociologists, and anthropologists have dominated current studies of parenthood.

Benedek (1960) viewed parenthood as a developmental phase, thus modifying the customary notion of libido theory that personality integration occurs in adolescence. Instead Benedek saw personality integration as extending into later development, where it is affected by the drive potentials of reproduction. For the woman, physiological and psychodynamic interplays during pregnancy and breast-feeding sustain a maternal drive organization toward mothering. Pregnancy is, naturally, endowed with individual, idiosyncratic meanings for the woman. As Benedek (1960) states:

> The foetus is a part of the mother's body. . . . In some cases it may represent the missing penis; in others, it is the admired beauty, or the envied pregnancy of the woman's own mother; most fequently the foetus is the

token of the loved self. . . . Many women identify the foetus with faeces and relive during pregnancy the ambivalent feelings and mysteries of the infantile sexual fantasy of the anal child. The mother's object relationship to her unborn child becomes ambivalent or strongly hostile when the fantasy projected on to the foetus is highly ambivalent. The foetus, then, becomes the representation of a hated and/or feared person, and motherhood becomes an overwhelming menace [p. 11].

Benedek uses the term *emotional symbiosis* to denote the structural changes in both mothers and children that emerge through identification and introjection. Under optimal conditions, the mother, gratified by her ability to nurture successfully, establishes greater self-confidence and a new integration of personality via the introjection that "good, thriving infant" equals "good mother-self." She thus attains a part of her ego ideal and is somewhat buttressed against the anxieties, fears, and frustrations that are inevitable in caring for a baby. Her own infantile experiences, including the oral dependence, can be relived and reconciled, permitting a new corrective emotional balance.

The father is similarly effected by a drive organization. "There need be no doubt that the male reproductive drive has psychic representations of instinctual, biological origin. . . . The adult male includes in his ego ideal the aspiration to complete his role in procreation by fatherliness" (Benedek, 1960, p. 398).

Reactions of both mother and father cannot be a mere reenactment of early psychic dramas; the infant, as a new member of the cast, strongly affects all the actors. Parenting also changes throughout the life cycle, and we cannot expect the mother to react to her adolescent children in the same manner as she reacts to newborn infants. The feelings of parenthood undergo slow, gradual transformations, so that the mother's affect at the time of her children's departure is very different from her earlier responses when they left for nursery school or camp. Finally, parents must adjust to each other's reactions to being a parent, thus complicating the situation even further and allowing for more variations. On a latent level, infants can trigger off dramatic, long-repressed feelings, both positive and negative. Unwelcome examples include envy, competitive feelings, fears of aggression and abuse, and jealousy. Positive outcomes include working through associations to the child's sex, sibling position, innate endowment, and temperament; and feelings of protectiveness and satisfaction in giving. The list is infinite.

The normative adaptation of both sexes—that is, projecting onto the child needs that would interfere with decent parenting—involves a not inconsiderable amount of self-sacrifice and, ultimately, a socially acceptable, adaptive projection onto the child of parental narcissisms. Gutmann (1981) notes that this is necessary for the survival of the species. The child becomes idealized as the mother views her offspring as an extension of herself, and the father projects grandiose fantasies onto his son or daughter. In general, Gutmann (1980) continues, when another person becomes the reservoir of one's feelings about oneself, the life of the other person becomes more important than one's own life. Personal death is made more acceptable because the child's survival has assumed first priority. Indeed, stories of parents willingly sacrificing their own lives for their children are legion and part of our folk wisdom. For Gutmann, then, becoming a parent answers many essential needs, including the most basic questions concerning the importance and meaning of existence, giving the person a raison d'être in the most fundamental sense. For many people, nagging, existential concerns can be put aside temporarily; indeed, one is often obliged to cast them off because of the constant, daily, consuming nature of child rearing.

Feminists, Gutmann predicts, will probably argue with his enunciation of gender distinctions, but he feels strongly that women have been given the more focused, close responsibility for child care, while men are obliged to cope with the larger, more peripheral external environment. The intimate, emotional nurturance offered by the mother leads to the building of emotional trust in the child, and the father's contribution leads to a feeling of physical security. Becoming either a mother or a father leads to alterations in the channeling and expression of basic aggressive impulses. Status for women has been traditionally derived from the home role, while men evoke esteem for their instrumentality. It follows, then, that males' aggression is externalized, and their passive dependency needs are vicariously satisfied through the projection of these needs onto his family. Dependence is then experienced by taking care of his dependents. In counterpoint to the masculine solution, the mother curbs her own active strivings and suppresses the anger that is routinely part of daily life with small children.

As one ages, this intrapsychic resolution of endowing another with a large part of one's narcissism begins to be less appropriate. Men and women are slowly freed from the extended crisis situation of parenthood as children assume responsibility for their own lives. In middle age, as we have seen, men may examine and reassess their intense, prolonged absorption in work activities, perhaps regretting the neglect of private, personal relationships. They may decide to concentrate on areas that were slighted, such as affiliation, aesthetics, or contemplation. The male empty-nest syndrome may then appear. The man's own dependency needs, previously projected onto his children, have to be dealt with. One possible solution is to project them again, this time onto his wife, with the formula: "I am not dependent. She is the one who must be depressed because her children have left, and now she needs me." In fact, many men decide on a divorce after the departure of their children and then, interestingly enough, begin another family.

In contrast, many women at this time permit themselves for the first time to express their inhibited, so-called masculine, aggressive impulses and now strive for achievement and dominance. They may become more outward in their orientation and may move away from dependence on the husband and the need to support the family emotionally. Some of the narcissism that has been invested in their children is then retrieved for individual self-expression. To the extent that the husband and family resist the alterations in the woman's orientation, they will attempt to force her back into her previous emotional alliances and priorities. The degree and effectiveness of her resistance to their pressure will determine the outcome of her empty-nest syndrome. Moreover, not only is it no longer necessary for the woman to express herself through others, if she does so she will be frowned on as a clinging mother. The midlife woman is faced with a Scylla and Charybidis situation, both solutions fraught with difficulties and conveniently labeled as female pathology.

Parenthood has other, more obvious social meanings that have to do with religion, sexual and gender identity, and instinctual needs. Many religions extol and enforce a moral obligation to have children and to refrain from birth control or abortion. It has been noted that the liberal groups that endorse individual decision making regarding the number of children in a family still refrain from urging zero population growth. On a national scale, even China, which exemplifies the professed right of the community to decide these matters, still limits coercive bans and permits families a sole offspring. As desirable as it might be, the government does not press for complete abstention from parenthood. In purely agrarian societies, of course, children are considered necessary replacements for dying workers. The value of producing progeny must be transmitted from generation to generation. A modern example of the use of a large family, in this case for the purpose of gaining entry into the power structure, might be the Kennedy clan, who also come from a religious group that is against birth control or abortion. If a woman has accepted religious or social notions about the rectitude of having children despite her own personal wishes, convictions, or needs, the departure of her progeny may constitute relief from a longtime burden.

It is commonly assumed that women possess more of an instinctual drive to have children than men do, and that women are more subject to control by their physical potential for reproduction. Some writers have postulated a need to be pregnant; Fletcher (1968), for example, views parental activity as a physiological response to hormones and sexual organs triggered by the perception of a human baby. In a further extension of this belief, Fletcher posits a homemaking instinct that encompasses the nuclear family, the wish to procreate, and the establishment of a home. Childlessness is, by definition, deviant and unnatural. This is a convenient idea. If we endorse it, social and psychological conditioning do not have to be explained, and symptoms of depression when children leave have a simplistic basis.

Finally, the acceptance of a consensually validated gender role is visibly demonstrated by an avowed wish for children. Masculinity and femininity are neatly stereotyped. Female gender identity is more closely bound to this concept than the male's. If sex is for the purpose of procreation, pregnancy unconsciously equals genital success and proof of potency for the man. More children indicates more intercourse. The lore that couples who cannot have children have coitus less frequently is still accepted.

POSITIVE ASPECTS OF THE EMPTY NEST

Why do negative stereotypes about the middle years in a woman's life continue to persist, despite all empirical evidence to the contrary? Neither menopause nor the empty nest, by themselves, are correlated with a decrease in well-being (Neugarten, Wood, Kraines, & Loomis, 1968; McKinlay & Jeffries, 1974; Lowenthal, Thurnher, & Chiriboga, 1975; Maas & Kuypers, 1975; Radloff, 1975; Campbell, Converse, & Rogers, 1976).

The most obvious explanation is the belief that a woman's centrality lies in her biological potential and that any aborting of those capabilities inevitably leads to psychic distress. The inability to further procreate is seen as even more burdensome when the children who do exist do not require constant care. By regarding the phenomenon of motherhood through such a distorted lens, investigators have been able to disregard the data that middle-aged women look forward to the departure of the children (Lowenthal et al, 1975); that women whose offspring have left have a greater sense of well-being than those living at home with small children (Radloff, 1975); and that "the marriage of the last child is to a notable extent negatively associated with emotional distress" (Pearlin, 1981, p. 184). Instead, they claim that the negative affect—that is, the postulated depression, fear, and anxiety—is not accessible to consciousness in the interview situation—a transparent misuse of psychoanalytic concepts! If the subject does not acknowledge the phenomenon but the investigator believes it to exist, the investigator's belief system is not in error, but rather denial is operating and precluding proof of the belief. Moreover, these observers perceive the assertiveness that many adult women manifest at this period of their lives as a return to the repressed rather than as maturational development and evidence of growth! The biases of the observer may determine the interpretation of the data. Perhaps other variables, such as ethnicity, social class, education, timing, and personality variations in the women, determine the conclusions of the investigations. For example, some mothers prefer different life stages in their children, and adolescence—the stage of children at this time in the mother's life—may be hardest for some.

As has been noted, midlife is generally considered a time for concentration on morals, superego concerns, the meaning of life—issues that had to be put aside because of child care responsibilities (Frenkel-Brunswick, 1968; Havighurst, 1973; Levinson, Darrow, Klein, Levinson, & McKee, 1976). Men often wait until retirement at age 65 to assess their personal belief systems. Women at midlife are in a better chronological place to slough off unwanted obligations, to concentrate on the future steps to be taken, and to be stimulated by changes. Given the current pronounced deemphasis and even denigration of the role of full-time mother—a role that probably involved a considerable sacrifice on the part of the middle-aged woman—the value of having children at all is a particularly poignant and pressing question for women at this time. However, for better or worse, *alea iacta est* (the die is cast);

the job is essentially completed, and the woman must consider the future. As a result of the woman's movement, independence and assertiveness are more highly valued for women than before (Barnett & Baruch, 1978). The middle-aged woman may return to issues of identity and autonomy that may have been only partially resolved in young adulthood, facilitating even further growth.

During this time of self-examination, the availability of free time can be restorative, providing an opportunity for subjective shifts in thinking. A heightened sense of mortality, a common awareness in midlife, is less terrifying when one has dealt with children and, often, the care of older parents. One can accept the knowledge of being separate and alone, even if closely tied to others, and proceed to develop and grow; or, one can retreat to the previous islands of safety, pouring time into grown children, grandchildren, and endlessly expanding household responsibilities.

Motherhood is not a unitary phenomenon—it cannot retain the same significance for the woman throughout her life. Middle age brings a perhaps welcome diminishment of the burdens of being central to a family's interactions, of being ever open to interruptions from others who require responsiveness and constant emotional sensitivity, and the inevitable daily tasks involved in the mere maintenance and mechanics of family life. Although mothering continues, it is on a less intense basis. This may connote a certain loss of power, since the mother plays such an important role in a child's early life; but the gain resides in the knowledge that all of one's actions are not so fateful and fraught with consequences. The woman is in greater charge of her own life. The feeling that one is not in charge is associated with depression.

Children are also in charge of their lives, and the parent is no longer the sole monitor of their behavior. Their departure causes daily life to become much less complicated. The charged presence of adolescents frequently generates a good deal of tension in the family and the time right before they leave is often marked by anxiety and internal conflict. Furthermore, many adolescents are sources of competitive envy, blessed as they seem to be by limitless vigor, attractiveness, and demands for financial and emotional support. The potential for envy rises proportionate to parents' feelings of inadequacy, negatively affecting family relationships. The children's departure permits the release of massive amounts of energy and narcissism that can be rechanneled. And finally, the sexual relationship between the parents is often more satisfactory than ever before. When parents are no longer fearful about conception and are not interrupted by the presence of children, they can experience sex for its mutual pleasure rather than solely as a procreative act.

Difficulties arise when the empty nest is refilled, either by returning children or aging, ill parents. For example, one middle-aged woman, the mother of three, stated during her session, "I've always watched everybody else growing." Returning to school after the last child had gone off to graduate work, she found herself depressed when a son came home from medical school at the very time of her own final examinations:

> I only saw his hungry mouth, waiting for me to feed him. I couldn't say, "I'm glad to see you." He put his laundry on the kitchen table, where I was working. My husband said to put some food on the table, but I told them, "Help yourselves." He screamed at me: "Is that any way to talk to your child?" This is my child who needed me all the time, was still hungry for milk, still wanting to be the baby.

CLINICAL ILLUSTRATIONS

Mrs. W. was a 55-year-old mother whose only child, a 36-year-old son, had just left his parents' home. This couple then faced about 20 years alone together—actually somewhat less time than the average two-parent family today, whose children usually leave when the parents are in their forties. In this instance, the presence of the son who aligned himself with the mother against the father, had diluted much of the very hostile interaction between the husband and wife.

Mrs. W. was reared in the European tradition, in which the matriarch was still important. The fact of the son's leaving, even at this age, was invested with a strongly negative aura: "I'm ashamed in front of my neighbors—they'll think he's a fairy." The family lived in an Italian section of the Bronx, as did Mrs. W.'s parents and her mother-in-law. Many of the foreign-born or first-generation American women there were somewhat isolated from the larger community and had not acquired a sufficient command of written English. Mrs. W. uses this lack to explain her inability to seek a job. In truth, her resources were limited, and the son had assisted her in the daily management in the larger environment; he filled out forms, dealt with community agencies, and performed many minor tasks for her. She, in turn, cared for all his physical needs and, to as great an extent as possible, cultivated and then satisfied his dependency wishes.

After he left, Mrs. W. called her son almost daily and sent money and all her credit cards, in line with her definition of a good mother. To her, a good mother was a constant, conscientious worrier—a worrier who can flexibly change the content of any particular concern should a particular situation be resolved. For example, for several sessions, Mrs. W. diligently focused on the perils of the son's geographical relocation: "I slept not at all last night because the TV reports there's an earthquake right where he lives. I know he's dead, or hurt, or messed up." When her son proved not to be a victim or even remotely connected to the event, Mrs. W. could easily reevaluate her emotional Richter scale by substituting another possible danger. Persistent attempts to help Mrs. W. understand the need to project onto the environment her own internal fears of disintegration, triggered off by her terror of separation, were therapeutically inadequate. We were able to successfully overcome some of the initial resistances in the form of conscious barriers—for example, Mrs. W. said that she was too old for treatment, that the therapist could not understand the Italian culture, that only bad people went to counselors. But we could not work through the essential need to experience herself as a separate person without her son, and treatment was aborted after the summer break. Mrs. W. reported the following last dream:

> I'm walking in an open air trench in the country, yelling for water. A man leans over and says the lines are cut off. He will turn it on for me to take a drink. I have to drink enough for two-and-a-half months. He turns the lines off again. I have to keep walking to the next state. I yell like crazy for water.

In the dream, the time period may relate to the summer vacation time for the analyst. The source of a life essential, water, is seen to be in the hands of a man. Mrs. W. is exposed, vulnerable, and needs to keep moving. Indeed, in regard to therapy, she literally "took a walk." But the relationship between her and her son is expressed in terms of warfare, on a male "turf," so to speak. And she is totally dependent upon him to cut the lines—the cords between them. She is at his mercy.

In an analogous situation, the therapist was able to help a similarly fearful woman who projected her panic onto a separating son. The woman subsequently became intensely involved with the nuclear freeze movement, successfully sublimating much of her anxiety. Unfortunately, different countertransferential feelings probably accounted for the variation in the success of the two women's treatment.

In another illustration, a 53-year-old woman came for psychoanalytic treatment, her initial encounter with therapy, because of a frightening, recurrent dream: "My breasts are hanging down – old, gnarled, and withered from too much giving." The last of her three children had left and she welcomed the freedom from the confinements of housework and daily child care, work that she had indeed found quite satisfying. In fine physical condition, intelligent and resourceful, she was eager to get started in a doctoral program in economics that would lead to her first job outside the home since her marriage. The night before her oral defense, she had the following dream: "My baby [actually the youngest of twin sons] is going down the bathtub drain."

Later in treatment, after she had begun to achieve prominence in her exacting field, the twin sons began to take turns in returning to the home, each for different causes. One returned with his lover, supposedly for financial reasons. This younger woman was running for political office, and the family became involved in a competitive electoral campaign; their energies were completely diverted by the temporary urgency of the campaign's demands. The patient's study, household help, and time were given over to others by her sons and husband. As this situation developed, the patient had to deal with her very real jealousy of the prospective daughter-in-law, her conscious wish to help another woman succeed, and her reluctant awareness that the husband, sons, and older daughter were using this opportunity to gently sabotage her new career. The nest had been refilled with even more demands. The patient then had the following nightmare: "It is very, very late out and I am running on a rainy, slippery sidewalk looking for a restaurant. I have to stop before I get to one, because there is a small baby lying in the gutter. I must pick him up. It is pitch black outside."

In her dream, this patient, unlike Mrs. W, was in charge of the male child. In analysis, this patient was able to work through her ambivalently experienced self-strivings, her sense of identity, and her fear of separation. She brought to her treatment excellent resources, a good external environment, and the ability as well as the motivation for intensive psychoanalysis.

POSSIBILITIES FOR THE EMPTY NEST

Obviously, two cases cannot even begin to explain the nature of the empty-nest syndrome, but they do serve to illustrate the complexity of the phenomenon. For far too long, we have been offered a facile explanation of midlife female psychology: Not having tiny people to take care of and boss makes women cranky and irritable. We must fill up our time until grandchildren can reabsorb our nurturing souls. Is this an exaggerated version of the theory? Perhaps only a quintessential Archie Bunker would put it so crudely. Perhaps, though, many women also secretly believe this antediluvian credo.

We need to scrutinize carefully what is really happening to the individual woman. Many variables need to be assessed. For example, timing is of considerable importance in any life event. Deviation from an internalized expectation of the timing of life events creates stress (Butler & Lewis, 1973). Age norms have recently become much more fluid, but we do have certain notions of when important milestones occur in the life cycle—when children should leave, for example. Having a time in mind provides us with an opportunity to rehearse the departure. Planning a wedding, for example, which is not a necessarily predictable ritual in today's world, provides an important *rite de passage*. We must also consider how accurately we can predict our life without the children—the extent to which we have correctly forecast the quality of life afterward may determine our reactions to it. Change qua change is not necessarily unpleasant—only if subsequent hardships must be endured is change intrinsically difficult.

The nest is often emptied only temporarily. Some women refill it deliberately, by taking on the care of foster children; some are obliged to take aging parents into their home; and some unconsciously urge, or at least permit, children to return to the hearth. In my own family, a dominant grandmother simply kept two of the daughters at home with her until her death, not too rare a solution in those days for female children. Finally, grandchildren may appear, fulfilling many needs, including the most obvious one—a sense of continuity.

Any psychological event that occurs within a family context must have implications for all family members. As noted, many midlife men make the transition to the more nurturing parts of themselves, discarding their prior strong faith in the world of work and learning to accept other perhaps frightening parts of themselves (Gutmann, 1977; Sears, 1977; Vaillant, 1977). Just at this point, they may have to cope with wives who seek increased work mastery and self-expansion (Sears & Barbee, 1977), and the women's movement exhorts them to encourage their wives in these pursuits. Many men in treatment face conflicts because they wish to retire from the pressures of the business world, move to a geographically more relaxed community, and pursue long-denied pleasures. Because of the usual age differential, their wives are just embarking on careers and prefer the intensity and competition of stimulating urban life. The family may be in disequilibrium. Who is the breadwinner and who is the homemaker? Validating the crossover of tasks may serve to bring couples closer together (Giele, 1981), as sex and age become less important in regulating behavior, or it may increase conflict.

The dependency needs of the husband may become more readily apparent without the children or wife to serve as targets for projection. He may then subtly encourage or actively evoke a depressive reaction in the wife to solve or mask his own intrapsychic conflicts. He can then become the head of the house once again, taking care of the wife. Another choice for him is to send equivocal messages to the children concerning their departure, exacerbating family conflict. If the children have served as compensation for other family discontentments, the field is ripe for difficulties. Often, the paternal figure can use money and influence, which he controls, to keep the children dependent on him. In this way, the husband tries to enter the interpersonal scene, which may have been preempted by his wife.

Some women may try to solve these marital dilemmas by attempting to exert more control over their children and spouse. Other women, however, reject what they perceive as the masculine component of themselves—that is, their striving for self-assertiveness. They fear their new aggression will diminish their attractiveness to men. In this situation, the children are often of great assistance to the mother in urging her to "do her own thing," to finally make herself number one. Perhaps, glad to have their mothers less intrusive in their own lives, they may encourage her to assert herself in the work arena.

The variations in the reaction to the departure of the children from the home are infinite. Older persons differ from each other more than any other age group, so that their responses to any given life event are also more varied than at earlier times. As this essay has shown, the woman of today whose children have grown is in no way doomed to feelings of loss and depression; indeed, the possibilities for growth and development are unlimited. With the 1984 presidential elections a woman has graphically demonstrated the options open to us at midlife by running for the office of vice-president of the United States.

REFERENCES

Barnett, R., & Baruch, G. (1978), Women in the middle years: A critique of research and theory. *Psychol. Women Quart.*, 3: 187–197.

Benedek, T. (1960), The organization of the reproductive drive. *Internat. J. Psycho-Anal.*, 41 (Part I): 1–15.

Butler, R. N., & Lewis, M. J. (1973), *Aging and Mental Health: Positive Psychosocial Approaches in the Adult Years.* St. Louis: C. V. Mosby.

Campbell, A. Converse, P., & Rogers, W. (1976), *The Quality of American Life.* New York: Russell Sage Foundation.

Colarusso, C. A., & Nemiroff, R. A. (1970), Some observations and hypotheses about the psycho-analytic theory of adult development. *Internat. J. Psycho-Anal.*, 60: 59–71.

Cumming, E. & Henry, W. (1961), *Growing Old: The Process of Disengagement.* New York: Basic Books.

Erikson, E. (1968), *Identity, Youth and Crisis.* New York: Norton.

Evans, R. (1981), *Dialogues with Erik Erikson.* New York: Praeger.

Fletcher, R. (1968), *Instinct in Man.* London: Unwin.

Frenkel-Brunswik, E. (1968), Adjustments and reorientation in the course of the lifespan. In: *Middle Age and Aging,* ed. B. Neugarten. Chicago: University of Chicago Press, pp. 77–84.

Freud, A., Nagera, H., & Freud, W. (1965), Metapsychological assessment of the adult personality: The adult profile. *The Psychoanalytic Study of the Child,* 20: 9–41. New York: International Universities Press.

Giele, J. (1981), Crossover tasks in adulthood. In: *Themes of Work and Love in Adulthood,* ed. N. Smelser & E. Erikson. Cambridge, MA: Harvard University Press.

Gould, R. L. (1980), Transformational tasks in adulthood. In: *Adulthood and the Aging Process,* ed. S. I. Greenspan & G. H. Pollock. Washington, DC: NIMH, pp. 55–89.

Gutmann, D. (1977), The cross-cultural perspective: Notes towards a comparative psychology of aging. In: *Handbook of the Psychology of Aging,* ed. J. E. Birren & K. W.

Schaie. New York: Van Nostrand Rheinhold, pp. 302–326.

_____ (1981), Psychoanalysis and aging. In: *Adulthood and the Aging Process*, ed. S. I. Greenspan & G. H. Pollock. Washington, DC: NIMH, pp. 489–517.

Havighurst, R. J. (1973), History of developmental psychology: Socialization and personality through the life span. In: *Life Span and Developmental Psychology*, ed. P. Baltes & K. W. Schaie. New York: Academic Press, pp. 4–24.

Heyman, D. K. (1970), Does a wife retire? *Gerontologist*, 10: 54–56.

Jaques, E. (1981), The midlife crisis. In: *Adulthood and the Aging Process*, ed. S. I. Greenspan & G. H. Pollock. Washington, DC: NIMH, pp. 1–24.

Kerckhoff, A. (1966), Family patterns and morale in retirement. In: *Social Aspects of Aging*, ed. I. Simpson & J. McKinney. Durham, NC: Duke University Press, pp. 173–192.

Kline, C. (1975), The socialization process of women. *Gerontologist*, 15(6): 486–492.

Kuhlen, R. G. (1963), Age and intelligence. In: *Middle Age and Aging*, ed. B. Neugarten. Chicago: University of Chicago Press, pp. 552–557.

Kutner, B. (1961), The social nature of aging. Paper presented to the American Psychological Association, New York.

Levinson, D. (1977), *The Seasons of a Man's Life*. New York: Norton.

_____ Darrow, C. M., Klein, E. B., Levinson, M., & McKee, B. (1976), Periods in the adult development of men: Ages 18–45. *Counsel. Psychologist*, 6: 1.

Liang, J. (1982), Sex differences in life satisfaction among the elderly. *J. Gerontol.*, 37: 100–108.

Lopata, H. Z. (1971), Widows as a minority group. *Gerontologist* (Spring, Part II): 67–77.

Lowenthal, M. F., Thurnher, M., & Chiriboga, D. (1975), *Four Stages of Life: A Comparative Study of Men and Women Facing Transitions*. San Francisco: Jossey-Bass.

Maas, H. S., & Kuypers, J. A. (1975), *From Thirty to Seventy*. San Francisco: Jossey-Bass.

McKinlay, S., & Jeffries, M. (1974), The menopausal syndrome. *Brit. J. Prevent. Soc. Med.*, 28: 108–115.

Michels, R. (1981), Adulthood. In: *Adulthood and the Aging Process*, ed. S. I. Greenspan & G. H. Pollock. Washington, DC: NIMH, pp. 25–35.

Neugarten, B. (1968), Adult personality: Toward a psychology of the life cycle. In: *Middle Age and Aging: A Reader in Social Psychology*, ed. B. Neugarten. Chicago: University of Chicago Press, pp. 137–147.

_____ & Gutmann, D. (1968), Age, sex roles, and personality. In: *Middle Age and Aging*, ed. B. Neugarten. Chicago: University of Chicago Press, pp. 58–71.

_____ Wood, V., Kraines, R., & Loomis, B. (1968), Women's attitudes toward the menopause. *Human Develop.*, 6: 140–151.

Pearlin, L. I., (1981), Life strains and psychological distress among adults. In: *Themes of Work and Love in Adulthood*, ed: N. Smelser & E. Erikson. Cambridge, MA: Harvard University Press, pp. 174–191.

Peck, R. C. (1968), Psychological developments in the second half of life. In: *Middle Age and Aging*, ed. B. Neugarten. Chicago: University of Chicago Press, pp. 88–92.

Radloff, L. (1975), Sex differences in depression: The effects of occupation and marital status. *Sex Roles*, 1: 249–265.

Rangell, L. (1953), The role of the parent in the Oedipus complex. *Bull. Menn. Clinic*, 19: 9–15.

Sears, P. & Barbee, A. H. (1977), Career and life satisfaction among Terman's gifted women. In: *The Gifted and the Creative: A Fifty Year Perspective*, ed. J. Stanley, W. George, & C. Solano. Baltimore: Johns Hopkins University Press.

Sears, R. R. (1977), Sources of life satisfaction in the Terman gifted men. *Amer. Psychologist*, 32: 119–128.

Sternschein, J. (1973), The experience of separation-individuation in infancy and its reverberations through the course of life; Maturity, senescence, and the sociological implications. *J. Amer. Psychoanal. Assn.*, 21: 633–645.

Thurnher, M. (1974), Goals, values, and life evaluations at the preretirement stage. *J. Gerontol.*, 29: 85–96.

Vaillant, G. (1977), *Adaptation to Life*. Boston: Little, Brown.

12
The Aging Woman: Confrontations with Hopelessness

Vicki Granet Semel, Psy.D.

Aging, which confronts women with the frightening realities of loss and death, also offers them the unique opportunity to learn to deal with the feelings of hopelessness that are so pervasive at this time of life. For women who have not developed adaptive mechanisms to handle such feelings, the confrontation with hopelessness in the aging process appears distinct from the experience of men.

Menopause, that stark reminder of the loss of childbearing functions, cannot be ignored by any woman. Its physiological aspects cry out for recognition. This biological fact of life constitutes a specific (although chronologically variable) mark denoting the commencement of the aging period for the female. In great contrast to the less somatically visible changes in men, this unmistakable event jars the woman in an obvious fashion and leads to an increased awareness of her body and its biological changes.

We must begin consideration of aging in women by admitting to the embryonic state of psychoanalytic research in this area. In one of the few early psychoanalytic studies on the aging female, Deutsch (1945) stated that menopause ushers in a "loss of femininity." Although many might refute Deutsch's notion that "femininity" disappears with menopause, the narcissistic blow of this development may still have a powerful effect on a woman's views of herself. Nevertheless, the idea that a female psychoanalyst equates ovarian functioning with femininity is profoundly significant. It indicates the way that the early psychoanalytic writings on aging, in their own pessimistic view of the elderly, suggest my thesis that aging, especially for the female, begets much hopelessness. As options become more limited, and the reality of impending death looms larger, the recognition of the psychic pain of hopelessness as an essential part of life leads to many both adaptive and maladaptive attempts to avoid or come to terms with despair. Thus, defenses against hopelessness or adaptive attempts to resolve incapacities deriving from hopelessness are central in any study of the aging female.

The portrait of the aging female, in this discussion is based on women whose ages spanned a 43-year-period – my patients who ranged in ages from 50 through 93. Clearly, such a span of years in the beginning of life would encompass several distinct maturational levels. The likelihood is that such distinct levels of development also exist between the younger, relatively intact aging person and the very elderly, seriously disabled individual. Yet the lack of such groupings in the literature reveals the nascent stage of our research in this area. This paper will use clinical examples from all along the spectrum of aging.

AVOIDING THE AGING

To regard aging as a spectrum adds complexity to psychoanalytic thinking on the subject as influenced by Freud, whose sparse commentary has led therapists to avoid the aging patient in traditional psychotherapy. In the early days of psychoanalysis, in fact, Freud (1904, 1905) made it clear that he thought his method of treatment and research should not be applied to those around the age of 50 or older. He believed that the amount of material that had to be verbalized and the growing inflexibility of the personality with increasing age made such a psychoanalytic undertaking inadvisable. King (1974), notes, however, that when Freud suggested this limitation, he himself was 49 years of age, with much of his creative theorizing and treatment still ahead of him. What later psychoanalysts then saw as a pronouncement *ex cathedra* was probably no more than some early thoughts of Freud's.

Freud's writings clearly contain some tentative theorizing about the crisis of menopause and aging. Freud (1912) noted the possible dislocating "sudden increases of libido . . . habitually associated with puberty and the menopause—with the attainment of a certain age in women" (p. 236). In addition to this theoretical suggestion, Freud (1914) also wrote of his frustration in "the case of an elderly lady who had repeatedly fled from her house and husband" and soon "decamped from me, too, before I had had the time to say anything to her which might have prevented this repetition" (p. 154). Again, in 1933, Freud described the case of a woman, "no longer young," whose goals were blocked by people's reaction to her as "too old to accomplish anything in [a] field" (p. 109). This led to an upsurge of masochism in the guise of accidents or somatic reactions that rendered her unable to proceed with her efforts. Thus, although Freud offered strong doubts about treating the elderly, one can also glean from his writings that he did work with such patients.

How does one explain, then, the ease with which therapists have abandoned the older patient, using Freud's partial statements, not the details evident in his writings, as proof that such patients are basically untreatable and incapable of change? I believe the basic reason has to do with the countertransference resistance of most therapists to handling the painful and disturbing feelings of hopelessness that constitute the core problem for the aging female patient. Such patients, then, induce in their therapists with equal intensity the feelings they have about themselves and their own condition. Such inductions from patients' unexpressed emotions in the countertransference reactions of psychoanalysts are often described (Spotnitz, 1976; Spotnitz & Meadow, 1976) as helpful information about the resistance operating in the treatment. Thus, the wholesale avoidance of such patients may result from an unwillingness to share the feelings of hopelessness brought about by the decreasing options and choices as the aging individual moves closer to death.

Part of this common pattern of avoiding the aging patient appears initially in the simple diagnostic formulation that is frequently followed. If symptoms in an aging individual involve cognitive impairment (memory deficits, retardation of thought); emotional disabilities (psychomotor retardation, narcissistic self-involvement); or somatic problems (bowel or bladder dysfunctions, gastrointestinal or eating problems), these problems *must* be related to organic processes, usually assumed to be senile dementia. Then, it automatically follows, the patient needs supportive treatment, since her state is accepted as organically irreversible – certainly a hopeless view of treatment. One compendium on the treatment of the elderly actually recommends that the bulk of treatment for the older patient be handled by the paraprofessional (Götestam, 1980).

Increasingly, however, therapists are recognizing that such symptoms can be related to psychological and emotional problems, more reflective of depression than of organic deficits. Berezin (1977) gives a recent example of the psychoanalytic treatment of a woman with all the signs of organic deficits, whom he decided to treat psychologically. His treatment of this particular woman rendered her memory clearer, and he came to the conclusion that her memory deficits were related to emotionally meaningful material involving "intense sexual fantasies" (p. 15).

Some psychoanalytically oriented therapists do express concern with the aging patient. The Boston Society for Gerontologic Psychiatry, mainly composed of psychoanalytically trained physicians, has been offering books (see, for example, Zinberg & Kaufman, 1963; Berezin & Cath, 1965; Levin & Kahana, 1967) and the *Journal of Geriatric Psychiatry* for at least 20 years. Jungian analysts have always worked with elderly patients (Zoja, 1983), as have a daring few other analysts over the years (Abraham, 1919; Grotjahn, 1940; Segal, 1958; King, 1974, 1980; Jaques, 1965; Sandler, 1978). Myer's (1984) recent review of his treatment of elderly patients concentrates on reactions to loss and to the ultimate loss – one's own death.

It seems that the most useful studies of the aging are those that permit us to keep an open mind. Atkin (1941) sets a fine example for such an approach in a reaction to a paper by Kaufman (1940). He tackles the assumption of personality rigidity in the elderly, which was Freud's warning against the likelihood of any success with them in treatment. In Atkin's work with an aging spinster, he found her mental inelasticity to be a defense against massive anxiety rather than an irreversible effect of the aging process.

Thus, it is important that hypotheses about the aging process in women leave future psychoanalytic researchers broad areas for exploration and encompass the variability and complexity of the aging process. Just as some recent clinical case studies have called into question the single path of the oedipal conflict and resolution for the female child (Parens, 1976), so, too, we can assume that aging does not carry a single path of development or a single resolution for the female.

The true gift of the psychoanalytic perspective is in allowing the patient to be heard in the deepest sense and at the deepest levels of the conscious and unconscious self. The psychoanalyst fulfills the Freudian destiny most clearly when he or she listens to the patient and develops ideas and theories on the basis of the information forthcoming from the interaction. The theoretical perspective is a suggestion during the psychoanalytic process, not a formula. In any work that seeks to understand the dynamics of the aging woman in today's society, it is important to make this distinction quite clear.

COMPLEXITY IN THE AGING PROCESS

As multiple variables influence the experience of aging for all adults, it would be premature to describe one theoretical line of development. An individual in good health, with few material losses and viable and sustaining interpersonal relationships may react quite differently to aging than would someone who is seriously ill and facing declining economic and social status and the death of a spouse or other family members and friends. Furthermore, the characterological substrate on which the crises of aging impinges must remain central to any discussion.

For example, King's (1974, 1980) conceptualization of aging as leading to a resurgence of the adolescent passage seems to describe certain adults. Most likely, this applies to those with relatively mature levels of functioning—perhaps those who had successfully surmounted at least the phallic stage of development. The preoedipal personalities who are more frequently seen in treatment—the borderline, the serious depressive, the somatizer, and the schizophrenic—may be expected to react quite differently to the crisis of aging. Whereas the oedipal personality might indeed regress to adolescent functioning, the preoedipally fixated adult may not have such a luxury. For such individuals, crises are likely to call forth the preoedipal defensive maneuvers more characteristic of an earlier style of development. Thus, strongly established character styles as well as reality factors are central to any approach to aging.

HOPELESSNESS AND HUMAN LIMITATIONS

Although learning to deal with hopelessness seems to be the major emotional task of the aging process, it is evident that hopelessness is nothing new in the human life cycle. Acceptance of the limitations of life begins with the infant's loss of the idyllic environment of the mother's womb. In their study of the psychological birth of the infant, Mahler, Pine, and Bergman (1975) note a period of "soberness or even temporary depression" (p. 213) when the toddler realizes his or her separateness from the mother and the concomitant loss of omnipotence. This short period of hopelessness results, however, in a vast increase in cognitive growth, balancing the loss with hopeful qualities that propel the toddler into childhood and the maturational potential of that period.

At this early point, the girl suffers an additional loss, compounding that experienced by the boy, for she must face the hopeless state of never having a penis. This realization seems to set her apart from the male child in her early experiences with hopelessness. Mahler, Pine, and Bergman (1975) note the anger and dependence that characterize the female toddler's relationships with her mother. They relate this frequently perceived pattern to the meaning the child gives the lack of a penis—the idea of being castrated or shortchanged by the mother. A more contemporary view of the conflict attributes the hostility between mother and daughter to the parent's view of the female as less favored. Emotional status based on gender appears as relevant as the actual absence of a penis.

Continuing experiences with loss, leading to the sense of hopelessness, are evident throughout life. During the oedipal period, the child comes to know that he or she has a hopeless wish to marry the parent of the opposite sex. The resolution of this conflict moves the child toward further success in the real world, developing peer relationships and increasing intellectual attainment. In the adolescent period, the resurgence of earlier issues involving separation-individuation and oedipal conflicts leads to both hopelessness and hope. The teenager learns the ultimate hopelessness of remaining a dependent member of his or her family, but the hopeful resolution leads to the establishment of a family and career of his or her own. When the individual moves into middle age, however, the balance between the hopelessness of unfulfilled wishes and the hope of fulfillable ones clearly shifts. Increasing hopelessness and the necessity of bearing the truth of diminishing potential now require mature acceptance of the limitations of one's life. This recalls Erikson's (1959, 1964) concept of life's final task as the attempt to achieve "integrity versus despair."

Three cases will be presented to examine the way three different women have dealt with the issues of aging and the confrontation with hopelessness. The first, Mrs. Z., was a woman in the relatively early stages of aging whose marital crisis brought her to treatment. In contrast, Mrs. A., a physically disabled but intellectually intact, professional woman of 73 had to deal with her own increasing infirmities and possible death. A final study of my oldest patient is presented to illustrate the impact of aging for an elderly, panicky, and somatically impaired woman.

THE CASE OF MRS. Z.

Mrs. Z., a devout Catholic and active in the church with her husband, had recently turned 57 and was about to send her fourth and last child to college. At this time, her husband, a lawyer in a large firm in New York, announced that he was planning to leave her for another woman, a colleague with whom he had been having an ongoing affair for six years. Mrs. Z. felt frozen with the shock and humiliation of his announcement and could not comprehend how she could not have known about this relationship.

After much equivocating, the husband fell into a serious depression and decided he wanted to remain with his wife. Initial forays into pastoral and then marital counseling led nowhere. Mrs. Z. insisted her husband have psychiatric care, and Mr. Z. began to work with a psychiatrist. When Mrs. Z. eventually sought a therapist, two years after the shocking announcement, she asked for a referral to a woman therapist who would be able to understand her more fully and help explain men to her. Her therapy with me has lasted for over three years of once-a-week treatment.

Mrs. Z.'s initial goal, to understand her husband, was a disguised communication that revealed the paranoid nature of her functioning, for much of what she discussed in the first two years of treatment was about her husband and his problems rather than focusing on herself. She was not interested in understanding herself, her reactions to this man's perfidy, or any contribution she might have made to the unrewarding state of their marriage.

A most unpleasant aspect of Mrs. Z.'s functioning was the continual rage she expressed at her husband. At one point, after she had begun to bring him to her sessions every other week, her raging reached such a crescendo that the workers in the office below rushed upstairs to see if I was being harmed! During the first two years of treatment, her fury was endless. Yet Mrs. Z.'s paranoid style led her to perceive her husband as furious. He, on the other hand, reacted to her assaults passively, fearfully, or defensively, which enraged her further at his weakness and unassertiveness. Mrs. Z. criticized her husband on many scores, such as his overinvolvement in his work and the terrible job he did with the children. She continually reminded him of his unfaithfulness, particularly when their relationship appeared to be taking a turn for the better.

Mrs. Z. had made child rearing her focus to such an extent that she found herself ill-equipped to go forward into the next stage of life without children. Her husband had an advanced degree and career, whereas she had obtained only a high school education and had briefly been a clerical worker. I began to wonder if her intense anger at her husband was, on the one hand, displaced from herself and her present unfulfilled condition and, on the other, a defensive maneuver against feeling her intense sadness at the loss of her children—her very purpose in life. Mrs. Z. even referred hostilely to the children as "hers" in front of her husband. Yet Mrs. Z., of course, saw only her husband's betrayal.

Mrs. Z.'s background was suspiciously vacuous. She spoke of an idealized mother and father who loved each other and nurtured her and her older sister. Yet unlike Mrs. Z., her sister had been college educated. Mrs. Z. frequently spoke of this lack, but was quick to absolve her parents of any blame for her limited education.

In one session I noted an interesting repetition: her father, whom everyone had trusted and idealized, had betrayed her mother by stealing money from a family member. The shock of the patient's mother at her husband's betrayal continued over years, paralleling Mrs. Z.'s own reaction. Both Mrs. Z. and her mother had been totally trusting of their spouses in all areas, and neither had expected such behavior.

Work with this woman was frustrating and slow. I began to feel annoyed and hopeless. When I realized that my annoyance with Mrs. Z. paralleled her own reactions to her spouse, however, I became more accepting of her defensive need to remain the way she was. I also wondered if my hopeless feeling about her ability to improve her relationship with her husband was also a parallel of her unexpressed and unexperienced emotion in the situation with Mr. Z. I simply accepted the feeling of hopelessness and continued to work with her.

Mrs. Z. continued to speak only of her husband and his problems, often projecting her reactions onto him. She was frequently unable to comprehend either his verbalizations or his behavior, as her paranoid style scrambled what she could understand. She seemed quite the reverse of the trusting person she described, instead appearing continually suspicious.

Therapy was directed toward helping Mrs. Z. pay some attention to herself in the sessions, describing how *she* felt and what *she* thought, apart from her husband. This ability to describe herself developed gradually. After 3 ½ years of treatment, instead of repetitiously complaining, "He has a problem in that area," or "He feels, . . . " Mrs. Z. might occasionally state, "I was annoyed when he . . . " or "I'm upset about our son." Mrs. Z. also began to recognize that verbal lashing out at her husband was both a reaction to his behavior and an expression of her anger at him, something she was unable to perceive in the past. Self-awareness seemed to be developing in this preoedipal patient.

Just before a two-week vacation break, Mrs. Z. arrived for her session appearing both sad and "slowed down." She began to talk about a physical ailment, a bursitus of her shoulder, which she described as "inflamed." She then went on to describe how upset she was about her husband and daughter's fighting. She also described her attempts to stay out of their argument and to control her annoyance with her husband. My immediate association was that in repressing her usual outbursts of rage, Mrs. Z. had begun to somatize. Once she restrained the acting out of her continual anger, Mrs. Z. became depressed and sad.

As she spoke further, it became clear that her disability had initially led to much anger with her husband—he could not function as a support for her and could do nothing right. She even wondered if he were not becoming senile like his father before him. The anger dissipated as she continued to speak, and, instead sadness about ever being nurtured by her husband became evident. Mrs. Z. acknowledged a sense of hopelessness, of time running out on the possibility that her marital relationship would ever offer her what she wanted.

Because Mrs. Z.'s major role for so many years had been as a mother—almost a single parent—it may well have been that nurturing her children had satisfied her own unmet needs for nurturance. With the passing of that role, these needs would now be left unfulfilled. Much of Mrs. Z.'s anger at her husband seemed related to this loss.

Once she was able to accept the hopelessness of her relationship—the fact that her husband would not nurture her or change his way of interacting with her—Mrs. Z. became noticeably less hostile toward him. He then became somewhat more assertive with her. Experiencing hopelessness, rather than avoiding and denying it, led Mrs. Z. to formulate somewhat less critical interactions with her spouse.

Therapy with Mrs. Z. still remains in the early stages, as a preoedipal patient with much paranoia will require many years of work. Her case, however, illustrates the effects of giving up the maternal role on women who have exaggerated motherhood out of proportion to all other roles. These women experience their lives as hopeless without children to raise. After a period of mourning, however, they can go on to make new choices and perhaps even find some life's work that gives them a sense of worth.

THE CASE OF MRS. A.

Mrs. A., a 73-year-old, seriously ill and physically disabled widow, was referred for consultation because of the vicious verbal abuse that she continually leveled against the nursing staff and administrators in a New York City nursing home. Her rages came from her perception that they were demeaning her and treating her without due respect. Although Mrs. A. was seriously impaired in her physical abilities, her cognitive functioning was extraordinary. She had traveled widely during her adult years, marrying three times, and working in media-related field that utilized her writing abilities. She experienced herself as superior to the other residents and sought to identify herself with the volunteers at the home, offering her services in an attempt to continue her role as an independent, functioning adult.

She willingly agreed to weekly sessions. She spoke freely yet tangentially of her physical ailments and of her difficulties with the staff. Slowly, she began to report details of her earlier life, never mentioning previous spouses, only the most recent one, who had died. She also never mentioned the death of two children during infancy.

It seems that in the course of her life, Mrs. A. had managed to alienate vast numbers of relatives and friends, who eventually disappointed her with their limited intellect or inferior, parochial values. As a world traveler and left-wing activist, she had many legitimate vehicles for touting her narcissistically needed superiority over others.

I quickly became an extension of the valued aspects of herself. I was seen as similar to herself, an intellectually superior world traveler, whose vacations from her therapy were spent in foreign lands, either traveling or giving papers on important psychological topics. I became her ally against the staff, about whom she complained bitterly and continuously, never describing her own role in their hostile interactions. I was clearly idealized and became a reflection of her worth and grandiose self. I totally enjoyed my work with Mrs. A. and listened believingly to her stories.

I began to understand the effects of the aging process on her present psychopathology. As a narcissistically disordered woman, whose narcissism was tied to intellectual talents and status rather than physical beauty or child rearing, Mrs. A. experienced anything less than idealization as a demeaning lack of respect – the ultimate attack on her narcissism. Ill health left her at the mercy of the "incompetents" of the world.

Mrs. A.'s physically deteriorating condition often led to hospitalizations. After one prolonged siege, during which physicians expected her to die, she instead became so outrageously demanding and hostile to the hospital staff that they returned her to the home, actually refusing to accept her as a patient in the future. This mobilization of aggression against the "ignominious peasants" of the hospital seemed a life-rejuvenating effort for her.

Yet Mrs. A. returned to the home confused and terrified of dying. The physician, eager to have some support for her during this difficult time, consulted me and asked for more intensive treatment. Seeing her twice a week during this period, I too felt confused by her apparent intellectual deterioration. She was demanding more and more special treatment from the dietary and nursing staff, antagonizing them even further. But her self-righteous battles seemed to be good for her health, and she slowly gained back some of her "fight."

During this period Mrs. A. appeared pathetic for the first time. She would apologize to me for her loss of "a good vocabulary." Her cognitive abilities seemed to be fading, which disheartened her considerably and led to a sense of hopelessness. She also wanted to distance herself from me so that I would not witness this radical change.

She began to talk about dying in a vague and indirect fashion. I helped her to articulate directly her growing belief that she was approaching death. She then reported with rage that her nemesis, a certain nurse with whom she had a running battle, had requested one of the small sculptures around her room to "remember Mrs. A. by." The thought that such an insensitive woman should actually begin to procure some of Mrs. A.'s belongings seemed to revive her. Although she took a turn for the better, Mrs. A. began to defecate in her bed, as an anally symbolic way of getting back at the nurse, who then became overtly enraged at the patient.

Mrs. A. mentioned her bowel problems only in the most delicate and subtle fashion. When asked why a lack of control bothered her, she admitted that it was rather fun to simply let go of everything. The patient's serious state reversed itself. It seems likely that there was a link between her overtly expressed aggression and a reestablishment of her narcissistic balance.

Slowly, I began to formulate a hypothesis about the effects of the aging process on this narcissistically pathological woman. During her earlier years, Mrs. A. was able to handle her intense aggression by "moving on." She did so both with relationships and actual physical mobility, as she migrated from husband to husband and country to country. Age took from her the ability to act out a defensive need that permitted her to control her aggressive impulses through physical and emotional mobility. She could handle radical disappointments in her younger years by dropping relationships and finding new ones relatively easily, since she presented a charming, intellectual exterior. Despite her immense needs for adulation, her skill in media work and her interpersonal charm made it possible for her to avoid dealing with hopelessness and deep interpersonal disappointments. She could continue to look for the ideal. But age took this hope from her in the form of serious physical incapacities. Mrs. A. then had an opportunity to grow inwardly, rather than simply moving on as she confronted the realities of her life and her approaching death.

Work with this patient remained incomplete because I moved to a different facility after approximately one year of treatment. Mrs. A. has called me occasionally, and we chat for a short time. She was still alive and fighting battles with the staff when we last made contact, nine months after the termination of treatment.

THE CASE OF MRS. K.

My oldest patient, a 93-year-old, uneducated factory worker, was referred because her extreme agitation and anxiety made her a behavior problem on a nursing home unit. Mrs. K. had been experiencing a decrease in sensory capabilities, first in the visual area, then in the auditory one. She had suffered many losses in her life, from the basic one of leaving her native land, to the deaths of her husband and an adult son, to the recent divorce of a daughter, which brought Mrs. K. to the nursing home. She remained, to a large degree, cognitively intact. Her agitation, which reached psychotic proportions and seemed of long duration, appeared to protect her from intense depression related to the various losses in her life. She also lived in terror of the dangerous actions of others over which she would have no more control than she had had over the pogroms of her native land. She often thought of the facility as a prison.

Mrs. K.'s panic was dreadful to see and even more difficult to experience, as she induced her agitation in me during the sessions. I longed to comfort her, but such actions were useless. Her desperation was intense. Hysteria would mount during important events such as medical crises or family contacts. She behaved like an infant, unable to assuage her anguish or to mitigate her agitation.

Mrs. K. always communicated the deepest sadness when she spoke of the death of her 27-year-old son, which occurred well over 40 years ago. Then the tears would fall and genuine mourning would replace her unfocused anxiety. Mrs. K. had been in a state of unresolved mourning for that son for nearly half a century. The feelings were as real now as the day the death had occurred. The recent loss of her husband and of her daughter, who was still alive but had abandoned her to the nursing home, paled beside the loss of her son.

As I listened to Mrs. K. over several months in a modified psychoanalytic approach, it appeared that her ego was simply overwhelmed by the multiple tragedies in her life. Although she had probably never experienced much self-esteem, she had worked to educate her children, one of whom had become a quite successful professional. She had been isolated from interpersonal ties except for her family. Schizoid in her dynamics, she was now confronted by large numbers of people sharing her space, her table, her environment. She was buffeted about by the intrusions of others, when all she wanted was to be shielded from stimulation, much like an infant who needs such protection. Her environment could not provide her with such insulation, however. For the schizoid woman who needed much distance from people, the overstimulation of the home was a barrage on her weakening defensive structure.

Mrs. K. could not permit herself to feel hopeless or to mourn deeply and fully the multiple losses of her life. She used intense agitation to defend against all feelings. She had a long history of psychotic-level anxiety, but when left alone and permitted to withdraw, she functioned far better. The nursing home, however, did not permit this defense to strengthen. Moreover, Mrs. K.'s loneliness became increasingly terrifying to her because she could no longer see or hear well. Mrs. K. often believed she was being abandoned or forgotten, as she was by her family.

Many women today share the dismal conclusion to life that Mrs. K. experienced. Their longevity leaves them without supporting relatives who might keep them at home. When they become disabled, they are among the first in their family's history to find themselves in nursing homes, rather than being cared for by their daughters. Mrs. K. often bemoaned that fact and wondered what she had done wrong that her daughter would not keep her in the house where she had lived for so many years. After all, Mrs. K. would moan, she had cared for her aging mother, had sacrificed herself for her dying father. Such comments were few and far between, however. Usually agitation and panic characterized the sessions.

Social realities have impinged on the psychological realities for this
woman and many others. Their daughters work or do not feel responsibility to care for their parents themselves, as was common in more
traditional extended families. The nursing home becomes the place for
the elderly who are physically or cognitively impaired, even if family
members are still alive. Experiencing the hopelessness of their abandoned condition is intolerable for these elderly people. They adopt defensive maneuvers in keeping with their individual characterological
patterns. For example, Mrs. K. became more panicky and anxious to
warn herself away from some unacceptable idea or feeling – probably
rage at her family for abandoning her or mourning for the various and
intense losses that marked her life.

CONCLUSIONS

These cases of women at distinct stages of the aging process illustrate
the multifaceted ways in which aging women handle the realities of
hopelessness and impending death. How to manage a meaningful life
in the face of these realities is the central issue for the aging female, who
so often outlive their spouse and friends. The crises of aging are more
evident for women, whose initial loss of child-bearing functions ushers
in the biological onset of aging.

The patients described here tended to be preoedipal rather than
oedipal in their levels of functioning. Each of these patients – who displayed a borderline condition, narcissistic disorder, and even a psychotic level of anxiety – offers a picture of the crisis of aging that is distinct from the experience of the neurotic or healthy female. For Mrs.
Z., permitting herself to feel hopeless and letting go of the defensive
rage she used to prevent her awareness of this feeling allowed her to
have a more satisfying relationship with her husband. For Mrs. A., the
only professional woman discussed, acknowledging the possibility of
her own death rather than repressing awareness of this likelihood re-
vived her fight against the nursing staff that she experienced as demeaning her. In the case of Mrs. K., her psychotic agitation and anxiety abated when she permitted herself to deeply mourn her lost son.

The ability of the therapist and the patient to acknowledge the
hopelessness of the aging condition – and then to continue to work

together—may be the route to helping the aging woman confront the realities of hopelessness and still have a useful life.

As the new generations of career woman age, they will have more choices and arenas to make themselves valuable members of society for considerably longer. It will be interesting to discover whether the dis-heartening effects of menopause, as the harbinger of aging, might abate for them. Nevertheless, as long as women continue to live longer and outlive their loved ones, they will be forced to confront the issues of hopelessness and death. Yet, these transitions provide women with opportunities to mature emotionally, even in the prime or twilight of their lives.

REFERENCES

Abraham, K. (1919), The applicability of psycho-analytic treatment of patients at an advanced age. In: *Selected Papers on Psycho-Analysis*. London: Hogarth Press, 1927, pp. 312–317.

Atkin, S. (1941), Discussion of Kaufman's paper. *Amer. J. Orthopsychiat.*, 10: 79–84.

Berezin, M. A. (1977), The fate of narcissism in old age: Clinical case reports. *J. Geriat. Psychiat.*, 10, 9–26.

_____, & Cath, S. H. (Eds.) (1965), *Geriatric Psychiatry: Grief, Loss, and Emotional Disorders in the Aging Process*. New York: International Universities Press.

Deutsch, H. (1945), *The Psychology of Women: A Psychoanalytic Interpretation*, Vol. 2: *Motherhood*. New York: Grune & Stratton.

Erikson, E. (1959), Identity and the life cycle. *Psychological Issues*, Monogr. 1. New York: International Universities Press.

_____ (1964), *Insight and Responsibility: Lectures on the Ethical Implications of Psychoanalytic Insight*. New York: Norton.

Freud, S. (1904), Freud's psycho-analytic procedure. *Standard Edition*, 7: 249–254. London: Hogarth Press, 1953.

_____ (1905), On psychotherapy. *Standard Edition*, 7: 257–268. London: Hogarth Press, 1953.

_____ (1912), Types of onset of neurosis. *Standard Edition*, 12: 227–238. London: Hogarth Press, 1958.

_____ (1914), Remembering, repeating and working-through. *Standard Edition*, 12: 145–156. London: Hogarth Press, 1958.

_____ (1933), New introductory lectures on psycho-analysis. *Standard Edition*, 22. London: Hogarth Press, 1964.

Götestam, K. G. (1980), Behavioral and dynamic psychotherapy with the elderly. In: *Handbook of mental health and aging*, ed. J. E. Birren & R. B. Sloane. Englewood Cliffs, NJ: Prentice-Hall, pp. 775–805.

Grotjahn, M. (1940), Psychoanalytic investigations of a seventy-one-year-old man with senile dementia. *Psychoanal. Quart.*, 9: 80–97.

Jaques, E. (1965), Death and the mid-life crisis. *Internat. J. Psychoanal.*, 46: 502–514.

Kaufman, M. R. (1940), Old age and aging: The psychoanalytic point of view. *Amer. J. Orthopsychiat.*, 10: 73–79.

King, P. H. M. (1974), Notes on the psychoanalysis of older patients: Reappraisal of the potentialities for change during the second half of life. *J. Analyt. Psychol.*, 19: 22–37.

_____ (1980), The life cycle as indicated by the nature of the transference in the psychoanalysis of the middle-aged and elderly. *Internat. J. Psycho-Anal.*, 61: 153–160.

Levin, S., & Kahana, R. J. (Eds.) (1967), *Psychodynamic Studies on Aging: Creativity, Reminiscing, and Dying.* New York: International Universities Press.

Mahler, M. S., Pine, F., & Bergman, A. (1975), *The Psychological Birth of the Human Infant: Symbiosis and Individuation.* New York: Basic Books.

Myers, W. A. (1984), *Dynamic Therapy of the Older Patient.* New York: Jason Aronson.

Parens, H. (1976), On the girl's entry into the oedipal complex. *J. Amer. Psychoanal. Assn.*, 24 (Supple.), 79–107.

Sandler, A. (1978), Psychoanalysis in later life: Problems in the psychoanalysis of an aging narcissistic patient. *J. Geriat. Psychiat.*, 11: 5–36.

Segal, H. (1958), Fear of death: notes on the analysis of an old man. *Internat. J. Psycho-Anal.*, 39: 178–181.

Spotnitz, H. (1976), *Psychotherapy of Preoedipal Conditions: Schizophrenia and Severe Character Disorders.* New York: Jason Aronson.

_____, & Meadow, P. W. (1976), *Treatment of the Narcissistic Neuroses.* New York: Manhattan Center for Advanced Psychoanalytic Studies.

Zinberg, N. E., & Kaufman, I. (Eds.) (1963), *Normal Psychology of the Aging Process.* New York: International Universities Press.

Zoja, L. (1983), Working against Dorian Gray: Analysis of the old. *J. Analyt. Psychol.*, 28: 51–64.

ISSUES IN THE THERAPEUTIC RELATIONSHIP

13

Women Feminist Patients and a Feminist Woman Analyst

Ruth-Jean Eisenbud, Ph.D.

*No one ever told us we had to study our lives, make of our lifes a study, as
if learning natural history,
or music*
— Adrienne Rich, 1978, p. 73.

Twentieth century feminism was an integral part of society's industrial, political and scientific revolution. Women's personal emancipation was impeded by vested patriarchal interests and by women's own
internalization of a patriarchal society. In time, the "establishment" of
classic psychoanalysis allowed its authority, evolving theory, research
and potent instrumental skills to be preempted. In an age of anxiety,
psychoanalytic treatment of women prospered by pacifying and
adapting woman to her secondary role (Eisenbud, 1959). Even the
most sensitive and devoted psychoanalyst accepted the rationaliza-
tions of vested interests and disarmed women patients who were
among the most advanced. In doing so, the good doctors inhibited the
advance of established psychoanalysis as well.

Many contemporary Freudian psychoanalysts now take a clear stand on the woman question. We reverse the game, and in the name of feminism, we claim the rich Freudian inheritance for our own revision and purposes. Its profound insights, empirical research, and extended discoveries daily inform our work (Person, 1982). We also claim the liberal realistic, pioneer spirit of early psychoanlysis. We find inspiration in the innovative post-Freudians and their focus on ego and adaptive defenses. We find validation of much that is new through the empirical observation and conceptualization of modern psychoanalysis. This essay will address some of the attempts at integration of actual intensive psychoanalytic treatment with woman's demands for truth and justice (Lytton, 1984).

OVERDEPENDENCE ON A MAN FOR SPONSORSHIP

Athena was in her thirties. She presented a slim, full-bodied, tall, sad appearance, a kind of goddess quality. Born in Greece, she was now a professor of economics as was her American-born husband. She came for help because, "for the first time in my life I am afraid."

She explained, as a girl she had been, courageously, a witness to street violence. She was a hard working child, a valiant champion of the family in their fight to survive under military oppression and dire poverty. She was now acutely ashamed of being a scared baby. She told me of her harsh, primitive and desparately overwhelmed mother who had always been tough with her many children. For example, her mother had sneered at Athena's "female cramps" at puberty, as Athena now sneered at herself for her shaking fear. Athena was the only one of her many sisters who stood up to her tyrannical, patriarchal, idealist father and she alone had moved away from home during her high school years.[1]

I asked if Athena remembered a recent dream. Yes, last night she had awoken with a feeling of dread and paralysis. She had dreamed she was a pretzel, twisted out of shape and unable to move. What came to her mind, thinking of the pretzel? The way she slept, curled and

---

[1]Biographical facts confided in treatment have been much changed to protect the patient's identity.

shrinking into herself. A double bed? Yes. So as not to touch her husband. She did not want him to push her away. He had not touched her all year, scorning her. He had been away from the house a good deal. He had always been a puritan like herself, but now he was drinking for the first time, he was in blue jeans, he wore beads, and so forth. No, there was no other woman! Athena declared she was walking on eggs. She would do nothing to force the issue. Her marriage must be saved at all costs (Cantor, 1982).

In the next session I learned that during the past year, Athena's husband had been appointed to a university in New York City and had commuted home most weekends. Even in the preceding year, there had been changes on her part. She had become more frivolous, cut her long hair, had become more merry and less scholarly. Her son had also gone off to college. During this past year her work had gone well. She had obtained a sabbatical, rented their home upstate, and had come to New York City to work and join her husband.

As we discussed Athena's easy open alliance with myself, her direct reporting to me in the office, her insight and poise, we realized her behavior in treatment was in strong contrast to her dependence and submission at home. Her ability to confront me and claim her own space, time and dress in the office seemed inconsistent with denial of her rage over abandonment and rejection at home and her dependence on her already suborned marriage. When she was at home her sense of personal responsibility and willingness to introspect were suppressed by "cognitive hysteria."

Athena reviewed her teenage life before she left Greece. She had been the mistress of a gentle, aristocratic older man, who had given her the doting tenderness her harsh, unkempt mother denied her. He taught her that in return she was to be beautiful and have high style. He trained her in a feminine, romantic, passive compliance, and to abandon herself to a passionate response to his lovemaking. This idealized self that she thus attained in her late teens was of essential importance to Athena as it rescued her from a negative identification with being a woman. She did not want to be either her mother, or the self reliant boy her mother wanted her to be.

I asked Athena if she was physically afraid of her husband. She was amazed to realize that she was. He had called her clumsy and stupid with mechanical things; he had bullied and belittled her homemaking. She had served him as she had her mother, and she feared him as she had feared her mother's rough hands and abuse. He had not been physically abusive, but had used cruel moral dominance (Weldon, 1974).

In their professional work, the couple formed an elite, productive enclave, held in high esteem. They were scornful of their colleagues, whom they considered fraudulent or softminded. Their advanced approach to economics was clean, pure, mathematical. Although Athena's work may have represented a self-image, it was not personalized, not self-referential. It was objective, instrumentally skillful, and absorbing (Bernay, 1982). To some degree, her work was creative and imaginative, her husband's organized, detailed, compulsive. As real as were her own achievements, when their partnership threatened to dissolve, her very life seemed in danger. The low self esteem and surrender of self that she played out in their private life made her husband's acceptance of her work seem doubly necessary.

Athena was dependent on her husband for her independence! Her dependence on men had begun as she depended on an alliance with her father and the larger world to which he belonged for individuation from mother. Of all the many siblings she alone won father's respect. Her father had shamed her mother and sisters in ugly ways. Her guilt and pity over her mother's suffering had delayed her individuation, as had the poverty and the closeness of the embattled family unit. As a young woman, she had been permanently imprinted by her dependence for sponsorship of tender sensuality and for elite status in society by her dominant romantic male lover. Finally, now in a foreign land she depended on her husband for membership in a special club with a space for her, a desk for her, a home in which she was "sponsored" in work and motherhood.

As she got in touch with her rage at her surrender and her husband's abandonment, Athena felt "afraid" no longer. Understanding her own projections of mother and her transferences to her husband, it was remarkable to see Athena shed cringing dependence and terror as completely as an infatuation peels off. She turned serious attention to the insecurities that had kept her in the marriage but suffered no further anxiety attacks.

At school in Greece Athena had been gifted, unusually tall, an ungainly colt, a righteous, lonely little girl. She had been unable to relax and play with the others, but had been recognized as a fine student. The children scapegoated or ignored her but she was chosen for special responsibilities and honors by her teachers, and her peers turned to her for help in every crisis. She was proud and aggressive and ached for forgiveness for needing love. Love was not forthcoming from sisters or mother, whom she often loathed but always protected. She depended on men for demonstrative love, on her husband for a place as a woman. Her overdependence on men had thus been overdetermined by interactions involving individuation, sensual happiness, regression, sponsorship of achievement, and forgiveness for being herself.

In the course of our work, Athena hated and shamed herself, forgave herself, hated her mother, protected her mother, and hated and shamed me in the transference as her mother. Finally, she allowed herself to experience what she felt to be my generosity, my reliable open feedback and warm presence, my acceptance and understanding as real and deserved, and she was able to internalize my sponsorship. Again and again we "worked through" her outsider self, her fighting self, her female self, her pride and scorn and her natural need for comradeship and love.

Together we reconstructed, reexperienced and analyzed her past. We gave priority, at first, to the inward and outward process of her emergence from her recent overdependence. Analytic work with Athena entailed an active stance, a strong sense of mutuality. She began to find herself, in relationship to me.

VALUE CONFLICTS – DEPENDENCE VS. AUTONOMY

Our modern ideal of a good relationship entails trustworthy disclosure and an interactive partnership. Mutuality also symbolizes to us liberation from tyrannical authority. It means respect for autonomy and equality. In therapy, mutuality is often part of the process of individuation.

Yet, the framework of psychoanalysis must be asymmetrical. Like Athena, all patients explicitly demand a primary dependent relationship when it comes to transference of infant needs. In the wished-for primary relationship, both members of the pair would be entirely engaged in the needs of one. The analytic process needs to stay basically asymmetrical, so that transferences of many kinds can emerge. It is in the mutuality of the working alliance that the asymmetrical non-mutual transferences can be worked through. Because of a mutual working alliance, both patient and analyst can hold and respect the basic asymmetrical model and still adventure in many ways.

Sometimes, in treatment, a woman patient's demand for mutuality may be an expression of both a search for identity, the core of woman's struggle for personhood, and a transference need for symbiotic merging. A break in the feeling of common trust can then seriously threaten the analytic alliance and even inflict critical narcissistic injury. During the 1970's, with women's consciousness-raising groups breaking new ground, woman patients seemed not to come alone to the office. Like adolescents, each was invisibly accompanied by her group. Unless the analyst would in effect become a dues-paying member of the group, she was considered an enemy; as in class war, there were no neutrals there.

For example, in that context, a young woman came into therapy one day with a question that had come up in her consciousness-raising group. In treatment, we had so far been engaged in understanding her sexual frustration in marriage, a symbiotic relationship with her little son, a submissive, dependent relationship to her parents, and her sensitivity to my possible criticism. Sitting up straight in her chair and speaking right out she now asked, "Are you a Freudian? My group wants to know."

What did she think? After all, we had already worked for eight months.

Never mind: she wanted to know, was this therapy Freudian?

Very well, I would answer. It emerged from her questions and my answers that my orientation was grounded in Freudian understanding, that my treatment modes were eclectic and related to new thinking. It emerged that I took great issue with Freud over his genius error of constructing basic feminine development on a foundation of penis envy.

Stop there! Did I believe in "penis envy"? What kind of penis envy did she mean, I asked. Did I believe in it?

Yes, a small child does feel primary envy about what another child is or has. A little girl can bitterly envy and overvalue the penis because in her experience it symbolizes masculine privilege and superiority. In a grown woman, a secondary bitter envy can be discerned in symbols, dreams, and personality and so, by inference, penis envy exists.

The patient froze, and when she could speak again, she said we could not work together ever again. She rose and left.

She returned on time for the next session, sat down, and picked up her work regarding her jealousy of her woman friend's "great" breasts. I intervened to inquire "What happened to my being a Freudian?" "Oh, that," she cooly responded, "no problem." She had simply decided, "not to bring in any 'Freudian material'!" Even if she had to call her own shots, she would stay in the game.

IS SOMETHING MISSING IN WOMEN?

Under such stresses as disparagement, exclusion, belittling, dismissed aspirations, is it not normal to respond neurotically? Masochistic surrender and identification with the aggressor, over-dependence upon another, a demand to merge, are attempts at crucial alliances. Angry demands for a dramatic role on another's stage, exhibitionistic attention-getting hysteria, or bitter martyrdom are all bids for important recognition.

Is woman really inferior? Has she a missing piece? Why does she so often lack confidence, achiever or underachiever, and why does she so frequently interpret the vicissitudes of life with self-reference and feelings of persecution? In fact there is a "missing piece" inside woman. *There is a missing piece of internalized sponsorship.* There is nothing missing in woman herself. There are parts of the self that are lost because they are not available to the woman without this internalized sponsorship. Her penis envy and overvaluation of the penis is an envy of sponsorship, an exaggerated sense of the sponsored other, and an underestimation of her own instrumental self.

Because the woman has experienced a lack in the course of development, analytic technique, must not have a missing vector. The analyst must be the lacking significant other, the sponsor, a primary source of feedback of the value of self. Finally the analyst must become an internalized, truthful, reliable caretaker when it comes to understanding the past and the present, the weaknesses and strengths of the self (Gedo, 1981). For women in our culture, through their mothers, through their fathers, through their early childhood, there has been something truly missing, sponsorship is missing; their unhappiness and their defensive measures are "normal." These defensive measures are also often destructive and limiting. They make the woman vulnerable, as was Athena, at critical junctures in life. When Roy Schafer (1984) wrote about woman's idealization of unhappiness, I wonder if he realized that because this unhappiness has an external reality there is a responsive misery that must be coped with? Perhaps woman's unconscious idealization of unhappiness has been one of the better ways of coping with what seemed a sad but necessary condition. To make a virtue of, even to idealize necessity, is a kind of solution. Woman's creativity, her flight to imagination, is a flight to a realm in which she can remold reality more closely to the heart's desire (Spacks, 1972). Her "heavenly hurting" may have been a counsel of despair but, like her art, offers a liberating, value-giving sense of self.

Aware that she must be sponsor to her children and family, and vulnerable to the myth of inferiority, the woman turns for solution to dependence on superiority and omnipotence of another. The woman analyst, failing omnipotence, is then often seen as another castrated person. She is accused of being herself someone with a missing piece, with an innate weakness. A patient engaged in a bitter lifelong struggle with a paranoid and sexually aggressive father, upon leaving the office one day, noticed my then slight limp, left over from early polio. At our next session she declared that I should have protected her and not let her see my limp. Now, she claimed, she would never be able to overcome her own emotional handicap (Rycroft, 1955).

Another young woman was in the course of breaking her strong oedipal bond with her patriarchal father. The struggle was expressed with both the past, internalized father and the present father. She became unswervingly and erroneously convinced that I was engaged in a liberating extramarital affair of my own. Her unconscious fantasy was that I had altered reality, and that symbolically, her poor mother was at last liberated from the submissive, subservient condition of her parents' marriage. With her "mother" liberated she could then free herself.

Many sessions with women deal with the external causes of the patient's feeling of inferiority as a woman. Many deal with an inner sense of something missing, a tragic inadequacy. Insecure, sensitive to criticism, forever demanding reassurance, women respond to life with an internalized belief that something is missing in them, an inner reality in their early years and later a reality in the external world. In analysis we can recognize this reality and engage and validate both the inner and outer sense of a missing piece. In some ways we can objectively supply what is subjectively missing.

FAMILY TIES, SPONSORSHIP AND EXPLOITATION

The value-giving responsiveness of babies and children, the very real need and crucial role that mother plays for children, the actual new group of mother and children and father, all provide the woman with some of the missing inner validation. The duet of love between mother and baby is of unique value to each. In the sense that penis envy may be equated with internalized envy of inspiring personal sponsorship, Freud is right again, and "baby equals penis."

But family ties also exploit. In therapy the woman cries, Why should *I* put aside my unhappiness? Why should *I* be the one not to fight because of the children? Why should *I* be the angel in the house who makes peace and a creative milieu? The man, she cries, can go scot-free. He can walk away if I withdraw my love. I am dependent on his love for my sense of self, my place in society. In such situations, the analyst, in the interest of the woman's self-fulfillment, must be careful not to err on the side of repeating injustice and endorsing surrender.

Are there times when wisdom is the better part of valor? Must the woman be the one to adapt to injustice or tear herself apart as she generatively sponsors family growth and happiness? At different stages, inner degrees of freedom of choice are limited by important factors: depth of relatedness, degrees of individuation, available identification, the presence or absence of profound disillusionment or the creative energy required for reinvestment. Shared honesty and clear perception by patient and analyst nurtures a process of changing resolutions of conflict.

THE EVOLUTION OF "CHANGE IT"

The history of change in the woman's movement resembles changes that take place in individual analysis. At first society told women to "Take it and like it." Women could aspire only to creativity, to active female responsiveness to male dominance, to imagination and art, to the idealization of unhappiness, and creative homemaking for children and husband (Spacks, 1972). When Ibsen's heroine Nora slammed the door of the "Doll's House," leaving home and children behind, woman's slogan became "Take it or leave it." She would get a job and leave her humiliation and man's hypocrisy. Finally, the feminist woman says "Take it and change it."

In feminist analysis, in a sponsored relationship, the "present" recites the past, discovers and works through the ardent struggle of life, dreams and all. As with natural history, in one sense the woman and the therapist take it and like it. But new options and aspirations and a stronger earlier sense of self emerge as impulses and memories are given voice. Risks, acting out, and sometimes alienation ensue. Woman finds she can *take it or leave it*. But it is her life, and hers to choose; she is both a female and a person. As a person, she can be different, she can take it and change it. To do so, she needs to learn, study, and practice in the office and in her life the instrumental, individuated self.

As we study our lives in therapy, we find good as well as bad objects of the past stored up inside us. As they become more freely available, they can be used as sponsors of change: the iconoclastic intelligence and warm sentimental culture of father, the laughter and courage and righteous passion of matriarchal mother, the love and sponsorship of effective brothers, the important aspirations of sisters.

PRIMARY LESBIANISM AND EROTIC TRANSFERENCES

Psychoanalytic understanding is very important in therapy with women of a primary lesbian orientation. Working in analysis with a woman of a truly primary lesbian choice, the analyst is dealing with transference from a preoedipal time. We recognize that an early strong "erotic" turn-on has resulted in a permanent erotic inner construction towards a female and a female's erotic response. In the course of treatment, if the erotic transference of a woman patient to a woman analyst is invalidated as a cover for some infant type of dependence, or as a mask for oedipal or heterosexual feelings, the patient experiences humiliation, hopelessness, deprivation, and rage. Such an interpretation does not do honor to the crucial fact that the little girl *took it* and by her precocity attempted to *change it*, to find the love she needed.

In a review of psychoanalytic theories of gender identity, Person and Oversay (1983) remind us that gender is early assigned and experienced, as early as 18 months, and the oedipal period organizes not gender but the little girl's sexual feelings around father. When sex is aroused in the preoedipal period, it organizes the world in a different manner. Mitchell (1974) calls our attention to the fact that in a patriarchal society, the father is of critical importance whether present or absent, and this is certainly true in the oedipal period. When there is sexual arousal in the preoedipal period, sexuality is organized around the mother (Eisenbud, 1981). Later the mother's relationship to the little girl may be of great importance in identification and for the resolution of the oedipal period, but in the preoedipal period it is crucial to precocious sexuality. In my article on Lesbian Choice (1981) I speak of ego development and precocious sexuality. I suggest there "that primary lesbian erotic love originates in a precocious turn-on of erotic desire mandated by the ego, and that it is progressive, not regressive. It occurs when the child feels excluded from good enough or long enough primary bliss, and seeks inclusion by a sexual bond and sexual wooing."

Classical psychoanalytic theory posited that a lesbian orientation came from negative oedipal experience and was a defensive attempt to rescue sexuality from frustration and inhibition. The lesbian woman was one who took it and left it, a defensive maneuver. This classic insight did not identify or describe the data of primary experience that I have been discussing. I found that respect and recognition of strength is communicated when the analyst engages with the patient in a reconstruction of early preoedipal struggle and the courageous innovations of the ego at that time. Although our basic strivings are sometimes used as defensive maneuvers in analysis, primary lesbian erotic transference must be respected and validated.

The lesbian woman is often resistant, suspicious, and withdrawn at the start of treatment. She considers regression to childhood as demeaning. She makes hostile denials of dependence. Then sudden change surprises the analyst. The patient confesses to a yearning for romantic intimacy with her beloved therapist. "The invitation to a love feast follows hard upon the sense of funeral loss and hopelessness she first laid at her therapist's door" (Eisenbud, 1981).

At the core of lesbian primary erotic orientation, achieved in preoedipal years, is a sense of exclusion from mother. I will sketch three different patterns in the analytic transferences that suggest three variations of context of this etiology. These examples illustrate the integration of new feminist understanding and psychoanalytic practice.

In its first and most direct form, the lesbian woman in treatment makes overt demands for proof of special love and inclusion in the woman analyst's life and offers a keen eroticized courtship. In this recapitulation of urgent need for erotic proof of "mother's" inclusion, the analytic alliance itself without extra inclusion, finally forms a "good enough" bond and a transference that gives a sense of "good enough" inclusion.

In the second context, reconstruction during analysis suggests mother herself encouraged her little daughter to serve her romantically, even to court her as an attentive lover might. But mother never rewarded the daughter with the promised reciprocal romantic attachment. In the transference the lesbian patient then interprets analytic acceptance and empathy as seduction. She responds by wooing aggressively, and will hear no denial. She is left with rage at being encouraged and then scorned, as long ago with mother. In treatment, insight into her mother's earlier double binding helps the Lesbian to let go the tough character armor formed over her hate. She becomes willing to risk love again, and to seek a love that can be returned.

In the third context, the mother sought fusion and was sensual and incorporative, threatening the little girl's ego with death by symbiosis. In this context the etiology of active primary lesbian choice is an attempt at reversal. Rather than be the victim in a passive surrender to mother, the child takes a compulsively active role, vigilant and lonely, to ensure individuation. In analysis with the woman, in the transference, a fierce struggle emerges with the analyst over control. Meanwhile, a struggle rages within the woman herself, between a lust for power over women and the need for intimacy and love. Transference interpretation, respect and empathy, and firm limit setting encourage new individuation.

With understanding of the three different patterns, recapitulations of mother and little daughter, each of the transferences can be worked through. Such resolutions provide a better foundation for adult lesbian sexual binding than a blind repetition of the past between analyst and patient (Fleming, 1984).

FRUSTRATION AND PERSECUTION

Women and men can adapt to a surprising amount of physical and emotional frustration and live through and recover. When stress is experienced as persecution, however, its effect is much more powerful and demands denial or counteraction for survival.

How does the experience of persecution differ from one of frustration? Noticeably, we or our group feel *helpless* and discounted in the hands of someone or of a group's power, the hurt is experienced as *intentional* and it feels *particular to us* or to our group.

Often in treatment, a woman who was an abused child must be taught to recognize injustice and to feel persecuted. Repression of responses of rage, rebellion, or revenge reinforces learned suffering and defensive helplessness. Analysis must elicit the persecutory aspects of the frustration by speculative reconstruction, associative memories, metaphors, dreams, and identificiation.

One patient had resources that were strong enough to afford an example of how effective such a breakthrough can be. Her father, a powerful older man, childless in two marriages, demanded that his third wife, a ballerina, give him a baby boy. With some indifference and narcissistic dismay, she did conceive and deliver a child, but it was a baby girl. Father's grief was mythic in the family, and also his pronouncement, "If she is a girl, she'll have to be a perfect girl." (This was in the 1970's, not in Victorian times.) The perfect girl came for analysis at 30 years of age, a stylish doll, smiling and charming. She had 8 years of a frigid marriage and faked orgasms, and 26 years of phobic "test anxiety." She came because she wanted to be sexually alive and to be more independent and to be a better mother for her son.

During her first four years of life, the patient had been a wild, happy, naughty little girl, too much for her undemonstrative mother. Only father could "handle her," enjoy her, spank and subdue her. Now her husband, a Navy officer, dictated her dress, her budget, her sports, and her sexual behavior. Their philosophy included vacations from marriage for himself. She felt guilty but rejecting toward her oldest son, and smothered her youngest son with catering love.

After a few weeks in analysis, the patient had a dream:

A small, feeble blind boy was feeling his way down a staircase. He was bedraggled and alone.

To this dream she associated her father's disappointment and decrees. She was also reminded of her oldest son. We spoke of the lost boy in her, her lost spontaneous, confident, impulsive self, the lost "4 year old giant." We reconstructed how she had defended herself against both her rage and punishment for boyish liveliness by "blinding" herself, by phobias, by compliance, and finally by projection of the be-draggled boy she herself had become to her eldest son.

There was some anxiety in myself, in the countertransference; she so rapidly reclaimed her bold assertive self, and so rapidly discovered the feminist world around her, and new attitudes of the sexual revolution. With the mild sponsorship of a few months of analysis, she broke through and released a screaming, angry, incorrigible rebellion in her marriage. She found she could take persecution or leave it, or reverse it, that she herself could be a powerful, autonomous "man," i.e., a person! She went to school.

Oh girl! Oh, girl! Sure enough, her husband proved threatened, jealous, beside himself, stayed ashore, and went for help. The couple found an incomparably richer and changed way of life.

On a detour, on her own during vacation from analysis, the patient risked separation and left home with a gentle, impotent lover of counterculture philosophy, who was gratefully responsive to her active erotic role. She was awakened sexually and remained a passionate woman.

Alas, a destructive introject can be much more deeply embedded, without the resources of personality in this patient, our "little" Navy wife. When a powerful, shaming mother, or important, idealized sneering father is the internal enemy object, life can become a tragic stage, however talented an achiever the woman may be, and a woman's envy and masochistic tears and self-hate and self-reproach are the signals of depression and despair. How then can the analyst sponsor inner change in such an individual? New approaches to masochism integrate modern analytic theory with treatment.

First, with the patient, we study the relinquishment of self as a defensive mechanism. Classically, this has been called an "identification with the aggressor," a mechanism that hopes to neutralize the enemy, to do the dirty to the self, to punish the self.

Secondly, the new conceptualizations of internalization of early relationships and situations as objects stored inside the subjective world is a powerful tool against masochism and depression. The analysis becomes the enemy of the biting bully, the self-hate within.

A third modern approach and important therapeutic tool is to recognize and honor the adaptive attempt to restore effectiveness that is hidden in the masochistic behavior. The masochist repeats defeat and hopes this time things will be different. This time she will win. For change to occur, however, something must change in the setup, or blindly, the same defeat is repeated. A vicious circle is set up, and a new loss of effectiveness again demoralizes (Eisenbud, 1967). Active encouragement to try unused degrees of freedom, new forms of behavior, a change of heart is needed to win a restored sense of effectiveness (White, 1963).

Fourth, masochistic behavior in marriage and work is well understood in the context of the process of individuation, the foundation of change. The treatment dyad affords a mutual proving ground for this process of growth and experience, for individuation allowed and encouraged (Cantor, 1982).

One patient, a rejected late child, having been hit by an automobile when she was 10 had been taken to the hospital by the police and had her broken arm set. The child begged them "not to tell my mother," but at last, as her fearsome mother came to the emergency room, she shouted to mother, "It was my fault, it was my fault!" She was still hoping to evade the shaming fury that would ensue.

In treatment this woman and I worked on understanding that she was identifying with the aggressor, that she was trying to wipe herself out, to make no intrusion or demands on her mother.

A second aspect of this approach, one of internalized object relation, emerged as we realized that this same patient, all but hypnotized by her mother, reflected in offense as well as defense her mother's angry rages and shaming vigilance. She rushed to the offensive at any hint of possible shame or scorn from another. She lived in a persecutory world. It was as if she were really "possessed," and in that context, treatment was far from only a sponsoring, ego-building, insightful operation. Vicious destruction of the self and of the other had been internalized and had to be encountered in the analysis. The patient's bitter, vengeful, internalized brutal mother must become ego alien instead of ego syntonic. Again and again we confronted the "just like mother" as well as the "surrender to mother" destructive wishes. She who lives by the sword dies by the sword.

It is also worth noting some of this woman's strengths, the internalized feelings and adventures that became our allies and afforded her courage. "Get out," her mother had said; and indeed she did, as much as possible, down the block and away, and found a roller-skating, traveling, comradely self, and later, for a husband, an outgoing regular fellow. Moreover, the sharp seeing, sneering, shaming mother had taught her to notice, watch, and learn. She found she could study, and design beauty, and aspire to change. As analyst, I fought the internalized mother actively, sneer for sneer, and there were many painful confrontations. But our empathy and alliance held. The defense and carrion comfort of depression and hate gave over as she courageously allowed me to fight by her side.

We see that persecutory feelings can stem from overdependence on sponsorship, lack of individuation, profound conviction that something is missing, the important blackmail of family ties, misunderstood erotic transferences, and the internalized abuse of early childhood. These feelings are reinforced by objective social injustice, irrational autocratic authority, denial of recourses, hypocrisy, and unfair double standards. How do these feelings show up in the analytic dyad during treatment?

Some persecutory feelings find a fit in the frame of therapy. Some are archaic distortions, invited in by the reliving of the past. Because persecution entails intentionality, special sensitivity to what is in the mind of the "important parent," the analyst, becomes a vital transference factor. Scorn, boredom, enjoyment of power, all take their turn as projections on the analyst and contribute a sense of ill-treatment. Indeed, the thoughts imagined in the mind of the analyst are experienced as ill-treatment itself, and have the magic power of inflicting pain.

When the "mother" analyst is experienced as separate at the time the patient is feeling an infant need for fusion, the analyst's separateness is felt to be a persecution. She is accused of "not feeling what I feel." She is a destroyer because she denies the patient a primary relationship without which a baby cannot live. When, on the contrary, the patient feels that the analyst recognizes and empathizes with missed needs for early infant nurturance, the adult woman may feel shamed and persecuted to be so reduced. She says, in effect, with Bugs Bunny, "Look out who you call a little gray rabbit!"

Sometimes in analysis the "working through," the confrontations with difficult psychic tasks, is experienced as a cops and robbers game. The patient feels caught at being neurotic. Although projection of cops and robbers may be more frequent when the analyst is a man, it also occurs with a woman therapist. When one woman therapist's choice of therapeutic orientation, and the demonstration of the correctness of that orientation seemed more important than did the patient herself, the therapist became a persecutor. This patient had a dream in which she attempted to sing a solo song, but was intentionally drowned out by her therapist accompanist!

When another patient seems "favored," and "chosen" above her, when fees or times or vacations seem arbitrary and cruel, as in childhood, the patient is bitter and helpless and cries, "Unfair!" Powerless to fight exclusion, as with oedipal jealousy, or exclusive early forceful parental intimacy, the patient relives painful jealousy, and experiences of helplessness, persecution and exclusion ensue.

Among the many ways in which the patient, in turn, can be the persecutor of the analyst, the theme of "something missing" often reappears. Sometimes this accusation of something missing in the analyst is made in honest desparation, sometimes it is for sport, sometimes the patient is working through the need for an ideal self. When the patient does not sponsor the analyst's effectiveness, but belittles and distrusts it, the analyst, she points out, is missing something. The analyst is not a faith healer, she does not produce a map for living, or she does not engage in changing real life for the patient. The analyst is not even a strict, orthodox classic analyst with true religion, a real doctor!

Although it is essential to respect and attend to these accusations, how do we finally undo persecution in modern analysis? If we give active recognition of real social injustice, does our new active stance, a kind of "fair employment" policy, preclude or impede transference, or deny and suppress it? By validation of the feelings of injustice, by representing a rational authority that holds itself to account, by clear and firm limit setting, by sharing mutual feelings, by empathetically reliving injustice and anger with the patient, by active interpretation and insight and explanation, by ongoing encouragement, we hope to give an experience of justice, a development of self, to counter the old experiences of injustice. This security allows the patient to return to reenact the past and reengage the present in and out of the transference. With generative empathy and acceptance and insight, the analysis can become both a room of one's own and a group of one's own for sponsorship of self.

REFERENCES

Bernay, T. (1982), Separation and the sense of competence-loss in women. *Amer. J. Psychoanal.*, 42 (4): 293–305.

Cantor, D. W. (1982), Divorce: Separation or separation-individuation? *Amer. J. Psychoanal.*, 42 (4): 307–313.

Eisenbud, R. J. (1959), Repudiation of the feminine self. Unpublished Ph.D. thesis, Radcliffe College, Harvard University.

_____ (1967), Masochism revisited. *Psychoanal. Rev.*, 54 (4): 6–25.

_____ (1981), Early and later determinants of lesbian choice. *Psychoanal. Rev.*, 69 (1): 85–109.

Fleming, J. (1984), *Lovers in the Present Afternoon*. Tallahassee, FL: Naiad Press.

Gedo, J. E. (1981), Notes on the psychoanalytic management of archaic transferences. In: *Advances in Clinical Psychoanalysis*. New York: International Universities Press, pp. 93–132.

Lytton, S. M. (1984), Report of a panel on value judgments in psychoanalytic theroy and practice. *J. Amer. Psychoanal. Assn.*, 32 (1): 150.

Mitchell, J. (1974), *Psychoanalysis and Feminism*. New York: Random House.

Person, E. S. (1982), Women working: Fears of failure, deviance and success. *J. Amer. Acad. Psychoanal.*, 10 (1): 67–84.

_____ & Ovesey, L. (1983), Psychoanalytic theories of gender identity disorder. *J. Amer. Acad. Psychoanal.*, 11 (2): 203–226.

Rich, A. (1978), *The Dream of the Common Language*. New York: Norton.

Rycroft, C. (1955), Two notes on idealization, illusion and disillusion as normal and abnormal psychological processes. *Internat. J. Psycho-Anal.*, 26: 81–87.

Schafer, R. (1984), The pursuit of failure and idealization of unhappiness. *Amer. Psychologist*, 39 (4): 398–405.

Spacks, P. M. (1972), *The Female Imagination*. New York: Avon Books.

Weldon, F. (1974), *Female Friends*. New York: St. Martin's Press.

White, R. W. (1963), Ego and reality in psychoanalytic theory. *Psychoanalytic Issues*, Monogr. 11. New York: International Universities Press.

14

When Men Are Therapists to Women: Beyond the Oedipal Pale

Stanley Moldawsky, Ph.D.

The literature on gender in psychoanalysis was sparse, if not nonexistent, until recently. Psychoanalysis has been gender blind as a result of a number of factors. First, psychoanalysis was a creation of a man who was a part of a sexist society, and the majority of analysts were male. Freud's concepts of penis envy and his notion of female development as phallocentric held sway in psychoanalytic theory for a long time before the feminist movement influenced many analysts to investigate female development afresh and correct early theorizing. Indeed, Horney's early rebellion against the concept of penis envy was criticized as evidence of its existence.

An earlier version of this paper was presented at the annual meeting of the American Psychological Association, Toronto, Ontario, Canada, August 1984.

The second reason for ignoring gender is that the transference is experienced in long-term analysis, when appropriate regression has occurred, regardless of the real attributes of the analyst, including gender. Thus, the analyst may be nurturant, giving, reliable, and warm, but, based on the patient's dominant perception of the mother, the analyst may be perceived as depriving, withholding, and unreliable, regardless of whether the analyst is male or female. The transference, then, is gender blind.

Third, although our knowledge is increasing, the paucity of research in the area of gender leaves us in the realm of anecdotal reports. With the growing number of female analysts, some have turned their attention to this difficult area. Data needs to be obtained on such questions as (1) Is the sex of the therapist a critical variable? (2) Is the *experience* of, say, a father transference to a male analyst the same as a father transference to a female analyst? (3) Is the *experience* of a woman in an early mother transference with a female analyst the same as with a male analyst? This article will report data from analyses that adds to our anecdotal lore; however, we are badly in need of definitive studies. It is a sign of the changes in our science as well as the changes in our culture that these questions are now being asked.

Psychoanalysis has generally taken the position that gender is not a crucial variable. Mogul (1982) reports on over 80 articles that deal with gender of the therapist in some way. She argues that the sex of the therapist matters least in traditional psychoanalysis with neurotic patients and matters most in face-to-face therapies that are less intensive. Karme (1979) concludes that early mother-child transferences can disregard the gender of the analyst. She notes that mother transferences with male analysts are always pregential. I shall report some data that corroborates this conclusion.

Person (1983) has written that the effects of gender may be subtle but pervasive in analyses. She notes that female patients are requesting female analysts more and more. Person suggests four conscious reasons for women's choice of female analysts:

1. Fear of sexism from a male analyst.
2. Avoidance of "faking it" – the need to please men, leading to constant ingratiating behavior.
3. Fear of erotic transference and countertransference.
4. A wish for a role model.

The first three reasons lead to avoidance of male analysts, the fourth impels a move toward female analysts.

In discussing the fear of sexism, Person reports a clinical vignette in which a male supervisee interpreted a woman's desire to work in symptomatic rather than adaptive terms. This particular woman had had a difficult relationship with her mother and was ambivalent about leaving her own children to return to work. Her desire to work was interpreted as a defense against closeness with her children, which immobilized her in guilt and uncertainty. After supervision the male analyst discussed his interpretation with the patient and corrected it, relieving her guilt.

I had a patient who chose me as her analyst because she noted that the name preceeding mine in the American Psychological Association Directory was my wife's. If I would *allow* my wife to be a professional woman then I would *allow* my patient to do likewise. This initial attitude permitted her to enter a relationship with me, and we analyzed the roots subsequently. Complicating the choice of a male as her analyst were experiences with her mother that left her feeling that only men were valuable and that women achieved in life only if they controlled and had power over men. Because of sexist attitudes in her upbringing, and despite her fear of sexism in some men, she could only value a male analyst. Thus, despite the trend toward women selecting female analysts, the underlying reasons for the choice are the most significant and ultimately will emerge in the transference analysis.

Regarding the second fear, many women have adopted an ingratiating facade toward men. This may be missed by a male analyst early in treatment but soon will be exposed as a character defense. When this defense was exposed in a patient of mine, a number of changes took place. First, she found it possible to express anger toward me when heretofore it had been impossible. Previous attempts at analyzing resistance to feeling and expressing anger had failed. The crucial resistance was the subtly ingratiating attitude. This woman, herself a therapist, also found her anxiety in treating men diminished when this resistance yielded. Her sense of her own genuineness increased, and she felt fully competent when she no longer had to "fake it." Although Person writes of this as a conscious reason for selecting a female analyst, it may be the very reason a female patient chooses a male analyst. That is, she needs to affirm her value by having a male once again succumb to her ingratiation.

Although some patients may fear an erotic transference toward a male analyst, sexuality ultimately must be analyzed. With a female analyst, the likelihood is greater that sexuality will be analyzed in terms of figures other than the transference figure. This, by definition, produces a different experience for the female patient. Themes of competitiveness will be experienced in the transference rather than themes of erotic yearning toward the analyst. (I refer here to the positive oedipal strivings.) Analysts are aware that these different experiences still permit the analysis of unconscious conflict, although the experience in the transference is different depending on the gender of the analyst.

PREOEDIPAL STRUCTURE AND ITS IMPACT

Freud's analyses were six-month, six-days-a-week experiences. They were essentially analyses of id contents, and analyzing the resistances to recognition and remembering infantile wishes was the focus of the work. With our increased knowledge of ego psychology, object relations theory, and countertransference, analysis today can be of eight years' duration or more. With greater investigation of preoedipal development (Mahler, Pine & Bergman, 1975), analysts are seeing patients less frequently – two, three, or four times a week for longer periods of time – and are involved in resolving early mother transferences. For Freud, the personality developed its major stamp between 3 ½ and 6 years of age, namely, during the oedipal period. All adult behaviors, problems, and conflicts were reduced to the vicissitudes of the Oedipus complex. Thus, the transference was always seen as an oedipal transference in one form or another.

What kind of regression is induced by the analyst of either gender? The male or female analyst will induce the same regression in the female patient by virtue of the nonintrusive, nonjudgmental, interested stance, focused on the patient's needs only. This produces an adult version of the early mother-infant situation in which the mother's needs are mostly set aside in favor of the child. This is repeated in all medical settings throughout life. Nowhere is there a more consistent nurturant atmosphere than in analysis. Hour after hour, the analyst sets aside his or her own interests and needs and devotes attention to the patient. This is a powerful inducement to regress and encourages the emergence of early transferences. Much has been written about the greater prevalence of preoedipal disturbances in today's clinical practice (Boyer and Giovacchini, 1967; Blanck & Blanck, 1979). An argument could be made that the analytic method is especially suited to permitting the flowering of preoedipal transferences; thus, we bring out in bolder relief the more primitive desires and earlier conflicts of our patients. The male analyst is therefore involved in a mother transference more often than not. Before discussing clinical examples we need to qualify the concept "Neutrality."

THE CONCEPT OF NEUTRALITY

When the analyst says in the beginning of treatment that he or she will try to help the patient, the analyst has aligned himself or herself with the patient's ego and thus has compromised his or her neutrality from the outset. Freud counseled that a position equidistant from the id, ego, and superego was the neutral spot for the analyst. I believe that our alliance with the patient's ego makes us not neutral at all. We have become allies in encouraging further development. This alliance also leads to countertransference problems, but these can be opportunities for creative work. The analyst becomes the sponsor of further development in the patient. Neutrality, then, refers to (1) not imposing the analyst's values on the patient, (2) not making choices for the patient, and (3) not assuming the role of counselor or advisor (Lieder, 1984).

A number of years ago I treated a 38-year-old Catholic woman who had had a previous catatonic episode. She was raised in a family that produced two siblings who suffered psychotic episodes. She was a nurse-educator and was working steadily when I met her. We developed a good rapport and to please me, as well as herself, she lost 100 pounds in the first year of therapy. Although I was seeing her only once a week, she developed a strong regressive transference and I could feel myself being wooed by her. I was aware that the love she felt was not of an adult heterosexual nature. Her wishes were to be held and cradled. This was pleasant to me and my response was a mixture of warmth and support and pleasure in her work achievements and weight loss. (Hardly neutral!) My neutrality was even further weakened when she shamefully admitted masturbating.

I commented to this Catholic patient, "You're 38, single, with no relationship. It's only natural that you would be loving yourself." She replied, "It's a sin according to the Church." I countered with, "Your

Church is wrong!" I had taken on the Catholic Church and strained my patient's loyalties. She went off to see her priest to help in her struggle with her desires and to deal with my unneutral stance (siding with her desires against her superego). Behold! She encountered a young priest who said, "You are 38, single—it's understandable that you would masturbate!" My patient was able to relax more now that both father (priest) and mother (analyst) had given her permission.

After we continued our work for six months, she called one evening for an emergency appointment. This was unusual, and I saw her the next day. She was in a panic. She had fallen in love and was convinced it was abnormal and disgusting. She had fallen in love with a woman, the mother of three children (like her own mother), with the same name as herself. Her overt concern was that lesbianism was pathological, and she was sure I would condemn her. It became apparent that she really wanted my permission; in transference terms, she wanted to know whether it was okay for her to love anyone but me. When I interpreted this to her, she associated to her family of origin, the tight clan that it was, and her mother's admonition that "it's a cruel world out there. Stay here with me, where we will all be safe." I was able to expose the conflicts between loyalty to her mother and separation and greater autonomy. The patient was not able to see, however, that at the same time, that she was fearful of loving anyone but her mother, she was also symbolically wooing her mother. Eisenbud (1981) has discussed the notion that lesbian love is an attempt to sexually woo a woman who symbolically represents the mother. She points out that the origin of the difficulty with mother is a feeling of being left out of the bond with mother, and the sexual wooing is an attempt to seek inclusion. I made no such interpretation to my patient, because it was being acted out and my interpretation would have been useless.

The patient's affair ended when the lover became afraid of losing her children to her husband in a divorce action if she was discovered. The patient rapidly formed another relationship with another single woman, and when they bought a house together, she ended treatment.

This case again illustrates how in a regressive transference the male analyst is cast in the role of mother. Men need to be comfortable with this. Analytic activity involves quiet listening and active interventions. Thus, the analytic work requires a capacity to be passive, receptive, and, I believe, nurturant. For the male, this must be non-threatening, which means personal analysis of any defenses against one's own identification with the mother as well as defenses against passivity.

In the case just cited, I did not analyze the conflict over masturbation, but rather acted as a counselor; whereas with the panic over the love affair, I analyzed the transference. I wish I could explain why I abandoned my analytic stance in the one instance and not the other. With preoedipal disturbances analysts primarily interpret, but we also are providing a relationship with nurturance, limit setting, and acceptance of impulses and compassion. I believe my nonneutral stance in the former instance was useful. I also think, because this patient characteristically did not free associate, that analyzing the masturbation conflict would have been impossible. In the second instance, she gave me barely enough associative material, but, with what I already knew of her history and the transference, I could do transference analysis.

In another clinical case, Alice, an attractive, bright, articulate, gifted woman came for analysis suffering from depression. She had been experiencing this on and off for four years following the death of her mother. She was married to a physician, and had two children. Alice was very dependent on her husband and had great fears of self-assertion, low self-esteem, and feelings of inadequacy as a parent. The intimacy of the analytic situation (we were meeting four times a week) aroused intense erotic desires, which were exposed and experienced with the usual frustration of the analytic process. Here was a man, listening to and discussing a woman's passionate desires, saying things like, "Tell me more about it," or, "What does that bring to mind?" There were moments when discussion was the furthest thing from Alice's mind; action was urged upon us. I encouraged her to tell me about her feelings and empathized with her frustration that she was not being loved in the way she wanted. Slowly, we *lived through* the intense, demanding, unrequited loving; associations and dream material brought forth the oedipal underpinnings of these feelings. The father was clearly in the picture, and many memories emerged. As this was happening, opportunities arose for Alice to relate to her estranged father. The contacts became less anxiety-provoking and took on a more realistic appearance.

This covered the first few years of analytic work. The patient then regressed further in the relationship, and the feelings became more warm, enveloping, close. Her wish to be held and tenderly loved came out strongly in her feelings toward me. Now the associative material and dream material pointed directly to the mother. We learned of early fears in her relationship to a mother who was suicidal during marital strife when the patient was four. Alice developed powerful feelings of closeness with me and vigorously denied the notion of separating and becoming autonomous. As we explored these feelings of closeness in the last two years of our work, we also discussed termination. Her fears of separating were intense. Despite these fears, the patient had been making many independent strides in relation to her children, her husband, and educating herself for a career.

In the last two years we worked through Alice's dreams that someone would die if we separated (the symbiosis), her fury that I expected her to be a separate person. This sophisticated woman brought me Chodorow (1978) to read on mothering to bolster her argument that women were different from men in their needs to separate from their mothers. Women had semipermeable membranes so they could sink back and forth into each other and not ever become separate. She felt I was imposing on her my male notion that separation was necessary. I interpreted these intellectual arguments as defenses to prevent her from leaving me. I empathized with her desire to remain in a cocoon with me. I reflected her anger that I was being a rejecting parent who insisted on her independence. Through all the interpretive work, I maintained my personal conviction that she must separate, that she had the ability to survive, and that she had the resources to grow and achieve.

My awareness that I was gently prodding my patient toward termination engendered doubts about my technical correctness—that I was analyzing the fears of separating and all the accompanying feelings without imposing my own plan for the patient. I overcame my doubts, and once we had agreed on a date I stuck to it as the patient wavered, saying: "After all, eight years is a long time. So what if we postpone it for a while just to be sure? Six months or so won't make a difference." I empathized with her uncertainty, her doubts, and her anger that it would soon be over. In fact, she set the date three months before my usual summer break. This was going to be her termination, not mine. Two sessions before we ended, she asked if she could bring her husband in to meet me. Her request came as the session ended, so I murmured the usual, "Why don't we discuss it next time?" Between the sessions, she telephoned to argue in favor of the meeting, and I agreed to it. (I have noted a tendency of myself as well as other analysts to be more easily swayed by talking on the telephone than by free associative material.)

The three of us met, and he and I sized each other up. We spoke of many things, including his pleasure with the results of his wife's analysis. She later told me that she felt as if she were the hypotenuse in this triangle, as her two men showed off. She compared it to when she visited her grandmother with her father. She liked sitting with them as they talked with each other. Although she experienced this feeling of being a child with her parents, she was also trying to effect a transition from her analyst to her husband and particularly to withdraw from the transference. Her last session was spent in analyzing our "acting out" (the inclusion of her husband).

My rationale for agreeing to the meeting was that this was an attempt to cope with termination and that it would be useful to remove some of the sense of secrecy regarding the analysis. My later association was to a marriage ceremony in which I, the parent (now the father), handed the patient over to her husband with my blessings. At least, I had the same feelings as I did when I went through such a ceremony with my own daughter.

THE RELATIONSHIP WITH A MALE ANALYST

In the two cases discussed, most of the analytic work was done in the context of a mother transference. Separation issues were present in both patients. Again, such transferences routinely develop with a male analyst, as long as he is open to working with the patient whenever she is in her regression. I once had an astounding experience of working with a schizoid woman who had had a previous psychosis and who was in a symbiotic relationship with me. One day she stared at me and said, "I can see you! There you are, and here I am!" Her recognition of my presence was symbolically like a birth experience. In this instance, the transference involved regression back to the earliest possible level.

I do not know whether female analysts have an easier time in living through a regressive mother transference with a patient. Perhaps there are analysts of either gender who reject the regression. The patient is exposing repressed affects and forgotten ideas. She feels, for example, angry or sometimes furious with the analyst, and although these feelings were experienced before with the parent in conflict, they were never worked through and integrated. But to risk experiencing strong affects and emerge unscathed and stronger is an exciting development.

In the analytic literature essentially since the 1950s the attempt to differentiate the real relationship from the transference has occupied such writers as Sterba (1934), Leowald (1960), Stone (1961), Winnicott (1965), Greenson (1967), and others. Grunes (1984) writes that for patients with object hunger, there exists a demand for relationship that should be responded to within the context of what he terms the "therapeutic object relationship." He sees this as a unifying clinical and theoretical concept. It aids us in realizing that developmental maturation as well as transference analysis is taking place. Grunes defines the therapeutic object relationship as the matrix of change in treatment. He considers it a relationship of "primal intimacy; increased permeability of boundaries between self and others; intensive empathic interaction; the evolution of self and object definition in a context of intimate relation with an object that is instrumental in this process . . ." (Grunes, 1984, p. 141). Like most of the analytic literature, Grunes does not discuss the gender of the analyst as a distinguishing variable.

The analytic relationship is a very special one which has a reality of its own as well as a repetitive transference aspect. Grunes' concept may be a very fortunate choice of words (therapeutic object relationship) which tries to include the real relationship within it, thus obviating the need for a separate concept of a real relationship. When we consider that the analyst is a quickener of development (or a sponsor) we have stretched neutrality further. The analyst is saying, "I value you, I care about your growth and development, you are important to me, I will not impose my values or plans on you. I will help you actualize yourself. You, as a person, count, be you female or male." Those attitudes come through the analyst in his or her intimate, empathic interaction with the patient. This conveys hope, optimism, and the prospect of change.

What does this mean to the female patient who has a male analyst? In the context of a long-term relationship, particularly when the woman suffers from low self-esteem and poor sense of self-worth, the growth in self-esteem stems from a new identification. In his valuing of the patient, the analyst, aside from helping to resolve conflict, helps the patient *value herself*. She accomplishes this by *identification* with the analyst. This may express itself in career choices, in her new self-confidence, or in her manner of relating to others.

More superficially, it may be a brand new experience for a "traditional" woman who is dependent according to family values, submissive to her husband, and feels inferior, and so forth to be challenged in these personality traits by a male analyst. It can be a truly novel experience for a woman to be sponsored in feminist values by a male. However, this is not as profound a role for the male analyst as being an object for the identification that takes place only in a long-term relationship.

DOES THE THERAPIST'S GENDER MATTER

My object in this paper was to show that a male analyst has something different and perhaps special to offer the female patient. After reviewing my clinical work with women, I can see why papers on technique are essentially genderless. The analyst's task is to permit the transference to flourish, to aid in the continued maturation of the patient, particularly with regard to preoedipal differentiation and separation. Karme (1979) states that early transferences can disregard the sex of the analyst. She also agrees with Blum (1970) and Zetzel (1970) that oedipal transferences always adapt to the gender of the analyst. With a male analyst, a woman's fantasies of oedipal involvement with the analyst are expected to emerge. With the female analyst, fantasies of the analyst's spouse or other outside figures emerge. The fantasies are influenced by the gender of the analyst so that the conflicted oedipal themes are exposed to analysis, but in different ways. Karme also suggests that female therapists rarely experience father transferences, whereas male analysts regularly experience preodipal mother transferences.

I have previously discussed the concept of *living through* (Moldawsky, 1982). It is similar to *working through*, which has both an intellectual and emotional aspect, but *living through* is a more comprehensive term that encompasses the therapeutic relationship. That is, the patient experiences affects, which had previously been repressed, in a *new* relationship (with the analyst). The patient then has the opportunity to live through the process of first, overcoming the anxiety; second, experiencing the conflicted affect; and third, allowing it to remain conscious and then remembering its roots and antecedents. Living through to integration is the new development made possible by the interpretive stance, tolerance, encouragement and alliance of the analyst.

This new experience of living through the range of affects with the analyst is *not* just a repetition of the past. It includes the repetition but goes beyond it. This is not an intellectual process in which the patient has figured out something about the past that is currently interfering in his or her life, any more than it is an intellectual figuring out done by the analyst. The empathic communication is a more comprehensive attitude on the part of the analyst, which includes avoiding the transference invitations while still experiencing them.

Can the female patient have the same living through experience in a preoedipal transference with a male analyst as when she is seeing a female analyst? I am convinced that the male analyst can help a female patient live through a preoedipal mother transference. I do not know, however, whether it is *experienced* the same way when both members of the dyad are female.

Gender should make a difference. Although the issue requires research that has not been done, the answer I finally come to is that certain feelings will be facilitated with an analyst of one gender but that, over the long term, all the conflicts will be experienced in the analytic relationship with an analyst of either sex. However, all the *feelings* may not necessarily be "lived through." The question for research, then, is whether or not this makes any difference.

I can well appreciate the role modeling that professional women offer their female patients. The capability for intimate, empathetic communication—the heart of the intensive analytic experience—goes beyond role modeling, however. This capacity must be highly developed in any analyst, male or female.

REFERENCES

Blanck, G., & Blanck, R. (1979), *Ego Psychology II: Psychoanalytic Developmental Psychology*. New York: Columbia University Press.

Blum, H. P. (1977), *Female Psychology: Contemporary Psychoanalytic Views*. New York: International Universities Press.

Boyer, L. B., & Giovacchini, P. (1967), *Psychoanalytic Treatment of Schizophrenic, Borderline and Characterological Disorders*. New York: Aronson.

Chodorow, N. (1978), *The Reproduction of Mothering: Psychoanalysis and the Sociology of Gender*. Berkeley: University of California Press.

Eisenbud, R. J. (1981), Early and later determinants of lesbian choice. *Psychoanal. Rev.*, 69 (1): 85–109.

Greenson, R. R. (1967), *The Technique and Practice of Psychoanalysis*. New York: International Universities Press.

Grunes, M. (1984), The therapeutic object relationship. *Psychoanal. Rev.*, 71 (1): 123–143.

Karme, L. (1979), The analysis of a male patient by a female analyst: The problem of the negative oedipal transference. *Internat. J. Psycho-Anal.*, 60: 253–261.

Leider, R. (1984), Report of a panel on the neutrality of the analyst in the analytic situation. *J. Amer. Psychoanal. Assn.*, 32 (3): 573–587.

Loewald, H. W. (1960), On the therapeutic action of psychoanalysis. *Internat. J. Psycho-Anal.*, 41: 16–33.

Mahler, M. S., Pine, F., & Bergman, A. (1975), *The Psychological Birth of the Human Infant: Symbiosis and Individuation*. New York: Basic Books.

Moldawsky, S. (1982), *Living Through*. Paper presented to the New York Center for Psychoanalytic Training, New Jersey Division, Cranford, NJ.

Mogul, K. (1982), Overview: The sex of the therapist. *Amer. J. Psychiat.*, 139: 1–9.

Person, E. S. (1983), Women in therapy. *Internat. Rev. Psycho-Anal.*, 10: 193–204.

Sterba, R. F. (1934), The fate of the ego in analytic therapy. *Internat. J. Psycho-Anal.*, 15: 117–126.

Stone, L. (1961), *The Psychoanalytic Situation*. New York: International Universities Press.

Winnicott, D. (1965), *The Maturational Process and the Facilitating Environment*. London: Hogarth Press.

Zetzel, E. R. (1970), The doctor-patient relationship in psychotherapy. In: *The Capacity for Emotional Growth*. New York: International Universities Press, pp. 139–155.

15

Childless Women Approaching Midlife: Issues in Psychoanalytic Treatment

Phyllis Ziman-Tobin

This chapter is devoted to some reflections about psychoanalytic patients who share a particular set of problems described by time, gender, and statistics. These patients range in age from 35 to 45. They are women. They are childless. They come into treatment for a variety of reasons, but all express the desire to be appropriately paired (or, more typically, married) and to bear children. Regardless of diagnosis, the women enter treatment anxious and depressed. Work with them requires a special alertness to the immediate reality with which they must cope: They are entering midlife—they are perimenopausal. More questions may be raised than answered here about the psychoanalytic treatment of this group, but an important purpose will be served by heightening awareness of the special problems that distinguish them.

MIDLIFE CURFEW

Since the 1960s, more women have defined their early adult life primarily in terms of their careers and have delayed childbearing. In their lives, marriage and children have been postponed until the future. These women operate under a psychological and physical curfew. Part of the post-World War II "baby boom," they come into treatment in the 1980s at age 35 or older. Aware of the limits of the time within which they can bear a child, they also know that their years affect their social desirability and make marriage increasingly unlikely.

Women seem, in a sense, to have been betrayed by the very liberating forces that pushed them to strive for something different from what their own mothers had (Scarf, 1980).

Women who have chosen to remain single and childless until "the future" are in a predicament. Their situation is different from that of their male counterparts because women have less time in which to settle into a more conventional, traditional family style. It is men who have benefited the most from those aspects of the "sexual revolution" and "women's liberation" that result in later marriage. From young adulthood on, men find that appropriate women sexual partners are now more available. These liaisons need not follow the traditional lines of courtship leading to childbearing and family. In regard to having children, certainly, men have much more time and much less pressure.

For women, differentiations of life phase are determined by reproductive and/or family cycles (Neugarten, 1968; Neugarten & Datan, 1974; Perlmutter, 1978; Notman, 1981). The longer a woman menstruates, the fewer follicles remain from which estrogen is produced; the decrease in estrogen is a corollary to increased circulation of gonadotrophic hormones. Although the actual neurohumoral physiology has not been clearly worked out, the net effect of these relationships becomes obvious in decreased fertility, a static, lower birthrate in women's early forties, perimenopausal symptoms, and manifestations of progressive tissue atrophy and aging. Menopause, defined as one year without menstruation, occurs in contemporary Western societies at a median age of 51.4 or an average age of 49 (Perlmutter, 1978; Eskin, 1980; Speroff, Glass, & Kase, 1982).

Menopause has been considered the dominant factor of midlife, but "midlife" is best defined with respect to the imminent cessation of re-productive capacity. The term should rightly be understood as cover-ing a fairly substantial time period, roughly age 35 to 55. Measured by fertility rates, reproductive capacity decreases roughly from 90 percent at age 35 to 10 percent by age 45. The change within this ten year pe-riod is striking (Tietze, 1957; DeCheney & Berkowitz, 1982; Fédéra-tion CECOS, Schwartz & Mayaux, 1982; Speroff et al., 1982).

Closer analysis of these changes reveals that "there is a decline of fer-tility with age but this decline is not precipitous until the woman enters her forties" (Speroff et al., 1982, p. 487). From 1970 through 1981, there was a trend toward increased first births among women aged 30 to 39. Most important, however, there was no change in the number of first births among women aged 40 to 45 (National Center for Health Statis-tics, 1982). Thus, it may be inferred that in the 1970s, women who had chosen to delay childbearing into their thirties, were doing so success-fully; those who waited until their forties had waited too long. It is likely that the same situation still prevails.

The woman of today whom the culture has permitted and even en-couraged to delay childbearing is confronted with a biological reality: after age 35 there are sharply decreasing fertility rates with increased risk to both fetus and mother (Naeye & Tafari, 1983). This has obvious implications for medical practice. In an editorial in the respected and widely read *New England Journal of Medicine*, DeCheney and Berkowitz (1982) urged physicians to counsel women in their thirties not only about increasing risks to the fetus of problems such as Down's syndrome, but also about significantly decreasing fertility. Women, they felt, should be encouraged to bear children in their thirties and discouraged from delaying childbirth until their forties. Citing the lines of Robert Herrick, "Gather ye rosebuds while ye may/Old time is still a-flying." Schneider (1980) put the problem of delaying childbear-ing a bit more lyrically: "The woman who postpones pregnancy for rea-sons of career, study, or finance must be told that for the ovum, Old time is still a-flying" (p. 99).

Perhaps more women are now becoming aware that postponement risks both significantly decreasing opportunities for both marriage and fertility. One would hope that a more sensible integration of career and family will evolve for women in our culture. Perhaps those who have elected a strategy of "family later" will eventually even disappear as a special group. For the present, however, many women are faced with this predicament and are owed the serious consideration of their plight.

THE CHOICE TO BEAR A CHILD

The psychological and psychoanalytic literature has, by and large, been concerned with the aspects of reproduction related to (1) *choices* regarding pregnancy, – that is, the right either *not* to have children or to plan when children are to be conceived, and (2) *mothering* as an issue of gender identity. Psychoanalysts have had little to say, however, about maintaining a prudent regard for the limits on one's capacity for childbearing.

Feminist literature (for example, Sturdivant, 1980; Eichenbaum & Orbach, 1983) is strikingly devoid of discussions of childbearing altogether. Biological facts and statistics about fertility in older women are often dismissed as malicious myths perpetrated by a male establishment (see, for example, Eichholz & Zuckerberg, 1980). Baruch, Barnett, and Rivers (1983), who examined the consequences of the various choices women make about having children, selected women age 35 and older because by that age, they claim, "the major aspects of life have settled into a stable pattern" (p. 5). A final choice *before* age 35 not to have a child, they allege, results in a sense of contentment. Even if this is the case, a decision before 35 is very different from choices made later and in the face of fading biological capacities.

Such studies, moreover, do not address the situation of women age 35 and older who either have not made choices, have been unable to realize their choices, or have merely rationalized their dilemma. Among the latter group, the wish to be married and bear children is entangled with unresolved issues relating to love (Scarf, 1980). The wish may be diverted into idealizations of marriage, forms of anti-establishment or unconventional life style, or a particular socio-political stance. (I am not, of course, suggesting that all such choices can be reduced to the consequences of frustrated intimacy and generativity).

Antiestablishment artists are not just a current phenomenon, of course. There is an apocryphal story of a great American artist who had already accomplished much in her twenties, when the influence of early psychoanalysis was already being felt on the arts and artists. At that time, she chose to give up sex, wishing to sublimate her libido exclusively to her creativity. Indeed, she continued her remarkable artistic ascent, without sex. When she reached her late fifties, she decided that sexual abstinence was no longer necessary; there was enough libido within her, she felt, for both her art and intimate sexual expression. To the astonishment of her colleagues and admirers, she thereupon became openly promiscuous. She asserted, so the story goes, that she was compensating for all the years of deprivation. Her creativity as a great artist continued.

If that story has a moral, it is that a choice about sex, per se, like many other choices one makes in life, can be reversed without significant consequences. There may be quantifiable experiential and dynamic changes, to be sure, but an aspect of life as important as professional achievement apparently could remain undisturbed throughout this major reversal. This is not so for the consequences of reproductive choice. A woman entering midlife has roughly five years, if that much, in which she must choose *and* act. The biological consequences are not reversible.

A biological clock governs us all, of course. Time is not retrievable and, in the existential sense, an opportunity lost is forever lost. The nulliparous 35-year-old women, however, is subject to a pressing temporal reality that requires a different psychoanalytic stance from the usual.

A TREATMENT PERSPECTIVE

Traditionally, psychoanalysts allow the patient to take the lead, set the tempo, and introduce material. We struggle to keep ourselves at a judicious, constructive distance. We may be particularly pleased when young people want treatment because we believe that the earlier the capacities for love and work are satisfactorily integrated, the better — but we still allow the patient to take the lead.

A supervisee of mine was rather startled by and skeptical about the request of her patient, an illiterate 55 year-old hard-core heroin addict in a methadone treatment program, who expressed the desire to learn how to read. She felt that he would not be reading a "decent" book until he was perhaps in his sixties. My response was, I think, typical for experienced psychotherapists, at least in the philosophy it reflected. If he learns to read *now*, I maintained, he will be five years more advanced in the books he will have read than if he begins at sixty. And he will be much further along than if he were to learn to read at 65. "Whenever" is better than later or never.

For a childless woman of 35 or more, "whenever" can all too quickly turn into never. Because time is literally running out for the choice, we must be unusually active and vigilant regarding the matter of childbearing.

As psychoanalysts, we are always balancing the focus of our work between the psychic organization of the patient's past and the patient's current reality. To say that we focus on one or the other is as unhelpful and as inaccurate as, for example, the now discredited dichotomies of mind-body or nature-nurture. People come to us because they are suffering. They are distressed with themselves as contributors to their own anguish, as contributors to unacceptable qualities in their own lives. It is our job to demystify their current lives by helping them to understand how their conflicts reflect the psychological organization of their early life experiences. The method is a constant contrapuntal reading of current reality in terms of antecedent psychic integration. The goal is to help patients free themselves to develop more creative and adaptive solutions that can improve the quality of their lives. We do not ignore any reality in a patient's life; reality is the *source* of the treatment issues.

An unmarried, childless woman who wishes to be married and bear children provides a reasonable focus for exploration. Her declining chances for fertility are the reality against which the resolution of dynamic issues proceeds. How she understands why she has thus far in her life been unable to fulfill her wishes is one starting point; how we as analysts understand it establishes the intersection from which the course of the treatment unfolds. Although it is not ideal, it is nonetheless true that the content and shape of the exploration depend, in great measure, on how the expressed desire to bear children is viewed by the analyst. One should of course be alert to signs of contagios despair emanating from either hopeless analyst or hopeless patient. But even at best, many alternatives present themselves to explain the desire for a child: it may be seen as an innate wish or instinct, an expression of penis envy, mother-daughter identification, intentional role training, or any combination of these or other possibilities.

The analyst who appreciates his or her patient's temporal reality may be presented with a technical dilemma: Patients who seem to be consumed by the awareness of their time-delimited state may also be understood as resisting the investigation of other, more important, perhaps characterological, issues. Does one analyze this "obsession" as resistance—this, of course, takes time—or, under the dictates of time, must one directly analyze what has interfered with fulfilling the patient's specific wishes to marry and bear children?

It is my opinion that the latter course is indicated. By allying ourselves with the focus of the time pressures, we do not collude with resistance, even though the time pressure may indeed also be resistance to other issues. Fertility is a reality that *cannot* be profitably analyzed later. Furthermore, the desire to have a child has to be accepted at face value, regardless of an analyst's theoretical orientation or bias and, of course, with clinical intelligence. To do otherwise would be counterproductive and, however well-meaning, wasteful and misguided.

Even for women who do not enter treatment to deal specifically with the decision to bear a child, the finiteness of reproductive capacity must be accounted for in the analysis. We cannot collude with the patient's avoidance of this temporally bound biological variable; it must be handled, one way or another, within a specific, crucial period of time.

Decreasing fertility must be taken, by both patient and analyst, as an issue governing the analysis. For patients who come to us already aware of their predicament and consciously struggling with it, the alliance will be strengthened by the analyst's acknowledgment of this priority. The measure of a successful analysis, however, is not one in which the patient terminates as both married and pregnant—there are, after all, factors beyond anyone's control and the influence of treatment. It is fair, however, to evaluate success by the patient's capacity to act sensibly on her own behalf toward fulfilling her wishes.

The specific group of women under consideration here wish to have children or to resolve conflicts they have about childbearing. Some may resolve such conflicts appropriately by choosing not to have children. This alternative is nowadays judged to be dynamically valid and sensible for an increasing range of women, not only for those whose deprivation early in life has been so severe as to render them virtually incapable of parenting an infant. It goes without saying that such decisions must be carefully assessed and clearly understood as irreversible.

Acknowledging the finiteness of reproductive capacity does create a bias within the treatment. Is it different, however, from the "bias" created by our response to a patient who arouses our suspicions that she is ignoring a possible malignancy? Not at all. In that instance, surely we become more focused on issues that would maximize her ability to take good, precautionary care of herself. The urgency of time may require shifting priorities in the flow of the analytic process.

Most analysts probably feel they can be more objective, neutral, less biased, and perhaps even more "analytic" around the question of diminishing reproductive capacity if, for example, the woman entering treatment is already married and has children. Such a case is less likely to require parameters. If a patient begins analysis unhappy in her marriage, the contract, typically, is to facilitate her decision about whether or not to remain in the marriage. In working through historical and transferential issues, one hopes that the course of treatment is relatively unbiased; whatever the analyst feels personally about the patient remaining with her husband can be kept from bearing significantly on the analytic work. In all cases, the analyst *does* care—very much, I daresay—about a patient's being able to make the most sensible, salutary choice for herself that may improve the quality of her life.

The married woman who already has children, however, is not necessarily under an inexorable temporal constraint. The sooner she makes her decisions, the better for her, of course, but she has more time to work through a wider range of issues than the 35-year-old woman who wishes to marry and bear children. *She* requires an analyst who understands that for the patient's ovum, "time is still a-flying." A passive style, whether from training or nature, may not interfere with one's ability to analyze a wide range of people. With some patients, it may even be advantageous. The group of women in question, however, may not be helped expeditiously enough by these psychoanalysts who doggedly wait, prompted either by temperament or by doctrine.

If a childless woman over age 35 chooses analysis, it is because she is aware, at some level, that her own personality or character contributes to her inability to have fulfilled her wishes thus far. An analyst must, of course, think very carefully about any patient who is assessed as having a particularly difficult reality problem that will deeply affect the work or a certain diagnosis that predicts an arduous course of treatment. Choosing to work with a patient with a reproductive dilemma requires a readiness to help the patient as soon as and however possible to act on her own behalf. Analysts must think twice before accepting such patients for analytic work.

The mutual understanding of what time means requires a shift in priorities. If a childless woman nearing midlife is accepted for treatment, one must be on guard not to be seduced by other facets of the patient that might provide the analysis with lengthy, exploratory excursions. Is the implicit contract, then, to do psychotherapy, not psychoanalysis? No. The depth work of uncovering historical and transferential material that will result in meaningful structural change can only come about by means of psychoanalytic technique, as well as understanding.

THE PERSPECTIVE IN PRACTICE

With the psychoanalytic contract and alliance established on the basis of an appreciation of the pressure of decreasing fertility, how does the content of the analysis change? The quality of relationships is, of course, the essential focus of our work. For these women, the resistances to be analyzed are those affecting appropriate coupling. For each individual, the dynamics no doubt vary, but I find that the primary focus for all will be on some combination of passivity and masochism, often experienced as helplessness. The two qualities are related in terms of the experienced locus of control, but they mean something different in terms of observable behavior. *Passivity* is the posture of waiting for someone else to act or something else to happen; *masochism* is remaining (figuratively and, in this case, literally) in unfruitful relationships.

It is no mean task to consider with a patient the quality of her relationships; one immediately involves the crucial issues of separation, individuation, autonomy, and attachment, among others. When the press of time is appreciated, the analyst becomes more vigilant about examining every act in the patient's current reality that detracts from appropriate coupling. The set toward the material is different from the way we normally work. We are typically more relaxed in allowing the flow of association, feeling that if something is important it will eventually resurface and need not be actively pursued. In the case of these women it is no less true that important issues will, of course, resurface. With them, however, we probe beneath the surface to meet the issue.

This stress on more actively analyzing the resistances to being involved in appropriate relationships has emerged from changes in my
own way of working. I noticed that in treating several women, as they
turned 40, I turned active. Why? To the best of my knowledge now, I
understood my patients' increasing despair regarding time to be both
realistic and relevant to the analytic work — not just as resistance or as a
reality impinging on life but irrelevant to the analysis. Concerned by
the possibility of countertransference, I shared my feelings with both
supervisors and colleagues. I found support from senior analysts for the
more active strategy I had adopted. Indeed, I was astonished, and in
some measure prompted to write this essay, when a number of competent women analysts told me that whether or not *they* bore children in
their forties was seriously affected by the differential sensitivities of
their own analysts to issues of decreasing fertility as they approached
midlife.

I began to concentrate more on selectively following certain issues
for analysis, several of which I knew I might have let pass a year or so
before. My sharpened and more vigorous focus seemed to be met with
relief by my patients, although not without ambivalence. We seemed
at last to be very clear about what we were doing in a strengthened alliance, experienced by each of us as a point of profound understanding.

As one woman patient was enviously describing a colleague who
seemed to have "so many men in her life," I asked whether the colleague was aware that the patient was interested in meeting men. She
grew silent. What emerged was anger and embarrassment. It was very
important to my patient that she be thought of as not needing anyone
or as being already coupled. The thought of being so active on her own
behalf brought into awareness many historical associations regarding
her competitiveness and her experience of being seen as "imperfect."
The result of this concerted exploration was a shift in the patient's
sense of her own contribution to her dearth of social contacts.

Another woman entered treatment in her late thirties with a severe
depression for which she had previously been treated primarily with
drugs. We had been working on the depression on many levels but, as
she turned 40, we began to concentrate on her singleness and childlessness. It is true that certain aspects of the depression had to be dispelled
before such work could begin, but I wonder how the course of treatment might have differed had I earlier pursued more vigorously her
problems with experiencing love. I now believe that such a program

would have favored her ability to be more active sooner on her own behalf.

Besides the specific issue of the quality of intimate relationships, attitudes about childbearing should be actively explored. A woman's relationship to her mother is the likely paradigm here, but it may be most expediently examined both consciously and unconsciously through the transference to a woman analyst. Again, even in this exploration, the tempo of the work should be governed by the reality of decreasing fertility.

There are female patients for whom working with the temporal issue of their fertility per se is not relevant. For example, there are those who, from a biological perspective, seek treatment too late. Others, although biologically "in time," are far from working out those issues that would psychologically facilitate their childbearing capacity. Some, finally, act out, becoming pregnant without having handled in depth relevant conflicts and disturbances. Alas, these situations confront us unfortunately perhaps more often than do those for whom expediting the treatment is valid and successful. In all cases, however, the analyst's attention to the reproductive time line is vital.

OTHER GOVERNING REALITIES

Both analyst and patient must confront the humiliation most women feel about being visibly "on the market." It is often so painful that it keeps many women (and men, I might add) in marriages that are grossly unsatisfactory. The "singles' scene" may be glamorized for both men and women with sophisticated fun and sexually liberating gimmicks, but it is an arena of shame for women who desire marriage, children, and family. Witness the self-mockery of the comedienne, Rita Rudner: "You know how I end relationships now? I just say 'I want to marry you . . . I want to have your children . . .' Sometimes they make skid marks" (Quoted in Berger, P., The new comediennes. *New York Times Magazine,* July 29, 1984, p. 27).

Even those who work through and understand, in terms of their past, why it has made sense to remain single and childless until now are hampered from changing by a painful reality. Where are the men with whom to couple? Here the social facts powerfully compound the pressure of the biological imperative.

Women in their late thirties or early forties who are newly able to establish intimate couplings are, in fact, at a demographic disadvantage. By age 35, women significantly outnumber men in the same age category. Psychologically, men—with no biological imperative quite analogous to the finiteness of woman's reproductive capacity—have different requirements for fulfilling their need for intimacy. Male age peers, particularly those who have been married before, are often interested in and successful with *younger* women. Men who have remained single, by and large, are ridden with many psychological problems and have poor prognoses (if only because relatively fewer of them seek therapy). Widowers who have had good marriages are more eager to pair off with age peers but less inclined to have second families. Even in this age range, at any rate, there are significantly more widows than widowers. Older men are, of course, fewer; they may find women at midlife more desirable, but they too are less likely to want to have a new family.

Like any reality, harsh or otherwise, the statistics of singleness and childlessness must be dealt with. Resistance and passivity in the face of that reality need to also be actively analyzed. Once again, one cannot ignore the omnipresent variable of time. The earlier a patient is "ready," the more chances she has to fulfill her wishes. For these women, enduring the double limits on potential fertility and potentially eligible partners requires the alliance of a concerned analyst.

A final word about another reality: the vulnerability of psychoanalysts. There are many communities of psychoanalysts, each with their own emphasis and espousing various social and political beliefs. A male analyst who respects the biological imperative of women patients may be as easily mistaken for chauvinist, pigeonholing women by their genotype, as someone unusually sensitive to women's issues. A female analyst dealing with patients in the fashion I have suggested might be condemned as having fallen prey to her own profound countertransference. All analysts know that in psychoanalytic circles, important controversies about theory and technique often take on a surprisingly personal face.

These problems nothwithstanding, I believe that a change in attitude and strategy is demanded from someone who treats childless women age 35 and older who wish to be married and have children. They are a special group and under a special constraint of time. Reworking, reanalysis or rethinking 10 or 20 years hence simply comes too late.

REFERENCES

Baruch, G., Barnett, R., & Rivers, C. (1983), *Lifeprints: New Patterns of Love and Work for Today's Women.* New York: McGraw-Hill.

DeCherney, A. H., & Berkowitz, G. (1982), Female fecundity and age. *New England J. Med.*, 306: 424–426.

Eichenbaum, L., & Orbach, S. (1982), *Understanding Women: A Feminist Psychoanalytic Approach.* New York: Basic Books.

Eichholz, A., & Zuckerberg, J. (1980), Later pregnancy. In: *Psychological Aspects of Pregnancy, Birthing, and Bonding,* ed. B. Blum. New York: Human Sciences Press, pp. 94–102.

Eskin, B. (1980), Aging and the menopause. In: *The Meonopause: Comprehensive Mangement,* ed. B. Eskin. New York: Masson.

Fédération CECOS, Schwartz, D., & Mayaux, M. J. (1982), Female fecundity as a function of age: Results of artificial insemination in 2193 nulliparous women with azoospermic husbands. *New England J. Med.*, 306: 404–406.

Naeye, R. L., & Tafari, N. (1983), *Risk Factors in Pregnancy and Diseases of the Fetus and Newborn.* Baltimore: Williams & Wilkins.

National Center for Health Statistics, S. J. Ventura (1982, May), Trends in first births to older mothers, 1970–79. *Monthly Vital Statistics Report,* Vol. 31, No. 2, Supp. (2). DHHS Pub. No. (PHS) 82–1120. Hyattsville, MD: Public Health Service.

Neugarten, B. L. (1968), The awareness of middle age. In: *Middle Age and Aging. A Reader in Social Psychology,* ed. B. L. Neugarten, Chicago: University of Chicago Press, pp. 93–98.

——— & Datan, N. (1974), The middle years. In: *American Handbook of Psychiatry,* Vol. 1 (2nd ed.), ed. S. Arieti. New York: Basic Books, pp. 592–608.

Notman, M. T. (1981), Midlife concerns of women: Implications of the menopause. In: *Women and Mental Health,* ed. E. Howell & M. Bayes. New York: Basic Books, pp. 385–394.

Perlmutter, J. F. (1978), A gynecological approach to menopause. In: *The Woman Patient,* ed. M. T. Notman & C. C. Nadelson. New York: Plenum, pp. 323–336.

Scarf, M. (1980), *Unfinished Business: Pressure Points in the Lives of Women.* New York: Doubleday.

Schneider, J. (1980), Age and the outcome of pregnancy. In: *The Menopause: Comprehensive Management,* ed. B. Eskin. New York: Masson, pp. 93–100.

Speroff, L., Glass, R. H., & Kase, N. G. (1982), *Clinical Gynecologic Endocrinology and Infertility* (3rd ed.). Baltimore: Williams & Wilkins.

Sturdivant, S. (1980), *Therapy with Women: A Feminist Philosophy of Treatment.* New York: Springer.

Tietze, C. (1957), Reproductive span and rate of reproduction among Hutterite women. *Fertil. Steril.*, 8: 89–97.

16

Women's Dreams: A Nocturnal Odyssey

Joseph M. Natterson, M.D.

Dreams are expressions of the unique complexities of the dreamer's life. Therefore, any assumption that women's dreams, in general, possess validly discernible characteristics that are distinctive and useful seems dubious at best and dangerous at worst. The new psychology of women could certainly use constructive contributions from dream studies, yet such efforts can become treacherous. Each woman's dreams are informed and influenced by her total life experience, including her gender, her sexual identity, her specific experiences of sexual intimacy, and the particular psychosocial triumphs and tragedies she has lived through. My experience in analytic work has helped me shape the ideas about the revelatory and transformational aspects of women's dreams that I shall set forth here.

EMERGING DIMENSIONS OF FEMININITY

The women's movement of recent years has liberated women from the bondage of traditionally defined lives as wives, cooks, and mothers. The amount of liberation women have achieved may also be a measure of society's general emancipation. It is possible that the special suffering women have endured will have constituted a long winter of humanistic germination, and that from the newly liberated women will emerge a moral renaissance for this increasingly dehumanized and amoral world. The painful subordination of women will have been like that of other oppressed and disenfranchised groups, a crucible wherein marvelous new essences of human experience and meaning have been created. This involves the notion that aggression is received, absorbed, transformed, integrated, and returned. Wolfenstein (1981) offers an analogous set of ideas about the creative transformation of aggression in the experience of American blacks. Kovel (1970) regards the dialectic between an individual's personalized experience and the fate of his or her sociopolitical group as an axis of shifts and transitions that result in creative maturational changes.

Women, according to the Freudian view, were passive, dependent, and masochistic. This traditional notion is now seen to have been a realistic appreciation of the psychological effects of the conditions in which women were obliged to live, but it also reflected a profound moral bias arising from male domination and the self-justifying tendencies inherernt in such domination. The current ideal of an aggressive and competitive woman represents a constructive variation from the traditional norm, but since such women are still regarded (and therefore regard themselves) as deviant, they continue to experience excessive guilt, anxiety, and depression for their deviation from the stereotype. It seems possible that the effort to create a new feminine identity through transformation into "superwoman," creates a different kind of false self. Yet this new ideal woman may be a necessary mediating condition on the path to a truer feminine self. Do the new, emerging dimensions of femininity reflect options potentially available to *all* of us? If so, will the addition of these developmental milestones not only reduce the age-old exploitation, damage, and sexual abuse of women, but also help establish a more generally nurturant use of aggression in the service of universal fulfillment?

An important new perspective on the issue of women's morality is offered by Gilligan (1982), whose landmark work is aptly titled *In a Different Voice*. In contrast to Freud's view that women's superegos are weak and corruptible and subject to the vagaries of the emotions — unlike the superior, "blind" impartiality of men's morality — Gilligan proposes that women's moral development be reinterpreted as mainly informed and directed by women's special experiences of interconnectedness and relatedness throughout life. Gilligan believes that such experiences are givens, not choices, for women. Thus, women follow a path to maturity built out of interdependence and empathic caring. Boundaries between self and other, subject and object, inevitably become blurred, engendering new experiential realities. From this, women develop an ethos of nurturance and responsible caring resting on a premise of nonviolence. Men, whose developmental path leads to autonomy and separateness, evolve an ethos of fairness and justice, based on a premise of equality. Gilligan believes that different moral emphases exist for men and women, both derived from experience, and neither superior or inferior to the other. Schafer (1974) proposes that we have erroneously reified the firm, objective, logical moral judgments of men as being the only "right" world view, thus incorrectly devaluing women's more relational and cooperative idea of morality.

Gilligan's contribution is powerful and important, so it requires careful scrutiny. Is Gilligan's voice really different? I believe so. Yet, she might be perilously close to singing the same old tune. Although the penis no longer inches out the other factors, women and their sociomoral development are still defined on the basis of intimate, relational functions that, in turn, arise from women's bodies and their roles as childbearers, nurses, and tender mothering persons. Is it possible that, although the key has been changed from minor to major, the name of the tune remains "Anatomy is Destiny?"

TODAY'S WOMAN AND THERAPEUTIC ACTION

As psychoanalytic theories of female psychology are changing, so, too, are the concepts of therapeutic action. A significant relationship may well exist between the two.

Traditionally, the analyst has been defined as detached, neutral, dispassionate. Newer ideas, from within and outside of the analytic mainstream, instead posit an analyst who provides a "holding" environment. This newly defined analyst is involved in an empathic, intersubjective experience with the patient, which draws on the passions, fantasies, and unconscious activities of both patient and analyst, constituting a unique and powerful unit of human interaction. The newer concepts of therapeutic action (Winnicott, 1965; Kohut, 1977; Gill, 1982; Schafer, 1983) are especially relevant to psychodynamic psychotherapy with women. The traditional authoritarian, paternalistic elements in therapy cannot effectively accommodate the new psychological realities of women's lives.

The dreams of women can illustrate the newer aspects of therapeutic action, and these may well be useful for patients of both sexes. But particularly for women in therapy, a more subtle, variable, less sharply polarized role assignment for therapist and patient provides greater opportunities for the enhancement of women's individuality and creativity.

The newer conceptual elements of therapeutic action are relevant to problems of early development, and they address the detachment and isolation so prevalent in the patients of today's narcissistic culture. They also link up with current trends in feminine psychology toward fuller understanding of women's early mother-child experiences and their effects on adult life (Mahler, 1963; Chodorow, 1978; Roiphe & Galenson, 1981).

The therapeutic matrix should be a finely tuned interpersonal environment that facilitates the attachment process, gradually leading to the patient's internalization of maternal-therapist functions. Concomitantly, the patient rediscovers hidden or stunted aspects of self, and self-definitional processes are active, leading to crucial and fulfilling self-transformations. The goal, somewhat simplistically, may be seen as the true self. The nondefensive, subjective availability of the therapist is crucial for the invocation of past images through which the patient learns new modes of relating to him- or herself—via new ways of relating to another. Although analysts have long decried insight, which is purely intellectual, and have reiterated the importance of experiential ingredients, the traditional formalities of psychoanalysis have somewhat limited the fuller exploration of experiential factors.

Most therapeutic moments derive their mutative effect from the *intersubjective* matrix in which they occur and from the unique interactions of the individuals whose convergence creates the matrix (Stolorow and Atwood, 1984). This premise establishes the possibility of therapist and patient uniting in mutual, empathic understanding. This use of empathy as neutrality can be effective in transforming the old psychic scars manifest in transference repetitions. They can become new personality structures, with associated new and complex values and meanings, accretions of association, and enrichment (not reduction) of transferences. This aspect of therapeutic action requires the therapist to be maximally available and flexible in perceiving and responding to the patient's developmental and subjective shifts and changes. Much of this process occurs unconsciously in both parties, or, if conscious, eludes verbal representation until its organization is well accomplished.

According to this view, empathic availability precedes and underlies the neutrality of the therapist, which can no longer be justifiably regarded as a formally imposed refusal to "take sides." Similarly, metaphors such as "parameter" or "frame" become of diminished referential value in psychotherapy.

In the treatment of women, the tendency for the therapist to offer himself or herself as clear, objective, neutral, and capable of resolving all ambiguities becomes a particular obstacle. Such a stance might well cause the therapist to evaluate the normally less well defined boundaries between the female patient and the significant others in her life, past and present, in a damaging way. The therapist might incorrectly view the blurred boundaries as evidence of an unconscious struggle by the patient to extricate herself from a symbiotic maternal stranglehold. This simplistic assumption might then be used to explain problems in social role and sexuality that in fact have different and more complex causes.

Schafer's (1983) analytic attitude devalues the positivist inclinations of the therapist. He maximizes the therapist's individual orientation, which will influence the selection of the questions raised and the evidence focused on. This will include mode of expression, voice tone, and affective style of intervention, plus many other visible and invisible contributions of the therapist. Schafer repeatedly emphasizes that the form and course of the analysis will depend heavily on the "narrative structure" that the analyst brings to the analysis. Obviously, Schafer's and related viewpoints reflect a departure from the traditional efforts to objectify and standardize some of the most crucial aspects of the analytic situation. The patient as object becomes an increasingly untenable notion. Instead, interactional and transactional emphases prevail, and a creative ferment occurs.

By emphasizing the interplay of the subjective experience of patient and analyst, a model of therapeutic action emerges that is analogous to the relationship of infant and mother, child and caretaker, (Winnicott, 1965; Loewald, 1970). This is an especially apt model for female patients, who in many instances – perhaps always – need to rediscover, redefine, and reappropriate authentic aspects of themselves that have been hitherto concealed by a false self. This will also mean, in some instances, the creation of new self-components, previously unformed. Although of the greatest importance, the mother-child model is probably insufficient to account for the full creative implications of therapeutic action.

Therapy may also validly be regarded as an artistic enterprise; this in no way invalidates the concept of a dynamic parent-child unit. The patient and therapist may be seen as creating a new self-portrait of the patient. Patient and therapist continuously offer one another shifting, oscillating, converging, and diverging perceptions. The yield consists of increasingly rich, complex, and satisfying self-images, which are added to the gestalt of consciousness and reformed psychic structures, both conscious and unconscious. Much of the material for these new self-perceptions comes from previously disowned and hidden components of self.

These therapeutic events cannot occur unless the therapist immerses himself or herself in the instability and ambiguity of the patient's psychological experiences. This passionate participation by the therapist facilitates the patient's search to find the old and familiar in the new, thus helping to achieve higher levels of creative individuality. This intersubjective experience possesses a keenly felt affective immediacy that helps the patient reduce her sense of alienation from self and world. As the process develops, patient and therapist ineluctably bring conscious and unconscious life experience, values, attitudes, reactions, and associations to the therapeutic encounter.

One might also think in terms of minidramas that are being continuously lived out between the two participants, while each separately experiences silent private dramatic fragments. The fragments converge regularly to provide power and shape for new dramatic interactions (not necessarily overt) between patient and therapist.

This description may provide some idea of the therapeutic matrix in which conflict is mobilized, discovery occurs, conflict is resolved, and integration is achieved with interpenetrating simultaneity. Out of the maze of perceptions and misperceptions, identifications, projections and introjections, the patient shapes the new self-definition and self-transformations leading to enhanced individuality.

Both Kohut (1977) and Loewald (1970) emphasize an important promising or prophetic role for the analyst. This may arise from the new self-images that the therapist can, figuratively, hold before the patient as an encouraging mirror. Kohut talks of the gentle, yet persistent, expectation that the empathic parent holds for the child's next maturational step. Such parents encourage but do not force. Loewald also alludes to the prophetic aspect of the therapeutic task. He notes that the therapist best understands the patient when the therapist is empathically attuned to the patient's unconscious and can perceive the patient's core object relationships beneath the defenses. The therapist accompanies the patient on the regressive path to the crucial points of pain and conflict, while also holding before the patient a picture of what the patient can become but has not yet become. Loewald's language is careful and traditional, but it clearly conveys the impression of a therapeutic process consisting of an intersubjective experience and resulting in creative self-transformation.

TRANSFORMATIONS IN WOMEN'S DREAMS

Therapists who approach patients with well-defined understanding, such as a confident a priori sense of the crucial components of a woman's personality and problems will, in all likelihood also smuggle in covert prejudices, rigidity, and stereotypes. This attitude will inevitably alienate rather than facilitate. This hazard speaks eloquently for an open, ambiguous, intersubjective, creative model of therapeutic action.

Such a model tends more toward process than cure. *Process* implies transformation, whereas *cure* suggests elimination. Transformation indicates structure. Life structures are established or dismantled at critical developmental points or moments, yet such structures are infinitely varied due to the uniqueness of each person's developmental experiences. Often, perhaps usually, the therapist performs a more useful function by discerning the presence and nature of transformations than by detecting isolated unconscious conflict.

Women's dreams are a rich source of discovery, definition, and therapeutic transformation of inner, psychological structures. The world, for everyone, is constantly undergoing rapid, powerful, and baffling change. But the world of women is probably changing at a particularly dizzy rate. Women's dreams, with their heuristic properties, are a consequently hopeful resource, because dreams often dramatize these profound psychological transformations in ways that provide excitement and incentive to both patient and therapist to clarify, integrate, and expand the range and power of the change. Without the prospect of change, neither therapist nor patient can maintain effective motivation for therapy.

THE CASE OF ETHEL

Ethel was in analytic therapy for over a decade and provided regular dreams throughout. She was in her early twenties when she entered treatment and had recently completed college. She reported that she had what seemed at the time a frighteningly tenuous hold on a newly obtained job in the field of child development. Ethel was socially quite isolated and dependent on her parents. She was still badly wounded by the recent violent death of her brother, who was adopted, as was she, although they were not consanguineous. Ethel was very anxious, depressed, and inhibited. Except when she occasionally erupted in defensive fury at me, her voice scarcely rose above a whisper. Ethel's dreams of this period are exemplified by the following retrospective composite:

> Ethel is in her bedroom. A male intruder approaches her. She is terrified, for his intentions are horrible. He begins to beat her, culminating the attack by hurling her about the room homicidally. She bounces off the walls, receiving broken bones and awful bruises—injured even unto death.

During this time, Ethel's psychotherapy was dominated by fears of discriminatory treatment and humiliation by authorities and by dismal expectations of failure in love and work. She had begun treatment at the same time that a rather unusual sexual relationship was ending, and she was feeling stunned. The man was quite famous and considerably older than the patient. Their rendezvous were to some degree managed by his subordinates. At first she had been swept away by romantic excitement; later she felt swept into the dust pan. In this early phase of therapy, if a young man happened to enter her life, she behaved whimsically, enjoying provoking the man and then abruptly dumping him. Any tendency of the patient to become closer and warmer to me would be followed by storms of rage and accusation, in which she saw me as a polite version of the nocturnal dream attacker, although from my standpoint, she seemed more the attacker than I.

From the intersubjective standpoint, these frenzied furies were quite important. Rather than observing the paroxysms with lofty detachment, I let myself experience an almost shameful feeling of incapacity at such times. These were quite painful, and I believe my subjective experience matched the chronic pain that afflicted this young woman. That she could inflict pain on me and that I quickly rebounded from her attack without serious damage was a crucial experience for the patient. This may have vividly demonstrated to her that she really possessed power, but her aggression was not necessarily lethal. Thus she began her gradual reclamation of her aggressive potential. As is so often the case, her therapy progressed very slowly. She seemed to become a little more self-confident, and the frightened, rageful eruptions toward me slowly diminished in frequency.

Despite intense misgivings, Ethel let herself be persuaded by friends and family to enter a doctoral program in her field, and she began her timorous pursuit of a Ph.D. In this program, she continued to believe that she was disliked and unwanted, and she insisted that she lacked the intellectual and psychological capability to complete the program. I directly indicated my belief in her, and I encouraged her to examine her terrible lack of belief in herself.

After several years of this supportive, but analytically oriented therapy, Ethel withdrew from me. She discontinued treatment, talking about her need for more directed, behavioral therapy. I did not hear from her for about two years, when she returned, telling me that she had spent the hiatus in virtual psychological hibernation. She had no dates with men, saw little of a couple of girl friends, did only scant work on her doctoral project, and spent much time with her parents at their home.

Nevertheless, the key dream with which she returned to psycho-therapy seemed to point in a new direction. Ethel reported: "I am going down an aisle happily. Then I am walking furtively down a dark corridor, clutching my purse to my breast." We readily perceived that important movement was indeed occurring in her life. In response to the patient's associations (and my own), I constructed the interpretation that the dream revealed her crucial feminine conflict over whether to become a confident woman with an open, legitimate sex life in marriage or some equivalent, as portrayed by "going down the aisle," or whether to remain severely constricted, frightened, and withdrawn, as in the second part of the dream. My interpretive style with her tended to be both empathic and discursive, with much repetition. This was my intersubjective antidote to her tense, laconic, half-whispered verbalizations. The vivid simplicity of the dream and its obvious meaning helped Ethel apply her cognitive skills to her life tasks, and the effect was very encouraging to a young woman who needed all the encouragement she could get. Without the crystal clear message of the dream, she might have been unable to realize how strong and effective her growth tendencies had become. This dream is an excellent example of the nodal, clarifying, and direction-pointing value of dreams. Although the second part of the dream suggests danger and fear, the violence in Ethel's dreams—and in her inner life—had diminished greatly.

My interpretive emphasis on Ethel's sexual dilemma, and my vote in favor of the positive side (going down the aisle) correlated with Ethel's entrance into her first serious and extended relationship with a man. It is a tribute to her growing hardiness that she undertook this relationship despite some realistic obstacles that might have daunted even a hardy veteran of the war between the sexes. I realized that I now was beginning to experience her as a beautiful young woman with considerable sexual capacity, rather than as a vulnerable child in need of continuous support.

Fortified by her success, particularly the stability of her love relationship, Ethel's defenses melted still more. The culmination of this warming phase was a dream of some two years later: "I am doing a sexual dance for you, gyrating voluptuously, removing one layer of silk after another, as you recline on pillows, very turned on. I am extremely aroused sexually." Here she was frankly erotic, gaining pleasure, assuming active responsibility, and not drenched with guilt. Her portrayal of me as a man who prefers Turkish delights, suggested an ironic inclusion of a continuing, traditional attitude about female-male relationships. Nonetheless, the dream denoted progress.

Dreams certainly do not constitute the only crucial surface and mirror of psychological change. Undoubtedly, a good deal of this patient's change could have been accomplished without the conspicuous role played by dream interpretations in treatment. Without the dreams, however, the therapy would have been more of a benign, shapeless drift to maturity. With the dreams, the therapy became a fascinating and creative chronicle of a young woman's journey to self-discovery and self-transformations. The dream work, which provided us with such vivid and graphic representations, sharpened our conscious perceptions, expanded our cognitive comprehension, and facilitated experiential learning.

The patient's dream odyssey did not end here. About one year later, a serious block developed in the therapy. Ethel was approaching the concluding tasks for her doctoral program; she responded by becoming anxious, hypochondriacal, depressed, and academically inactive. Our discussion indicated that once more she was misconstruing constructive activity as destructive because, in childhood, she had so feared the violence of her brother's behavior that she concluded the only way to be good and safe was to be passive and compliant. But this, of course, meant she would also have to be ineffective and unhappy. In the face of the current challenge, she had regressed to her traditional defense. For several weeks, my interpretations of this did not seem to be helpful.

I finally proposed that perhaps ten years of therapy was excessive for her and for me and that perhaps she would find a new, female therapist more helpful. She responded with the following dream: "I am in a boat, not pulling my oar. The captain, an older man, firmly orders me to do my job, or be left behind. Frightened of being thrown overboard, I comply." My approach to the blocked therapy may have left a little to be desired, but that is not the issue of the moment. The dream basically provided the necessary data: Ethel was shirking her therapeutic duty out of fear, but her superordinate motivation was to continue to go forward with me. She was validating my expectations of a high level of accomplishment. Her therapy did quickly resume its course toward the appropriate goals.

Ethel now began to resolve her chronic disabling inhibitions and to seriously believe for the first time that she could regard herself and be regarded by others as an effective person. It was fitting that she then began to have a revised version of her initial dreams:

> I am at work in my apartment. A male intruder approaches me. At first, I am very frightened because he obviously intends to harm me. But then I begin to talk with him and succeed in changing his intentions. He becomes friendly, I am no longer frightened, and I set him to work helping me with the household chores.

I assumed that this dream indicated that she had now reappropriated the aggression she had previously projected on the exterior world. In the case of sexualized aggression, men understandably became the evildoers of her dreams.

The violent dream turned civil indicates a decisive psychological accomplishment. It reflects the task most urgently required of all individuals and of all social aggregates: the taming and civilizing of human aggression. Sexual liberation is not damaging, but the contemporary proliferation of destructiveness is obviously much more complex and much more menacing than the simple unleashing of hitherto repressed potentials. Stabilizing and hope-providing institutions and values are increasingly eroded in our society, and the mediating family is collapsing. From such a childhood, the new, dangerous narcissistic man is emerging.

Ethel's dreams reflect the universal experience of women. The violence visited on women is internalized, then projected, and must somehow be reclaimed — but in a transformed state. I believe that those who have been the recipients of violence and aggression may be particularly capable of accomplishing the urgent sociomoral task of converting aggression into a constructive force.

THE CASE OF BETTY

At the other end of the spectrum of feminine experience from Ethel is the woman who suffers without visible pain. Here, denial and manic defenses prevail, with peppy cheerfulness excluding subjective suffering, until the yawning depths of depression suddenly become visible through unexpected cracks in the surface of good cheer.

Betty, a woman in her midfifties, was such a patient. Her 20-year-old daughter had died of leukemia three years earlier, and her husband, whom she saw as the center of her life, left her shortly thereafter for a younger woman.

After about two years of intensive analytic therapy, Betty reported the following dream, which had occurred about one year prior to beginning therapy: "I am caring for my infant daughter, and I lift her out of the crib. I am astonished now to see myself lying under her — also an infant." The daughter she dreamed about was the daughter who had died. On the day before the dream, which was a relatively short time after the daughter's death, she tried to arrange with the cemetery to be buried next to her daughter when she died, but because of crowding at the cemetery, they arranged for her to be buried beneath the daughter.

This recollection of a dream which occurred before she began therapy with me was important for several reasons. This woman utilized manic defenses and denial. In the two years before she reported this dream, I had relied on her personal history and my understanding to make "intellectualized" interpretations to her. (They were "intellectualized" because they were remote from her conscious experience.) Among these was a very elaborate, four-tiered interpretation. The first layer was her cheery, hypomanic, denying surface. The second layer was a guilty, anxious, eroticized involvement with the father, including identification, producing the third layer: pregenital rage, guilt, and symbiotic preoccupation with the mother, leading to depression. The bottom layer was her true self.

Her dream, which occurred before this interpretation but was reported after the interpretation, seemed to me to confirm my intuitive notion of the burial of her true self under several, more superficial personality layers. It also supported my intuitive decison to make experience-remote interpretations until the patient could become closer to her inner experience.

The quality of relatedness between Betty and me was significant and stemmed from the commencement of treatment. Betty had had some modestly successful psychotherapy several years previously. Immediately prior to beginning with me, she had been referred by a relative's therapist to still another therapist because of her deepening depression. Although this therapist was experienced, Betty found this person stiff, insensitive, and formulaic. The referring therapist then gave Betty my name. She called me and decided on the telephone that I had to be her therapist, even though I assured her I had no available time. By coincidence, one of her dearest friends was a woman whose daughter had also died of leukemia and who had also been my patient. This woman contacted me and prevailed on me to accept Betty as a patient.

Betty maintained an unremitting belief in me as a loving person who could be trusted to restore her well-being and who would, if necessary, subordinate conventional therapeutic formalities to her particular needs. This attitude evoked counterpart parental (probably maternal) rescue, alter-ego potentials within me. Thus, my decision to render intellectualized, experience-distant interpretations was based on an intuitive decision to do Betty's hard psychological thinking for her until she could reappropriate this necessary faculty. Perhaps this decision can be understood better as part of a comprehensive approach of immersing myself in her suffering. Another facet of this approach was the repeated experience of sitting and shedding tears with her as we listened to audio tapes made by her daughter during her terminal illness. Crucial to this approach was the blurring of boundaries between the two of us, with therapeutic reexperiencing of profound conflict in her early relationship to her mother. I viewed the report of her dream as the fruit and the validation of our prior two years of work.

Betty had many issues inappropriately situated in her mind. For instance, she thought she missed her husband more than her daughter, but as therapy progressed, she realized this was not so. In fact, she had to exhume the corpus of painful memories of her dead daughter in order to find herself. This was the prophetic message of her dream.

Betty had two older sisters and a brother who had died before the patient's birth. Her mother was an extremely depressed woman who made suicide attempts and required some hospital treatment for psychotic depressions. Betty's father was an energetic, life-loving person who was probably somewhat indifferent to his wife's emotional needs. The patient became the designated boy in the family, her father's favorite. In high school she became a national champion in athletics. She loved her tomboy status as the only one of the boys who was a girl. Her two sisters were both depressed. One committed suicide in middle age.

Betty could not initially accept my interpretation that her pseudo-male identification had saved her from the more severe, overt depressions of her sisters, who had to rely on their identifications with the seriously ill mother. Nevertheless, I persisted in making interpretations of her depressive response to her identification with her mother. I also emphasized her rage and guilt toward this frustrating mother, whose empathic, nurturing availability was limited by her depressive constitution, reinforced greatly by continuing grief over the death of her little son. Betty listened to all this and understood, but she assured me that it had no psychological meaning for her. For many, many months, she talked, and we argued over my interpretations, which consciously were derived from her personal history, some of her dream material, and some basic psychodynamic assumptions. Her repudiation of my interpretations was coupled with a profound respect for me, which was very sustaining for her. Another interpretation was to point out her exceedingly high development of human qualities, accompanied by an incongruous inability to use these qualities in her cognitive approach to her own life – but not to the lives of others. This interpretation of a massive inhibition always felt right to her.

The example of the dream of being covered by the daughter shows how a therapist who is highly attuned both to the patient and to women's experiences of submerging their aggression and sense of self will perceive the buried themes before they are articulated. The notion of burial of the self, as portrayed in the dream – that is, the unconscious submersion of one's identity, one's true self – may well be one of the major disruptive life themes of women in an unfair world.

In the psychoanalytic or psychotherapeutic relationship, the therapist appropriately subordinates himself or herself to the therapeutic needs of the patient. In mothering, the effective, fluent mother must do the same to herself relative to the child's needs. Perhaps this fact was represented in Betty's dream. She was beneath, subordinated to her daughter. Thus, she sustained her child – in life and in death. Perhaps this inevitablility also determines the relatively higher levels of nurturing and empathy in women but as a sometimes unavoidable side effect may mean a loss of autonomous identity for the mother. Perhaps in certain women the intersection of normative maternal requirements (self-subordination) and the personal history of the particular woman may lead to a quantity and quality of self-subordination that becomes tantamount to self-burial. The mothering capability may require an inevitable but submerged agony, which, if denied, may induce a baffling and bewildering depression.

THE CASE OF CATHY

A married professional woman with two small children, in her midthirties, Cathy had been in psychoanalysis for a number of years. She had made many constructive changes: great improvement in her definition of her psychological self; the establishment of a lasting and productive relationship with a man; good development of her career; becoming a mother and discovering that she was quite content in the mothering role; and considerable reduction of a complex, painful, ambivalent, symbiotic attachment to her family of origin. However, Cathy still suffered with severe insomnia, inability to discuss sexual matters except in general terms, an unwanted aversion to the establishment of close female friendships, and strong feelings of being devalued by me, as well as by other authority figures on whom she needed to depend. She reported three dreams:

> 1. Charles Manson is on his way to his execution, and he decides to kill three more people. And my father is one of the three who are killed. Wanda S. tells me that my father was shot in New York.

> 2. Laura W. asks me for chocolate whipped cream, which I express from a container. I squeeze some on to Laura's blouse. I didn't realize I was doing anything wrong. But Laura becomes enraged, and she screams at me. I am horror stricken, I feel awful, I've lost my boundaries. Laura changes clothes. I remain confused. I didn't know what I did wrong.

> 3. I enter your office; you are running in, wearing tennis clothes. It's a huge suite, with many therapists and secretaries. I yell and scream that you don't care about me. Someone, either you or I, yells, "Let's talk about sex." It's all mayhem and confusion.

Charles Manson seemed to be a reference to Cathy's mother, whom she regarded as the parent who created psychological devastation in the family. The father was shot where Cathy's eldest sister lived, and she felt this sister was the mother's psychological substitute. Cathy regarded Laura both as an immature woman who relished pregnancy and as a mother substitute. The chocolate cream on the blouse, Laura's rage, and the patient's helpless, horrified loss of boundaries all point to deep, anal and oral, destructive ambivalence between mother and child. The third dream reminded both Cathy and me of the presence of these dynamics in the therapeutic situation and of how her pregenitally derived depression bred a defensive cynical therapeutic resistance (saying I didn't care). The dream also suggests that until these more basic existential issues were resolved, she would continue to be unable to deal with her sexual inhibitions.

Cathy and I knew that her mother's destructiveness had eventually driven her father from the home. We also agreed that, although Cathy was critical of her father's aloofness, she also loved him and found it possible to maintain a reasonably good relationship with him. However, something new emerged from these dreams. I began to feel very close to the patient, as though I had "lost my boundaries." Then I became aware that I felt very sorry for the father and very protective of him. I realized that these were Cathy's feelings; just as the older sister, represented by Wanda, was the mother's ally in the family warfare, so Cathy was a member of her father's guard. I was very moved and felt like crying. In a choked voice, I told Cathy that she was a soldier loyal to her father, and that her innocent, but ambivalent action toward Laura in the second dream was an infantile effort to protect or avenge him. Laura's response represented psychological murder by the enraged mother. These dreams revealed a major new dimension of understanding; that Cathy saw her father in mortal danger from the mother and that she saw her duty as sacrificing herself to save her father—hence the stunning psychological blow which she sustained in the second dream. The validity of this interpretation seemed established by Cathy's sobbing release of feelings and rush of confirmatory associations. She had never previously realized the alliance she felt with her father.

Her nocturnal, vigilant sleep deprivation, her inability to fully acknowledge her sexuality, and her feelings of being relatively friendless and isolated were all possible corollaries to the role of devoted member of her father's guard. In fact, the sessions after we discussed these dreams were laden with discussion of these issues, and the problems were noticeably reduced.

DISCUSSION

Each of the women whose dreams were presented, may be seen as emblematic of a specific variety of the common experience of female suffering. Ethel lived in hiding from the dangerous world. Her perception of the human experience was clearly conveyed by her recurrent dream of the nocturnal rapist-murderer. Her capacity for transformation of this dismal view of life was shown by the progressive changes in her dreams during the following decade.

Betty's dream also revealed a view of life involving suffering, but with considerable difference. She perceived her role as enormously self-submerging (being under her daughter in the dream), yet she added a defensive dimension, in effect averring that there was nothing to complain about. Denial, smiles, good cheer had to prevail. The refusal to acknowledge hate and cruelty was supposed to abolish these very features of human life. In therapy, Betty gradually became aware that her denial of aggression rendered her the unwitting accomplice of the damaging forces in both biological life and human culture. Her new willingness to appreciate the unavoidable elements of hostility in her own psychology (such as resentment toward mother and husband) became a powerful lever in lifting and releasing her essential self from the layers of dutiful pain under which she was buried.

Cathy's dreams revealed still another variant of womanly suffering. She was like Betty in her self-sacrificial urges and similar to Ethel in feeling like a depreciated child. But unlike them, she neither denied her pain nor developed terrorized shyness. She never projected and disavowed her aggression as massively as the two other women.

It seems to me that these three women's dreams reveal something of value. Are they not the fantasy counterparts of the traits designated as special for women by Gilligan (1982)? Self-sacrifice may well be the inescapable concomitant of effective empathic and caring responses. On the other hand, excessive suffering may also have had the opposite effect, that is, an ultimate reduction in the capacity for empathic caring. This would be especially evident in Ethel's case.

Moreover, my informal, but I hope informed, impression of men's dreams is that they usually do not possess the continual wholesale, subjective painfulness of these women's dreams. In order to know pain and how to relieve it, painful experience must be felt.

I believe these three women, although quite dissimilar, enjoyed a commonality of therapeutic "cure." All three benefited from the discovery, definition, and transformation of their shared experience of aggression. In such a process, the therapist perforce needs to reclaim his or her own feminine legacy of suffering, which, through the powerful agency of identification, is surely present in all of us. This dimension of therapy requires that the therapist become enough of a caring mother or sister to reestablish an intratherapeutic ethos of caring and hope, which is gradually appropriated and internalized by the patient.

It should be obvious that the "good life" is not and never has been a given. It is a goal closely associated with the humanistic view of the human condition. Perhaps women's dreams, which portray endless suffering in infinite permutation, are addressing this goal and the effort to reach it by repeatedly demonstrating how huge the gap is between the "good life" and the average expectable experience for people at this time.

This creative model of therapeutic action contains many opportunities for therapeutic error as well as for fluent human connection. "The momentary lapse will reveal the therapist's lack of perfection and omnipotence. How the patient reacts to this offers further material for exploration" (Horner, 1984). Caretaking requires continuous identification, which in turn requires sustained immersion in frustration, pain, hurt, dread, depression, and all the agonies for which dependent people require help. Out of this matrix emerge women's dreams of suffering and their accompanying sharpened vision of humanistic goals.

REFERENCES

Chodorow, N. (1978), *The Reproduction of Mothering: Psychoanalysis and the Sociology of Gender*. Berkeley: University of California Press.

Gill, M. (1982), *Analysis of Transference, Vol. 1: Theory and Technique*. New York: International Universities Press.

Gilligan, C. (1982), *In a Different Voice*. Cambridge, MA: Harvard University Press.

Horner, A. (1984), *Object Relations and the Developing Ego in Therapy*. New York: Jason Aronson.

Kohut, H. (1977), *The Restoration of the Self*. New York: International Universities Press.

Kovel, J. (1970), *White Racism*. New York: Vintage.

Loewald, H. (1970), Psychoanalytic theory and the psychoanalytic process. In: *Papers on Psychoanalysis*. New Haven: Yale University Press, 1980, pp. 277–301.

Mahler, M. S. (1963), Thoughts about development and individuation. In: *The Selected Papers of Margaret S. Mahler*, Vol. 2. New York: Aronson, 1979, pp. 3–19.

Roiphe, H., & Galenson, E. (1981), *Infantile Origins of Sexual Identity*. New York: International Universities Press.

Schafer, R. (1974), Problems in Freud's psychology of women. In: *Female Psychology*, ed. H. Blum. New York: International Universities Press, 1977, pp. 331–360.

——— (1983), *The Analytic Attitude*. New York: Basic Books.

Stolorow, R., & Atwood, G. (1984), *Structures of Subjectivity*. Hillsdale, NJ: The Analytic Press.

Winnicott, D. (1965), *The Maturational Process and the Facilitating Environment*. New York: International Universities Press.

Wolfenstein, E. (1981), *The Victims of Democracy*. Berkeley: University of California Press.

17

Creative and Reparative Uses of Countertransference by Women Psychotherapists Treating Women Patients: A Clinical Research Study

Ellen Bassin Ruderman, Ph.D

Few American women today can have avoided internalizing the negative attitudes toward women that prevailed in the sociocultural milieu they were raised in. These attitudes were, and to a distressing extent still are, transmitted during the earliest phases of a woman's development and within the most intimate framework of her object relations. The culture then reinforces them.

This article is based on the author's Ph.D. dissertation, "Gender Related Themes of Women Psychotherapists in Their Treatment of Women Patients: The Creative and Reparative Use of Countertransference as a Mutual Growth Experience," Institute for Clinical Social Work, June 1983.

Female psychotherapists cannot pretend to have escaped that pattern. Both they and their female patients are likely to be dealing as best they can with similar sets of unresolved issues and conflicting attitudes about their femininity and their attempts to balance the social, familial, and professional aspects of their lives. The chief difference between them is that, presumably, the therapists have acquired greater insight and better tools for coping with social and personal issues. Nevertheless, many questions remain concerning how therapists resolve those issues. Since so many women today seek treatment with female psychotherapists, it seems essential to know what inner experiences, feelings, and attitudes about women's issues psychotherapists bring to their role. Because, presumably, the depth and extent of these attitudes can profoundly affect the psychotherapeutic process, it is justifiable to inquire about the female psychotherapist's self-experience—her countertransference—while she conducts psychotherapy with women patients.

The woman therapist is confronted with an internal paradox. Although she may intellectually agree with expanding notions of women's role in society, feelings that derive from her archaic experiences may persist as an undercurrent beneath her new attitudes and become reactivated in the countertransference. If they emerge, the same therapist who encourages her female patient to claim equal treatment with men as her birthright may be wrestling silently with her own unresolved conflicts about familial and professional roles, competitive anxiety, and fears of success.[1] This paradox—a focal point of the author's research—cannot avoid entering into the dynamic interplay between patient and therapist.

Although the literature on women's issues contains many surveys of attitudes and feelings of psychotherapists—about sex biases, sex-role stereotyping, orientation to psychotherapy, and so forth—few self-report studies of psychotherapists' countertransference have been undertaken. The study reported here describes and discusses the nature and content of countertransference reported by a group of women therapists treating women patients. Countertransference is defined here as the therapist's consciously felt attitudes, experiences, and attributes as evoked by the stimulus of the psychotherapist-patient rela-

---

[1] In microcosm, her experience may mirror the deepest intrapsychic fears of most women about their changing roles. The failure to ratify the Equal Rights Amendment in 1982 may be partly attributable to such fears.

tionship. It reflects the therapist as a total person – her age; her stage of life development; her life experience and performance in multiple roles; and her experience of acute life crises, separations, and losses. It is the sum total of what she feels toward the patient and within herself in the context of the treatment process.

THE LITERATURE

This study considers issues in two major areas of theory: female development as it relates to women's issues and conflicts; and the countertransference of therapists in their treatment of patients. The conceptual framework for this study is drawn principally from psychoanalytic perspectives; the literature reveals numerous points of view and diverse approaches to female development.

Female Sexuality

Selected aspects of three psychoanalytic conceptual frameworks are especially pertinent to any discussion of women's development and conflicts. They include Freud's theories of female sexuality and oedipal themes (1925, 1931, and 1933); challenges and modifications to Freud's theories as reflected in the work of Schafer (1968a, 1968b, 1974, 1978), Horney (1924, 1926, 1933, 1935), Galenson and Roiphe (1977), and Stoller (1963, 1968, 1972); and the contributions of Mahler (1954, 1964, 1970, 1975, 1981) to an understanding of early development, particularly the "rapprochement" crisis of the separation–individuation phase. Significant recent contributions to female psychology are also relevant; these include the contributions of Horner (1968, 1972a), Hoffman (1972, 1974), Chodorow (1978), and Gilligan (1982).

Freud deserves credit for opening the doors to ongoing psychoanalytic attempts to discover the origins of women's early identities. In his paper on "Female Sexuality" (1931), he describes the strength and duration of the little girl's preoedipal attachment to the mother: "We see . . . [that] the phase of exclusive attachment to the mother which may be called a pre-oedipus phase, possesses a far greater importance in women than it can have in men" (p. 221).

Freud's general stance was that the path to development of femininity opened to the girl only after she had passed through the phallic phase, the observation of anatomical difference, the castration complex, a sense of inferiority and penis envy, and finally entered the oedipal period, turning away from her mother toward her father. These ideas characterize his writings from 1908 through 1938.

Horney (1924, 1926, 1933) and Jones (1927, 1933, 1935) were strong critics of Freud's theory, proposing that instead of femininity representing thwarted masculinity, both femininity and masculinity predated the phallic phase and had pre-oedipal origins. In contrast, Freud believed that a girl's reaction to the discovery of sexual distinction was decisive not only for female sexual development, but for the personality traits he associated with femaleness: passivity, masochism, and narcissism.[2]

Stoller (1968) shared the view of Horney and Jones that gender consciousness is integral, but he did not view masculinity and femininity as parallel constructs. In his theory, gender identification precedes the child's discovery of sexual distinction. Stoller perceived the roots of primary femininity in the earliest phase of life for both boys and girls, because of both sexes' primary identification with the mother in that phase. Greenson (1958) suggested that this poses a special problem for boys because they must disidentify with the maternal object in order to achieve an appropriate masculine identity.

Commenting on the uses of aggression in the service of separation-individuation, Mahler (1981) points to the difficulties of resolving mother-daughter conflicts in the preoedipal, oedipal, and postoedipal periods. In highlighting the difficulties women experience in differentiating from their mothers, she says:

> When separation from the postsymbiotic mother becomes a necessity, the boy has the father to support his attainment of personal and gender identity. Under ordinary circumstances, the father offers uncontaminated personality traits, traits in particular which fit the gender identity needs of the boy. The girl also has to disidentify herself from part-object representations of her mother, and goes through a tortuous and complicated splitting, repressive, and reintegrative process to attain and maintain her self and gender identity [p. 628].

---

[2]Freud may have drawn exactly the wrong conclusion from his theory. If, on account of her different constellation of castration concerns, a girl does not develop the implacable superego that a boy does, then at least in this respect, she might be better suited than a boy to develop a basis for moral decision making that is enlightened, realistic, and consistently committed to a conventional form of civilized interaction among people (Gilligan, 1982).

Smith and Smith-Blackmer (1981) note especially the daughter's need to revisit her relationship with her mother in order to explore and develop her own identity. The findings of their study clearly foreshadow the needs of female therapists to continually rework and reexamine their relationships with their mothers, particularly with reference to themes of separation and individuation. In his response to Freud, Schafer (1974) says: ". . . one must see the girl and, later, the woman, as being in a profoundly influential, continuously intense and active relationship, not only with her real mother but with the idea and imagined presence of her mother and with her identification with this mother" (p. 485).

Horner (1965, 1972a, 1972b) and Hoffman (1972, 1974) shed glaring new light on women's inhibitions and fears of success. Horner saw the avoidance of success as an internal psychological surrender to the dominant societal stereotype, which frowns on competence, independence, competition, and intellectual achievement as unfeminine and therefore unhealthy for women, but lauds those qualities in men and associates them with mental health. Hoffman concluded that women fear success because they fear that affiliative loss will result from it.

Similarly, Galenson (1977) studied the fear of competition among women in its manifestation as "examination anxiety," a problem far more common among women than men. Impending school examinations prompted strikingly similar clinical features among a group of young, ambitious, and intelligent women patients. The anxieties expressed by these women included fear of object loss, guilt and self-reproach, deep concerns about bodily integrity, and feelings of intellectual imperfection. Several patients expressed regressive wishes for an earlier dependent relationship as a way out of a competitive showdown. These symptoms appeared to subside when exams were over. In understanding these inhibitions, sexual and competitive anxiety, and prohibition of actualizing efforts, Galenson and Roiphe (1976) cite the effect of the early castration reactions of the preoedipal girl on developing object ties. Galenson (1977) says:

> Early castration reactions take place precisely during the era when intellectual functioning has begun to assume some characteristics of secondary process thought. Various presymbolic forms, such as gesture and semi-symbolic play are developing during the second year of life, and speech is just emerging. . . . It would appear, then, that the budding in-

tellectual function is involved, in many little girls, with their concern over genital intactness, as well as the older renewed anxieties of object and anal loss [p. 17].

Chodorow (1978) did an analysis of contemporary child-rearing practices. She noted the importance of emotional relational bonding in young women, whereas abstract, work-oriented ties to the social world are valued in the rearing of male children. In Chodorow's view, girls have a more difficult time separating from mother than do boys:

> Because they are the same gender as their daughters and have been girls, mothers of daughters tend not to experience these infant daughters as separate from them in the same way as do mothers of infant sons. In both cases, a mother is likely to experience a sense of oneness and continuity with her infant. However, this sense is stronger and lasts longer, vis-à-vis daughters. Primary identification and symbiosis with daughters tend to be stronger and cathexis of daughters is more likely to retain and emphasize narcissistic elements, that is, to be based on experiencing a daughter as an extension or double of a mother herself, with cathexis of the daughter as a sexual other usually remaining a weaker, less significant theme [p. 109].

It is clear that object loss – the loss of the significant other – is a focal point in the basic theories of female development. It is a source of concern for all women, but especially for women who excel, who succeed, or who actualize intellectual and creative potential. As demonstrated in the work of Mahler, Galenson, and Roiphe, certain of the origins of this conflict around female separation and autonomy and female achievement have their roots in the earliest separation-individuation experience. Thus, it is to be expected that core countertransference themes experienced by women therapists treating women patients will be associated with separation-individuation and object loss, with special references to the maternal relationship, fear of success, and role conflicts related to masculinity and femininity.

Countertransference

Unlike the literature of female development, the literature on countertransference tends to be more generic, focusing on the process and manifestations of countertransference as a phenomenon in psychotherapy and less explicitly on its gender-linked content.

Kernberg (1965), for example, distinguishes between two forms of countertransference: "classical" and "totalistic." What he terms classical countertransference derives from Freud's descriptions of the psychoanalyst's unconscious reactions to the patient, which Freud viewed as neurotic conflicts to be overcome. In contrast, totalistic countertransference is viewed as the total emotional reaction of the psychoanalyst to the patient in the treatment situation, both conscious and unconscious. Totalistic countertransference incorporates not only the analyst's reactions to the patient's reality and transference to the analyst, but also the analyst's own reality needs, which exist in addition to neurotic needs.

The study reported here examines totalistic countertransference, in accordance with Sullivan's conclusion (1953) that the analytic situation is an interactive process in which the past and present of both participants fuse into a unique emotional position involving both of them. Racker (1968) elaborated on this idea by suggesting that the analyst can find his or her countertransference reactions useful for obtaining important information about the patient's inner emotional constellation, besides using them as a barometer of the ongoing analytic process. Seen in that way, countertransference is a normal, natural, interpersonal event — not an idiosyncratic phenomenon and certainly not the hindrance to the therapeutic relationship that it was formerly thought to be.

In the same vein, Searles (1979b) speaks of the need for therapists to be open and honest with themselves about their countertransference. He emphasizes that the danger is not so much having countertransference feelings as it is not being in touch with or not being honest about them. Both Searles and Langs (Langs & Searles, 1980) agree that therapists can gain rich material for their own growth through attentiveness to countertransference.

METHODS AND LIMITATIONS OF THE RESEARCH

This examination of countertransference themes among women therapists treating women patients included two corollary questions: Does the therapist's attentiveness to countertransference offer possibilities for mutual growth and repair for both therapist and patient? and Do the countertransference themes of women psychotherapists have a gender-linked component?

Twenty psychoanalytically oriented women psychotherapists consented to be the subjects of this study. The criteria for choosing them included licensure; sufficient clinical experience to use countertransference as an essential contribution to the treatment; current practice of psychoanalytically informed psychotherapy; and past or present experience as a patient in psychoanalysis or psychodynamic psychotherapy.

The participants ranged in age from 38 to 59 years (one of them preferred not to state her age). Six of them had practiced psychotherapy for 21 to 25 years, 8 for 15 to 20 years, and 6 for 10 to 13 years. Nineteen of the 20 subjects teach and supervise mental health professionals in training. Six therapists were divorced; 13 were married, and 1 was single. Four were childless, and 16 had children ranging in age from 2 to 34 years.

Using a tape recorder, the author conducted semistructured, open-ended, in-depth interviews, lasting 1 ½ hours with each therapist. Each therapist was asked to present the case of one female patient with whom she had worked for at least six months. The author emphasized that the primary interest of the study was not the treatment itself but rather the therapist's countertransference. The interviews were intense, emotional, and often consultative and cathartic – to the point that some of the women lamented that they were "not long enough."

Data analysis consisted of a line-by-line review of the transcripts. All subjective statements pertaining to countertransference were grouped into one of two categories: major themes or secondary themes. Because issues often were not stated explicitly or in uniform terminology, the author was forced to exercise considerable judgment, make interpretations, and impose uniformity.

Although the emphasis was on consciously felt countertransference themes and issues, the author made inferences about a number of covert themes and issues that she believed to have been part of the self-report data collected in the interviews. Just as the therapists' statements in the interviews derived from their own perceptions and descriptions and not necessarily from "hard facts," it must be understood that the study's findings rely heavily on the author's understanding and interpretation of the data. The findings are therefore the residuum of two subjective filterings, with all the hazards and vulnerabilities attendant upon such a process.

Another limitation of the study is that the 20 subjects came from similar sociocultural backgrounds, and all but one or two were in the same midlife phase of their life cycle. They were chosen from among members of the author's somewhat closely linked informal professional network. The author cannot claim that this sample necessarily represents the larger psychotherapeutic community or that the study's results are generalizable to that entire community. However, the sheer homogeneity of the subjects produced a provocative set of perspectives, and it is reasonable to presume that they are at least common.

Restricting the study to women psychotherapists treating women patients leaves completely open the question of whether male psychotherapists undergo analogous experiences with their male patients. It also avoids completely an attempt to understand the nature of treatment issues between male therapists and female patients, and female therapists and male patients. These are valuable questions but must be left to other researchers.

FINDINGS: FIVE COUNTERTRANSFERENCE THEMES

Five major themes emerged among the therapists, all related to issues on which they were currently working or had resolved in their everyday lives or in their therapy or analysis. These were (1) the therapist's relationships with her mother, especially with respect to separation-individuation and identity; (2) fear of success, as manifested by the therapist's empathic identification with her patient's inhibitions, conflicts over ambition, and devaluation of self-worth; (3) role conflicts around needs regarding family and relationships versus career pursuits and around feminine-masculine role stereotypes in professional roles; (4) envy in the countertransference, as related to either feelings of dependence or to mourning; and (5) the life stage of the therapist.

These themes are treated separately in this study, but of course they form a single stream whose ultimate source is in the early maternal experiences of both therapist and patient. It is also intuitively clear that this research offers an elaboration of women's intrapsychic conflicts, even though they are viewed through the narrow lens of therapist countertransference. It is the author's basic assumption that these intrapsychic fears and conflicts prevent women from fully acknowledging and experiencing gratification in their creative and intellectual pursuits. This, in turn, perpetuates the barriers erected by society, which blows its trumpet a bit too loudly over the progress it has allowed, while it continues to devalue women and to undermine their efforts to achieve legitimate recognition and equality.

THEME 1: THE THERAPIST'S RELATIONSHIP WITH HER MOTHER

Separating and individuating the self is a dynamic process that continues throughout life. Similarly, the process of discovering one's identification as a woman builds cumulatively through the moving away from one's mother and returning to her in memory. The whole relationship of a woman to her mother is extremely complex (and becomes all the more so when the woman becomes a mother herself). It seems to transcend the relationship with the mother and become the model for every relationship of intimacy and closeness.

All the therapists in the study became transferential persons of significance for their patients; and for many of the therapists, the feelings and issues evoked in the treatment of women patients impinged strongly on their own identification and separation processes. The therapists were thus given an opportunity to contribute healthier resolution of these issues for their patients and at the same time benefited themselves from their own reworking process. A common thread among the therapists was the need to repair aspects of their relationships with their mothers. As therapist Margaret Jones[3] said:

> My work with [the patient] really reworked something for me. Here was the first time in a treatment situation I allowed a woman total aggression and ventilation, and now I've emerged on the far side of it with her. . . . Her mother was a depressed, withdrawn woman, and she won the oedipal victory. So I did free her, and she helped me to free something in myself.

Ms. Jones noted that every woman must be able to stand apart and look at her mother from some distance, but to achieve separateness, one must first have become close to the mother:

---

[3]All therapists' names are fictitious to protect the confidentiality of subjects in this study. Any resemblance to the actual names of any psychotherapists or patients is purely coincidental.

Actually, I had more than one mother. I was raised by my grandmother, so that my mother was floating somewhere out there and I had to pull her back in to me to see who was my mother. My mother ran away all the time. She was off traveling with my father, and my grandmother stayed home and took care of me. My patient also kept running away from me, so she represented the mother who ran away – but I also became the mother who stood still for her, and let her run away.

Therapists constantly rediscover their mothers in working on aspects of their maternal identification. Therapist Anne Smith commented: "The capacity to facilitate another woman's development is very rewarding, probably because it wasn't something that happened for me with my mother. I always had a feeling that she loved me, but I didn't think she knew square one about what would promote my development." Ms. Smith recalled that one of ther mother's concerns had been, "If you go to college, you're gonna look down on us." By improving herself, Ms. Smith felt she was devaluing her mother – and her mother did indeed feel threatened by her daughter's achievements. About her patient, Ms. Smith said, "I've been conscious all along of wanting her to be as successful as she can be."

Therapist Carol Evans described her efforts to help her patient resolve conflicts about her female identification. She identified several issues related to her own difficulties in separating from her mother:

Every bid my patient made to individuate . . . caused her mother to get sick. And of course that reminded me of my own mother. When I went into my career she got a bleeding ulcer. Every move I made in the service of individuation was like a cardinal sin. And so this female patient reminded me of myself, and of the girl I would wish to be. . . . I helped her to realize herself as my mother could never comfortably help me. . . . I guess in helping her [the patient] to individuate from a controlling, martyring, self-sacrificing mother, I identified with her to an extent, I'm quite sure, and I maybe further freed myself in the process of freeing her.

Therapist Jones, Smith, and Evans demonstrate the pattern in which learning, growth, and repair have taken place for many of the female psychotherapsits in this study.

At the same time, Ms. Evans reflected on the hazards of allowing psychotherapist countertransference to remain unchecked:

When I said that in the countertransference she was very much a daughter to me, and it was reparative, what was hardest for me in my life was not having a child, and it was reparative to the extent that I would do for this child what her mother could not do. I was so proud of her and I got my wounds healed. Okay, you don't have your own child, but you can still contribute to the next generation, which is part of what you need to do. . . . At the same time, if I hadn't been aware of my feelings toward her, I could have derived too much self-satisfaction out of being her model, and gotten in the way of my patient's picking up what was positive in her mother. In order to be a whole person, she has to selectively identify with her mother. If I stand in the way of that, I would be doing her a great disservice. So I had to back off: she was not my child.

THEME 2: FEAR OF SUCCESS

From the standpoint of clinical practice, fear of success is often hard to discern because it is tightly interwoven into the fabric of women's conflicts, choices, and decisions. Fear of success is linked to the earliest relationship between women and their mothers; all subsequent conflicts about women's roles—family versus profession; autonomy versus dependence; stifled ambition, assertiveness, and creativity—emanate from that source. Combined with a restrictive sociocultural milieu, these fears create a barrier to success and self-satisfaction. Freud (1925) linked fear of success with guilt reactions engendered during the oedipal period; the child experiences growth and development as rivalrous and fraught with violence. Applegarth's (1977) study of women analysts suggests that the conflict in women reflects guilt and fear at surpassing the mother. Hoffman (1972, 1974), in reviews of child development studies, suggested that females have high needs for affiliation, which influence and sometimes block their achievement motives and behavior. Girls, she believes, receive less encouragement than boys for independence, are protected more by their parents, and receive less encouragement to develop separate identities and explore their environments.

Clinically, female patients experience the fear of success when, for example, their pursuit of intellectual and professional achievement in a career conflicts with building a significant love relationship in which they are to play (by one definition or another) a "feminine" role. Many young women patients complain that their choices are becoming more polarized. One young woman commented, "If a woman wants to succeed, she has to be prepared to give up a lot. We wind up career bound but alone. Men are simply uncomfortable at the least, threatened at the most, and where does that leave us?"

In her interview, therapist Barbara Hill described two of her patients as young, unhappy, and depressed. Both worked beneath their capabilities. Both feared "going beyond" their family and friends. They saw success as causing enmity and envy, inflicting pain, destroying relationships, and devaluing those they would be leaving behind. The therapists in the study said they strove to endow women patients such as these with freedom from fear through an experience that they themselves had enjoyed in their own therapies: the support of a consistent, patient person who remained "there" and "at home" while their patients explored, discovered, and expanded new internal and external dimensions of themselves.

Therapists' countertransference issues about fear of success run parallel to the conflicts and issues presented by their patients. For example, therapist Marjorie Green revealed her own discomforts with ambition, aggression, innovation, and creativity. She noted that she avoided work on articles she had agreed to write for publication two years previously. Even with a deadline, she procrastinated. In her work with her patient, both were able to achieve a deep recognition of how much each had feared hurting or devaluing their mothers by failing to live out their mothers' expectations. She reflected:

> I've often felt guilty, conflicted, like I was betraying my mother as I went ahead in my professional career. But another part of me felt that she really would have enjoyed seeing me do all of this. She would have gotten vicarious pleasure in my achieving. And I think, in that sense, it's quite different from my woman patient, because I think for my patient's mother, it's very threatening to see her daughter achieve and do well. She's proud of her in one sense, wants to show her off and say, "Look at my daugher, the doctor," but she's quite envious and uncomfortable as her daughter becomes successful, aggressive, and self-sufficient. I think she feels intimidated by her daughter, worries that she no longer has any control over her, that her daugher will leave her, not take care of her, do for her. My own mother was more subtle. Her fears were not the fears that I would leave her, but that my role was properly first and foremost to be successful as a mother and as a wife to my husband.

Several of the therapists felt that their own experiences in therapy had led them to bring an unwavering, therapeutic optimism to the treatment of their patients. This enthusiasm communicated a willingness to stay with the patient for the duration of the therapeutic work. The therapist felt that this form of encouragement in the transference relationship helped to clarify many of the anxieties associated with their patients' fear of success.

Therapist Lisa McKay understood her encouragement of her female patient in terms of her own past: "I felt totally alone, as if no one quite understood me for who or what I was. No one understood my creative, sensitive part." Reflecting on her childhood in a family that neither recognized nor encouraged her talents, she said: "My music teacher had to tell them how talented I was. My mother would go to the concerts, but she would not read the program notes. She was never really involved in the concerts, or in that part of me." Acutely attuned to her patient's need for support, Ms. McKay became a kind of mentor for her patient, discovering, encouraging, and enhancing the patient's creativity. She passed on to her patient the gift she had received from her own music teacher: the ability to value herself, to lend legitimacy to her creative side. Ms. McKay commented on the uniqueness of a shared understanding of the creative process with the patient:

> There was something about that mutual kind of creativity, you know, that part of us that is common among artistic-type people that does not necessarily have to be verbalized. There is something that is "meta-communicated" to each other. It is like being in a special kind of family which most people could not understand, but we do, intimately.

In summary, the therapists' countertransference identification with their women patients can be seen clearly in the empathic and sometimes frustrated feelings they expressed. They viewed themselves in the mirror of women patients who were constricted, inhibited, and caught in internal dilemmas related to their sense of emotional well-being and self-actualizing potential as women. At the same time, they saw and experienced the need to become mentors to their young women patients, either because an older woman mentor had been significant to them or because they had needed, but had never received, such mentorship. In working with women patients who present conflicts leading to creative inhibition, the woman therapist may thus be offered the chance to rework similar aspects of her own identity.

THEME 3: ROLE CONFLICTS

A major theme that emerged for the therapists in these interviews related to their conflicts in balancing career aspirations with family and social relationships. Role conflicts were also related to both intrapsychic and societal definitions of masculinity and femininity. These often emerged in material having to do with the ambitions of patients and therapists and their resulting confusion about traditionally prescribed and proscribed behavior for women. The expansion of choices for women appeared to be helpful in resolving some of the confusion. Therapists spoke of their mothers as having had few options other than their traditional roles, such as the Germans' *Kinder, Kuche, Kirche* (children, kitchen, and church). This concept of the female role was passed on to them by their mothers. Later, in adolescence and early adulthood, they regretted not having been encouraged to explore other options. Many of the therapists expressed envy of and admiration for their younger patients, who now live in a cultural context that is less grudging about options for women; but they were also keenly aware of the intrapsychic conflicts that precluded many of their patients from exercising these expanded options.

Therapist Sarah Scott commented on how essential it had been for her to sit back and allow her patient to unfold in her own good time: "I think one of the major problems we, as women therapists, have with women patients is when we identify and, therefore, want to encourage their assertiveness too quickly. That's more in the service of our needs, not necessarily theirs." In reflecting on her temptation to move too fast, Ms. Scott said she had felt concerned about her patient's level of ambition and aspirations: "Her seeming to have so little ambition was a big mystery for me. Somehow, in this bright woman, who could have been anything she wanted, she wanted so little for herself. Somehow, her ambition got stopped!"

In working out role conflicts, women may tend to seek out a particular kind of role model in another woman. Several therapists in this study indicated that their female patients had specifically chosen to work with them because the therapists not only had achieved professional stature but were also married and the mother of children. Describing her patient, therapist Ruth Wells said: "She felt that with me she had a chance to be both successful, professional, and feminine. She saw me as a more feminine person than her other analyst, and fresh flowers in my office had a great deal of significance for her."

The burdens of becoming a role model, with its incumbent idealization, reverberates in the therapists' countertransference. Therapists Karen Randall and Barbara Hill commented on their struggles to balance family and career needs. Ms. Randall talked about guilt feelings when the balance shifted from mothering to career: "If I am away from home or too involved with my work I get confused: Am I going to do to them [her children] what my mother did to me?" Ms. Hill said, "Sometimes it's hard to give to both [patients and children]. I feel like I'm not a good mother to either one."

Within women, role conflict seems to be intraphysically structured so that, when they experience enormous barriers to aggressive and productive strivings, they are unable to locate the origins of their guilt, unease, and uncertainty. Although their talents and capacities are constricted, they remain subservient to spouses and tied to children in order to preserve important relationships.

Because of their own life experiences, therapists Catherine James, Nancy Alexander, and Ruth Wells expressed deep empathy for their patients' needs to make their own choices. They all felt they had been denied similar opportunities in their own upbringing. Commenting on the countertransference issue, Ms. Wells said:

> I knew I had a positive wish for her, but I also knew that it must not pass the boundaries of neutrality. I could also have slipped into the shoes of her controlling and intrusive mother, were I to lead her in any way, even away or on a path which might seem more beneficial to her. . . . I had to be so very aware of my own countertransference at all times, partially because I was so identified with her, partially because one would have to be, at any cost.

It is worth considering whether the extent to which a woman therapist has balanced her professional and relationship needs will influence the course of treatment with her women patients. The issue may not be so much the perfection of the balance as it is the therapist's sensitivity to its constant fluctuation.

THEME 4:
ENVY IN THE COUNTERTRANSFERENCE

Envy in the countertransference was associated with the reactivation in the therapist of dependency wishes, conflicts about autonomy, and mourning for lost or absent opportunities for gratification in her past life. Envy has its productive and constructive elements; if resolved, it leads to admiration and awe. It can also lead naturally to a process of mourning, in which the therapist reevaluates and rediscovers her feelings about the past and present and, perhaps, her sense of direction for the future. If mourning for what was, what was not, and what can never be is successfully accomplished, life can progress, producing new developments that bring satisfaction and an increasing sense of self-value, reducing the subsequent envy that one feels toward the accomplishments of others.

In reviewing her envious feelings, therapist Elizabeth Edwards discussed the defensive functions of her maternal countertransference:

> It was crucial to effective treatment. I would not be able to make proper interventions around her conflicts because I would not see them as conflicts. . . . As I continue to resolve these areas, my envy of feelings about my patient reduce. I am very aware of them, and am clear that my role as a facilitator is not a defensive one. The more I clear up for myself, the more I become more comfortable with her, and see her more as she really is with her own conflicts.

Ms. Edwards described her patient as an exceptionally bright environmental physicist, the highest-ranking graduate from a local university. Ms. Edwards said:

> My envious feelings focused on her youth and the opportunities open to her, because of the constellation of dynamics that left her unconflicted in areas that were conflictual for me—for example, in the area of intellectual exhibitionism. And also the greater freedom that was afforded her by a society which, today, has to some extent widened its horizons for females. She was moving ahead in her mid-twenties, while I, so many years later, was plodding through areas that I wish I could have plodded through in my mid-twenties.

Ms. Edwards' patient had a natural confidence, had achieved success in her profession, and had won awards for her professional work. Ms. Edwards commented:

All of this stirred up intensive reactions in me. Characteristically for me, I responded with maternal feelings, part of a defensive maneuver against the competition and envy, but in part they were also precursors to adopting a genuine facilitating mode. . . . This case enabled me to identify the areas in which competition and envy emerge for me. . . . It is almost exclusively in some area of intellectual achievement. . . . This case crystallized that realization for me, which had never really been in the forefront of my consciousness.

Like many of the other therapists, Ms. Edwards compared herself with her patient:

It makes no sense, really, because of our differences in age, the different cultures we grew up in. We're years apart, but dynamics are dynamics, and there is a universality and that is the common bond. I don't know how much I've learned through this patient about myself, but I have come to a greater sense of respect for the unique and individual struggle one has in one's own life, and the unfolding that really defies comparison with any other person — even with one's peers. What is most difficult for me with my woman patient is some of the mourning process I am going through, along with other issues of what never was and what never will be.

THEME 5: THE THERAPIST'S LIFE STAGE

In these interviews, the impact of the therapists' midlife stage was very forceful. Discussion often centered on the patient's age and then on the therapist's reflective evaluation of her changing personal values, feelings, and needs, as well as changes in her therapeutic work and thinking. This focus recalls Levinson's (1978) concept of the life-structure, developed in his study of the life stages of men in this society, and the impact of sociocultural, intrapsychic, and interpersonal aspects of their lives. The life-structure is an individual's unique pattern of living in the world with others, including aspects of the sociocultural world, intrapsychic world, and transactions between the self and world. Levinson speaks of the consequences for women who in their thirties choose career over relationship, and in their forties and fifties often deal with loneliness and alienation. Several therapists in the present study, reflecting on the position that women occupy in the current sociocultural milieu, similarly noted that although women have gained considerable independence in the last decade, they are ending up poor and lonely. Therapists Jane Gardner and Helen Robinson, for example, who were struggling with their own midlife issues, spoke of the difficulties for the single, divorced, middle-aged woman in a society that idealizes youth and "togetherness" and stigmatizes women who are single, divorced, middle-aged, and alone.

The interview with therapist Grace Black illustrates the work of midlife mourning and working through of the therapist's life experience. Ms. Black described her intense inner responses to her patient's youthful and flowering life. Ms. Black recalled that the abundant options now available to her woman patient had not been open to Ms. Black and her generation. Her feeling of deprivation fed considerable grief to the mourning process. In reflecting on her own life's imperatives, Ms. Black saw that they had been marriage and family. Her parents had overlooked her intelligence and her potential in other areas. She regretted her lack of options, and she regretted the lack of a person to encourage her as she encouraged her patient.

Ms. Black also realized that she had, in the past, been far too glib in telling some female patients—and herself—that they had as many choices as men. In looking back on her own life, she had neither realized nor wanted to admit how often she had sacrificed her professonal wishes for the sake of maintaining a healthy family life. She was all too aware that her marriage would have taken a completely different turn had she not been so compromising and had she done what she really wanted to do.

Of paramount interest is how therapists transmit certain values, encouragement, and attitudes to their patients at certain phases of the therapists' lives, and how those elements may shift and change. To some extent, such changes are a function of changes in the mental health professions as a whole. New approaches, new theoretical considerations (for example, changing perspectives on homosexuality), and views of male and female roles have repeatedly altered many traditional beliefs and approaches to treatment.

Changes in the profession intersect with changes in individual psychotherapists. The interview with therapist Jane Gardner exemplifies this process. Returning from out of state after several years of absence, and resuming treatment of a patient she had seen ten years previously, Ms. Gardner felt alone and isolated and, hence, she also felt increased appreciation for family and friends. As a result, her covert message to her patient stressed the importance of relationships and family ties. This message was vastly different from her clarion call in the previous decade to separate, differentiate, and move out into the world. In the earlier therapy, Ms. Gardner had encouraged her patient to break out of the symbiotic and constrictive relationship she had with her husband. Ms. Gardner was simultaneously engaged in dissolving her own marriage. During the more recent encounter with the same patient, Ms. Gardner was vastly more circumspect with respect to this particular issue. Values have changed in the outer world, and it is difficult for a bright, sensitive, middle-aged woman to find a spouse with similar attributes.

Therapist Susan Andrews summarized her sense of the impact of life stages on therapeutic issues by saying: "Perhaps at certain times in our lives we have needs that lean in one direction more than the other. . . . What we must do is focus always on the impact of our own developmental stages on ourselves as well as others around us, and be aware that life is never static, nor are we."

DISCUSSION OF FINDINGS

In addition to the specific content of the five major countertransference themes described above, some general conclusions can be drawn from these interviews. First, and perhaps most striking, is the extent to which women psychotherapists experience profound resonance with their women patients. This resonance appears to go beyond simple empathy; it seems to come from a commonality of life experience and feelings that creates a strong and potentially healing mutual bond. Women seem increasingly drawn to the potential of what one woman can offer another, a tendency perceivable in the extent to which women seek as psychotherapists other women, who may serve not only as healers but also as professional and personal role models.

Second, the study seems to offer an implicit warning that unacknowledged or mishandled countertransference can lend a destructive valence to the treatment or, at best, may perpetuate oppressive sociocultural attitudes. Countertransference, then, not only is a reflective vehicle through which the patient's conflicts can be mirrored and worked through, but also can be a valuable source of material with which the psychotherapist can resolve conflictual material of her own.

A third finding in the study—startling at first, but ironically consonant with its dominant theme—was that 18 of the 20 women psychotherapists interviewed undervalued their obviously excellent therapeutic work. They did not share the author's view of them as sensitive, aware, empathic, and highly skilled practitioners. Furthermore, they were not aware of this attitude in themselves, nor did they link it to the five countertransference themes described in the preceding sections. This self-devaluation cut across all five countertransference themes and persisted as a profound undercurrent to most of the feelings of patients described by the psychotherapists. It thus is a sixth, albeit unconscious, theme of psychotherapist countertransference in this study.

A corollary question of the study was whether the countertransference themes described in the interviews have a specifically gender-linked component. Although there appears to be abundant justification for hypothesizing a gender link, more precise validation of such a component in countertransference themes can only take place through research involving a four-celled analysis of countertransference to male and female patients among male and female therapists. Still, the special quality of "feeling understood" that often exists between a woman patient and her woman psychotherapist points to the existence of a gender component in the therapist's countertransference.

Finally, an important image arising from this study is the immeasurable respect the therapists in this study displayed for their female patients as a result of their prudent and concerned awareness of countertransference themes. By allowing their patients the widest latitude to make their own choices and unfold in their own way, the therapists displayed what is, at all times, the height of caring in the psychotherapeutic relationship: one person aiding another to win freedom of choice and action as a self-determining individual, rather than one who is subservient to the will of other people or to unconscious forces.

IMPLICATIONS FOR CLINICAL PRACTICE

A number of this study's findings have implications for the clinical practice of psychotherapists in general and female psychotherapists in particular. First, the female therapists envinced a serious concern about their countertransference, based on the wish to know as much as possible about their deeper feelings. Interest in countertransference alone, however, is not necessarily sufficient to produce self-knowledge that will either enlighten the therapist or promote the treatment of patients. The depth and intensity of feelings that are provoked in the treatment situation between women therapists and their patients strongly underscores the need for psychoanalysis or psychoanalytic psychotherapy as a prerequisite for all therapists who engage in intensive psychotherapeutic treatment. All psychotherapists should also receive ongoing consultation, regardless of their years of experience or amount of personal therapy, either in the form of individual or peer-group consultaton or supervision. For female psychotherapists in particular, the women's issues discussed in this study reactivate disturbing memories and produce intense emotions. These issues must be prudently considered by therapists as a part of their professional work.

Second, based on the experience of this study, attitudes toward countertransference are still prevailingly negative in the therapeutic culture. The author was struck by how often the therapists in this study devalued themselves and their work when they were confronted with their countertransference to their patients. One would wish psychotherapists could take the work of Rackler, Searles, and others more to heart and view countertransference as an exciting learning experience as well as a route to profound discovery for both therapist and patient. Despite the therapists' emphasis that countertransference explorations had led many of them to important growth experiences, they still tended to criticize the evidence of countertransference in themselves.

Finally, the female therapists in this study, and perhaps women in general, resonate in a particular way with each other. They have much to share, and many steps to climb together. Even beyond therapy or analysis, women appear to need a place where they can continue to dig deeper into self-discovery. That was certainly true for the women therapists in this study; many initially consented to these interviews merely as a courtesy to the author, but found them so personally exciting and rewarding that they repeatedly urged their continuation in other forms, such as group meetings. The scope of clinical practice may need to be broadened to allow for such collective ways of working together.

REFERENCES

Applegarth, A. (1977), Some observations on work inhibitions in women. In: *Female Psychology: Contemporary Psychoanalytic Views*, ed. H. Blum. New York: International Universities Press, p. 266.

Blum, H. P., & Galenson, E. (1978), The psychology of women. *J. Amer. Psychoanal. Assn.* 266: 163–177.

Brodsky, A. E. (1980), Psychotherapy and women: Priorities for research. In: *Women and Psychotherapy*, ed. A. E. Brodsky & R. Hare-Mustin. New York: Guilford Press, pp. 385–386.

Chodorow, N. (1978), *The Reproduction of Mothering: Psychoanalysis and the Sociology of Gender*. Berkeley: University of California Press.

Chodoff, P. (1966), Feminine psychology and infantile sexuality. *Sci. Psychoanal.*, 10: 28–44.

Freud, S. (1905), Three essays on the theory of sexuality. *Standard Edition*, 7: 125–143. London: Hogarth Press, 1962.

_____ (1914), On narcissism: An introduction. *Standard Edition*, 14: 73–102. London: Hogarth Press, 1962.

_____ (1923), The infantile genital organization: An interpolation into the theory of sexuality. *Standard Edition*, 19: 139–145. London: Hogarth Press, 1961.

_____ (1924a), The dissolution of the Oedipus complex. *Standard Edition*, 19. London: Hogarth Press, 1961.

_____ (1924b), The economic problem of masochism. *Standard Edition*, 19: 159–170. London: Hogarth Press, 1961.

_____ (1925), Some physical consequences of the anatomical distinction between the sexes. *Standard Edition*, 19:241–258. London: Hogarth Press, 1961.

_____ (1931), Female sexuality. *Standard Edition*, 21: 225–243. London: Hogarth Press, 1961.

_____ (1933), New introductory lectuures on psycho-analysis. *Standard Edition*, 22: 5–182. London: Hogarth Press, 1964.

Galenson, E. (1977), Examination anxiety in women. Paper presented at the Los Angeles Psychoanalytic Institute, Los Angeles, CA.

_____ & Roiphe, H. (1977), Some suggested revisions concerning early female development. In: *Female Psychology: Contemporary Psychoanalytic Views*, ed. H. P. Blum. New York: International Universities Press, pp. 29–59.

Gilligan, C. (1982), *In a Different Voice*. Cambridge: Harvard University Press.

Greenson, R. R. (1958). Dis-identifying from mother: Its special importance for the boy. *Internat. J. Psycho-Anal.*, 49: 370–374.

Hoffman, L. W. (1972), Early childhood experiences and women's achievement motives. *J. Soc. Issues*, 28(2): 129–155.

_____ (1974), Fear of success in males and females: 1965 and 1971. *J. Consult. Clinic. Psychol.*, 2(3): 353–358.

Horner, M. S. (1968), Sex differences in achievement motivation and performance in competitive and non-competitive situations. Unpublished doctoral dissertation, University of Michigan.

_____ (1970), Feminity and successful achievement: A basic inconsistency. In:

Feminine Personality and Conflict, ed. J. Bardwick, E. M. Douvan, M. S. Horner, & D. Gutmann. Belmont, CA: Brooks-Cole, pp. 167–188.

_____ (1972a), The motive to avoid success and changing aspirations of college women. Unpublished manuscript, Harvard University.

_____ (1972b), Toward an understanding of achievement related to conflicts in women. *J. Soc. Issues*, 28 (2): 155–175.

_____, & Rheom, W. (1968), The motive to avoid success as a function of age, occupation and progress at school. Unpublished manuscript, University of Michigan.

Horney, K. (1924), On the genesis of the castration complex in women. In: *Feminine Psychology*, ed. H. Kelman. New York: Norton, 1967, pp. 147–161.

_____ (1926), The flight from womanhood: The masculinity complex in women as viewed by men and by women. In: *Feminine Psychology*, ed. H. Kelman. New York: Norton, 1967.

_____ (1933), The denial of the vagina. *Internat. J. Psycho-anal.*, 14: 57–70.

_____ (1935), The problem of feminine masochism. In: *Feminine Psychology*, ed. H. Kelman. New York: Norton, 1967.

Jones, E. (1927), The early development of female sexuality. *Internat. J. Psycho-anal.*, 8 (4): 458–473.

_____ (1933), Original papers—The phallic phase. *Internat. J. Psycho-anal.*, 14(1): 1–33.

_____ (1935), Early female sexuality. *Internat. J. Psycho-anal.*, 16(3): 363–373.

Kernberg, O. (1965), Notes on countertransference. *J. Amer. Psychoanal. Assn.*, 13: 38–56.

Langs, R., & Searles, H. F. (1980), *Intrapsychic and Interpersonal Dimensions of Treatment: A Clinical Dialogue*. New York: Jason Aronson.

Levinson, D. (1978), *The Seasons of a Man's Life*. New York: Knopf.

Mahler, M. S. (1954), Some theoretical considerations on the problem of mother-child separation. *Amer. J. Orthopsychiat.*, 24: 471–483.

_____ (1964), Thoughts about development and individuation. *The Psychoanalytic Study of the Child*, 19: 196–221. New York: International Universities Press.

_____ (1981), Aggression in the service of separation-individuation: Case study of a mother-daughter relationship. *Psychoanal. Quart.*, 625–637.

_____ & Bergman, A. (1975), Symbiosis and individuation. In: M. S. Mahler, F. Pine, & A. Bergman, *The Psychological Birth of the Human Infant: Symbiosis and Individuation*. New York: Basic Books, pp. 39–109.

Racker, H. (1953), A contribution to the problems of countertransference. *Internat. J. Psycho-anal.*, 34: 313–324.

_____ (1968), *Transference and Countertransference*. New York: International Universities Press.

_____ (1981), The meanings and uses of countertransference. In: *Classics in Psychoanalytic Technique*, ed. R. Langs. New York: Jason Aronson, pp. 197–201.

Roiphe, H., & Galenson, E. (1981), *Infantile Origins of Sexual Identity*. New York: International Universities Press.

Schafer, R. (1968a), *Aspects of Internalization*. New York: International Universities Press.

_____ (1968b), On the theoretical and technical conceptualization of activity and passivity. *Psychoanal. Quart.*, 37.

_____ (1972), Internalization: Process or fantasy? *The Psychoanalytic Study of the Child*, 27: 411–436.

_____ (1974), Problems in Freud's psychology of women. *J. Amer. Psychoanal. Assn.* 22: 459–485.

_____ (1978), Impotence, frigidity, and sexism. In: *Language and Insight.* New Haven: Yale University Press, pp. 141–171.

_____, & Wimpfheimer, M. (1977), Psychoanalytic methodology in Helene Deutsch's "The Psychology of Women." *Psychoanal. Quart.*, 45(2): 287–319.

Searles, H. (1979a), The analyst's experience with jealousy. In: *Countertransference: The Therapist's Contribution to the Therapeutic Situation*, ed. L. Epstein & A. Feiner. New York: Jason Aronson, pp. 305–329.

_____ (1979b), *Countertransference and Related Subjects: Selected Papers.* New York: International Universities Press.

Smith, M. O., & Smith-Blackmer, D. (1981), The mother-daughter relationship: A dialogue continued. *Clinical Social Work Journal*, 9(2): 57–68.

Stoller, R. J. (1963), The sense of femaleness. *Psychoanal. Quart.*, 37(1): 42–55.

_____ (1968), *Sex and Gender.* New York: Science House.

_____ (1972), The bedrock of masculinity and femininity: Bisexuality. *Arch. Gen. Psychiat.*, 26: 207–212.

_____ (1974), Facts and fancies: An examination of Freud's concept of bisexuality. In: *Women and Analysis: Dialogues on Psychoanalytic Views of Femininity*, ed. J. Strouse. New York: Grossman, pp. 343–363.

_____ (1976), *Sex and Gender*, Vol. 2: *The Transsexual Experiment.* New York: Jason Aronson.

Sullivan, H. S. (1953), *Interpersonal Theory of Psychiatry.* New York: Norton.

Author Index

Subject Index